MW00526508

WITHDRAWN

Diaspora, Development, and Democracy

Diaspora, Development, and Democracy

THE DOMESTIC IMPACT OF INTERNATIONAL MIGRATION FROM INDIA

Devesh Kapur

PRINCETON UNIVERSITY PRESS

PRINCETON AND OXFORD

Copyright © 2010 by Princeton University Press

Requests for permission to reproduce material from this work should be sent to
Permissions, Princeton University Press

Published by Princeton University Press, 41 William Street, Princeton, New Jersey 08540

In the United Kingdom: Princeton University Press, 6 Oxford Street, Woodstock,
Oxfordshire OX20 1TW

All Rights Reserved

Library of Congress Cataloging-in-Publication Data

Kapur, Devesh, 1959–
    Diaspora, development, and democracy : the domestic impact of international migration
from India / Devesh Kapur.
        p.   cm.
    Includes bibliographical references and index.
    ISBN 978-0-691-12538-1 (hardcover : alk. paper)
    1. India—Emigration and immigration.   2. India—Emigration and immigration—
Economic aspects.   3. India—Emigration and immigration—Political aspects.   4. East
Indians—Foreign countries.   I. Title.
JV8501.K37 2010
304.80954—c22   2009053054

British Library Cataloging-in-Publication Data is available

This book has been composed in Sabon

Printed on acid-free paper. ∞

press.princeton.edu

Printed in the United States of America

10   9   8   7   6   5   4   3   2   1

TO MY FAMILY AND FRIENDS

Who made it all possible

Contents

List of Figures and Tables

Tables

Acknowledgments

WHEN ONE HAS been working on any project over many years, one collects many debts—and I have more than my fair share.

My interest and research on the impact of international migration on the countries of origin began when I was a faculty member in the government department at Harvard University. With support from the Center for Global Development in Washington, DC, and working jointly with a colleague in the economics department, John McHale, we wrote a monograph looking at this issue worldwide, *Give Us Your Best and Brightest: The Global Hunt for Talent and Its Impact on the Developing World* (Washington, DC: Center for Global Development and Brookings Institution, 2005).

Since then, I have worked with John on a range of papers on this subject, some jointly, some with other colleagues (notably Ajay Agrawal and Mihir Desai). Throughout, John's intellect and openness and his personal warmth and decency have deeply influenced my thinking, and the framework in chapter 2 owes much to John's conceptualization of the issue.

Over the years my thinking on these issues has been influenced by a number of friends and colleagues: Arun Abraham, Michael Clemens, K.P. Krishnan, Atul Kohli, Pratap Mehta, Partha Mukhopadhyay, Karthik Muralidharan, Urjit Patel, Lant Pritchett, Anand Shah, Arvind Subramanian and Richard Webb. Discussions with Steve Wilkinson were particularly helpful in sharpening my arguments and improving the manuscript. Wendy Pearlman meticulously read the page proofs and not only helped correct errors in style and judgment but also in making me think of the sorts of thing I should have done.

The project began with seed funding from the American Institute for Indian Studies, for a year-long stay in India. I spent a year at the Indian Institute of Management, Ahmedabad (IIM-A), where I was hosted by Professor Pankaj Chandra and his family, whose friendship and hospitality are unbounded. Professor Errol D'Souza (also at IIM-A) generously helped educate me on some of the conceptual issues of the macroeconomics of remittances, with his characteristic clarity. Ambassador Jayant Prasad helped to bring me up to speed on official Government of India thinking.

Subsequently, funding from the Asia Center, the Weatherhead Initiative, and the Milton Grant (all at Harvard); the Macarthur Foundation; and a gift from the Diego Hidalgo Foundation were all extremely helpful in supporting the project.

Rebecca Thornton, then a graduate student at Harvard, was instrumental in designing the survey questionnaires. The Indian surveys were added to the Indian Readership Survey. I am deeply grateful to Ashok Das, managing director at Hansa Research, and his staff for their enormous help in making this possible. The list of unique Indian last names was put together from phone directories in India by P. K. Kapoor and his team, to whom I owe much gratitude. The database of Indian Americans was built with the help of proprietary databases of InfoUSA. I am especially grateful to Bill Hippen, who time and again worked with me in building this database. The phone survey (and data entry) of Indian Americans was managed by ORG-Marg in Mumbai.

The large survey data sets that were specifically built for this project were checked and analyzed by Randy Akee, Vaibhav Gujral, and Atul Pokharel, who all spent long hours helping me with this when they might have been doing something better!

The case study of the role of the Indian diaspora in the development of the diamond industry in India in chapter 4 owes much to the interviews conducted by Mihir Seth in Belgium and India. The database on India's elites in chapter 5 was developed by Arjun Raychaudhuri, at the time a Rhodes scholar in Oxford. Arjun organized a team to painstakingly craft this database with his characteristic good humor and care. Some of the findings from this data set were presented at a conference at SAIS at Johns Hopkins and part of which appeared in the journal *India Review*. I am grateful to Ramchandra Guha and Sunil Khilnani for correcting my historical errors.

For chapter 6, Diego Miranda helped research the concept of elites and how Indian elites historically differed from others around the world, especially Latin America, a region with which he was deeply familiar. This chapter has also benefited from comments and suggestions made by seminar participants at the University of Texas—Austin, University of Pennsylvania, Princeton, Cornell, and Brown.

The discussion of the role of the Indian diaspora in Indo-U.S. relations in chapter 7 draws heavily on interviews by Manik Suri for his senior thesis at Harvard, which I supervised. Manik was very generous in sharing the interview material and later in reading, commenting on, and editing not just this chapter, but the entire manuscript, for all of which he has my deep gratitude.

I am indebted to Radu Tatucu for the analysis in chapter 8. Given the sensitivity of the questions, it was important that the person be technically adept, but also, hopefully, not have strong priors about India and specific Indian ethnicities. As a Romanian national with strong statistical skills, Radu fit the bill perfectly and worked tirelessly to get the nuances of this analysis correct. Partha Mukhopadhyay and Shubham Chaudhary were very helpful in their suggestions and comments on the statistical aspects and interpretations, and the limits to the claims that could be made. Bharat Ramamurti helped put together the survey of Indian diasporic philanthropy.

A year's leave at the Princeton Institute for International and Regional Studies under the aegis of the Program in Democracy and Development allowed me time to finally complete the manuscript. I am deeply grateful to Atul Kohli and Deborah Yashar for making that possible. Several students helped enormously in putting the manuscript together and rectifying the many inevitable glitches. I am grateful to Katia Alexander, Megan Crowley, Deepa Iyer, Ritu Kamal, Sagar Raju, Anjali Salooja, Yashas Vaidya, and Shreya Vora.

Working with Chuck Myers and his colleagues at Princeton University Press (especially Sara Lerner) has been a pleasure. His patience and commitment helped draw this long project to a close and his many thoughtful suggestions considerably improved the manuscript. Jennifer Harris copyedited the manuscript and Sherry Smith created the index, both with admirable care and meticulousness.

Finally, my wife, Sadhana, and children, Maya and Kunal, patiently and good-humoredly bore my long absences from their lives—but as I bring this to an end, I hope to make amends!

Diaspora, Development, and Democracy

CHAPTER 1

The Missing Leg of the Globalization Triad: International Migration

INTRODUCTION

IN RECENT YEARS, the analysis of globalization—its multiple causes, manifestations, and complex consequences—has become a staple of discussion within academia and public discourse. The innumerable facets of
globalization have given the term a certain elasticity and made it difficult
to reconcile its multiple complexities. There is little disagreement regarding the reality of the unprecedented growth (at least since World War II)
of cross-border flows of capital, goods, and services. However, there is
less agreement as to the relative importance of the various factors and
mechanisms that are facilitating and driving these flows. On the one
hand, many agree that technological changes, which have resulted in a
sharp decline in the transaction costs of global goods and services trade,
whether containerization (in the case of manufactured goods) or information technologies (in the case of services), have undoubtedly played an
important role. There is less agreement, however, as to how technological
changes have interacted with other driving or intermediary variables,
such as the role of ideas (particularly the triumph of so-called neoliberal
economic ideas), the role of international organizations (especially the
Bretton Woods institutions and the World Trade Organization [WTO]),
the role of major powers (particularly the United States), and last, changes
within countries themselves. There is least consensus on the welfare
implications of globalization, both among and within countries, as well
its links with contemporaneous complex phenomena such as climatic
changes and terrorism.[1]

---

[1] The literature on this subject is vast. For some of the more lucid (and contentious)
analyses, see Jagdish Bhagwati, *In Defense of Globalization* (New York: Oxford University Press, 2004); Nayan Chanda, *Bound Together: How Traders, Preachers, Adventurers,
and Warriors Shaped Globalization* (New Haven, CT: Yale University Press, 2007); Dani
Rodrik, *Has Globalization Gone Too Far?* (Washington, DC: Institute for International
Economics, 1998); Jeffrey D. Sachs and Andrew M. Warner, "Economic Reform and the
Process of Global Integration," *Brookings Papers on Economic Activity* 26, no. 1 (1995):
1–118; Joseph E. Stiglitz, *Globalization and Its Discontents* (New York: W.W. Norton &
Company, 2002); Martin Wolf, *Why Globalization Works* (New Haven, CT: Yale University
Press, 2004).

However, whatever the debate regarding the causal mechanism of globalization and its normative consequences, few would question the reality that cross-border flows of products (goods and services) and financial capital have transformed the global economic and political landscape over the last half-century. Yet the burgeoning literature has paid limited attention to the third leg of the globalization triad: the flow of labor. The premise of this book is that cross-border flows of human capital are likely to play an equally influential role in shaping the political and economic landscape over the next fifty years. While a variety of factors—demographics, technologies, economic structures, domestic politics, institutional structures, and national security concerns—will mediate the specific characteristics and magnitudes of these flows, there is little doubt that these flows will have a profound and transformative impact on both sending and receiving countries.

The consequences of such potentially large immigrant inflows have prompted much debate and analysis in advanced industrial countries. There is also substantial literature (especially in sociology and cultural studies) on diasporas themselves and the phenomenon of transnationalism.[2] But another reality has received short shrift: what will be the consequences on the *sending* country of large cross-border flows of people? This book seeks to understand the political and economic consequences of international migration and diaspora formation on the *country of origin*, focusing on India.

What Do We Know about International Migration?

The last few centuries have witnessed four significant waves of international migration: the forced migration from Africa to the Americas in the seventeenth and eighteenth centuries; the transatlantic migration from Europe to the Americas in the late nineteenth and early twentieth centuries; the labor migrations from China and India to other parts of Asia, Africa, and the Caribbean (and from China to the Americas); and the mass movements of populations in the aftermath of World War II.

In more recent years, three significant migrant streams have been reshaping the global landscape. First, there were the forced migrations resulting from civil war and ethnic cleansing, as in Afghanistan, Africa, and

---

[2] Journals such as *Diaspora, International Journal of African and Black Diaspora Studies,* and *Chinese Southern Diaspora Studies* examine the cultural and social aspects of diasporas. On transnationalism, see Arjun Appadurai, *Modernity at Large: Cultural Dimensions of Globalization* (Delhi: Oxford University Press, 1997); Thomas Faist, *The Volume and Dynamics of International Migration and Transnational Social Spaces* (Oxford, UK: Oxford University Press, 2000); Peggy Levitt, *The Transnational Villagers.* (Berkeley: University of California Press, 2001).

the Balkans. Second, we must count the multiple streams of unskilled and semiskilled labor migration: from South Asia to the Middle East; from Central America and Mexico to the United States; from Indonesia and Myanmar to Thailand and Malaysia; from the Maghreb to Southern Europe; and so on. Third, there is skilled migration from lower income countries, particularly within Asia and Africa, to industrialized countries in Europe and the Americas.

International migration in the latter half of the twentieth century has been strikingly different from the great migrations of a century earlier in one crucial respect. From a hemispherical perspective, in the nineteenth century, there were two separate streams of international migration—North–North and South–South—exemplified by the migration from Europe to the "New World" and from China and India to other countries in the South. In the more recent period, while international migration also has two main streams—South–South and South–North—the migrants in both cases are from developing countries. As a result, the foreign-born population in industrialized countries has increased significantly from 1965 to 2000 (table 1.1). It has more than doubled in North America (from 6 to 13 percent) and increased by a third in Australia and New Zealand (Oceania). Across industrialized regions, the sharpest increase has been in Europe (from 2.2 to 7.7 percent), and even more in Western Europe (from 2.2 to 10.3 percent).

TABLE 1.1
World Migration, 1965–2000

	Africa	Asia	Latin America	North America	Europe	Oceania	World
			Migrant stock (millions)				
1965	8.0	31.4	5.9	12.7	14.7	2.5	75.2
2000	16.3	50.0	5.9	40.8	56.1	5.8	174.9
			Percentage of world migrant stock				
1965	10.6	41.8	7.9	16.9	19.6	3.3	100.0
2000	9.3	28.6	3.4	23.3	32.1	3.3	100.0
			Migrant stock as percentage of population				
1965	2.5	1.7	2.4	6.0	2.2	14.4	2.3
2000	2.1	1.4	1.1	13.0	7.7	19.1	2.9

Source: Timothy J. Hatton and Jeffrey G. Williamson, *Global Migration and the World Economy: Two Centuries of Policy and Performance* (Cambridge, MA: MIT Press, 2005).

This significant shift in the levels and selection characteristics of immigrants has created deep concerns in industrialized countries. There is growing literature on the effects of international migration on labor markets,[3] national security,[4] and social security and welfare systems.[5] Immigration has had increasingly significant effects on domestic politics in industrialized countries, demonstrated, for instance, through the revival of extreme right-wing nativist parties in several European countries. All this has contributed to deep uneasiness about the implications of immigrants on the "core" national identity of the receiving country, an uneasiness reflected, for example, in Samuel Huntington's analysis[6] of Hispanic migration to the United States and the furor over the banning of headscarves worn (mainly) by Muslim schoolgirls in France.

In contrast to the scholarship on the countries that receive migrants, discussions of the implications of migration for sending countries and societies have been relatively limited. These include studies in economic history examining the effects of the large outflows of labor from Europe in the late nineteenth century on labor markets in source countries;[7] the celebration of international diasporic networks as the "commons of mutual interest" divorced from the "commons of place and local resources";[8] the effects of diasporic networks as channels of influence for "values";[9] the role of the Chinese diaspora (the "bamboo network") in channeling trade and investment into China; and a burgeoning literature on the effects of financial remittances.[10] A small but emerging literature has begun focusing on the political effects of international migration on countries of origin.[11]

[3] George J. Borjas, Richard B. Freeman, and Lawrence F. Katz, "Searching for the Effect of Immigration on the Labor Market," *American Economic Review* 86 (1996): 247–51.

[4] Charles King and Neil J. Melvin, "Diaspora Politics: Ethnic Linkages, Foreign Policy, and Security in Eurasia," *International Security* 24, no. 3 (1999): 108–38.

[5] Devesh Kapur and John McHale, *The Global War for Talent: Implications and Policy Response for Developing Countries* (Washington, DC: Center for Global Development, 2005).

[6] Samuel Huntington, *Who Are We? The Challenges to America's National Identity* (New York: Simon and Schuster, 2004).

[7] Kevin H. O'Rourke and Jeffrey G. Williamson, "The Heckscher Ohlin Model between 1400 and 2000: When It Explained Factor Price Convergence, When It Did Not, and Why," National Bureau of Economic Research Working Paper No. 7411 (1999), http://ideas.repec.org/p/nbr/nberwo/7411.html.

[8] Joel Kotkin, *Tribes: How Race, Religion, and Identity Determine Success in the New Global Economy* (New York: Random House, 1993).

[9] Yossi Shain, *Marketing the American Creed Abroad: Diasporas in the U.S. and Their Homelands* (Cambridge, UK/New York: Cambridge University Press, 1999).

[10] Murray Weidenbaum and Samuel Hughes, *The Bamboo Network* (New York: Free Press, 1996). James E. Rauch and Vitor Trindade, "Ethnic Chinese Networks in International Trade," *Review of Economic Studies* 84, no. 1 (2002): 116–30.

[11] Some examples include Devesh Kapur, "The Janus Face of Diasporas," in *Diasporas and Development*, eds. Barbara J. Merz, Lincoln Chen, and Peter Geithner (Cambridge,

A recent analysis of a specific segment of this migration—namely, the consequences of skilled labor flows on developing countries—argues that mounting demographic pressures in industrialized countries and resulting increases in dependency ratios will put unsustainable fiscal pressures on the social security systems of industrialized countries.[12] This, in turn, will increase the demand for labor from developing countries and is likely to translate into immigration policies designed to draw the "fiscally attractive" section of the population—specifically, individuals in the midtwenties to midforties age group who have higher education and demonstrated skills. Additionally, for cultural, political, and economic reasons, immigration policies in industrialized countries will favor temporary migration— where migrants are likely to return to their country of origin—especially for less-skilled laborers. Last, national security and neighborhood concerns will affect which sending countries are favored and which are not. Industrialized country decision makers face the prospect of either allowing more immigration from culturally heterogeneous countries or looking on as skilled, white-collar jobs move outside the country. For firms within industrialized countries, the degree to which services are tradable, lower-cost skilled labor is available overseas, and international contracting is feasible will lead them to contract overseas; the more this happens, the greater the pressure will be in industrialized countries to target selective immigration.

Why Is Emigration Understudied, and What Are Its Implications?

In contrast to the substantial literature on the political economy of financial flows and trade, discussions on the political economy consequences of international migration for the country of *origin* are virtually absent. The key reason appears to be the absence of data on international migration. Unlike the other two legs of the globalization triad, international migration data are woeful. In the case of capital flows, the past few decades have seen huge leaps in the quantity and quality of data, which now include duration (maturity), type (debt/portfolio/foreign direct investment

---

MA: Harvard University Press, 2007); Silvia Pedraza, *Political Disaffection in Cuba's Revolution and Exodus* (New York: Cambridge University Press, 2007); David Fitzgerald, *A Nation of Emigrants: How Mexico Manages Its Migration* (Berkeley : University of California Press, 2009); Jonathan Fox, "Exit Followed by Voice: Mapping Mexico's Emerging Migrant Civil Society," in *Alternative Visions of Development: Rural Social Movements in Latin America*, eds. Carmen Diana Deere and Fred Royce (Gainesville: University Press of Florida, 2009).

[12] Devesh Kapur and John McHale, *The Global War for Talent: Implications and Policy Response for Developing Countries* (Washington, DC: Center for Global Development, 2005). The pioneering work is this area was Jagdish Bhagwati, *International Factor Mobility* (Cambridge, MA: MIT Press, 1983).

[FDI]), and conditions (interest rate, currency structure, etc.), and distinguish between stocks and flows and sources and destinations. International organizations (the Bretton Woods institutions, the Bank for International Settlements, the Organisation for Economic Cooperation and Development [OECD], and the United Nations Conference on Trade and Development [UNCTAD]) have played a key role in data access, comparability, and comprehensiveness. In the case of trade flows, the data are equally good, although data on trade in services are weaker compared to data on trade in goods. Once again, international organizations such as the United Nations, Bretton Woods institutions, and more recently, the WTO have played a key role in developing high-quality, comparable, cross-country data.

However, in the case of the third leg of globalization—international migration—data comparable to that for goods and capital flows simply do not exist. The sending country cannot capture data on migrants since they are no longer in the country, and data on migrants in receiving countries are limited by the variables of interest in that country. Most economic studies of international migration focus on labor market effects; hence, the selection variables they are interested in include education, gender, age, and earnings. These data are often available from sources similar to the census. However, even these data were not available cross-nationally until very recently, and they remain imperfect even now.[13] For instance, only a very gross reading of education data is possible, as the data set tracks only levels of education—there are no data on the type or quality of education. The loss of a migrant with a tertiary education could potentially be much greater if she studied medicine as opposed to a more general liberal arts program (depending on the definition of "loss"). Similarly, the data cannot distinguish between an individual who graduated from an extremely selective educational institution from another who went to a mediocre one. Consequently, the only way to gauge the loss of the quality of human capital to the country of origin is to impute it from earnings, a very imperfect measure for migrants, which in any case is often unavailable.[14] Equally (if not more importantly), the real significance might be in the unobservable characteristics of the migrant, such as whether the individual is a risk taker, is an institutional builder, or has leadership qualities. In the aforementioned example, while the loss of a

[13] For an excellent overview of what needs to be done on international migration data, see the recommendations of the Commission on International Migration Data for Development Research and Policy, *Migrants Count: Five Steps toward Better Migration Data* (Washington DC: Center for Global Development, 2009).

[14] Migrants face numerous employment barriers arising from a lack of the requisite language skills, weak access to informal networks, barriers posed by trade unions, or because their educational credentials are not recognized.

doctor will have a more negative impact on public health, the loss of a liberal arts graduate, who may have gone on to shape public policy or had the leadership potential to build institutions, might have more deleterious effects for the sending country more broadly. As you will see in chapter 2, the effects on the sending country depend critically on the selection effects: *who leaves, how many leave, why they leave, the legal basis on which they leave, where they go, how they fare,* and *how long have they been gone.* Thus, the political effects of migration from Nigeria on that country may depend on (among other variables) the religion, ethnicity, and region from which migrants are drawn and whether they left through legal or illegal channels. Unfortunately, however, there simply do not exist any data at that level of detail.

I argue in this book that the absence of analytical attention to the third leg of globalization has severe consequences for our understanding of the political economy of developing countries and encompasses a wide range of questions. Goldberg and Pavcnik's survey of the effects of trade liberalization on inequality and poverty in developing countries is compromised by a severe attribution problem: during the 1990s, as Latin American countries were undertaking drastic trade liberalization, they were also receiving increasing amounts of migrants' remittances, most of which were accruing to lower income groups.[15] Drawing causal links between trade liberalization and changes in inequality and poverty, while ignoring inflows of tens of billions of dollars to relatively poor households, can result in a severe attribution problem.

In addition to these economic effects, the political implications of migration can also be substantial, but the precise effect depends on who leaves, how many, and why. One explanation of the extension of the franchise in Western societies in the nineteenth century attributes the move to strategic decisions by the political elite to prevent widespread social unrest and revolution.[16] However, this was also a period of unprecedented emigration from these societies, a trend that increased stability in these countries by lowering population pressures, raising wages, and removing troublesome groups (ranging from convicts to minorities). Following the massive workers' uprising in Paris in 1848, the Assembly voted to "clear the capital of subversive elements." The solution? Provide free land grants to such elements in Algeria.[17] In the absence of these "vents for surplus

[15] Pinelopi Goldberg and Nina Pavcnik, "Distributional Effects of Globalization in Developing Countries," *Journal of Economic Literature* 45, no. 1 (2007): 39–82.

[16] Daron Acemoglu and James A. Robinson, "Why Did the West Extend the Franchise? Democracy, Inequality, and Growth in Historical Perspective," *The Quarterly Journal of Economics* 115, no. 4 (November 2000): 1167–99.

[17] David B. Abernethy, *The Dynamics of Global Dominance: European Overseas Empires, 1415–1980* (New Haven, CT: Yale University Press, 2000).

populations," would the gradualism in the extension of the franchise have been undermined by more severe instability?

In more recent times, the pressures of "incidents of voice, actual exit and exit's politicising influence" precipitated the collapse of the German Democratic Republic.[18] An analogous argument has been made in case of Bulgaria. The flight of more than a quarter of a million Bulgarian Turks to Turkey in 1989, a response to years of discrimination, is often cited as a factor contributing to the fall of the communist regime later in that year.[19]

In other cases, such as in Cuba and Zimbabwe, authoritarian regimes have sought to maintain political stability through the deliberate use of a strategy of "venting disgruntled groups" through emigration. Between 1959 and 2004, Cuba lost between 12 and 15 percent of its population in four waves of emigration, beginning with upper-class white elites in the earliest wave, to the largely black working class in the final one.[20] In Zimbabwe, the iron grip of Robert Mugabe and the sharp deterioration of the economy led to a hemorrhaging of the country's middle class, which fled to South Africa. The result, according to an opposition politician in Harare, "makes [Mugabe] a very, very happy dictator. . . . He gets rid of his opponents and they in turn send back money to their families in Zimbabwe and that keeps things ticking over."[21] Zimbabwe's loss has been South Africa's gain, which needs the middle-class professionals (especially after losing much of its own, largely white, middle class to emigration) for its growing economy, one reason perhaps why South Africa has not been particularly interested in putting pressure on Mugabe to reform.

History is replete with examples of the political consequences of nonvoluntary migration—from the African slave trade to the numerous instances of forced migration and ethnic cleansing in the twentieth century.[22] Nunn's study of the impact of forced migration—the slave trade—found significant negative long-term political and economic effects for Africa. The parts of Africa from which the largest number of slaves were taken are today the poorest parts of Africa, and this could not be explained by selection effects. The least developed societies were not the ones selected

[18] Jonathan Grix, *The Role of the Masses in the Collapse of the GDR* (Basingstoke/New York: Macmillan/Palgrave, 2000).

[19] Mary Neuburger, *The Orient Within: Muslim Minorities and the Negotiation of Nationhood in Modern Bulgaria* (Ithaca, NY: Cornell University Press, 2004).

[20] Silvia Pedraza, *Political Disaffection in Cuba's Revolution and Exodus* (New York: Cambridge University Press, 2007).

[21] Sue Lloyd-Roberts, "Zimbabwe's Precarious Survival," *BBC News*, September 8, 2007, http://news.bbc.co.uk/2/hi/programmes/from_our_own_correspondent/6982183.stm.

[22] John Thornton, *Africa and Africans in the Making of the Atlantic World, 1400–1800* (London: Cambridge University Press, 1998); Chaim D. Kaufmann, "When All Else Fails: Ethnic Population Transfers and Partitions in the Twentieth Century," *International Security* 20, no. 4 (1996): 136–75.

into the slave trade. Instead, the more developed and more densely populated societies supplied the largest numbers of slaves.[23]

Even where explicit force is not deployed, severe prejudice and bias can create pressures for the selective migration of particular ethnic groups, thereby reshaping domestic politics. If those who leave are more liberal than those left behind, their absence may remove voices for moderation. Alternatively it might affect politics by changing the ethnic and religious diversity of the population. Again, ignoring migration-induced changes in a political culture can lead to the misspecification of causal factors. For instance, the literature on the robustness of authoritarianism in the Middle East[24] does not consider the long-term political consequences of the emigration of Christians from Egypt in the 1950s, Palestine in the 1990s, and Iraq more recently.[25]

A related consequence of international migration is its effects on what constitutes a political community. The debates on democratic transitions and regime change, for instance, have emphasized the importance of the "stateness" variable. Stateness problems, most evident in the application of theories of democratic transition and regime change in post-Communist states, arise when "there are profound differences about the territorial boundaries of the political community's state and . . . who has the right of citizenship in the state."[26]

International migration with dual citizenship and voting rights is also likely to fundamentally alter the nature of political communities—but with what implications for democratic processes and practices? Some of the most well known work on the international sources of domestic politics has ignored international migration as an important international variable affecting domestic politics.[27]

[23] Nunn N, "The Long-Term Effects of Africa's Slave Trades," *Quarterly Journal of Economics* 123 (2008):139–76.

[24] Eva Bellin, "The Robustness of Authoritarianism in the Middle East: Exceptionalism in Comparative Perspective," *Comparative Politics* 36, no. 2 (January 2004): 139–57.

[25] The Christian population in present-day Jordan, Syria, Lebanon, Israel, and the Palestinian territories dropped from 26.4 percent in 1914 to 19.1 percent in 1945 to just 8.7 percent in 2007. Don Belt, "The Forgotten Faithful," *National Geographic*, June 2009, 78–97. The Christian population in Iraq is estimated to have dropped from 1.4 million in 1987 to one million before the Iraq War to 850,000 in September 2004, leading to fears that it was "robbing Iraq of a politically moderate, socially liberal, and largely pro-Western population at a critical juncture." Yochi Dreazen, "Iraq Sees Christian Exodus," *Wall Street Journal*, September 27, 2004, A17. On the effects on Palestine, see Charles M. Sennot, *The Body and the Blood: The Middle East's Vanishing Christians and the Possibility for Peace* (New York: Public Affairs, 2004).

[26] Juan Linz and Alfred Stepan, eds., *The Breakdown of Democratic Regimes: Crisis, Breakdown and Reequilibrium* (Washington, DC: Johns Hopkins, 1978): 17.

[27] Peter Gourevitch, "The Second Image Reversed: The International Sources of Domestic Politics," *International Organization* 32 (autumn 1978): 881–912, 931.

While the contentious debates surrounding the consequences of Mexican migration into the United States point to the growing importance attached to this phenomenon, they miss out on a critical point. Sam Huntington had famously argued that Mexican immigrants are likely to fundamentally affect the core national characteristics of the United States.[28] However, emigration from Mexico will in all likelihood have profound effects on Mexico itself, from large amounts of financial remittances empowering particular communities to the effects on Mexico's demographics (such as the fertility decline in Mexico that has accompanied the sharp growth in migration to the United States) and democratic processes in the country (from indirectly influencing voting behavior of households with family members abroad to the more direct effects consequent to dual citizenship). Thus, it is not clear whether international migration from Mexico to the United States will remake the American Southwest in the image of the former or whether northern and central Mexico will begin to mirror the latter—or neither. The transborder movement of people may well be one of the most important mechanisms of "soft power," but for which country—the source country or the destination country?[29]

International migration also leads us to rethink the most basic concepts in the vast literature on international trade. In the classic Mundell-Fleming framework, trade and migration are substitutes, whereas in any political economy model, they are rarely so. Labor flows are critically different from goods in their political effects for the most basic of reasons: people have agency; goods do not. When people cross borders, the one who gains most is the migrant himself or herself; when goods cross borders, it is those who receive and send them that gain. People can vote, reproduce, pay taxes, collect social security, and return home—goods cannot. And when people leave, their departure affects social relationships and the social fabric of a society—goods are incapable of such effects.

Consider the idea of "openness," which is generally measured by a country's trade–to–gross domestic product (GDP) ratio. Let us take two countries with similar endowments and capital-to-labor ratios, where one exports labor-intensive products and the other exports labor. In the first case, the export earnings add above the line to the trade-to-GDP ratio, supposedly with many virtuous consequences. In the second, the worker sends remittances, which may be greater than the net foreign exchange earnings from his counterpart making and exporting shoes. He may also be exposed to a new world of ideas, changing both his expectations and

[28] Samuel Huntington, *Who Are We?* (2004).

[29] The term "soft power" was coined by Joseph Nye, *Soft Power: The Means to Success in World Politics* (New York: Public Affairs, 2004).

those of his family in the "home" country. Is a country with substantial trade, but with few citizens who move around the world, really more "open" in a broader (perhaps more intuitive) sense than a country where trade is more limited but whose citizens live and travel internationally, thus remitting foreign exchange and ideas to a much greater extent?

Indeed, the benefits of international trade accrue not just because of Ricardian comparative advantage and the benefits of competition but also through the flow of new products and technologies. If trade is the principal source of the diffusion of technologies embodied in "hardware"— i.e., new products, especially capital equipment—migration has historically been a critical mechanism for the transmission of ideas and practices. Historically, travel and migration have been the conveyer belts that transmit the more tacit elements of knowledge. For millennia, migration helped diffuse plant species and domesticated animals across the Eurasian landmass, and where this was not possible because of geographical barriers, the diffusion was much less.[30] In the last two millennia, travel helped diffuse transformative ideas and technologies as wide-ranging as the printing press, gunpowder, and the magnetic compass from China, the decimal system from India, and edible plant species such as tomato, potato, and corn from the Americas.

Travelers and sojourners in varying guises—pilgrims, explorers, diplomats, merchants, students, and exiles—have long been agents in the transmission of ideas.[31] Across religions and over space and time, pilgrimages have been more than simply scripturalist imperatives to perform religious rituals. They have played a key role in linking the spatial and the cultural, piety and identity.[32] The intellectual linkages between travel and knowledge are as old as the concepts themselves. The Arabic literary genre of *rihla* is comprised of books that recount travels, particularly those undertaken in the pursuit of knowledge. Comparing the travels of Rifaʻa Rafiʻ al-Tahtawi (a young man appointed *imam* for an Egyptian student mission to Paris in 1826) to Alexis de Tocqueville's travels to the United States, Euben argues that while the two men differed in "background, genre, discipline, and reception," they shared a stake in claiming the authority of pedagogical *theoria,* the notion that one may travel to faraway places "in search of political wisdom to bring home."[33]

[30] Jared M. Diamond, *Guns, Germs, and Steel: The Fates of Human Societies* (New York: W. Norton & Company, 1997).

[31] Nayan Chanda, *Bound Together: How Traders, Preachers, Adventurers, and Warriors Shaped Globalization* (New Haven, CT: Yale University Press, 2007).

[32] Simon Coleman, *Pilgrimage: Past and Present in the World Religions* (Cambridge, MA: Harvard University Press, 1995).

[33] Roxanne L. Euben, *Journeys to the Other Shore: Muslim and Western Travelers in Search of Knowledge* (Princeton, NJ: Princeton University Press, 2006).

Historically, travel played an important role in the cognitive construction of India, especially in the case of pilgrimages.[34] Pilgrimage centers from antiquity continue to thrive, and the spatial patterns of Hindu sacred spaces and basic pilgrim circulatory routes have persisted over two millennia.[35] The pilgrimage sites gave Brahmin priests access to networks of travel and communication, further empowering them within Indian society. The empty spaces in the cultural map drawn up by Hindu pilgrimages, coinciding with its forested plateau regions in the center and east, were the sites of tribal regions—which India is still struggling to integrate. The long-term marginalization of these regions from India's cultural migration routes also meant the economic and political marginalization of the inhabitants of these regions.

In the nineteenth century, a revolutionary mode of travel was introduced in India by the British. The building of the railways by the British was both a system of imperial control and a driving force in forming a conception of national space.[36] But by sharply increasing the possibilities of travel for Indians, it helped kindle a new cognitive imagination about their political community—and a nascent pan-Indian identity.

After India became independent, it created a large public sector. Although its performance as measured by conventional indicators (such as productivity or financial indicators) has arguably left much to be desired, a critical contribution of the public sector—particularly institutions associated with the central government—may have been its role in creating "Indians." Government employees, whether in the armed forces, the bureaucracy, or public sector organizations like the railways, perforce had to physically move all over India. The spatial mobility of their children in their formative years diluted their parochial ethnic identities and created a more pan-Indian identity. The lack of congruence between the ethnic identity of the parents (from one part of India) with the region where their children grew up (in another part of India) meant that the identity that became more prominent in the repertoire of the next generation was "Indian."

Yet while the cognitive effects of a spatial mobility that crosses political and cultural boundaries may be real and substantial, it is much harder to pin down why it occurs in some cases but not others. In 1952, two young men, Alberto Granado and Ernesto Guevara de la Serna, set out on an

[34] For an argument on these lines in the region now known as the state of Maharashtra, see Anne Feldhaus, *Connected Places: Region, Pilgrimage, and Geographical Imagination in India* (New York: Palgrave Macmillan, 2003).

[35] Surinder M. Bhardwaj, *Hindu Places of Pilgrimage in India* (Berkeley: University of California Press, 1973).

[36] Manu Goswami, *Producing India: From Colonial Economy to National Space* (Chicago: University of Chicago Press, 2004).

8000-kilometer motorcycle trip across much of Latin America. The latter wrote about his experiences during the course of that trip, but his journal was forgotten until it was rediscovered in 1993. By that time, the author had been dead for a quarter-century and "Che" Guevara's iconic status assured that *The Motorcycle Diaries* would become a classic. It is clear that his long journey over the continent was a life-changing experience for the young medical doctor and that sojourns can serve as the crucible from which political understandings emerge. Yet there are difficulties in drawing any broad, generalizing conclusions: Was it the travels that changed Guevara or was the very fact that he was willing to undertake this arduous trip a signal that this was his nature from the start? Travel has often been seen as a metaphor for discovery and exploration. In Henry Miller's words, "One's destination is never a place but rather a new way of looking at things."[37] But as Jawaharlal Nehru noted, this will only occur if "we seek them with our eyes open."[38] And even if external exposure makes a difference, what type of exposure, and at what age, produces what change? To translate the question about Che Guevara into academic jargon: was there a selection effect at work, or a treatment effect? If this were a controlled experiment (which it clearly was not), the fact that his companion did not become a revolutionary simply underlines the conjoint nature of "travel" and "type." In this case, two young friends set out: one, a biochemist, changed little; the other, a doctor, became a revolutionary. Surely the cognitive impacts (on Guevara) of traveling mattered more at a time when other sources of information were so meager. In an era awash with information, from print to visual to electronic, would the marginal impact be as dramatic?

The history of twentieth-century politics in much of what is known as the developing world is replete with examples of political leaders whose exposure to new perceptions in the course of their foreign sojourns sparked a political awakening that would alter the course of their own countries. From Nehru and Nkrumah to Lenin, Ho Chi Minh, and Deng Xiaoping to contemporary leaders like Karzai in Afghanistan and Allawi in Iraq, an extraordinary number of transformative figures have had direct and extensive personal foreign exposure. "Why do nations or democracies rely on the agency of foreignness at their vulnerable moments of (re)founding, at what cost, and for what purpose?" asks Bonnie Honig.[39] Her answer, that "the novelties of foreignness, the mysteries of strangeness,

---

[37] Miller, *Big Sur and the Oranges of Hieronymus Bosch* (New York: New Directions Publishing, 1957), 25.

[38] Jawaharlal Nehru, *Selected Works of Jawaharlal Nehru*, ed. Sarvepalli Gopal (New Delhi: Jawaharlal Nehru Memorial Fund, 1993), 211.

[39] Honig, *Democracy and the Foreigner* (Princeton, NJ: Princeton University Press, 2001).

the perspective of an outsider may represent the departure or disruption that is necessary for change," points to the possible effects of living abroad—circulatory migration—even though the nature of the precise mechanisms may be hard to prove.

Furthermore, an inattention to migration also risks significant attribution problems as we discuss the forces behind a range of contemporary political phenomenon, from economic reforms to global governance. "Technopols"[40]—i.e., the often U.S.-trained returning economists—may well be more effective drivers of economic reforms in their source countries than the Bretton Woods institutions. In addition, in focusing on the visible strands of global governance—supplier networks, epistemic communities, network governance[41]—scholars have tended to neglect the informal diasporic networks that are a critical strand of transnational civil society.[42]

This book argues that an important explanation of the development successes or failures of low-income countries lies in the varying effects of international migration and diasporas. International flows of people are critically shaping a range of complex phenomena. The rapid growth of countries allowing dual-citizenship and financial remittances from emigrants are two manifest effects of the growing influence of diasporas. But when are diasporas likely to be more influential, and how does this influence affect the well-being of people in their country of origin? Is the dominance of skilled migration leaching out human capital in countries where it is already scarce (the oft-cited "brain drain")? Or, paradoxically, does it have beneficial long-term effects, not merely because of transnational "networks" but also by creating increased incentives for people to seek education in order to secure greater expected returns from migration?

How do diasporas shape national identity? What are the effects of long-distance nationalism? Do diasporas amplify or attenuate cleavages in the country of origin—might they even fuel *intranational* conflict (as with the Sri Lankan Tamil diaspora and Sri Lanka)? And similarly, do diasporic networks tend to support more hard-line political parties in the country of origin, thus fueling *international* conflict as well (such as in Armenia, Croatia, and Eritrea)? Or do they instead create conditions that provide a

---

[40] Jorge I. Domínguez, *Technopols: Freeing Politics and Markets in Latin America in the 1990s* (University Park, PA: Penn State Press, 1997).

[41] Anne-Marie Slaughter, *A New World Order* (Princeton, NJ: Princeton University Press, 2004).

[42] Recent scholarship addressing this lacuna includes Michael Smith and Matt Bakker, *Citizenship across Borders: The Political Transnationalism of El Migrante* (Ithaca, NY: Cornell University Press, 2008); Jonathan Fox and Xochitl Bada, "Migrant Organization and Hometown Impacts in Rural Mexico," *Journal of Agrarian Change* 8, nos. 2 and 3 (2008): 435–61.

countervailing force to nationalism, as is the case with the extensive cross-border business investments that the Chinese diaspora has been constructing throughout Asia and increasingly in other regions of the world?

This study seeks to address these questions by focusing on the impact of international migration and the Indian diaspora on India. The past few decades have seen an upsurge of migration from India, both low skilled and skilled, first to the Gulf and more recently to North America. Until the 1980s, the Indian government's policies and the diaspora's attitudes reflected mutual apathy and even disdain. The Indian government did little to press for better treatment of the diaspora when it faced discrimination or expulsion (as in Uganda). Following independence, India's fears of the outside world were reflected in not only its policies toward international trade and foreign direct investment (FDI) but also an apathy bordering on resentment toward its more successful diaspora. In the 1990s, the transformation of the ideological climate in India and the success of the diaspora, especially in the United States, instilled much greater self-confidence in both, leading to a strengthening of bonds that have transformed relations between the two. In 2003, the Government of India (GOI) organized the first *Pravasi Bharatiya Divas* (Celebration of Overseas Indians), officially sealing India's recognition of its diaspora.[43] In 2005, the Citizenship Act of 1955 was amended to allow for registration of persons of Indian origin holding foreign citizenship as "Overseas Citizens of India" (OCIs). Whether and how this changes the diaspora's self-identity and relationship with India remains to be seen. However, given India's demographics and those of industrialized countries, international migration from India will continue to grow, as will the diaspora's reshaping of both India and its destination countries, lending these questions even greater import in the future.

The title of this book serves as a metaphor and mnemonic for how a key component of globalization—namely, international migration ("Diasporas")—has important consequences on the sending country: its impact on domestic politics ("Democracy") and on its economy ("Development").

OUTLINE OF THE BOOK

Chapter 1. The Missing Leg of the Globalization Triad:
International Migration

In this chapter, I address why it is important to understand the complex effects of international migration on the country of origin. Why is

[43] Devesh Kapur, "The Indian Diaspora as a Strategic Asset," *Economic and Political Weekly* 38, no. 5 (2003): 445–48.

international migration, the missing leg of the globalization triad, again playing an important political and economic role in global affairs, one hundred years after its heyday in the late nineteenth century? What do we understand about flows of human capital and what stills remains poorly understood? What explains the increasing salience of diasporas to their countries of origin, especially in lower income countries? What are the implications of international migration and diasporas for the political economy of source countries and how we study them?

Chapter 2. Analytical Framework and Research Methodology

In this chapter, I first present an analytical framework outlining four key channels through which international migration affects sending countries:

1. The *prospect channel* captures the way in which a prospect or an option of emigration affects the decision-making of households and whether they actually end up emigrating. The prospect of emigration affects decisions ranging from skill acquisition to the incentives for the exercise of voice to linguistic preferences.

2. The *absence channel* focuses on the effects on those left behind (TLBs) in the case when individuals actually leave; this channel clearly depends on the characteristics of those who leave. This is particularly important in a multiethnic society like India, where differential rates of emigration can alter its ethnic balance. The social and political implications in turn will depend on the structure of institutions and cleavages already present in society. The *absence* of workers will also have strong political economy consequences. The more emigrant selection is biased toward skilled workers, the greater will be its effects on skill premiums and fiscal losses with consequent increases in inequality. Most importantly, this might affect a country's capacity to build domestic institutions.

3. The *diaspora channel* speaks to the impact of emigrants on the country of origin from their new position abroad. Emigrants can be a source of augmented trade, investment, and financial flows, but also of new ideas, practices, and technologies to source country economies. Their transnational social capital may result in strengthening international civil society, manifest in diasporic philanthropy, or result in something very different: long-distance ethnic nationalism. The political effects of the former are likely to be more diffuse and long term. The latter, however, can have a more immediate political impact, whether in shaping the policies of the country of residence toward the country of origin or through the support of more extreme political groups in the country of origin.

4. Last, the *return channel* looks at how returning emigrants can affect the domestic political economy differently than if they had never left. In a narrow sense, they typically return with greater financial wealth, augmented human capital, and access to global networks. In a broader sense, overseas experiences change expectations as well as preferences.

The second part of this chapter lays out the research design. The analysis in the book relies on five unique data sets constructed specifically for this project:

1. The Survey of Emigration from India (SEI). This random survey of 210,000 households was conducted in fall 2003 in India and was designed to understand household migration preferences, migrant characteristics, and links with the country of origin.
2. A comprehensive database of the Asian Indian population in the United States (410,000 households), covering nearly three-fourths of this group residing in the country at the time.
3. The Survey of Asian Indians in the United States (SAIUS) conducted in spring 2004. This phone survey of 2200 households was based on a random sample drawn from the Asian Indian database. This survey was designed to understand migrant characteristics and the intensity and nature of links of the U.S.-based diaspora with India.
4. A database on Indian political, administrative, business, and scientific elites, designed to understand a different facet of "openness"—the degree of foreign exposure of a country's elites is determined by measuring their foreign education and work experience. This data set was compiled from various individuals in *Who's Who in India* over the last half-century as well as the backgrounds of all 5000-odd members of India's elite Civil Service.
5. A survey of Indian diaspora nongovernment organizations (NGOs) in the United States to understand the scale and scope of diasporic philanthropy and the nature of transnational social capital.

Chapter 3. Selection Characteristics of Emigration from India

A central feature of the analytical framework established in chapter 2 is that the consequences of migration depend on the characteristics of the migrant. In this chapter, I first give a brief historical overview of migration from India, drawing on historical analyses of the big wave of late-nineteenth-century migration as well as new evidence on post-independence migration. Subsequently, drawing from a variety of data sources—in particular, the aforementioned surveys—I examine the characteristics of contemporary international migrants from India (including age, gender, education, occupation, religion, region, ethnicity, destination country, reasons for leaving, political beliefs, and socioeconomic group). Having established the characteristics of Indian emigrants, in subsequent chapters I analyze the consequences and causal mechanisms linking these characteristics to particular effects.

Chapter 4. Economic Effects

This chapter examines three mechanisms through which the economic effects of emigration and the Indian diaspora are most manifest: financial flows, global networks, and the diaspora's role as reputational intermediaries. I then analyze how these mechanisms shaped the success of India's information technology (IT) sector and the Indian diamond industry, while also affecting interregional and household inequality.

Financial remittances, which emerged as an important part of India's balance of payments (BOP) in the mid-1970s, constitute the diaspora's most visible economic contribution to India. By the late 1990s, remittances were about six times net capital transfers from international capital markets and official sources such as the World Bank, and by 2008 they exceeded $50 billion, amounting about 4 percent of India's GDP. This is in contrast to the Chinese diaspora, which tends to invest directly in the country of origin through FDI. What explains the different portfolio mix of financial flows from the Indian diaspora compared to its Chinese counterpart?

This chapter first examines the multiple effects of financial remittances, ranging from increased consumption levels to provisions for social insurance, at both the household and national level, by mitigating the effects of external shocks. For instance, remittances enhanced the Indian state's ability to withstand sanctions imposed in the aftermath of its nuclear tests. Financial remittances have also had considerable distributional consequences, affecting income inequalities across states, social groups, and households. In the state of Kerala, remittances account for nearly a quarter of state net domestic product and appear to have had considerable policy incentive effects as well, by reducing pressures for policy change. Using survey data, I examine who receives remittances and the effects of remittances on inequality among communities and regions.

This chapter subsequently examines a second mechanism of economic impact: the role of diaspora networks. The extreme selectivity of recent Indian emigration and the success of migrants abroad transformed the "brain drain" into a "brain bank." Has this resulted in broader spillover effects for India? Under what conditions do diasporic networks act as reputational intermediaries and as credibility-enhancing mechanisms for domestic Indian economic actors, and with what effects? I analyze these hypotheses by examining the cognitive impact of the Indian diaspora's success in Silicon Valley on global perceptions of India. By the 1990s, India's human-capital-rich diaspora, especially in the United States, emerged to become an international business asset for the country. Its success in Silicon Valley provided broader externalities, including improved perceptions of Indian technology businesses. As reputational intermediaries and as credibility-enhancing mechanisms, this diaspora favorably influenced global perceptions of India, reflecting the reputational spillover effects of succeeding in the most powerful country's leading technology sector.

In addition to information technology, Indian diasporic networks (mostly Gujarati Jains) have also played an important role in India's emergence as a world leader in the diamond industry. Through an ethnographic study of the Indian diamond merchants in Antwerp, Belgium, and their cutting and polishing plants in Gujarat, I demonstrate the critical role of the diaspora in building an industry that employs more than one million people and exports $10 billion annually.

Chapter 5. Social Remittances: Migration and the Flow of Ideas

Building on earlier historical work on Italy[44] and more recently the Dominican Republic,[45] this chapter examines the subtle and dynamic effects of migration's "social remittances" on reshaping political understandings, expectations, and norms, particularly of national elites. I analyze this issue both through historical analysis and by drawing on a database I have developed on India's business, intellectual, political, and scientific elite over the past half-century that examines the extent and nature of these elites' overseas experience. I argue that the distinctively elite characteristics of modern Indian emigration have amplified these "social remittance" effects, both because of the diaspora's overseas success and their access to influential institutional channels to transmit these ideas. Consequently, Indian political leaders, both local and national, are paying more attention to the policy preferences of the Indian diaspora.

Chapter 6. International Migration and the Paradox of India's Democracy

Although most of the attention on the political effects of emigration is given to the diaspora's financial contributions to a range of political actors,

[44] Donna R.Gabaccia, *Italy's Many Diasporas* (Seattle: University of Washington Press, 2000).

[45] Peggy Levitt, "Social Remittances: Migration Driven Local-Level Forms of Cultural Diffusion," *International Migration Review* 32, no. 4 (winter 1998): 926–48.

be they political parties, reactionary social and religious groups, or separatist movements, a systematic empirical verification of this proposition is not feasible. I discuss long-distance nationalism in chapter 8 and argue that while its effects are undoubtedly important in specific regions and time periods, in the Indian case the diaspora has not had *systemic* effects. In contrast, in this chapter I argue that the selection characteristics of who leaves have had systemic implications for Indian democracy: in particular, it at least partially explains the paradox of the endurance of India's democracy despite overwhelming odds.

Indian emigrants are positively selected from the social and economic elite (whether measured by caste, class, or education and skills). This elite emigration has lubricated the political ascendancy of India's numerically dominant lower castes. The introduction of universal franchise in India following independence signaled the death-knell of the political hegemony of India's high castes. In recent decades, as the inexorable logic of numbers has reshaped the political landscape of India and lower and middle castes have gained a greater share of political power, they have sought to use this newfound access to redistribute economic resources. The vast social churning engendered by Indian democracy has led to hitherto socially marginalized groups coming into political power and challenging the entrenched political power of upper castes. The question was not *if* this would happen, but *when* and *at what cost*. No group gives up its privileges without a fight, and the "silent social revolution"[46] in India could have been much more contentious but for the possibility of exit open to India's elites—both to the private sector, and ultimately, outside the country.

In the 1950s, when higher castes in South India were squeezed out of government jobs and higher-education opportunities, they began migrating to other parts of India (often to central government jobs). Since the late 1960s, upper-caste elites began to exit first the public sector, moving increasingly to the private sector, and eventually the country. While the inevitable pressures of democratic politics forced the Indian elite to loosen their grip on political power, palatable exit options made it easier to relinquish their centuries-old privileges. In 1990, India was reeling in the aftermath of a policy decision by a minority government to sharply increase affirmative action in government jobs and education. A decade later, the issue had faded away so quietly that few could recall what the riots had been about. I argue that an important reason for this change was greater exit options for India's upper-caste elites. The exit possibilities inherent in international migration, whether for jobs or education, mitigated the

---

[46] Christopher Jaffrelot, *India's Silent Revolution: The Rise of the Lower Castes in North India* (New York: Columbia University Press, 2003).

economic insecurities of India's elites—thereby making them less implacably opposed to the political ascendancy of hitherto marginalized social
groups. In turn, this has made Indian politics less contentious than it
might otherwise have been in the absence of possibilities of exit for elites
(and their progeny). It is in this contribution to the strengthening of India's democracy, even if inadvertent, that international migration may
have had its strongest impact on India.

However, I argue that contrary to Albert G. Hirschman's famous
formulation,[47] actual exit (and not simply the threat of exit) has not
weakened in any significant way the political voice of India's upper castes.
At the same time, the elite basis of Indian emigration has also had implications for the quality of Indian democracy. Exit has implied a reduced
incentive to exercise voice, particularly for public goods such as health
and education that have been the very basis for mobility of Indian elites
(i.e., human capital). Thus, while international migration has allowed an
exit mechanism that has created less contentious political space for lower
castes, it has also maintained differences in material well-being among
different social groups.

*Chapter 7. The Indian Diaspora and Indian Foreign Policy:
Soft Power or Soft Underbelly?*

Whereas chapter 6 examines the domestic political consequences of migration, in this chapter I examine its external consequences—in particular, the impact on India's foreign policy. Based on the SEI survey, I examine the preferences of Indian elites regarding the future geographic
location of their children in a globalizing world and how this may be reshaping their preferences in areas such as foreign policy. Although preferences are the cornerstone of explanations of state behavior, "scholarly
attention to the sources of national or subnational interests—or, as we
call them, preferences—is wrought with confusion."[48] The survey is a
novel method to understand how elite preferences in foreign policy might
change and test the dominant theoretical approaches (strategic choice,
cognitive, and constructivist theories) that seek to explain foreign policy
preferences. I argue that the global family portfolios of Indian elites are
affecting Indian foreign policy principally because the attention of elites
is overly focused on countries where their children are located to the
detriment of reduced attention paid to other parts of the world.

[47] Hirschman, *Exit, Voice and Loyalty: Responses to Decline in Firms, Organizations,
and States* (Cambridge, MA: Harvard University Press, 1970), 76.

[48] Jeffry Frieden "Actors and Preferences in International Relations," in *Strategic Choice
and International Relations*, eds. David A. Lake and Robert Powell (New Jersey: Princeton
University Press, 1999).

Chapter 8. Civil or Uncivil Transnational Society? The Janus Face of Long-Distance Nationalism

Although transnationalism is in vogue, its Janus face presents a puzzle: under what conditions are diasporas a form of international social capital (with its implied positive virtues), and when do they represent a more contentious long-distance nationalism? To put it differently, are diasporas a form of "bridging" social capital that helps strengthen the matrix of international social capital? Or are they more prone to ethnic long-distance nationalism, supporting more extreme groups and political parties? These questions are important because if diasporas are a form of international social capital, they are likely to have, much like their national equivalent, beneficial effects on global governance.

This chapter examines the variance in the intensity and forms of long-distance nationalism, both in the case of Hindu nationalism as well as among some subnational groups. While the evidence that Indian Americans harbor prejudices against Muslims is compelling, the evidence that the Indian diaspora is a primary or even an important factor in fueling religious conflict in India is weak.

Chapter 9. Spatially Unbound Nations

This book contributes to our understanding of the political economy of development in several ways. First, it treads new ground by demonstrating the effects of a hitherto neglected facet of India's engagement with the outside world—international migration—on the country's political economy. Second, it adds to the comparative literature on the political economy of diasporas, offering insights into why the intensity and form of engagement between diasporas and the country of origin varies across countries and time. Third, it contributes to our understanding of how notions of what constitutes a political community are changing and, with it, the acceptance of dual citizenship in many countries. Last, the book contributes to the literature on globalization by helping us understand the role of migration and diasporas as both a key cause and consequence of globalization.

CHAPTER 2

Analytical Framework and Research Methodology

INTRODUCTION

IT IS ONE thing to recognize that international migration and global diasporas may have significant effects on migrants' countries of origin. Yet understanding the nature of these effects, their relative magnitude, the specific mechanisms through which they work, and of course, why they vary across countries and over time, presents a challenging research agenda. Are the effects broad-based or sector and region specific? To what extent do economic effects mediate the political impact? Or does the causal chain run the other way? How does selection of the migrants themselves matter and why? How are the effects magnified or attenuated by specific institutional features of the country of origin and destination?

The range of these questions is complex, and addressing them would require an ambitious research agenda. Rather than develop an overarching theory, in the first half of this chapter I outline an analytical framework and specify the principal causal mechanisms through which international migration can affect the country of origin. In the second half of this chapter, I describe the research methodology of this study—in particular, the surveys that are the critical empirical pillars of this project.

ANALYTICAL FRAMEWORK

Kapur and McHale identify four channels by which emigration affects the country of origin: prospect, absence, diaspora, and return.[1] I adopt this framework and, next, outline the mechanisms through which each of these channels affects the country of origin.

Prospect Channel

The prospect channel focuses on how forward expectations affect current behavior. For instance, at the individual level the possibility of emigration leading to a higher expected return to human capital could lead to greater

[1] Devesh Kapur and John McHale, *The Global War for Talent: Implications and Policy Response for Developing Countries* (Washington, DC: Center for Global Development, 2005).

human investments, such as evidenced in the nursing sector in the Philippines or information technology (IT) sector in India. This can result in the paradoxical situation whereby an ostensible "brain drain" actually results in a net "brain gain." While the possibility of leaving induces more people to invest in human capital, due to variety of institutional constraints (such as visa restrictions) only a few can actually leave. As a result, the country could actually find itself with greater human capital than a scenario in which emigration was not possible at all. But the investment in internationally tradable skills need not be in education per se. For example, young men "invest" much more in soccer skills in Senegal because they are driven by the opportunity to play in lucrative European soccer leagues; similarly, in the Dominican Republic, young men overinvest in baseball skills hoping that they will be able to migrate and play in U.S. baseball leagues.

The possibility of emigration not only alters the level and form of human capital accumulation but also has other behavioral effects. If, for the reasons mentioned earlier, emigration results in an increase in net human capital accumulation in a country, it might also paradoxically increase the unemployment rate and cause a shift in occupational priorities. Normally, emigration should reduce the labor supply and therefore, *ceteris paribus*, the unemployment rate. However, the prospect of migration also increases the reservation wage. In Central American countries with high levels of emigration to the United States, young men seem unwilling to enter the labor force at prevailing wages, preferring to remain unemployed until an opportunity to leave presents itself. And in the Philippines, which has a reputation as the world's preeminent exporter of nurses, about 80 percent of the country's government doctors, according to one estimate, have become nurses or enrolled in nursing programs, hoping for an American green card.[2]

The prospect channel may also affect other aspects of the social and financial capital of forward-looking individuals. For example, if a person expects to leave, how likely is he or she to invest in local relationships or, on the other hand, to politically disengage? The increasing levels of migration from Mexico appear to be affecting the political attitudes and behaviors of those left behind: individuals in high-migration municipalities appear to be less politically engaged than their counterparts in towns with a smaller incidence of migration—lower voter turnout rates and less participation in politics, even as they participate in local community groups with transnational links to the Mexican diaspora.[3]

[2] Dugger, Celia. "U.S. Plan to Lure Nurses May Hurt Poor Nations." *New York Times*, May 24, 2006.

[3] Gary L. Goodman and Jonathan T. Hiskey, "Exit without Leaving: Political Disengagement in High Migration Municipalities in Mexico," *Comparative Politics* 40, no. 2 (January 2008): 169–88.

It may even lead to strategic behavior in identity formation. In recent decades, several groups in India's northeast (especially from the states of Mizoram and Manipur) have pressed their claim that they are one of the Ten Lost Tribes of Israel (the tribe of Menasseh) and, accordingly, have formally converted to Judaism from Christianity. On that basis, many have emigrated to Israel. For the settler movements in Israel located in Gaza and the West Bank, "the Bene Menashe were [a] godsend—frontline troops for the demographic war with the Palestinians."[4] At the margin at least, it seems doubtful that the change in identity among these tribal groups would have occurred so rapidly and to such a degree in the absence of any prospect of emigrating to Israel. At the same time, the settler groups in Israel might also have been less enthusiastic in recognizing the claims of these tribal groups were it not for pressing demographic reasons.

The most significant political effects of the prospect channel may, however, occur when elites see the future of their children outside, rather than within, the country. In particular, elites are less likely to lend their voice on the sort of public goods that are particularly important for parents—the quality of higher education, for instance. In most countries, privileged groups have a much higher access to the best public higher-education institutions. Many economists and institutions such as the World Bank have strongly argued that this amounts to a subsidy to the rich.[5] However, once elites move their children out (for instance, to study abroad), they also have a lesser stake in maintaining high-quality public institutions. Consequently, elite exit may actually result in better targeting of subsidies and less regressive transfers, but those who now avail of services are likely to be accessing a lower-quality product.[6]

Absence Channel

The absence channel centers on the following question: what happens to those left behind when people who would otherwise be present are now absent? The most obvious effect is that the country's labor supply falls, a trend that should result in increased wages for those left behind. The

---

[4] Tudor Parfitt, "Tribal Jews," in *Indo-Judaic Studies in the Twenty-First Century*, ed. Nathan Katz (New York: Palgrave MacMillan, 2007), 189. The emigration efforts have been aided by two organizations in particular—Amishav and Kulanu.

[5] See for example, *Priorities and Strategies for Education: A World Bank Review* (Washington, DC: World Bank, 1995).

[6] For an analysis of this in the Indian case, see Devesh Kapur and Pratap Bhanu Mehta, "Mortgaging the Future? Indian Higher Education," in *India Policy Forum 2007–08*, eds. Suman Bery, Barry Bosworth, and Arvind Panagariya (New Delhi: Sage Publications, 2008): 101–57.

great transatlantic migrations of the late nineteenth century were the single most important factor in wage convergence between Europe and the United States.[7] In that case, however, the migration was predominantly low-skilled labor. If, on the other hand, skilled labor leaves, as with many developing countries in the late twentieth century, the economic effects range from larger skill premiums to fiscal losses, diminished scale economies, and greater income inequality.[8]

Needless to say, the effects of the absence channel are strongly mediated by the characteristics of who leaves, but also by how many leave, from where (sectors, regions, communities), and the destinations to which they go. The late nineteenth century witnessed two large-scale international migrations: one from Europe and the other from China and India. While these two migrations were of comparable absolute number, the former was much larger in relative numbers and its destination was to other temperate countries, in contrast to the latter, in which migrants mainly went to other tropical countries. The consequences, as Arthur Lewis argued in his classic essay, were starkly different for the sending countries and set the path for the evolution of the international economic order in the twentieth century.[9]

Nonetheless, as with immigration, an inordinate focus on labor markets risks missing out on possible systemic implications. Skilled international migration can have severe adverse consequences for domestic institutions. The critical role of institutions in explaining large differences in living standards across countries is well recognized,[10] as is the role of incentives in the creation of institutions.[11] But necessity is the mother of invention only when there are certain basic capabilities—in particular, human capital. The worse the institutional quality in a country, the more likely potential institutional builders are to leave, resulting in a low-equilibrium institutional trap.

The loss of human capital can adversely affect a country's institutions in several ways. The option to emigrate can make younger people less willing

[7] Kevin H. O'Rourke and Jeffrey G. Williamson, "The Heckscher Ohlin Model Between 1400 and 2000: When It Explained Factor Price Convergence, When It Did Not, and Why," National Bureau of Economic Research Working Paper No. 7411 (Cambridge, MA: NBER, 1999).

[8] Kapur and McHale, 2008.

[9] Arthur Lewis, *The Evolution of the International Economic Order* (Princeton, NJ: Princeton University Press, 1984).

[10] Dani Rodrik, Arvind Subramanian, and Francesco Trebbi, "Institutions Rule: The Primacy of Institutions over Integration and Geography in Development," National Bureau of Economic Research Working Paper No. 9305 (Cambridge, MA: NBER, 2002).

[11] D. Acemoglu, S. Johnson, and J. A. Robinson, "Reversal of Fortune: Geography and Institutions in the Making of the Modern World Income Distribution," *Quarterly Journal of Economics* 117, no. 4 (2002): 1231–94.

to invest in skills that are most relevant to local institutions, preferring instead to invest in skills that are more internationally marketable—for example, becoming computer programmers rather than lawyers. Critically, the absence of talented individuals affects the *supply* of institution builders.[12] By "institutions," I mean not simply a set of rules that shape incentives, but institutions in their organizational incarnation such as universities, hospitals, banks, government statistical systems, and the like, which need professionals with the managerial and technical capabilities to run them well. As Fukuyama notes, "public agencies with poorly trained staff and inadequate infrastructure will have difficulty delivering services."[13] The implications of the loss of already scarce educated individuals may go beyond the loss of their human capital, as narrowly defined: it also undermines social capital and, with it, the more informal parts of the country's institutional infrastructure.

In addition, absence can also impact the *demand* for better institutions. The very individuals who are capable of being successful in high-quality institutional environments are also the ones who have the strongest interest in seeing these institutions built. While by no means universally, historically, the middle class—professionals and intellectuals—has played an important role in democratization.[14] The more educated (and internationally marketable) are often better positioned to exercise "voice" and press for changes in the status quo. (Although it is certainly possible that highly talented individuals have a stake in the continuation of bad institutions that allow them to extract rents.) Emigration can thus rob the country of influential voices for reform, especially those with internationally marketable talents and those who are not in the business of rent extraction at home.

Absence can also have direct and important political effects by simply creating political space for new groups. If elites leave—often the case in the aftermath of revolutions—the political space opens up for new elites, as has been the case with Cuba and Iran. Thus, *inter*-national spatial mobility can affect *intra*-national political and social mobility. It also affects domestic spatial mobility. External migration drives internal migration, and in a multiethnic society this has ramifications for subnational political dynamics. In India, rising incomes and external migration from certain states have fueled demand for labor from other parts of the country, gradually altering the ethnic and religious mix in these states. If politics is organized along religious and ethnic cleavages, then these differential

[12] Kapur and McHale, 2005.

[13] Francis Fukuyama, *State-Building: Governance and World Order in the 21st Century* (Ithaca, NY: Cornell University Press, 2004), 65.

[14] Charles Kurzman and Erin Leahey, "Intellectuals and Democratization, 1905–1912 and 1989–1996," *American Journal of Sociology* 109, 4 (January 2004): 937–86.

selection effects of who leaves the state and who comes in will have political consequences.

Diaspora Channel

The diaspora channel captures the effects of emigrants (and their descendents) living abroad on the country of origin. To put it differently, it
captures the effect of the deterritorialized nation on the territorial nation.
An optimistic view of diasporas is that they represent the "commons of
mutual interest" divorced from the "commons of place and local resources," despite being scattered over the globe.[15] The central idea is that
an emigrant retains certain connections to the home country and consequently should not be viewed as "just another foreigner" from the perspective of the home country. Since diasporas reside outside their kin-
state yet often claim a legitimate stake in it, they challenge the traditional
boundaries of nation-states. Foner argues that "immigrants are seen as
maintaining familial, economic, political, and cultural ties across international borders, in effect making the home and host societies a single arena
of social action." They demonstrate "continuing commitment to the
norms, values, and aspirations of the home society," even as they put
down roots in the new country. And today's cheap and fast communications and transportation make it possible "for the first time for immigrants to operate more or less simultaneously in a variety of different
places."[16]

However, as Ong and Nonini argue in their discussion of the "cultural
politics" of the Chinese diaspora, diasporas do not just "transcend" or
"subvert" the nation-state's political and economic discipline and liberate
their agents—in fact, they are just as likely to strengthen them. Diasporas
can perpetuate old forms of exploitation or invent new ones and grant
them extraterritorial impunity: "one should not assume that what is
diasporic, fluid, border-crossing, or hybrid is intrinsically subversive of
power structures."[17] But when do diasporas attenuate or amplify state
power? What are the effects of international migration on the nation-
building project? And when (and how) are diasporas themselves used as
political resources by origin and destination countries?

As actors that straddle national boundaries, members of a diaspora
have recourse to autonomous resources and values. Moreover, unlike most

[15] Joel Kotkin, *Tribes: How Race, Religion, and Identity Determine Success in the New
Global Economy* (New York: Random House, 1993).

[16] Nancy Foner, "What's So New about Transnationalism? New York Immigrants Today
and at the Turn of the Century," *Diaspora* 6, no. 3 (1997): 354–75.

[17] Aihwa Ong and Donald Macon Nonini, *Ungrounded Empires: The Cultural Politics of
Modern Chinese Transnationalism* (New York: Routledge, 1997): 325–26.

domestic actors, they can more easily interact with other actors across state boundaries and therefore facilitate international financial and technology flows. A diaspora can be a direct source of advantage to the country of origin when its members have the desire and ability to trade with, invest in, and outsource to domestic businesses. The persistence of "home bias" (the result of international trade costs) observed in international macroeconomics[18] may also indirectly explain the behavior of diasporas especially if social (or ethnic) proximity can substitute for distance.[19] A diaspora can also be an indirect source of advantage to the country of origin when its members act as reputational intermediaries—matching trading partners, supporting contracting by leveraging long-term relationships with people from their new and former homes, and possibly most importantly, overcoming negative national stereotypes through demonstrations of their capabilities abroad.[20] At the same time, this "home bias" can also result in political activism in the country of origin ranging from support to political parties, activist, and advocacy groups; to voting and running for elections; to financing extremist organizations.

The principal focus with respect to the economic effects of diasporas on the country of origin has been on their substantial financial contributions through remittances—private transfers from migrants to their families. There is now increasing evidence that in a large number of low-income countries, remittances are the single largest source of net foreign exchange flows, whether compared to flows from official sources (such as the Bretton Woods institutions) or private sources (whether foreign direct investment or portfolio flows).[21] In many cases, foreign exchange receipts from remittances are comparable to those from exports.

A few notable exceptions aside (and in contrast to the vast literature on the other sources of financial flows), the political economy effects of

[18] Maurice Obstfeld and Kenneth Rogoff, "The Six Major Puzzles in International Macroeconomics: Is There a Common Cause?" National Bureau of Economic Research Working Paper No. 7777 (Cambridge, MA: NBER, 2000).

[19] For evidence on this based on patent data citations, see Ajay Agrawal, Devesh Kapur, and John McHale, "How Do Spatial and Social Proximity Influence Knowledge Flows? Evidence from Patent Data," *Journal of Urban Economics* 64 (2008): 258–69.

[20] Saxenian (2000) examines the economic effects of Indians and Chinese in Silicon Valley on India, Taiwan and China, while Kapur and McHale (2005) examine the effects of the Indian, Irish, and Israeli diasporas on the development of the software sectors in these countries. Devesh Kapur and John McHale, "Sojourns and Software: Internationally Mobile Human Capital and High-Tech Industry Development in India, Ireland, and Israel," in *From Underdogs to Tigers: The Rise and Growth of the Software Industry in Some Emerging Economies*, eds. Ashish Arora and Alfonso Gambardella (New York: Oxford University Press, 2005).

[21] Devesh Kapur, "Remittances: The New Development Mantra?" in *Remittances: Development Impact and Future Prospects*, eds. S. M. Maimbo and Dilip Ratha, (Washington, DC: World Bank, 2005): 331–60.

remittances have been weakly analyzed. Remittances may have direct political effects if they are used to fund political parties, extremist groups, or subnational movements. But their indirect political effects, while more subtle, are arguably at least as important. Kiren Chaudhry investigated the process of institutional development and business–government relations in cases of reliance on two types of external capital in the Middle East.[22] She found that financial inflows into Yemen in the form of labor remittances from temporary migration failed to buttress an already weak Yemeni state by bypassing both state institutions and the formal banking system and going directly to millions of Yemeni migrants. On the other hand, oil rents strengthened the Saudi state by creating a huge, financially autonomous distributive bureaucracy. Thus, the different sources and channels of external financial inflows differentially affected state–society relations.

Alternatively, to the extent that there are strong selection effects in who migrates (by ethnicity and religion), remittances can induce differentials in income and consumption, thereby rapidly reorienting social and political hierarchies in societies receiving the money. Remittances are often used to build visible markers of new wealth, be it gaudy and ostentatious housing or places of worship. These serve to signal to other members within the community as well as to other communities the shifts in wealth and power. Consequently, the cognitive effects of this form of consumption can increase conflict.

The complex long-term political effects of migration are evident in Wood's analysis of democratic transition in El Salvador.[23] The landed oligarchy had long suppressed democratization, leading to a near civil war in the 1980s. The resulting political instability led to a large outflux of uprooted peasants (especially to the United States). Agricultural exports dropped, and by 1991 remittances exceeded export earnings. The burgeoning foreign exchange inflows resulted in Dutch disease effects.[24] As the upward pressure on the exchange rate undermined the competitiveness of Salvadoran exports, it further propelled elites out of agriculture. Increasingly over the decade, Salvador's political economy was driven not by export agriculture and its processing but by international

[22] Kiren Chaudhry, "The Price of Wealth: Business and State in Labor Remittances and Oil Economies," *International Organization* 43, no. 1 (winter 1989): 101–45; Kiren Chaudhry, *The Price of Wealth: Economics and Institutions in the Middle East* (Ithaca, NY: Cornell University Press, 1997).

[23] Elisabeth Jean Wood, *Forging Democracy from Below: Insurgent transitions in South Africa and El Salvador* (Cambridge, UK: Cambridge University Press, 2000), 62–65.

[24] "Dutch disease" refers to the phenomenon when sudden and large increases in financial inflows lead to upward pressures on a country's exchange rate, making its exports less competitive and shifting resources from tradable to nontradable sectors.

assistance and remittances from overseas. The shift in elite interests re-shaped Salvadoran politics: the new winners were sectors that controlled significant shares in courier companies that transferred remittances, for-eign exchange financial intermediaries, retail sectors that provided con-sumption goods, and real estate and construction companies. The broad shift in elite economic interests from agriculture to services in turn abated the severity of rural repression and shifted elites to adopt a bargained in-stead of a coerced resolution toward conflict.[25]

To the extent that international migrants come from poor households, remittances will then benefit these households, giving them autonomous sources of income and liquidity. In turn, this can undermine existing pa-tronage networks and therefore impact on clientelist politics. Evidence from Mexico suggests that this mechanism has resulted in making elec-tions more competitive.[26]

Remittances are just one mechanism through which the diaspora chan-nel has a political impact on the country of origin. Diasporas are also capable of influencing the residence country's policies toward the country of origin.[27] The importance of this mechanism increases with the degree of political cleavage between the diaspora and the governing regime in the country of origin. In those cases when cleavages are not important, a diaspora's economic and political impacts are greatest in its "insurance role," through enhanced financial flows when the country of origin faces a crisis, be it a natural disaster, external pressure, or an economic crisis. But members of diasporas participate in the politics of their country of origin in a variety of ways. In some cases, they have the right to vote, ei-ther as dual citizens or as citizens residing abroad. Perhaps more impor-tantly, they influence the voting preferences of kin in the country of ori-gin, an influence that is amplified if they send financial remittances. In other cases, they return and run as candidates themselves. Where direct participation is ruled out, diasporas may attempt to influence politics in the country of origin through financial contributions to political parties and candidates. The impact of these contributions depends both on the relative magnitude of these contributions as well as on the groups and parties to which they are made.

A diaspora can also affect the politics of its country of origin through its cognitive impact and its role as a channel for the flow of ideas. Peggy Lev-itt shows the power of "social remittances" at the household and societal

[25] Wood, *Forging Democracy from Below*, 62–65.

[26] Tobias Pfutze, "Do Remittances Promote Democratization? How International Migra-tion Helps to Overcome Political Clientilism," available at http://www9.georgetown.edu/faculty/tp95/jmp_1.pdf.

[27] Yossi Shain and Aharon Barth, "Diasporas and International Relations Theory," *Inter-national Organization* 57 (2003): 449–79.

level.[28] But is there a political counterpart? Is it, in fact, the less visible, nonquantifiable, and intangible remittances or the flow of ideas that have a more critical impact than the flow of money? For instance, diasporas may influence policy changes in the country of origin. They can do so directly, particularly on issues where the diaspora has strong economic interests or indirectly, as Wood's study shows, by reshaping the policy preferences of elites. Thus, a developing country's political economy might be affected not only by the usual sources of influence—be it the Bretton Woods institutions, international financial markets, or the U.S. Treasury—but also by its diaspora—in particular, if the latter enjoys legitimacy and points of contact with decision-making elites in the country of origin. Thus, there is a wide range of mechanisms of influence. But how important are the different mechanisms, and how does this importance vary with the characteristics of the diaspora, the host country, and the country of origin? This study will seek to offer insights to better address such questions.

A very different mechanism through which diasporas can affect the country of origin is through their role as facilitative role in global criminal networks.[29] There are several factors underlying the growing role of diasporas in international criminal activities. Much like any international industry, many criminal networks rely on expatriated populations to help facilitate their activities abroad. As with any business, international criminal activity also requires enforcement mechanisms and trust, and diasporic networks can more easily internalize these mechanisms. Increased migration—much of which stems from states with weak economies and political instability—has created a large demand for both financial support and larger global networks. In many cases, the strength of such networks is compounded by diasporas' weak integration into host societies. Last, forced repatriation of felons (e.g., from the United States to Central America) has also strengthened international criminal networks. While the impacts on both source and destination countries are large, the effects are understandably much greater on the former. These transnational links provide domestic criminal groups in source countries with substantial financial resources that are often large enough to allow the groups to emerge as significant political actors with the power to destabilize weak states. Profits from drugs, often funneled through diasporic networks, have played an important role in Haiti's narco-coup in 2004, the ongoing violence in Colombia, and the warlordism in Afghanistan.

[28] Peggy Levitt, *The Transnational Villagers* (Berkeley and Los Angeles: University of California Press, 2001).

[29] According to UN estimates, international crime is a $1 to 1.5 trillion annual industry, with drug trafficking, illegal arms trade, human trafficking and smuggling (especially women and children for prostitution and servitude), and money laundering constituting the principal activities.

TABLE 2.1
Diaspora-Based Global Criminal Networks

Organized Crime Group	Country of Origin	Global Presence
Italian Mafia	Italy	Europe, Central and South America, Caribbean, United States, Canada
Russian organized crime	Russia	Nearly 60 countries but especially Eastern and Central Europe
Albanian criminal groups	Albania	European Union, Eastern Europe
Chinese Triads	China, Hong Kong, Macao, and Taiwan	Netherlands, United Kingdom, Germany
Nigerian criminal groups	Nigeria	Over 80 countries in West Africa, Europe, North America
Latin American criminal groups	Colombia, Central America	Europe, United States

These activities bring in billions of dollars of revenue to source countries each year, but they also increase these countries' economic dependence on drug trafficking, prostitution, and other forms of illegal activity. Virtually all international criminal networks—whether Albanian, Italian, Colombian, or Chinese—rely upon their respective diaspora as a base for their activity (table 2.1).

A key political effect of the diaspora channel is the phenomenon of long-distance nationalism. Indeed, nationalism as a modern phenomenon of imagined communities is an idea that often grows in the minds of diasporic elites. In the Italian case, the diaspora helped in the creation of a national identity, as Italy's many disparate, regional diasporas were slowly consolidated into a single, national diaspora identifying primarily with the Italian nation. But the form of the diaspora's nationalism was not *creatio ex nihilo*. Mussolini worked hard to win widespread support for fascism from the nine million Italian diaspora living abroad, implementing many initiatives for migrants, even as his nationalistic government restricted emigration.[30] A similar historical process of convergence unfolded among diasporic Armenians. In this case, the diaspora sought to influence domestic and foreign policy development in the country of origin (in the Armenian case, this was most true in post-Soviet Armenia), while the latter tried to influence the diaspora in turn, seeking to tap its resources and regulate

[30] Donna Gabaccia, *Italy's Many Diasporas* (Seattle: University of Washington Press, 2000).

its activities in the homeland by circumscribing the diaspora's political involvement and instead emphasizing financial and cultural exchanges.[31]

Diasporic identities range from the cosmopolitan to virulent ethnic nationalism; it should therefore not be surprising that the actions of a diaspora toward the country of origin manifest themselves in complex ways. The act of migration and living abroad affects identities, attenuating some and amplifying others, but the questions remain: which identities and why? Most arguments that seek to explain why diasporas engage in long-distance nationalism recognize cognitive explanations centering on identity issues as the driving force. However, these theoretical explanations are of little help in understanding the intensity of a diaspora's nationalism relative to that in the country of origin, the intensity of one diaspora's nationalism relative to others, or the forms this long-distance nationalism takes, especially whether it manifests as ethnic or civic nationalism. Diasporas engage in civic nationalism—ranging from lobbying the government of their adopted country on foreign policy to sending funds during a natural calamity—yet they also support (to varying extents) ethnic nationalism, whose consequences can be deeply inimical but can also be easily exaggerated. An important factor explaining the variance in outcomes is whether (and to what degree) a diaspora is alienated from the governing regime—which in turn is a function of why they left in the first place.

The role of diasporas in ethnic violence and civil wars in the country of origin has drawn particular attention, given the serious implications of this involvement.[32] Historically, however, as was the case with the Greek, Polish, Irish, and Slovak diasporas in the nineteenth and twentieth centuries, or the communities of Russian Socialists throughout Western Europe at the start of the twentieth century, the long-distance nationalism of these diasporas has been portrayed in a more benign and positive light as "freedom fighters." Context works to make an ideology appear threatening or not: while diasporas in the earlier period were fighting multinational nondemocratic empires, today they are battling democratic states, and hence are perceived as more threatening. When this is not the case, as in Cuba and Iran, diasporas appear to enjoy greater international forbearance.

In recent years, diasporas have played a particularly important role in sustaining insurgencies. The roles of the Palestinian, Irish, and Sri Lankan Tamil diasporas in helping foster strong insurgencies are well known. The sudden upsurge in strength of the Kosovo Liberation Army (KLA) during the summer of 1998—at the expense of more compromise-oriented Kosovo elites—may have been at least partially due to fundraising

[31] Razmik Panossian, "Between Ambivalence and Intrusion: Politics and Identity in Armenia-Diaspora Relations," *Diaspora: Journal of Transitional Studies* 7, no. 2 (1998): 149–96.

[32] Yossi Shain and Martin Sherman, "Dynamics of Disintegration: Diaspora, Secession and the Paradox of Nation-States," *Nations and Nationalism* 4, no. 3 (1998): 321–46.

efforts by the Albanian diaspora in the West. The Croatian diaspora was quite effective in helping to swing the international community behind the Croats in their conflict with the Croatian Serbs in the mid-1990s. Collier and Hoeffler find that, all other factors being equal, the risk of conflict starting after at least five years of peace is six times greater in nations with the largest diasporas as compared to those with the smallest. Moreover, "after peace has been restored, the legacy of conflict-induced grievance enables rebel movements to restart conflict by drawing on the support of their diasporas."[33]

Diasporas have emerged as important actors and supporter of civil insurgencies, militant movements and terrorism around the world, especially after the end of the Cold War. A survey of support for insurgent movements covering seventy-four active insurgencies between 1991 and 2000 found that forty-four received state support of a magnitude critical to the survival and success of the movement; another twenty-one movements received significant support from refugees, nineteen received significant support from diasporas, and twenty-five gained backing from other outside actors, such as Islamic organizations or relief agencies.[34] Table 2.2 lists diaspora support for extremist causes (including insurgencies) in the country of origin. Nonstate actors, including diasporas, apparently play a particularly important role in funding. Not only is their contribution substantial, but it is also more reliable, for it is less susceptible to the rapid changes that frequently characterize state support. Still, although this study also presents suggestive evidence that diasporas are an important factor in fueling domestic conflict, their importance relative to other factors continues to be disputed.

A different research question centers on why certain diaspora-fueled conflicts ebb while others continue to simmer. For instance, in South Asia, conflicts within Punjab (in India) and Sri Lanka led the Sikh diaspora in the former and the Sri Lankan Tamil diaspora in the latter to actively support armed groups. Yet, while overseas support for the Khalistan movement has waned, overseas Sri Lankan Tamil communities continue to finance the Liberation Tigers of Tamil Eelam (LTTE). What explains this divergence? Christine Fair argues that an important factor was the differences in the geographical and political reach of the two diasporas.[35] However, it is likely that the changes in the domestic context that gave rise to these movements in the first place were even more important.

[33] Paul Collier and Anke Hoeffler, "Greed and Greviance in Civil War," World Bank Policy Research Working Paper No. 2355 (Washington, DC: World Bank, 2000).

[34] Daniel Byman, Peter Chalk, Bruce Hoffman, William Rosenau, and David Brannan, *Trends in Outside Support for Insurgent Movements* (Santa Monica, CA: Rand, 2001).

[35] C. Christine Fair, "Diaspora Involvement in Insurgencies: Insights from the Khalistan and Tamil Eelam Movements," *Nationalism and Ethnic Politics* 11, no. 1 (2005): 125–56.

TABLE 2.2
Diaspora Extremism since the 1990s

Country/Region of Origin	Examples of Ultranationalist/ Extremist Groups	Country/Region of Settlement
Afghanistan	Taliban	Pakistan
Algeria	Islamic Salvation Army (AIS), Armed Islamic Group (GIA)	France
Azerbaijan	Armenian separatists in Ngorno-Karabakh	Armenia, North America, European Union
Croatia/former Republic of Yugoslavia	Croatian nationalists	Croatia, Germany
Cuba	Cuban exiles	United States
Egypt	Gamaat Islamiyya (IG)	Middle East, United Kingdom
India	Vishwa Hindu Parishad	United States, United Kingdom
India (Kashmir)	Hizb-ul-Mujahideen, Harkat al-Ansar, Lashkar-e-Taiba	Pakistan
Indonesia	Free Aceh Movement (GAM)	Libya, Malaysia
Israel	Zionist Organization of America, Jewish Defense League	United States
Israel (occupied territories)	Palestinian Islamic Jihad (PIJ), Popular Front for the Liberation of Palestine (PFLP)	Middle East
Kosovo	Kosovo Liberation Army (KLA)	Albania
Lebanon	Hezbollah	Americas, Middle East
Russia	Chechen rebels	European Union, Middle East
Rwanda	Forces Armees Rwandaises	Burundi
Sri Lanka	LTTE	Canada, European Union
Turkey	Kurdish Workers Party (PKK)	European Union (especially Germany)
United Kingdom	IRA, PIRA, Islamic groups	United States, Pakistan

Source: Devesh Kapur, "The Janus Face of Diasporas," in *Diasporas and Development,* eds. Barbara J. Merz, Lincoln Chen, and Peter Geithner (Cambridge: Harvard University Press, 2007), 99, table 1.

While India succeeded in the restoration of democracy in Punjab and the elimination of militants there, Sri Lanka was unable to do so for nearly three decades. The Sri Lankan Tamil diaspora's support for a separatist case will undoubtedly wane with the military defeat of the LTTE in 2009 but might find other channels if the post-conflict political process does not address discrimination against the community. A similar case could be made of Northern Ireland, where concessions and agreements made by the British government, together with changes in the international context post–September 2001, led to a sharp decline in the Irish diaspora's support for militant groups there.

The factors that affect the likelihood, form, and intensity of diasporic long-distance nationalism—for example, the finely detailed characteristics of the diaspora and its reasons for leaving, and the countries of origin and settlement—need better understanding. The conventional wisdom is that diasporic nationalism is a consequence of the failure of immigrants to identify with the host society: it fills their identity "needs" in the host society primarily because of low levels of assimilation. Thus, Alejandro Portes argues that the preoccupation with the country of origin is greatest among those immigrants who intend to return (e.g., political exiles and migrant laborers) and least among those immigrants who have made a long-term commitment to the host society (e.g., professionals and immigrant entrepreneurs).[36] Others argue that ethnic identity will be salient even among professionals if they experience discrimination.[37] Similarly, another view argues that loss of status is a driving force behind diasporic transnational political activity; Michael Jones-Correa, for instance, argues that Latino males face a significant loss of status upon migrating to the United States and consequently are more likely to participate in political activities in the country of origin.[38] While these theories argue that diasporic nationalism is linked to levels and aspirations regarding assimilation, John Kenny argues that support for diasporic nationalism is strategically adopted by particular groups within the immigrant community as a means of generating support for their own local goals in the host society.[39]

Be that as it may, ethnic diasporas have been empowered in recent years because of their growing size, visibility, and impact within the international

[36] Alejandro Portes, "Globalization from Below: The Rise of Transnational Communities," in *The Ends Of Globalization: Bringing Society Back In*, eds. D. Kalb, M. van der Land, and R. Staring (Boulder, CO: Rowman and Littlefield, 1999).

[37] Ernest Gellner, *Nations and Nationalism* (Ithaca, NY: Cornell University Press, 1983).

[38] Michael Jones-Correa, *Between Two Nations: The Political Predicament of Latinos in New York City* (Ithaca, NY: Cornell University Press, 1998).

[39] John Kenny, "Mobilizing Diasporas in Nationalist Conflicts" (PhD thesis, University of Chicago, 2000).

system. Diasporic communities now have more mechanisms to call attention to issues of interest in their home countries. The ongoing communications and information technology revolution allows nonstate actors to more easily fundraise, mount international public relations campaigns, or exert pressure on governments in host countries. In addition, global banking nets make it easier, faster, and cheaper to move money than ever before. Clearly, for better or worse, diasporas have emerged as one of the most important nonstate actors in the international system, and consequently the diaspora channel represents a key mechanism by which international migration impacts sending countries.

Return Channel

The return channel works when those who left come back home, often with augmented human capital, financial capital (savings), foreign connections, ideas, and changed expectations. Return migrants are often viewed as negatively selected, i.e., those "who did not make it." The reality is more complex. While in some cases, such as in the case of scientists, this may be true, there are often greater incentives for elites to return than those lower down in the social and income hierarchies. Indeed, the propensity of the skilled to return may be greater when the income distribution in the country of origin is more unequal. For some, it may just be a preference to be a big fish in a small pond rather than a smaller fish in a big pond. For others, it may be forward expectations, as seen in the increase in return migration when countries as diverse as South Korea, Taiwan, Ireland, China, and India began to grow rapidly. A smaller subset of those who return are those who may be more intensely nationalist and more committed to national building—exemplified by the leaderships of anticolonial nationalist movements, virtually all of whom had studied and lived abroad.

Going abroad reshapes attitudes, expectations, and identities. America's worst race riots—the Tulsa race riots in Greenwood, Oklahoma, in 1921—resulted in part because of the participation of the town's African American soldiers in World War I. According to Alfred Brophy, the cognitive dissonance between the rhetoric about fighting for freedom abroad and its lack at home made Greenwood residents who had served in the war, as well as those who looked proudly on as their friends and relatives participated in it, more assertive in pressing for freedom and equality.[40] Veterans also brought ideas to Greenwood; they had seen and lived in a world where blacks were asked to fight to defend freedom and where

[40] Alfred L. Brophy, *Reconstructing the Dreamland: The Tulsa Riot of 1921, Race Reparations, and Reconciliation* (New York: Oxford University Press, 2002).

they were given more of it than white Oklahomans would generally allow. White Southerners were bothered by the increasing status and attitudes of blacks and found that "Negroes were becoming independent and no longer servile."[41]

In a parallel situation, it is not surprising that the first mass movement in India's freedom struggle occurred in 1919 in the state of Punjab, where nearly 60 percent of the British Indian army was recruited. The British Indian army had been a critical source of manpower for maintaining the empire.[42] However, until World War I, the British had been very careful not to use the army in any action against whites, worried that success might undermine the mystique of carefully nurtured racial hierarchy. In addition, British Indian troops had never been placed in a white social milieu such as Europe. This was the principal reason why in the Boer War, despite heavy casualties, the British Indian army was used only in support functions. This was not possible in World War I, and as David Omissi documents in his compilation of letters from Indian troops serving in France, the British had reason to be worried.[43] The effects of the experience of both living in France and fighting the Germans come out vividly in the letters. These observations range from the social (more balanced gender relations) to the economic (the wonderment at the lack of haggling in the market). But it is the political observations that are perhaps the most striking. Wounded soldiers convalescing in British hospitals were struck by how the British treated each other in that country, in contrast to how they interacted with Indians in India. On the frontline, meanwhile, victories over the Germans instilled greater self-confidence among the Indian soldiers.

Returnees have also played a critical role in the development of "Africa" as a consolidated political and cultural space: "The idea of Africa as a single place and of the African—the person of color, the Negro—as a single kind of person was conceived in the diaspora. . . . These conceptions, which were to become the Pan-Africanism of Nkrumah and his

[41] "Are We Entitled to the Moral Leadership of the World?" *Black Dispatch* 4, August 15, 1919, quoted in Brophy, *Reconstructing the Dreamland*, 6.

[42] At the outbreak of World War I, the combatant strength of the Indian army, including reserves, was 194,000 Indian ranks; enlistment during the war period totaled 791,000, making a total combatant population of 985,000. Of this number, 552,000 were sent overseas. In the case of noncombatants, the prewar strength was 45,000; an additional 427,000 were enrolled during the war; and 391,000 were sent overseas. The total number of Indian personnel was thus around 1,457,000, of whom 943,000 served overseas. India army personnel were deployed in France, East Africa, Egypt, and most importantly in Mesopotamia. Aravind Ganachari, "Purchasing Indian Loyalties I: Imperial Policy of Recruitment and 'Rewards,'" *Economic and Political Weekly* 40, no. 8 (February 19, 2005): 779–88.

[43] David Omissi, *Indian Voices of the Great War: Soldiers' Letters, 1914–18* (New York: St. Martin's Press, 1999).

generation of African leaders, came back to Africa with the returnees. Nkrumah learned them in Pennsylvania and in London; but in Liberia and Sierra Leone, men like Blyden [who had been born in the Virgin Islands and arrived in Liberia from abroad at around age 18] were already teaching them in the nineteenth century."[44]

Foreign education, especially in Western universities, has been a key mechanism for the transmission of ideas of modernity, be it political regimes or economic systems. Although foreign-educated individuals are a very small fraction of their native populations, there is evidence to suggest that they promote democracy in their home country, but only if the foreign education is acquired in democratic countries.[45] From the nationalist leaderships of newly emerging countries following decolonization to the economic technocrats of the 1990s who were the stewards of economic reforms in many developing countries, returning elites have played a singular role in shaping the destinies of their countries. This mechanism highlights the role of migration in developing new skills and changing preferences and expectations, particularly through higher education abroad. The "Berkeley mafia" in the case of Indonesia, the "Chicago boys" in the case of Chile, and a set of elite universities in the case of Mexico are all examples where technocrats returned to their countries in positions of responsibility and then spearheaded neoliberal reforms in them.[46]

While international education has been growing by leaps and bounds (there were an estimated 2.9 million international students in 2008),[47] the political economy consequences are not well understood. Despite all the positive stories, there is no reason to believe that skills and ideas acquired abroad necessarily have positive consequences. Pol Pot (who studied in Paris) and Sayyid Qutb (the spiritual leader of the Islamic fundamentalism

[44] Kwame Anthony Appiah, "What Was Africa to Them?" *New York Review of Books* 54, no. 14 (September 27, 2007).

[45] Antonio Spilimbergo, "Democracy and Foreign Education," *American Economic Review* 99 (March 2009): 528–43.

[46] On Chile, see Juan Gabriel Valdés, *Pinochet's Economists: The Chicago School of Economics in Chile* (Cambridge,UK: Cambridge University Press, 1995). For an account of the transformation of the Mexican economic technocracy from its nationalist left-leaning heyday in the 1960s to a bastion of neoliberals trained in elite U.S. universities such as MIT, Harvard, Stanford, University of Chicago, and Yale, and their impact on Mexico, see Sarah L. Babb, *Managing Mexico: Economists from Nationalism to Neoliberalism* (Princeton, NJ: Princeton University Press, 2001). On the Berkeley Mafia, see "Celebrating Indonesia: Fifty Years with the Ford Foundation 1953–2003," available at http://web.archive.org/web/20070403150613/www.fordfound.org/elibrary/documents/5002/toc.cfm.

[47] *Atlas of International Student Mobility*, Institute of International Education, retrieved June 2009. Available at http://www.atlas.iienetwork.org/?p=48027.

movement who studied in Colorado), while very dissimilar, are two examples of precisely the opposite outcome. The new skills of return migrants could lie as much in the organization and techniques of violence as in new agricultural techniques. Pakistanis and Yemenis, who migrated to Afghanistan to fight in the wars there and have since returned, have brought with them a set of new ideas that are unlikely to be beneficial to their countries. Similarly, gang members of Central American origin in the United States who were deported back to their countries have been observed to be much more adept in the use of guns. This appears to have increased the levels of violence in their countries when they return.[48]

Interaction between Channels

The preceding categorization of the principal mechanisms through which international migration affects the sending country is not to suggest that these channels operate in isolation from one another. For instance, the importance of the prospect and diaspora channels is likely to amplify the effects of the absence channel. In contrast, an increase in the salience of the return channel might dampen the effects of the other three channels.

The almost canonical theoretical framework for analyzing the political effects of international migration, a framework that (implicitly) emphasizes the absence channel, is Albert Hirschman's well-known treatment of "exit, voice and loyalty." Hirschman argued that "exit has been shown to drive out voice" and that "voice is likely to play an important role in organizations only on the condition that exit is ruled out."[49] But despite the elegance and perceptiveness of Hirschman's insight, it has been difficult to generate testable hypotheses.[50] If international migration is a form of exit from a country's polity, does exit via emigration increase or decrease political instability? East Germany and Cuba provide two contrasting examples: while in the former case migration precipitated severe political instability, resulting in the downfall of the regime, in the latter case it has enhanced regime stability.

According to Hirschman's framework, while the *threat* of exit enhances voice, once exit occurs (e.g., through international migration), it should

[48] Freddy Funes, "Removal of Central American Gang Members: How Immigration Laws Fail to Reflect Global Reality," *University of Miami Law Review* 63 (2008): 301–38.

[49] Albert O. Hirschman, *Exit, Voice and Loyalty: Responses to Decline in Firms, Organizations, and State* (Cambridge, MA: Harvard University Press, 1970).

[50] Keith Dowding, Peter John, Thanos Mergoupis, and Mark Van Vugt, "Exit, Voice and Loyalty: Analytic and Empirical Developments," *European Journal of Political Research* 37 (2000): 469–95.

result in a loss of voice and a waning of political influence. This idea makes intuitive sense: one cannot influence a game if one leaves the field. However, as I demonstrate later in this study, this is hardly inevitable— exit does not always lead to loss of voice. When emigrants "exit" a country, it is usually *not* the case that they snap their links. Indeed, since emigrants often have greater access to important resources, ranging from remittances, skills-transfer through returns, and networks, as well as symbolic and cultural capital, they may well enhance their voice in the country of origin.

My hypothesis is that *international exit, in contrast to domestic exit, can actually amplify the domestic voice of groups that exit.* The degree to which this will occur depends on the following:

1. The selectivity characteristics of the migration
2. The institutional structures of the country *from* which exit occurred
3. The institutional structures of the country *to* which exit occurs

The effects of international migration on the country of origin depend on the characteristics of the migrants as well as both the country of origin and the country of destination. The following discussion highlights the large number of variables and the complex interaction among them, as well as the mechanisms by which international migration impacts the country of origin. At the most basic level, the effects depend on the following:

1. **Who leaves?** Selection effects are crucial. The more demographically concentrated migrants are—in terms of ethnicity, age and gender, education, income, religion, and region—the greater the effects. The effects of migration and diasporas are very different if the migrant streams are elite or non-elite (table 2.3). By "elite," I mean not just the highly skilled, but also those who come from a stratum of society that gives them certain attitudes and access to influential networks.

However, as I pointed out in chapter 1, some critical dimensions of this variable, such as leadership potential, entrepreneurship, or tendency toward institution-building, are likely to be unobservable.

2. **How many leave?** The effects of *who* leaves are amplified by the *size* of the migration. Thus, while diasporas from countries like Germany and Chile have higher educational levels compared to those from many other countries, their small size makes them marginal actors. Relative numbers matter more for the "absence" effect, while absolute numbers have a greater impact on the "diaspora" effect. Small island economies or countries with a small tertiary-educated population are particularly vulnerable to the "brain drain." On the other hand, while the relative numbers are

TABLE 2.3
Typical Characteristics of Contemporary Voluntary Migrant Streams

	Elite	Non-elite
Absolute numbers	Small	Large
Relative size	Large	Small
Selection bias (education)	Extremely high positive selection	Low–medium positive selection
Distance of migration	Far	Close (neighboring countries)
Destination country	Upper income	Lower income (high income only if proximate)
Occupation in country of migration	Medium to high skill	Low skill
Income in host country	Medium to high	Low
Age at time of migration	Greater age dispersion, with a bias to young	Young
Investable wealth (generation)	First generation	Third generation (or later)
Political effects (source country)	Substantial at national level	Substantial at local level, but if the size is large, then also at the national level
Political leverage (destination country)	Medium	Small

much less for China and India, the sheer absolute number of emigrants matters much more in creating transnational networks and flexing political muscle in the receiving countries.

3. **Why did they leave?** The relative importance of political and economic factors underlying migration decisions will affect the nature and intensity of engagement with the country of origin after departure. The relationship of political and refugee diasporas with the country of origin are likely to be quite different from those who left for economic reasons. If there are sharp political and ethnic cleavages in the country of origin and the diaspora was forced out for political reasons, then it is likely to leverage its role to undermine the political regime in the country of origin. Cuban Americans, East European immigrants in North America prior to 1990, or Sri Lankan Tamil immigrants in Canada are all examples of this phenomenon.

4. **When did they leave?** It might appear that the greater the vintage of a diaspora, the less intimate its links with the country of origin, but this relationship may not be linear in the short and medium term. Vintage effects are likely to be mediated by age effects. Migrants are often young, but even if the strength of their ties to the country of origin are strongest immediately after they leave, their ability to have a greater influence usually increases with time (subject to specific family circumstances). Moreover, this variable is being affected by technological changes, which have made it much easier to travel and maintain communication and cultural links. Another impact of this variable can be seen in the cohort effect. Early waves of migrants may be more positively selected compared to subsequent migrant streams. For instance, migrants from Mexico to the United States in the 1980s appear to be more positively selected than those who came in the new millennium.

5. **Where did they go?** The destination country plays an important role because it affects the economic well-being of the migrants and the activities in which they engage: skilled versus nonskilled labor; tradable versus nontradable sectors; economic sectors that are "sunrise" industries versus mature industries, etc. The more economically successful a diaspora is, the greater its effects on the country of origin—and these effects are amplified by the global salience of the destination country. Controlling for other characteristics, ethnic lobbying on foreign policy has a greater potential payoff if the host country is the United States than if it is New Zealand. Moreover, the destination country's political regime can also have significant effects. Migrants to countries with authoritarian regimes are more likely to be temporary compared to those who move to countries with democratic regimes, and length of stay, in turn, affects migrant behavior. Furthermore, in democratic countries the diaspora can engage more openly in political activities affecting the country of origin. Indeed, the possibility of emulation by diasporas means that over time, they tend to learn about the political practices, such as forms of political participation and organization, in the destination country. The more open the political system, the greater the learning and the content of what is learned—and the larger the likely effects on the country of origin.

6. **How did they leave?** Even controlling for other migrant characteristics, the manner of entry will affect a migrant's prospects and therefore the impact on the country of origin. This is most obvious in comparing legal versus illegal migrants, but even within the former, those who enter as students have much better labor market prospects than those who come in through asylum or family reunification, even though they may have similar levels of education.

7. **Country of origin characteristics.** The difference between the *potential* importance of a diaspora and its *realized* influence will depend

principally on policies and politics in the country of origin. For instance, to whatever extent the Chinese diaspora has played a role in China's economic miracle, its influence became possible only after China opened up.[51] The contrast with the African diaspora of more recent vintage makes clear that the country of origin has to be prepared to make use of the remittances and/or investments of the diaspora by ensuring political stability and economic policies conducive to economic development. If domestic political cleavages are on ethnic lines, this will mediate any ethnic selection effects of migration. A diaspora's attitude is likely to change along with the evolution and prospects of the country of origin. Moreover, to the extent that diasporas are an informal channel of influence, their influence is likely to be greater the weaker formal institutional structures are in the country of origin. Diasporic networks straddling the European Union and North Africa are likely to be more consequential than intra-EU diasporas.

The list of variables discussed here emphasizes the range of migrant characteristics that a researcher must take into account in order to get a handle on the consequences of migration. However, in practice such data simply do not exist. Consequently, there is little option but to generate these data from scratch. This study has sought to bridge this research lacuna through an intensive data collection and analysis effort. I now turn to the methodologies developed to collect data on the characteristics of international migration from India.

METHODOLOGY

The key innovation underpinning this study has been the generation of new data on international migration and migrants from India, principally through three large surveys. The first was a household sample survey of emigration conducted in India. The second was a household survey of Asian Indians (or Indian Americans) in the United States. The third was the construction of a database on international mobility of Indian elites over the past half-century.

[51] Constance Lever-Tracy, David Fu-Keung Ip, and Noel Tracy, *The Chinese Diaspora and Mainland China: An Emerging Economic Synergy* (New York: Macmillan Publishing Company, 1996). The authors emphasize the importance of timing for the opportune economic relations between China and its diaspora: "Had it delayed a decade, it is possible that diaspora capitalism, with too limited investment opportunities, would have by then lost its industrializing drive and degenerated too deeply into paper shuffling and speculation" (p. 284). Presumably, this is because they would have followed on the tail end of Western MNCs that subsequently entered China in droves.

Survey of Emigration from India (SEI)

The SEI was inserted as an additional module to the Indian Readership Survey (IRS) and conducted from July 2004 to February 2005. The IRS is one of the largest and the most comprehensive media and market research surveys in India. Appendix I provides survey details, including coverage, sampling, household and individual selection, and the survey instrument.

Suffice it to say, the household survey is both sufficiently large as well as nationally representative. The survey had a sample size of 210,000 and covers about 1100 towns and 2800 villages in 22 of India's 28 states. The excluded states—Arunachal Pradesh, Manipur, Mizoram, Nagaland, Sikkim, and Tripura (the small states of the Northeast)—account for less than one percent of India's population of 1.028 billion as per the 2001 census. The IRS even reaches villages without electricity, attesting to its wide coverage. Given its purpose, the IRS sample has an urban bias: the sample is approximately two-thirds urban and one-thirds rural, the inverse of India's population distribution. However, this is suitable for the purposes of this study, since in contrast to internal migration, international migration from India is largely an urban phenomenon. The sample was weighted to correct for certain demographic variables—namely, age and gender (available from the 2001 census)—adding to the statistical validity of the survey.

Survey of Asian Indians in the United States (SAIUS)

A fundamental problem in conducting a survey of an immigrant group is how to construct a random sample without incurring prohibitive costs. In rare cases where the immigrant group is present in large numbers and is spatially concentrated—for instance, in the case of emigrants from Mexico in the United States—this is possible. But in most cases, the numbers of emigrants are small relative to the population. Thus, although emigrants from India were among the top five groups coming to the United States during the 1990s, by the end of the decade they still accounted for just 0.6 percent of the population. Simply conducting a random sampling of the population would require an extremely large sampling frame. In principle, one can improve on this by sampling only those areas where Indian Americans are spatially concentrated. According to the 2000 U.S. Census, half of Indian Americans live in five urban areas, three-fourths in twenty, and four-fifths in thirty. However, the share of the Indian American population in these urban areas is still meager—1.91, 1.39, and 1.25 percent, respectively. The highest density is the San Francisco/Oakland/San Jose urban area (4.81 percent). However, sampling in a single urban area (which encompasses Silicon Valley) would not be representative of the Indian American population, since an unusually high fraction of the Indian American population in this area are engineers engaged in high-tech occupations.

Another route is to tap immigrant organizations for member lists. This route has obvious problems. Constructing the universe of such organizations and persuading them to share information about their membership lists is nontrivial and creates sample bias as regards members of those organizations who are unwilling to share this information. Most critically, however, since members are self-selected, sample bias is a major problem, and it is unclear how one would be able to determine the extent of the bias and how to correct for it.

The survey methodology I adopted was in principle quite simple. I first built from scratch a comprehensive database of Indian Americans in the United States. Second, I drew a random sample from this database. Third, I constructed the survey instrument. And fourth, I conducted a phone survey of this random sample using a call-center in India.

The single biggest obstacle in following this route was how to build a comprehensive database of Indian Americans to ensure that the random sample drawn from this population was representative of the population. Fortunately, Indian last names proved to be an excellent instrument to analyze international migration. Indian last names are (for the most part) unique, which makes it relatively easy to track people of Indian origin. Appendix II describes how the database was built and the different robustness checks to ensure that the database indeed captured the underlying population.

Survey of Indian Elites

The database on national elites focuses on the overseas exposure of India's political, business, bureaucratic, and scientific elites—those who may have a potential impact on the political economy of India in some direct way. Although overseas exposure can encompass a range of experiences, the database focuses on education. While I explain the rationale in detail in chapter 5, the basic logic is that education has been the key mechanism for constructing new elites. Elites are educated to govern, and academic training and education have been central to the creation of new bureaucratic elites.

The database of Indian elites covers four critical decision-making groups: politicians, bureaucrats, scientists, and industrialists. Education was measured on two dimensions: the level to which the individual studied, and the place from where the degree was obtained. The time period covered was 1950 to 2000. Unlike in most other developing countries,

Indian politics has been characterized by unusual regime stability, which meant that elite mobility took place gradually but steadily through democratic politics. Consequently, elites would not change annually, and hence the data covers three points in time: 1950, 1980, and 2000. The methodology—in particular, problems of consistency over time and sources for the database—is elaborated in appendix IV.

CONCLUSION

The central claim of this book is that international migration and diasporas transform the political economy of sending countries. The staples of the vast literature on the political economy of development have largely ignored the effects of international migration, in large part because of the analytical and empirical challenges it poses. In this chapter, I have laid out an analytical framework and empirical research strategy to address some of these challenges, which will be analyzed in greater detail in the remainder of the book.

Clearly, the empirical strategy is not without its limitations. For instance, one could question the focus on Indian migration to the United States instead of the Gulf, since the magnitude of Indian migration to the latter has been greater. There are four reasons for choosing the former over the latter. First, migration to the United States is pan-Indian, while migration to the Gulf is dominated by one state (Kerala). Second, migration to the Gulf is temporary, while that to the United States (and other Western countries) is a mix of temporary and permanent. Third, the Gulf is not a homogenous entity. For instance, there are significant differences between the streams of Indian migration and their local positioning between the United Arab Emirates and Kuwait, with the former pointed toward South Asia and the latter toward the Middle East.[52] Thus, a much wider net would have to be cast to try to capture the effects of Indian migration to the Gulf. Last, due to political sensitivities, data collection problems in that part of the world are much more severe. This point underscores the fact that the analytical advantages of a comparative approach can by stymied by practical concerns. Additionally, one would ideally want panel data, while in this study we have only cross-section data. Consequently, many of the dynamic long-term effects of international migration cannot be precisely estimated. Such research limitations

[52] See, for instance, Karen Leonard, "South Asians in the Indian Ocean World: Language, Policing, and Gender Practices in Kuwait and the UAE," *Comparative Studies of South Asia, Africa and the Middle East* 25, no. 3 (November 2005): 677–86.

notwithstanding, the approach undertaken here offers valuable analytical insights into the political economy effects of international migration in the Indian context.

In order to develop these insights, the following chapter begins by examining a critical variable determining the impact of international migration on the sending country: the characteristics of international migrants from India.

CHAPTER 3

Selection Characteristics of Emigration from India

INTRODUCTION

THE IMPACT OF international migration on the country of origin is critically dependent on the characteristics of the migrants: who leaves, for where, when, and why? However, as you saw in chapter 2, even trying to assess something as seemingly evident as *who leaves* is anything but easy. For instance, focusing on just one attribute of a migrant group—say, their education—reveals the complexity surrounding this line of research. Most of the information we have on emigrants pertains to their level of education. This is certainly important, but so is the type and quality of that education. The loss of a migrant with a college degree in the humanities from a mediocre university will likely be quite different from the loss of a graduate from a highly ranked and reputed engineering institution. Even this level of specificity fails to capture the complete impact, since the effects could be substantially different if those who leave are concentrated at the top ten percent or at the bottom ten percent of their class. Consider a country that loses roughly one percent of its college graduates. Taken alone, that may seem like a trivial number, yet it was a loss of just this magnitude from Germany in the mid-1930s that changed the locus of global science and deprived Germany of some of the world's best scientists and intellectual minds.

Furthermore, education is only one of many emigrant characteristics that have significant consequences for the home country. The age of the migrant has implications for the dependency ratio and the "fiscally attractive" population (i.e., those of working age). Gender and marital status can affect the migrant's household in the home country, as well as the intensity and nature of links. A different set of variables concerns the characteristics that have political economy implications: the religion, region, ethnicity, class, and caste from which an immigrant is drawn. If international migration from India is selectively greater from the poor inland states of the North and East, remittances would ameliorate the growing interstate inequality. If, however, they come from the wealthier coastal states in the West and South, then remittances would amplify inequality. Effects on income inequality would be similarly manifest if the migrants came from India's urban professional elites or from the large number of poorer rural households.

Detailed empirical evidence regarding the specific characteristics of Indian emigrants is critical to understanding the implications of this migration for India. In this chapter, I analyze the characteristics of Indian migrants through a range of data sources—in particular, two surveys, the first conducted in India in 2004–2005 (Survey of Emigration from India, or SEI) and the second conducted in the United States in mid-2004 (Survey of Asian Indians in the United States, SAIUS). In addition, I supplement data from these surveys with other primary data sources–namely, the Census and Current Population Surveys in the United States and the limited data available from the National Sample Survey, the Protector of Emigrants in the Ministry of Labour (GOI), and passport information from the Ministry of External Affairs.

I first provide a brief historical overview of Indian emigration and the differences between the large-scale migration in the late nineteenth century and that in the late twentieth century. Next, I examine the evidence on the selection effects of emigration from India. I then provide evidence on the selection characteristics of a key destination of Indian emigrants in recent years—the United States. I conclude by comparing the salient selection characteristics of the two great emigration streams from India in the latter half of the nineteenth and twentieth centuries.

HISTORICAL OVERVIEW

Although Indians have been migrating to other lands for thousands of years, large-scale migration began only following the end of slavery in British colonies in the 1830s. Most migrants at the time went to South or Southeast Asia—about 42 percent settled in Burma, another 25 percent in Ceylon, 19 percent in British Malaya, and the rest in Africa, the Caribbean, and the Pacific.[1] The vast majority of Indian emigrants went as indentured laborers. Contract length varied with distance—accordingly, short-term arrangements were more common within South and Southeast Asia. The *kangani* system (the *kangani*, or head-man, was a professional recruiter, who often recruited whole gangs from a given village) characterized migration to British Malaya and Ceylon, while a variant of this practice, know as the *maistry* system, played a similar role in migration to Burma.

[1] Kingsley Davis, *The Population of India and Pakistan* (Princeton, NJ: Princeton University Press, 1951). An exception was the migration of the Roma people from Northwest India at the turn of the millennium.

Although British colonies (Burma, Ceylon, and Malaya nearby, as well as distant Trinidad and Tobago, Guyana, and Fiji) were the primary destinations for overseas migration, Dutch and French colonies in Reunion Island, Guadeloupe, Martinique, Mauritius, and Suriname also became home to considerable numbers of migrants.

In addition to their tendency to serve as indentured laborers in South or Southeast Asia, these migrants were also mostly unskilled and from the lower castes. While the migrants to geographically proximate regions (Burma, Ceylon, and Malaya) were from the Eastern coastal regions (Andhra Pradesh, Tamil Nadu, and Orissa), those going to more distant lands (the Caribbean, Fiji, and Mauritius) hailed primarily from the United Provinces (present-day Bihar and east Uttar Pradesh), and those to East and South Africa hailed from Gujarat and Punjab. As with the great transatlantic flows of the nineteenth century, a substantial wage difference—migrants could make between five to eight times what they earned in India—was the key driver of emigration.[2] The risks were large, with high mortality rates during passage, routinely abused contracts, and high suicide rates.[3] These unfavorable conditions might partly explain the high return rates: of the 30.2 million people who left India between 1834 and 1937, 23.9 million returned, resulting in a net migration of 6.3 million.[4] As with contemporary migration, migrants sent remittances using postal savings. They also returned with considerable savings: the average cash savings brought back by indentured Indian migrants returning from Mauritius in the late 1870s was equivalent to about four years of income at home.[5]

The second wave of migration was the "free" or "passage" migration of traders, clerks, bureaucrats, and professionals, mostly to East and South Africa and, in smaller numbers, to the other British colonies where indentured laborers had settled earlier. This migration continued in small numbers into the first half of the twentieth century. Following the end of World War II, post-war reconstruction and an acute labor shortage created a large demand for unskilled and semiskilled workers in the United Kingdom. These labor shortages drew large numbers of Indians, mainly from Punjab and Gujarat. A modest number of professionals and traders also migrated during this period. These numbers were considerably supplemented by "twice migrant" East African Asians (especially of Gujarati origin) into the United Kingdom in the late 1960s through the early 1970s.

[2] David Northrup, *Indentured Labor in the Age of Imperialism, 1834–1922* (Cambridge, UK/New York: Cambridge University Press, 1995).

[3] J. Geoghegan, *Note on Emigration from India* (Calcutta: Office of Superintendent of Government Printing, 1873); Hugh Tinker, *A New System of Slavery: The Export of Indian Labour Overseas, 1830–1920* (London: Oxford University Press, 1974).

[4] Davis, *The Population of India and Pakistan.*

[5] Northrup, *Indentured Labor in the Age of Imperialism*, 137.

Two unrelated events sparked the next major flow of emigration from the late 1960s onward. First, the sharp increase in oil prices and the resulting economic boom created a large demand for overseas labor in the Middle East. The majority of emigrants were unskilled or semiskilled, although in comparison to earlier migration waves there were considerable numbers of skilled migrants as well. Since the policies of the Middle East countries made permanent settlement extremely difficult, Indian migration to this region was inherently temporary. Migrants to these countries, especially women, have also been vulnerable due to limited civil rights and protections. While most eventually returned home, some skilled migrants often moved on to countries like the United Kingdom and Canada.

Second, the liberalization of U.S. immigration law in 1965 led to a large emigration of highly skilled professionals and students seeking to study in, and eventually immigrate to, the United States. The large demand for information technology (IT) workers in the United States in the late 1990s led to another wave of young professional immigrants. However, since most came with temporary work visas, a relatively large, although still modest, fraction returned home. The Indian-born population in the United States grew from around 13,000 in 1960 to nearly one million by 2000 and 1.5 million by 2007.[6] The Asian Indian population (the classification used by the U.S. Census Bureau to categorize the Indian-origin population in the United States) grew to nearly 1.7 million in 2000 and 2.8 million in 2007. Starting with a trickle in the early 1960s, by 2007 the Indian-born population became the fourth largest immigrant group in the United States (after Mexico, China and the Philippines).[7] This migrant stream has been the most highly educated, both in comparison to other immigrant groups into the United States and to any other Indian migrant streams. Since the 1990s, increasing numbers of skilled emigrants from India have also been moving to Australia, Canada, New Zealand, and Singapore— English-speaking industrialized countries whose higher-education systems are an important mechanism to attract and screen potential immigrants.

By the beginning of the new millennium, it was estimated that the Indian diaspora consisted of about 20 million people and spanned over 110 countries. There were 10,000 or more overseas Indians in 48 countries, and 11 countries had more than half a million residents who were of Indian origin.[8] More than fourth-fifths of the diaspora lived in middle- and

[6] Campbell Gibson and Emily Lennon, Technical Paper No. 29 (U.S. Bureau of the Census, 1999), table 3, available at http://www.census.gov/population/www/documentation/twps0029/tab03.html. The Indian-born population in the United States was 12,296 according to the 1960 census.

[7] Source: 2007 American Community Survey (ACS), U.S. Census Bureau.

[8] Government of India, *Report of the High Level Committee on the Indian Diaspora* (New Delhi: Ministry of External Affairs, 2001).

high-income countries, and more than 90 percent of those who lived in low-income countries were concentrated in just one, Myanmar. While the diaspora from the first two waves of migration has enjoyed mixed fortunes, this more recent immigrant group, on average, is better off in terms of income per capita, when compared to both the society from which it emigrated as well as, in many cases, that into which it settled. The latter holds true for many countries where there is a significant Indian-origin population. (Malaysia is a notable exception.) On the other hand, the diaspora suffers from ethnic tensions in many countries and, periodically, has been politically disenfranchised, especially in countries where migration occurred prior to independence (in the Caribbean, East Africa, Fiji, Malaysia, Myanmar, and in South Africa under the apartheid regime). The large "generational distance" of this diaspora means that its economic and family ties to India are quite weak, but it continues to draw religio-cultural sustenance from its roots in India.

Selection Characteristics of Contemporary Indian Migration

Evidence from India

Empirical evidence on contemporary international migration from India is surprisingly limited, even though opinions on the subject abound. The Indian government mounted a major initiative to build closer links with the Indian diaspora culminating in the first *Pravasi Bhartiya Divas* (Overseas Indian Celebration) in January 2003. As part of this initiative, an official commission was formed, but their thick report had little in the way of empirical analysis other than estimates of the numbers of overseas Indians by country.[9]

The only other sources of official data on the subject are the National Sample Survey (NSS) and passport data from the Ministry of Labour. Although the NSS is one of the world's leading household surveys, it has limited information about migration and even less on international migration.[10]

Passport data are an indirect way to gauge differences in international migration across different states. A passport-holder is likely to travel abroad, but need not. And if or when the passport-holder does travel, in

---

[9] Ibid.

[10] There have been several NSS surveys that have collected data on migration, notably the 49th round (January–June 1993) and the 55th round (July 1999–June 2000), but the questions have been limited. The questionnaire in the 64th round (July 2007–June 2008) is somewhat more comprehensive. However, at the time of completing this book, the data were yet to be released.

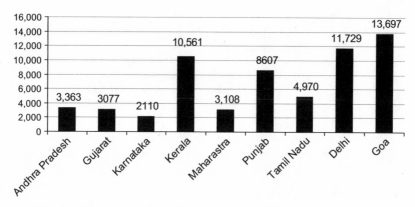

Figure 3.1. Average passports issued per million residents, 1997–2000. Note: The preceding graph shows data for the top seven states. Source: Ministry of Labour, GOI.

many (if not most) cases, it is for a variety of purposes, of which emigration is only one. Nonetheless, these factors are common across states, and hence the variance in the issue of passports across Indian states is suggestive of the regional selection effects of international mobility and, indirectly, of international migration (figure 3.1).

In order to protect Indian unskilled and semiskilled laborers traveling abroad for work from unscrupulous contractors, these laborers are required to register with the Protector of Emigrants. (These regulations do not apply to students, those traveling for business and pleasure, and skilled workers.) In principle, this office should have some data on Indian labor going overseas for work, but individual-level data are not accessible.

One exception in India is the Migration Monitoring Survey carried out by the Center for Development Studies in Trivandrum, Kerala, every five years. According to data from the last survey conducted in 2007, Kerala had approximately 1.85 million international migrants, 89 percent of whom were living and working in the Gulf region.[11] These periodic surveys are a rich source of data, but they are limited because of the focus on one state, migration from which is concentrated in the Middle East and is of relatively low skill.

The SEI survey, as a result, is the first attempt to specifically understand the characteristics of broader international migration from India. Methodological details of the survey are given in chapter 2 and appendix I.

[11] K. C. Zacharia and Irudaya Rajan, "Migration, Remittances, and Employment: Short Term Trends and Long Term Implications," Working Paper Series No. 395 (Trivandrum, Kerala, India: Center for Development Studies, 2007), 17.

TABLE 3.1
Indian Households with Global Connections
through the Diaspora

	Family Members	Extended Family	Friends
Overall (%)	1.7	2.9	0.8
Urban (%)	2.8	5.7	1.7
Rural (%)	1.2	1.7	0.4

Source: SEI.

SOCIOECONOMIC STATUS AND URBAN BIAS

Respondents were asked "Do you know any family members, extended family, or friends who live abroad?" and "How many [within each of these categories] that you personally know live abroad?" The responses point to three key characteristics of recent emigration from India.

First, the overall numbers are small. For a country of India's size, this is not surprising. Barely 1.7 percent of households have family members abroad, and only 2.9 percent have extended family abroad. Even fewer have "friends" abroad.

Second, there is a strong urban bias in households that have global links through migration (table 3.1). Urban households, on average, are 2.3 times as likely to have members of their immediate family abroad, 5 times as likely to have members of their extended family abroad, and 4.25 times as likely to have friends abroad compared to rural households. These findings are not surprising, since urban centers are the window through which a country's global links are woven.[12] They are more cosmopolitan and also have substantial numbers of high-income households—all of which are more likely to contribute to greater out-migration.

And third, the more "elite" the socioeconomic status of a household in India is, the larger its global networks. While the network size increases with income, it does so much more sharply at the highest end (figure 3.2). As one would expect, the *number* of members abroad also increases with income (figure 3.3), in both urban and rural areas, with the richest rural households (R1 and R2) having a greater likelihood of members abroad than poor urban households (A4 and A5). The survey's findings that for all groups, the number of households with one family member abroad is always greater than those with two members abroad, which in turn is always greater than those with three members (since the graphs do not

---

[12] Saskia Sassen, *The Global City: New York, London, Tokyo* (Princeton, NJ: Princeton University Press, 1991).

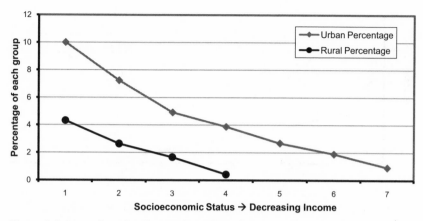

Figure 3.2. Immediate family members abroad. Source: SEI. $N = 467{,}112$.

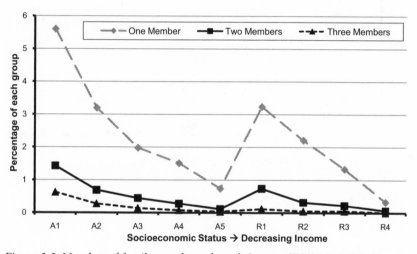

Figure 3.3. Number of family members abroad. Source: SEI. $N = 467{,}112$.

intersect or cross each other at any point), is both intuitive as well a good corroboration of the data.

The results are similar when we extend the analysis from immediate to extended family members (figure 3.4). Again, urban households tend to have more than two or three times as many extended family members abroad than rural households (5.7 percent compared to 0.6 percent). While all classes have fewer members of the immediate family abroad than the extended family, there is a sharp decline from the highest socioeconomic

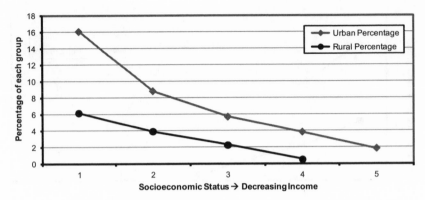

Figure 3.4. Extended family members abroad. Source: SEI. $N = 467,112$.

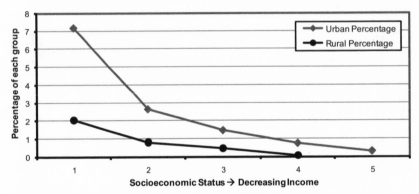

Figure 3.5. Friends abroad. Source: SEI. $N = 467,112$.

class (SEC 1) to the next (SEC 2). This shows the amplification of global networks at the most elite level.

In addition, the data shows that the likelihood of having a friend abroad increases with income; this is particularly marked at the highest socioeconomic class (figure 3.5).

Data on the number of extended family members and friends abroad are broadly similar. In both cases, the numbers increase sharply at the highest income levels, and the wealthiest rural group (R1) has substantially greater overseas networks compared to poor urban groups. In figures 3.6 and 3.7, I present data that aggregate overseas networks, including immediate and extended family members as well as friends. The results are striking. Nearly 32 percent of households in SEC A—largely India's urban professional elites—know someone abroad (figure 3.6). At the other extreme, within

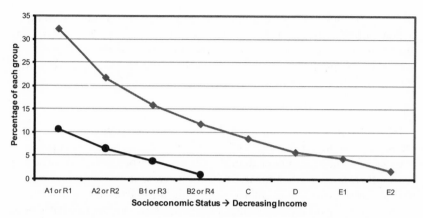

Figure 3.6. Households with global networks. Source: SEI. $N = 467,112$.

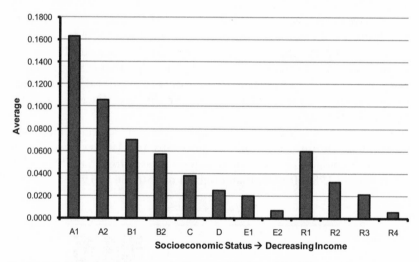

Figure 3.7. Size of global network. Source: SEI. $N = 467,112$.

rural labor (R4), virtually no household knows anyone outside the country (figure 3.7).

In summary, three points should be noted. First, for a given size of the overseas network, the likelihood of households having a network falls with income. Second, urban households are more likely to have global networks. Last, the richest rural households are more likely to have an overseas network than poor urban households. While these results may seem intuitive, they are the first firm empirical evidence that households in the highest socioeconomic classification have substantially greater global portfolios arising from international migration compared to other socioeconomic groups. Whether, and to what extent, these global networks preserve and enhance socioeconomic status as well as serve as an insurance against risk (both economic and political) in the home country, is examined in chapter 6.

VINTAGE

Nearly 90 percent of all households with a member outside the country report that the member left after 1990 (figure 3.8), with the rural percentage (92.2) somewhat higher than the urban (86.4 percent). For all socioeconomic groups, there appears to be an increase in international migration in recent years. Thus, international migration from India is of recent vintage. This matters, since migrants' links with the country of origin decay with time. The relatively recent vintage of migration from India implies stronger links with the country of origin, and in turn, more significant effects.

The survey's findings accord well with the limited macromigration data from India. Of the two broad streams of migration from India, the Gulf migration has high return rates, since permanent settlement there is exceedingly difficult. Hence, the stock of Indian migration in that region is constantly replenished by new migrants rather than natural growth. Data from the GOI's Ministry of Labour confirm the recent increase in labor migration (table 3.2).

In the case of migration to industrialized countries, skilled migration increased significantly, especially in the 1980s and 1990s. Thus, the Indian-born population in the United States increased from 51,000 in 1970 to 206,087 in 1980. It more than doubled to 450,406 in 1990 and again

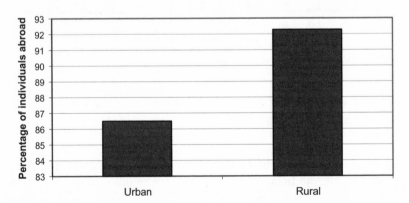

Figure 3.8. Emigrant vintage: share of post-1990 migration. Source: SEI. N = 322,499.

TABLE 3.2
Total Outflows for Employment (× 1000)

Year	Number of Workers
1999	199
2000	243
2001	279
2002	368
2003	466
2004	475
2005	549
2006	677
2007	809
2008	849

Source: Ministry of Labour, GOI; Ministry of Overseas Indian Affairs Annual Report 2004–2005, 2005–2006, 2008–2009.

Note: The data apply only to workers requiring emigration clearance from the office of the Protectorate of Immigrants. This group encompasses unskilled and semiskilled labor going to nonindustrialized countries. It should be noted that the data reflect the number of workers granted emigration clearance rather than actual outflows.

to over one million in 2000 and 1.5 million in 2007—of which two-thirds arrived after 1990.[13]

GENDER

An overwhelming majority of households reported that the family members who lived abroad were male (81.8 percent). This gender bias is largely because of the importance of Middle East migration, which is overwhelmingly male. Although the share of female migrants in urban households is almost triple compared to rural households (13.3 and 4.7 percent, respectively), it is still quite low (figure 3.9). In general, the percentage of female members abroad increases with household socioeconomic status.

The significant male bias is likely to have notable effects on households, with long-term social consequences. The precise effect depends on family structure, especially if the migrant is married and if the spouse is the head of household in the home country, as is the case in a nuclear family, or is part of another household (usually the in-laws or parents). Evidence from Kerala seems to suggest that female empowerment is greatest in the former case, when the migrant is a married male and his

[13] Gibson and Jung, "Historical Census Statistics on the Foreign-Born Population of the United States," 2007 American Community Survey (ACS), U.S. Census Bureau.

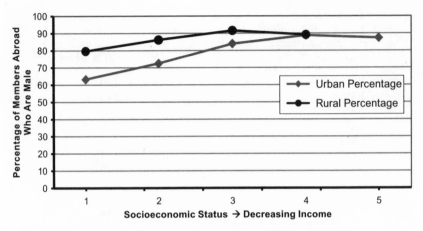

Figure 3.9. Emigrant gender composition. Source: SEI. $N = 467,112$.

wife is the head of household, since in her husband's absence she begins to make autonomous financial decisions.

MIGRANTS' AGE

Most of the family members abroad are in the prime working age group—nearly 83 percent of migrants from urban areas and 89 percent from rural areas are in the 20 to 50 age group, with the largest number from the 30 to 39 age group. Since this is the economically most active age cohort, the absence effect of this cohort is also likely to be greatest.

EDUCATION

Overall, approximately 57 percent of family members abroad have not had an education beyond high school (figure 3.10). There is a marked difference between education levels in urban and rural households, with two-thirds from the former having some tertiary education, while for rural areas this figure was only approximately 30 percent (figure 3.11). In the richest demographic segment (SEC A), however, the percentage of migrants with just high school education is a mere 14.1 percent, those with a college education is 84.2 percent, and those with a postgraduate degree is 78.3 percent (figure 3.12). Education significantly affects selectivity into the country of migration. Quite simply, the highly educated migrate to industrialized countries, while the less educated go to the Middle East. Thus, the selection effect of who leaves is amplified by where they go. The education level of the emigrant is strongly linked to household income and in turn affects the selection of the country of migration.

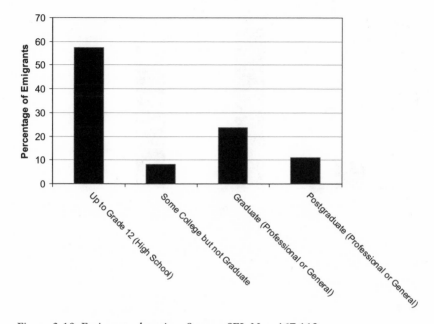

Figure 3.10. Emigrant education. Source: SEI. N = 467,112.

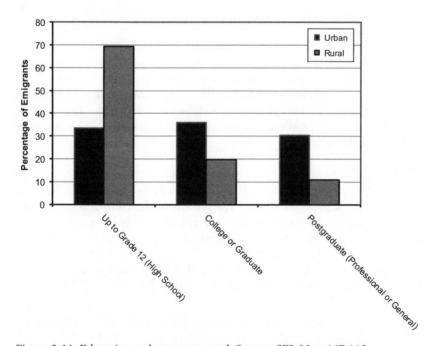

Figure 3.11. Education: urban versus rural. Source: SEI. N = 467,112.

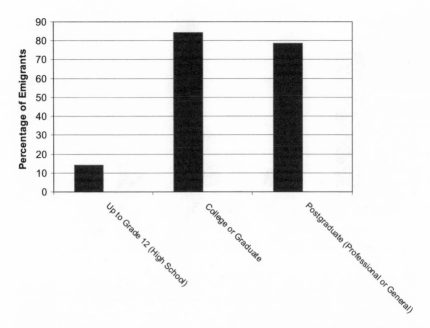

Figure 3.12. Education of emigrants from SEC A households. Source: SEI. $N = 467,112$.

Recent estimates of the emigration rate from India for those with tertiary education is 42 times those with primary and 14 times those with secondary education (table 3.3—these estimates are based on emigration only to the Organisation for Economic Cooperation and Development [OECD] countries). This is understandable in light of the fact that in 2000, just 3.3 percent of the 25+ population in India had completed postsecondary education.[14]

COUNTRY OF STAY

Overall, approximately half (50.2 percent) of migrants from India were in the Middle East, with about 19.7 percent in the United States. However, the results vary significantly for urban and rural areas. Among households with international migrants, 31.8 percent of urban but just 8.2 percent of rural households have family members abroad in the United States, while 39.3 percent of urban households and 60.6 percent of rural households have family members in the Middle East (figure 3.13).

[14] Robert J. Barro and Jong-Wha Lee, "International Data on Educational Attainment: Updates and Implications," Center for International Development Working Paper No. 42 (Harvard University, 2000).

TABLE 3.3
India: Recent Emigration Rates[a] by Level of Education

	Primary Education (%)	Secondary Education (%)	Tertiary Education (%)	All Education Groups (%)	Brain Drain Change (Rate in 2000/Rate in 1990)
1999	0.1	0.2	2.6	0.2	1.6
2000	0.1	0.3	4.2	0.3	

Source: Frederic Docquier and Abdeslam Marfouk, "Measuring the international mobility of skilled workers (1990–2000)—Release 1.0," World Bank Working Paper 3381, 2004.

[a] Emigration rate is the ratio of the emigration stock to the number of remaining residents.

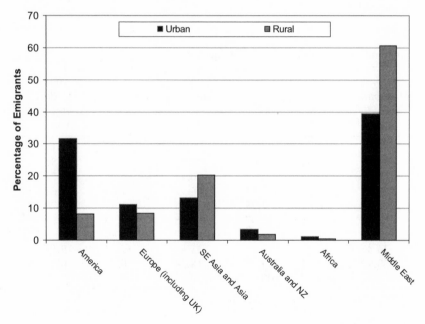

Figure 3.13. Emigrant destination countries. Source: SEI. $N = 467,112$.

Conditional on a household having a family member abroad, migration to the United States is a very strong increasing function of household income, while that to the Middle East is the opposite (figure 3.14). In general, the higher the SEC classification is, the greater the likelihood that the country of stay will be an industrialized country (table 3.4).

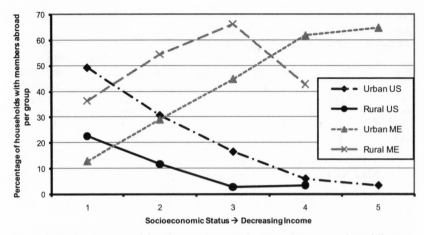

Figure 3.14. Percentage of family members in the United States and Middle East. Source: SEI. $N = 467,112$.

TABLE 3.4
Indian Emigrants: Destination by SEC Classification

SEC	Overall Distribution in India (%)	United States	United Kingdom	Australia, New Zealand, Canada	Europe (Except UK)	Asia (Including Southeast Asia)	Middle East
A	2.84	43.54	21.35	7.73	29.46	25.15	4.50
B	5.11	23.00	17.62	8.82	22.62	14.52	8.59
C	6.31	9.09	8.40	10.45	9.00	16.72	9.57
D	6.95	2.39	5.51	6.92	1.68	8.61	9.54
E	8.49	0.82	2.95	4.75	1.97	2.78	6.03
R1	2.61	8.78	13.07	6.28	2.93	12.69	5.63
R2	7.84	6.79	9.55	11.37	12.40	0	12.57
R3	26.36	4.06	17.05	25.44	19.94	19.53	36.36
R4	33.47	1.53	4.50	18.24	0	0	7.21
Total	100.00	100	100	100	100	100	100

Source: SEI survey. For SEC classifications, see appendix I.

The most skewed migration in this respect is that to the United States (although patterns are similar in other Anglo-Saxon destinations). While SEC A comprises just 2.84 percent of India's population, it accounts for more than 43.54 percent of all Indian emigrants to the United States. SEC R4 (the lowest rural socioeconomic group) accounts for a third of India's population, but just 1.53 percent of the Indian American population. In contrast, migration to the Middle East is much more representative of

India's population. The region is less attractive for India's high-skilled workers and mainly attracts unskilled and semiskilled workers who for the most part lack access to industrialized countries' labor markets. One implication is that Indian migration to the United States exacerbates intergroup inequalities—i.e., across socioeconomic groups—while that to the Middle East exacerbates intragroup inequities—i.e., within socioeconomic groups.

RELIGION

Another interesting variation is emigrant destination by religion. There is virtually no data on this sensitive subject. Since the U.S. Census does not ask religious affiliation, the size of the Muslim population in that country is much disputed. The SEI survey did not directly ask respondents their religious affiliation. However, all respondents who had a family member abroad were coded on their religion from their names. This creates some biases—for example, Jains and Sikhs could be identified as "Hindu," or Hindus could be classified as "Unidentified." For Muslims and Christians, the errors are likely to be smaller.

Tables 3.5a and 3.5b give the distribution of Indian emigrants by religion both across and within countries. While more than half of all Muslim

TABLE 3.5A
Distribution of Indian Emigrants by Religion across Countries and Regions (%)

	United States	Middle East	Canada, New Zealand, Australia	Africa, Latin America	Other Asia	United Kingdom	Europe (Other than UK)	Other Countries	Total
Muslim	14.27	52.27	4.09	2.9	16.09	3.09	3.27	4.45	100
Christian	14.92	56.71	3.48	2.48	10.2	2.98	3.48	5.72	100
Hindu	38.7	25.16	6.84	2.48	14.13	5.65	3.46	3.55	100
Unidentified	36.73	33.33	8.16	4.08	10.2	1.36	3.4	2.72	100

TABLE 3.5B
Distribution of Indian Emigrants by Religion within Countries and Regions (%)

	United States	Middle East	Canada, New Zealand, Australia	Africa, Latin America	Other Asia	United Kingdom	Europe (Other than UK)	Other Countries
Muslim	10.02	33.94	15.25	24.42	25.07	14.34	21.05	25.13
Christian	3.83	13.45	4.74	7.63	5.8	5.06	8.18	11.79
Hindu	82.69	49.7	77.62	63.36	66.99	79.74	67.83	61.02
Unidentified	3.45	2.89	4.067	4.58	2.12	0.84	2.92	2.05
Total	100	100	100	100	100	100	100	100

migrants are in the Middle East, this is also the case with Christians (perhaps reflecting the dominance of migration from Kerala to that region). Unsurprisingly, within each country, Hindus are the dominant emigrant group (although less than their share in the Indian population), with the United States and the Middle East showing the highest and lowest relative percentages of Hindu migrants, respectively.

The Particularly Strong Selectivity in the Migration of Indian Elites

A striking feature of recent Indian migration is its elite nature.[15] To put it differently, Indian elites have extremely high migration rates compared to the general population. The exceptionally high rates are also true of Indian elite institutions—in particular, educational institutions, where elites have a much higher rate of representation.[16]

Estimates on emigration rates of the graduates of the Indian Institutes of Technology (IIT) provide a good illustration of this evidence. The acceptance rate in these institutes is between one and two percent, from a pool that is already highly selective. An analysis of the "brain drain" of the graduates of IIT Mumbai in the 1970s revealed that 31 percent of its graduates settled abroad, while the estimated migration rate of engineers more generally was 7.3 percent.[17] Furthermore, the migration was significantly higher in those branches of engineering with higher ranked entrants to IIT: thus, the percentage who went abroad with degrees in electrical engineering (which was more selective in those years) was nearly 43 percent, while only 20 percent of those with degrees in metallurgical engineering (which was relatively less selective) went abroad. Similarly, while the percent abroad was 43 percent in the top quartile of the graduating class, it was 27 percent in the rest of the class.

The United States is strikingly dominant as the preferred overseas destination of graduates of the IIT's flagship undergraduate engineering

---

[15] Chapter 5 discusses the concept of elites in some detail. A statistical definition of "elites" would be a highly selective drawing from the upper-tail of a distribution.

[16] For a good account of skilled migration from India, see Binod Khadria, *The Migration of Knowledge Workers: Second-Generation Effects of India's Brain Drain* (New Delhi: Sage Publications, 1999).

[17] See S. P. Sukhatame and Indira Mahadevan, "Brain Drain and the IIT Graduate," *Economic and Political Weekly* 23, no. 25 (June 18, 1988): 1285–93. The survey population was students who graduated from IIT Mumbai between 1973–1977 and was conducted in 1986. Students taking the entrance exam for the IITs are ranked based on their performance in a written exam. Based on their rankings, the students rank both their choice of institute and branch of engineering, and once these are filled, the lower ranked students choose from the remaining disciplines.

programs. In 2004, IIT-Kharagpur had 4007 registered alumni in India, 3480 in the United States, and another 739 spread over 59 countries.[18] The total number of graduates from IIT-Kanpur by 2004, from all its degree programs, was 19,630.[19] Of the 8936 registered alumni, 1897 were in the United States and another 186 spread in other countries. Since its inception to 2004, IIT-Madras had awarded 27,193 degrees, of which 11,237 were undergraduate engineering degrees (BTech). About 6000 of the alumni were in the United States, another 500 in other countries, and about 20,000 in India.[20] About four-fifths of overseas alumni were from the prestigious undergraduate program, and the remaining one-fifth from the various postgraduate programs. Roughly seven out of eight of the overseas graduates of the IITs were in the United States.

The severe selection bias in emigration of engineers from India also exists in other disciplines. In medicine, while migration rates for doctors was about three percent during the 1980s, it was 56 percent for graduates of the All India Institute for Medical Sciences—India's most prestigious medical training institution—between 1956 and 1980, and 49 percent in the 1990s.[21] And in management training, a recent analysis of graduates of India's premier management school found that the typical recruit in the international sector has a cumulative grade point average (CGPA) that is "significantly higher" than his counterpart in the domestic sector.[22]

The preceding evidence that the more elite a group, the greater the likelihood of international migration from India, is supported by data from a very different group—the most senior officers of the Indian Army.

---

[18] IIT Foundation, "Directory Statistics," available at http://www.iitfoundation.org/directory/stats/ (accessed September 3, 2004). Because of selection bias in who becomes a member of the alumni association, overseas numbers are likely to be overrepresented.

[19] As of September 2004, out of 19,630 graduates from IIT Kanpur, 9074 were from its flagship BTech program. Of the remainder, 1797 were MSc graduates, 6883 MTech graduates, 1802 PhD graduates, and the remaining 124 had degrees like MPhil, DIIT, MBA, and MDes. Source: IIT-K Alumni Association, September 22, 2004.

[20] Data for IIT-Madras is from P. M. Venkatesan, Executive Secretary, IIT Madras Alumni Association, September 21, 2004.

[21] For figures between 1956 and 1980, see Binod Khadria, "Of Dreams, Drain, and Dams: Metaphors in the Indian Emigration of Talent," India International Center Quarterly 26, no. 3 (1999): 79–90. According to a report of the Comptroller and Auditor General, 49 percent of doctors trained in the All India Institute of Medical Sciences leave for foreign jobs. Rajya Sabha. "Synopses of Debates, Proceedings other than Questions and Answers," available at http://164.100.24.167/rsdebate/synopsis/193/22082001.htmlhttp://parliamentofindia.nic.in/rs/rsdebate/synopsis/193/22082001.html.

[22] Debashis Bhattacharjee, Karthik Krishna, and Amol Karve, "Signalling, Work Experience, and MBA Starting Salaries," Economic and Political Weekly 36, nos. 46 and 47 (November 24, 2001): 4369–74.

I chose the army because it is the predominant institution in the Indian armed forces, and it is much larger in size compared to the air force and navy, meaning that the number of retired senior officers is also larger. In general, information about the Indian army is not easy to obtain. In his landmark work on the Indian armed forces, Rosen cites an Indian army officer stating that the Indian armed forces "are perhaps one of the most secretive armies among democratic nations."[23] For security reasons, information about serving senior officers in the armed forces is closely held. (It is illegal to possess a list with names, phone numbers, and contact information of serving generals.) Even some serving officers of the rank of lieutenant general do not have access to a complete list with contact information of serving/retired officers of equivalent or higher seniority. For this reason, I chose to examine all officers of rank lieutenant general or above who had retired in the decade between 1994 and 2003. By choosing retired officers, but of recent vintage, I could ensure that the information was of contemporary relevance but nonetheless adhered to legal requirements and security sensibilities.

The survey covered 102 officers of the Indian army of rank lieutenant general who retired between 1994 and 2003. In each case, I ascertained the number of children, whether the children were above eighteen years of age, whether they currently resided in India or abroad, and if abroad, the country of residence. Out of the 102 generals in the sample, slightly under 50 percent were interviewed, and the remaining were either not contactable or traveling for extended periods.

The data are a strong affirmation of the trends observed in the SEI survey: elite households have a much greater likelihood of having a family member abroad, and conditional on the family member being abroad, the household is much more likely to be in an industrialized country, with the United States the clear front-runner (table 3.6). As you saw earlier, about eight percent of households in the highest SEC group (SEC A) have at least one member of their immediate family living abroad. The findings from the current survey clearly show that the percentage is much higher than this for the elite members of the Indian Armed Forces.

Might the strong selection effects of Indian migration, especially of its elites, have any political consequences? In chapter 6, I examine the effects of caste selection on the resilience and quality of Indian democracy, and in chapter 8, I discuss the religious and regional selection effects on long-distance nationalism.

---

[23] Steve Rosen, *Societies and Military Power: India and Its Armies* (Ithaca, NY: Cornell University Press, 1996).

TABLE 3.6
Location Choices of the Children of Senior Indian Army Officers

Total number of generals in survey	102
Not contactable (due to change of address, traveling, etc.)	47
Unwilling to disclose information	12
Percentage of children in India	55
Percentage of children abroad	45
Percentage of officers with at least one child abroad	59

Country location of children (% of total)

United States	54
Other English-speaking industrialized countries	23
Europe (excluding UK)	9
Middle East	3
Other Asia (excluding Middle East)	11

SELECTION CHARACTERISTICS OF CONTEMPORARY INDIAN MIGRATION

Evidence from the United States

One can complement data on emigrant outflows by analyzing data on immigrant inflows, comparing Indian immigrants in a nation with other immigrant groups as well the native-born population. In this section, I analyze data on Indian immigration to the United States, where data on some characteristics of the Indian-born population are available in the Current Population Survey (CPS) and on the Asian Indian population as a whole from the U.S. Census. In earlier joint work, which analyzed data from the CPS for the years 1994–2001, we found that the Indian-born population was distinct in its concentration in the prime work-age population, and strikingly so in terms of its education distribution.[24] More than half of the Indian-born were in the 25- to 44-year-old age group, compared to around 30 percent of the native-born (i.e., those born in the United States) and 44 percent of the other foreign-born. Moreover, while the dependency ratio (dependents under 18 or over 64) was just 15 percent or less for the Indian-born population in each of the years covered, it was about 40 percent for the native-born population. While this compression of the age distribution might be expected for immigrants relative to the native-born, the Indian-born differ markedly from other foreign-born as well.

[24] Mihir Desai, Devesh Kapur, John McHale, and Keith Rogers, "The Fiscal Impact of High-Skilled Emigration: Flows of Indians to the U.S.," *Journal of Development Economics* 88 (2009): 32–44.

The educational achievement of the Indian-born population is even more distinctive. Between 1994 and 2001, the average share of the native-born population with a bachelor's degree or higher was 26.5 percent—compared with 70.8 percent for the Indian-born. In contrast, the share of other foreign-born was similar to the native-born with an average share of 24.7 percent. The share of the Indian-born with post-bachelor's degrees—master's degrees, professional degrees, and doctorates—is also high at 36.8 percent, compared to 8.5 percent and 8.6 percent for the native-born and other foreign-born, respectively (figure 3.15).

These distinctions in age and education for the Indian-born in the United States translate into a distinctive income distribution relative to the native-born and other foreign-born. While median incomes for the Indian-born and native-born were approximately the same at the beginning of the 1990s, the Indian-born significantly outpaced both native and other foreign-born in earning power during the 1990s. The income distribution of the Indian-born shifted rightward far more strongly than for the native-born and other foreign-born since 1990, reflecting both the increased inflows of highly educated Indians as well as their concentration in the high-technology sector. By 2001, the total income of this group had escalated to over $40 billion (about 10 percent of India's GDP but just 0.1 percent of its population at the time), driven by a growing component of self-employment and nonearnings income, thus demonstrating a growing level of accumulated wealth.

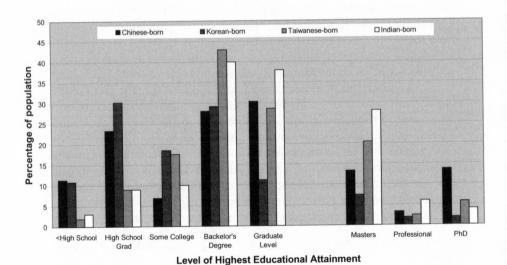

Figure 3.15. Education of Indian-born versus other Asian-born in the United States (2001). Source: 2001 CPS.

In summary, Indian immigrants to the United States are relatively younger, are more educated, and have higher income compared to the native-born and other foreign-born populations. From the late 1990s onward, these trends were amplified, largely due to the large influx of H-1B visa holders. Between 1998 and 2008, 27.6 percent of all H-1B visas (1,135,581) were issued to Indian citizens.[25] In contrast to both Indian-born immigrants from the 1980s and other foreign-born immigrants, the Indian-born immigrants from the 1990s were significantly more educated, with a particular concentration among those individuals having earned a master's degree. Last, Indian-born immigrants during the 1990s contributed to the compression of the age distribution of Indian-born residents, as these recent immigrants were considerably more likely to be in the 18- to 44-year-old age group relative to previous Indian-born migrants and other foreign-born migrants. Thus, while 33 percent of the Indians who came during the 1990s and were still in the United States in 2000 earned more than twice the native-born median for 2000, only 17 percent of those who came during the 1980s and were still in the United States in 1990 earned more than twice the native-born median for 1990.

While the CPS provides data on those born in India (and residing in the United States), more comprehensive data on Asian Indians, which includes those born in the United States, can be obtained from the U.S. Census. If we turn to the characteristics of the Asian Indian population in the United States, nearly 60 percent of which was born in India, data from the 2000 U.S. Census confirms the distinctive characteristics of this group (table 3.7). It has the highest median family income, a function of the highest levels of education (nearly two-thirds have a college education or higher), the highest labor participation rates (71 percent), and the highest fraction engaged in a high-skill occupation (more than half).

Given its selectivity with respect to the U.S. population, it should not be surprising that this selectivity is an order of magnitude greater compared to the population from which it is being drawn. In her analysis of educational selectivity of immigrants to the United States, Cynthia Feliciano finds that while nearly all immigrants are more highly educated than their home-country populations, they vary considerably in the degree of selectivity depending on the country of origin.[26] Understanding this selectivity is important since, as she argues, it "reveals the fallacy in attributing characteristics of immigrants to their national groups as a whole." Of the 32 largest immigrant-sending countries to the United States, *the most positively selected group* (by education) was Indians.

[25] Numbers based on data from DHS Yearbook of Immigration Statistics for years 1998–2008, available at http://www.dhs.gov/ximgtn/statistics/publications/yearbook.shtm.

[26] Cynthia Feliciano, "Educational Selectivity in U.S. Immigration: How Do Immigrants Compare to Those Left Behind?" *Demography* 42, no. 1 (2005): 131–52.

TABLE 3.7
U.S. Ethnic Groups and the Asian Indian Population, 2000: Selected Characteristics

Characteristic	Whites	Blacks	Latinos	Asian Indians	Chinese	Filipinos	Japanese	Koreans
Not proficient in English	0.7	0.8	30.3	8.4	31.3	7	10	32.9
Less than high school	15.3	29.1	48.5	12.6	23.6	13.1	9.5	13.8
College degree	25.3	13.6	9.9	64.4	46.3	42.8	40.8	43.6
Advanced degree	3	1.2	1.6	12.5	8.5	4.3	4.6	5.6
Median personal income (US$)	23,640	16,300	14,400	26,000	20,000	23,000	26,000	16,300
Median family income (US$)	48,500	33,000	36,000	69,470	58,300	65,400	61,630	48,500
Living in poverty	9.4	24.9	21.4	8.2	13.1	6.9	8.6	15.5
Public assistance	1.3	4.5	3.5	0.9	1.8	1.6	0.9	1.6
Married, spouse present	64.5	38	56.3	74.9	67.1	62.7	60.7	69
In labor force	63.6	59.8	61.5	71	65.1	68.3	58	62
High-skill occupation	21.4	12.3	9.6	51.6	41.9	29.7	32	27
Median SEI score[a]	47	44	26	65	65	46	62	52

Source: C. N. Le, "Socioeconomic Statistics and Demographics," *Asian-Nation: The Landscape of Asian America*, http://www.asian-nation.org/demographics.html, accessed 22 July 2004.

[a] The Socioeconomic Index (SEI) indicates "social status" and is calculated by combining individuals' income levels, educational attainment, and occupational prestige, as measured by the census's "occupational score."

While 71 percent of Indian immigrants to the United States had some college education (figure 3.16) just 3.42 percent of Indians in India were college educated—a more than *twentyfold* difference.

The positive selection is due to three principal factors: the tertiary-education bias in India's education system; U.S. immigration policy changes in 1965 that favored skilled immigrants; and the fact that the vast majority of Indian immigrants to the United States are economic migrants, a group especially prone to high selectivity.[27] When asked, "Why did you decide to leave India?" 78 percent of respondents cited economic reasons, 23.4 percent family reasons, and the rest (3.8 percent) noted "social and political reasons."[28] When the data are disaggregated by gender, 90 percent of males cite economic reasons and 47 percent of females cite family reunion as the reason for leaving India.

All the evidence cited overwhelmingly points to the same direction: Indian migration to the United States is very strongly selective by education. One study estimates that the overall emigration rate from India, for those with a tertiary education, was 2.6 percent in 1990 and 4.2 percent in 2000.[29] Nonetheless, we cannot say just how selective the migration is among those with a tertiary education (i.e., what is the distribution within the tail?). This matters because the more selective this migration is, the greater the likely consequences.[30] To put it differently, at this tail end of the talent distribution, the consequences are highly nonlinear to the loss of that talent.

Earlier in this chapter, I cite microlevel evidence from India's elite educational institutions that show the very high degree of emigration of graduates of these institutions. But the data are at best simply suggestive, not systematic. Instead of focusing on emigration selectivity by analyzing "input" measures—namely, education—I have chosen to get evidence on "extreme selectivity" by examining an output measure of emigrants' quality—namely, patents. In work conducted jointly with two colleagues, we examined patents issued by the U.S. Patent and Trademark Office

[27] B. R. Chiswick, "Are Immigrants Favorably Selected?" in *Migration Theory: Talking Across Disciplines*, eds. C. B. Brettell and J. F. Hollifield (New York: Routledge, 2000).

[28] The response percentages are greater than 100 because some respondents cited more than one reason.

[29] Frederic Docquier and Abdeslam Marfouk, "Measuring the International Mobility of Skilled Workers (1990–2000): Release 1.0," Policy Research Working Paper No. 3381 (Washington, DC: World Bank, 2004).

[30] Statistically, this could possibly be modeled using Extreme Value Theory (EVT), a statistical distribution that captures the relative frequency of extreme events. EVT models extreme deviations from the mean of probability distributions. Extreme value distributions are the limiting distributions for the minimum or the maximum of a very large collection of random observations from the same arbitrary distribution.

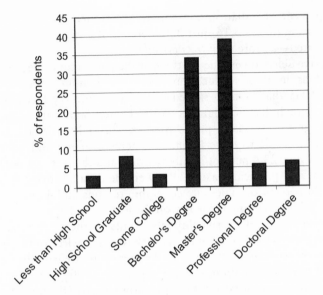

Figure 3.16. Education profile of Asian Indians. Source: SAIUS survey.
N = 2132; DK/CS (don't know/can't say) = 0.

(USPTO).[31] Using a unique data set of Indian last names, developed for the SAIUS survey, we extracted all inventions with one or more Indian-origin inventor. Table 3.8 illustrates the increasing importance of Indian-origin inventors over time. The share of total USPTO-issued patents that have at least one Indian-named inventor has been rising steadily approximately in line with the expanding Indian-born population.

In contrast, the number of patents filed by Indians from India grew from a mere 47 in 1997 to 177 in 2001, an annual average of 110 over the period. Is the focus on patents filed in the United States misleading? Could it be the case that Indians resident in India are indeed very inventive but that they file patents in India instead? I examined data on patents filed by the Council of Scientific and Industrial Research (CSIR), the apex scientific body that oversees a network of thirty-eight National Laboratories and Institutes and employs more than 5000 scientists. In the two fiscal years 2000–2001 and 2001–2002, the CSIR filed 820 patents in India and 1032 patents abroad. In 2002, it had 767 patents in force in India and 341 in force abroad.[32] Given the dominance of CSIR in Indian

[31] Ajay Agarwal, Devesh Kapur, and John McHale, "Defying Distance: The Role of the Diaspora," 2004.

[32] Council of Scientific and Industrial Research, available at http://www.csir.res.in/External/ Utilities/Frames/aboutcsir/main_page.asp?a=topframe.htm&b=leftcon.htm&c=../../../ Heads/aboutcsir/about_us.htm.

TABLE 3.8
USPTO-Issued Patents by Application Year

	1976	1980	1985	1990	1995	2000
Total	71,040	72,129	78,646	108,684	156,777	164,340
One or more Indian-origin inventors	651	788	1041	1934	4557	5334
Percent of patents of Indian origin	0.9	1.1	1.3	1.8	2.9	3.2
Indian-origin population in United States	—	387,223	—	815,447	—	1,678,765
Indian-origin population in United States (% of total)	—	0.17	—	0.33	—	0.60

Source: Agrawal, Kapur, and McHale, USPTO, 2004.

research and development, one can rule out the possibility that focusing on patents filed in the United States misses out on patenting in India.

The number of Indian-origin inventors residing in the United States (averaging over two years, 1995 and 2000) was 4945. Normalized by the population in the two countries, *the ratio of patents filed by Indian-origin inventors resident in the United States and those resident in India is 26,696.* Even discounting the fact that the ratio reflects not just ability but also very different opportunities (e.g., the availability of research facilities) as well as the reduced incentives for India resident inventors to file patents in the United States, the ratio is so hugely skewed that it speaks volumes of Indian emigrant quality at the tail end of the distribution.

RELIGION

Since the U.S. Census does not report data on religious belief, obtaining data on this characteristic is exceedingly hard. The methodology underlying the SAIUS survey is likely to underreport Indian American Muslims, but not hugely. Relative to their share in the Indian population, Indian Muslims are likely to be underrepresented in the United States for two key reasons: lower levels of education (table 3.9) and greater selectivity of educated Muslim migration to the Middle East (table 3.5a). The enormous education selectivity of migration to the United States means that those religious groups with higher levels of human capital are selectively much more likely to be represented in that country. In the aftermath of Partition, the Muslim community, especially in North India,

TABLE 3.9
Religious Composition and Literacy Rates

Religion	Share of Population in India (%)ᵃ	Share of Indian American Population (%)ᵇ	Share of Indian American Population (%)ᶜ	Literacy Rate (%)
Buddhist	0.77	0	0	72.7
Christian	2.33	5.3	4.8	80.3
Hindu	80.5	80.0	72	65.1
Jain	0.41	2.0	1.8	94.1
Muslim	13.4	1.3	10	59.1
Parsiᵈ	0.007	0.3	0.27	97.8
Sikh	1.85	5.7	5.1	69.4
None/other		5.4	4.9	

ᵃ Data on population share and literacy rates by religion are from Census of India, 2001. The total population of India was 1028 million.
ᵇ SAIUS data. 4.2% responded "none" and 1.2% "other."
ᶜ SAIUS data adjusted by SEI data (showing that 10% of emigrants to the United States are Muslim).
ᵈ The Parsi population in India has dwindled from 115,000 in 1961 to just 69,600 in 2001.

suffered a significant loss of its elite, who migrated to Pakistan. Since then, the community's educational attainments have lagged, even behind the slow rate of change in India. Still, as is shown in table 3.5a, the share of Indian Muslims in the Indian American population (10 percent) is not too different from its share in India.

Moreover, even the out-migration of educated Muslims to the Middle East has been relatively greater than out-migration from India in general. Thus, the maximum number of overseas alumni of Aligarh Muslim University (AMU), a premier institution of higher learning for Muslims in North India, are located in Saudi Arabia, apparently the largest number from any higher education institution in India in that country.[33] The overseas location of alumni is suggestive of the selection bias resulting from the religious and skill backgrounds of migrants. Thus, while the number of overseas alumni of AMU in Saudi Arabia are between three and four times those in the United States, the overseas location of the alumni of the well-known IITs (where Muslims are underrepresented) are a stark contrast—roughly 0.1 percent of the total in the United States.

POLITICAL PARTISANSHIP

The SAIUS survey revealed that Asian Indians overwhelmingly identify themselves as Democrat compared to Republican, while a sizable number

[33] In mid-2009, there were 1847 alumni in Saudi Arabia and 933 in the United States; available at http://www.amudirectory.com/ (accessed June 17, 2009).

do not have a strong partisan identification. This is in sharp contrast to both the native population as well as public opinion in India. While there is no direct comparable survey data on views regarding U.S. political parties in India, a survey conducted in India about the same time as the SAIUS survey is revealing. This survey in India was part of a large cross-national survey conducted in 35 countries, as regards overseas views on the U.S. presidential race.[34] The results of this survey reveal that a majority preferred John Kerry to win the 2004 U.S. presidential election. On average, Kerry was preferred by a two-to-one margin, including when the countries were weighted for variations in population. Approximately one-third said that it made no difference to them who won or did not answer either way. Respondents in only three countries preferred George Bush (Nigeria, Poland, and Philippines). In two others, India and Thailand, views were evenly balanced, with 33 percent in India preferring Bush and 34 percent Kerry. The survey found that negative feelings in response to U.S. foreign policy and support for Kerry were greater among those with higher education and income levels. Since the Indian American population is unusually educated and has high incomes, even compared to urban India (where the survey was conducted), this might explain the much greater support for Democrats among the former compared to the latter. Moreover, Kerry's stance against outsourcing undoubtedly had a negative fallout in India.

ETHNICITY

Ethnic selection in emigration from a multiethnic state can have important consequences. In figures 3.17 and 3.18, I give data on the share of different states and linguistic groups from which emigrants are drawn, as well as their share in the Indian population. Thus, while residents from Gujarat, Maharashtra, Punjab, and Tamil Nadu are "overrepresented" in the United States (compared to the share of these states' populations in India), using data by linguistic group modifies this story. Gujaratis, Punjabis, and Tamilians are even more overrepresented, while Marathi speakers are underrepresented. This is because many emigrants from Maharashtra are Gujaratis and Tamilians from Mumbai rather than Marathi speakers.

[34] The poll was conducted in 35 countries with 34,330 respondents from around the world. The margin of error ranged from +/–2.5 to 5%. The survey in India was carried out between July 7–19, 2004; the sample size was 1016 (unweighted) and was confined to four Indian cities (Mumbai, Delhi, Calcutta, and Chennai). Steven Kull and Doug Miller, "Global Public Opinion on the US Presidential Election and US Foreign Policy" (Program on International Policy Attitudes/Globescan, September 8, 2004), available at http://www.pipa.org/OnlineReports/Views_US/USElection_Sep04/USElection_Sep04_rpt.pdf.

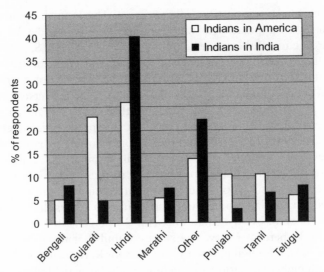

Figure 3.17. Distribution of population by linguistic group. Source: SAIUS survey. $N = 2132$; DK/CS (don't know/can't say) $= 0$.

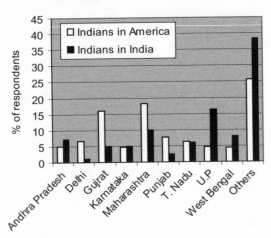

Figure 3.18. Distribution of population by state of origin. Source: SAIUS survey. $N = 1844$, DK/CS (don't know/can't say) $= 17.5\%$.

CASTE

This is an analytical category *sui generis* to the Indian subcontinent. Increasingly, the primacy of caste has shifted from a social to a political phenomenon, from a marker of ritualistic hierarchy to a basis for political mobilization. While there is a strong correlation between caste and class, it is by no means isomorphic. While neither the SEI nor the SAIUS survey picks up any information about caste, the database on Asian Indian households allows one to construct the caste composition of the Asian Indian population by matching last names to caste and weighing them by frequency of occurrence in the United States.[35] Of the 13,418 last names used to construct the database of the Asian Indian population, just 7.9 percent of names accounted for 90 percent of the Asian Indian population. All last names with a frequency greater than 163 were coded. (This represented 73 percent of the survey population of 405,000.) From the remaining names (representing 27 percent of the population), I randomly generated 30 names to see if their caste representation matched that of the main sample (which they did). The results are given in figure 3.19. High castes dominate, with dominant castes as the second largest group.[36] Some high castes are also dominant castes. The dominant caste data in figure 3.19 include only those who are not high castes. While the use of names to impute caste can be only a rough guide to the composition of the population, the data are strongly suggestive of underlying trends. Access to resources in India increases the probability of immigrating to the United States. The representation of members of the most socially marginalized groups, India's scheduled castes and scheduled tribes, who comprise more than one-fifth of the country's population, is at best a couple of percent in the India origin population residing in the United States. Lower-caste groups, who comprise roughly half of India's population, are also severely underrepresented. Underlying political trends in India are likely to result in a change, but not in the short term. In late 2004, the chief ministers of Bihar, Madhya Pradesh, and Uttar Pradesh (three states accounting for 31 percent of India's population) were Yadavs—a community that constitutes one of the largest "castes" in India (it has come to recognize itself as such in recent times) and has considerable political clout. Yet at the time

[35] I am grateful to Yogendra Yadav for sharing the caste coding of last names developed by the Center for the Study of Developing Societies (CSDS), New Delhi. Where necessary, this coding list was supplemented by referring to the "Peoples of India" project of the Anthropological Survey of India. It must be emphasized that caste is a somewhat elastic identity, and consequently last names do not always precisely reveal a person's caste. In the years around independence, when lower castes were emulating the higher castes (a process known as "Sanskritization"), one might have expected lower castes to adopt high-caste last names; in more recent years, the opposite is more likely, as higher castes try to avail of affirmative action benefits for lower castes. However, and importantly, this is unlikely to produce a systematic bias in the coding.

[36] Dominant castes (e.g., the Jats in Northwestern India, the Patels in Gujarat, Vokkaligas and Lingayats in Karnataka, Kapu and Kamma in Andhra Pradesh, and Marthas in Maharashtra) were upper or intermediate cultivating castes that controlled large areas of land, were numerically large as well, and hence held a preeminent position in the rural economy. M. N. Srinivas, Social Change in Modern India (Delhi: Orient Longman, 1995). They were often not ritualistically high caste.

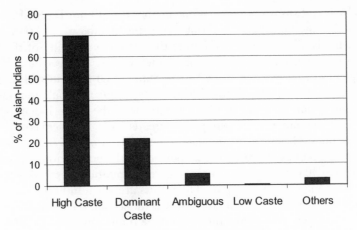

Figure 3.19. Caste composition of Asian Indian population.

of my survey, there were just barely a few hundred Yadavs in the United States, compared to an estimated 30 million in India.[37]

CONCLUSION

In the previous chapter, while outlining the principal mechanisms through which international migration impacts the country of origin, I argued that these effects depend critically on specific characteristics of the migrants: Who leaves? Where do they go? Why do they go? When did they go? Migrants are seldom representative of the population they are drawn from, and their selection characteristics are key to understanding the consequences for those left behind.

In this chapter, I have tried to establish the principal characteristics of emigrants from India. The empirical evidence on the characteristics of international migration from India reveals a stark contrast between the late nineteenth and late twentieth centuries. While migrants in the nineteenth century came from poorer socioeconomic groups and poorer parts of the country and went to relatively poor Southern countries, a century later virtually the opposite was true—migrants came from richer and more educated socioeconomic groups, from wealthier parts of the country, and

[37] The size of the Yadav community in India is based on the following estimates: about 5 percent in Rajasthan and Haryana, about 8 percent in UP, and about 13 percent in truncated Bihar. Yadavs are also present in Madhaya Pradesh, Maharashtra, Andhra Pradesh, West Bengal, and Orissa (between 1 and 4 percent of the population of these states). I am grateful to Yogendra Yadav for this insight. Personal communication, October 7, 2004.

TABLE 3.10
Selection Characteristics of International Migration from India

Selection Criteria	Time Period	
	Late Nineteenth Century	Late Twentieth Century
Caste	Lower	Higher
Class	Low	Medium–high
Destination	Low-income tropical zone (except South Africa)	Industrialized temperate zone (except Middle East Malaysia, and Singapore)
Education and skills	Illiterate and low skills	Skilled (industrialized countries) Low–medium skills (Middle East)
Gender imbalance	Severe	Severe (Middle East) Moderate (industrialized countries)
Income	Low	High
Region	Interior states (United provinces); Madras Presidency; Gujarat	Rim states in south and west; Punjab
Sector	Rural	Urban

with the significant exception of the large migration to the Middle East, primarily went to industrialized countries (table 3.10).

Paralleling these changes in the patterns of international migration and migrant characteristics from India has been an acceleration of India's economic growth and a "silent revolution" that has transformed the social basis of political power in the country, resulting in a gradual but perceptible political ascendency of hitherto socially marginalized groups.[38] Are these changes in the patterns of international migration on the one hand and the major macrochanges in India itself on the other merely coincidental? What would have been the counterfactual had this migration not occurred? I turn to addressing these questions—the consequences of international migration on India's political economy—beginning with the economic effects of migration in the next chapter.

[38] The term "silent revolution" borrows from Christophe Jaffrelot, *India's Silent Revolution: The Rise of the Lower Castes in North India* (New York: Columbia University Press, 2003).

CHAPTER 4

Economic Effects

INTRODUCTION

IN WHAT WAYS does international migration impact the sending country's economy? What are the mechanisms through which these effects are amplified or attenuated? In this chapter, I address these questions using evidence from India, while specifying the mechanisms that transmit and leverage migrants' economic effects on the home country: the diaspora's overseas network, their role as reputational intermediaries or credibility-enhancing agents for domestic economic actors, and their impact through financial flows including foreign direct investment (FDI) and remittances.[1]

First, I analyze the trade- and investment-enhancing effects resulting from the Indian diaspora's network and their role as reputational intermediaries. This analysis focuses in particular on two sectors where India has done well in the recent past: information technology (IT) and diamond cutting and polishing. I demonstrate that the diaspora's success in Silicon Valley created broader positive externalities for the domestic Indian IT sector. As reputational intermediaries and credibility-enhancing agents, the diaspora favorably influenced global perceptions of Indian technology businesses and thereby had a catalytic impact on the growth of this sector. Additionally, its success enhanced the legitimacy of entrepreneurship within India, particularly among social groups that had hitherto looked down on such activities. Indian diasporic networks have played a significant role in driving the growth of India's burgeoning diamond-cutting industry, which employs more than one million people and exports $10 billion annually.

Subsequently, I examine the impact of another mechanism—the diaspora's financial flows (particularly remittances) into India. Drawing on work by other scholars as well as individual-level data from the Survey of Emigration from India (SEI) and Survey of Asian Indians in the United States (SAIUS), I examine the multiple effects shown of remittances, both at the individual level as well as the macro–political economy consequences.

[1] An earlier comprehensive analysis on international migration from India and resulting financial flows, covering the period prior to economic liberalization, is Deepak Nayyar, *Migration, Remittances and Capital Flows: The Indian Experience* (New Delhi: Oxford University Press, 1994).

Last, I analyze the effects of international migration on human-capital formation in India. In some instances, migration has had a positive "brain gain" impact by promoting greater skill-seeking behavior domestically as well as through the transfer of innovative technologies and ideas back home. However, migration has had considerable negative impacts as well, contributing to the shortage of skilled, technical labor in research. More importantly, by denuding Indian universities of quality faculty, it has contributed to serious weaknesses in Indian higher education, with disquieting implications for the country's future.

TRADE AND INVESTMENT EFFECTS

Diaspora Networks and Reputational Enhancement

Historically, diasporas have played an important role in facilitating global trade. Indeed, merchant and trading communities from non-Western societies played a significant role in the so-called globalization of modern economic life, often in the shadow (and sometimes independently) of the colonialism and imperialism of prominent Western powers. Business, especially international business, requires enforcement mechanisms and trust, and diasporic networks, adept at internalizing these mechanisms, were especially successful in services such as trade, finance, and shipping.[2]

The role of diasporas in contemporary economic life can be better understood if markets are seen not just as price-making mechanisms but, in the broader Coasian sense, as social institutions that facilitate exchange. Networks embedded in social institutions mimic market structures through signaling and informational exchange among participants. Networks affect the flow of information in fundamental ways, shaping content, access, and credibility of information. Their role in employment and labor markets, as well as in immigration and immigrant entrepreneurship, is well documented.[3] Once in place, networks create self-sustaining migratory flows that gradually delink from the conditions that generated immigration in the first place. The resulting "chain migration" is an important explanation for why ethnic groups with very small numbers in the overall population concentrate, both spatially and in occupations and trades. Employers have strong reasons to hire individuals with a credible imprimatur, and referral by existing employees is an important mechanism. Hiring

---

[2] Ina B. McCabe, Gelina Harlaftis, and Ioanna Pepelasis Minoglou, eds., *Diaspora Entrepreneurial Networks: Four Centuries of History* (New York: Berg, 2005).

[3] For instance, Mark Granovetter, *Getting a Job: A Study of Contacts and Careers* (Chicago: University of Chicago Press, 1995).

new employees or contractors from networks that have delivered reliability in the past reduces search costs. In addition to employment, these networks provide access to informational and financial resources.

Given the multitudes of diasporic networks, however, why do some seem to be more important than others? Large countries have larger diasporas and, hence, larger networks. Since the benefits of networks increase rapidly with network size, for a given rate of immigration, large countries are more likely to benefit from the network advantages of diasporas. But network size is just one factor. The strategic location of diasporas is equally important because of the brokering role they play. The Chinese diaspora played that role in labor-intensive manufacturing exports from China, and the Indian diaspora is playing a similar role in tradable services—especially software and IT-related services. Diasporas seem to be playing an important role in the diffusion of knowledge and technologies—as well as fads, fashions, and "inappropriate technologies" (for instance, the capacity to engage in violence).

Diasporas can have reputational externalities for the country of origin. Firms and institutions in less developed countries (LDCs)—be they manufacturing firms or health or education service providers—face severe reputational handicaps arising from a "country-of-origin" effect. By "reputation," I mean the prior beliefs of buyers of products and users of services. These prior beliefs can be based on information stemming from previous transactions and experience—in which case, the reputation, whether good or bad, will be deserved. On the other hand, the buyer's prior judgments may be based on his or her experience with other firms similar to the firm in question—for instance, the reputation that a particular Nigerian firm is "stuck with" may derive not from its own past performance, but from the past performance of other Nigerian firms. A second aspect of these prior beliefs is how precise they are. If prior beliefs are based on past experience, the thicker the nexus of transactions is, the more precise the buyer's priors. A risk-averse buyer will care about the precision of her priors, and hence a seller who is a newcomer into a market will be at a disadvantage simply because he has no "reputation." (This is analogous to the widely observed phenomenon of individuals not being able to get credit unless they already have a credit history.)

LDC firms face reputational barriers to entry in export markets because buyers often have limited information about the quality of their products and service reliability. Since, by definition, buyers in major export markets will have had little prior experience of dealing with these firms, they may be reluctant to do business with them. This places newcomers at a reputational disadvantage relative to established firms, effectively creating a reputational barrier to entry. The reputational barriers to entry faced by LDC firms are principally twofold: situations where an individual firm is unfairly "stuck with" an unfavorable reputation because of the poor performance of other firms with which it is thought to be similar, and situations where a firm is at a disadvantage simply because little is known about it because it is a late entrant.

The importance of reputational barriers is likely to vary across industries and across segments within industries. Reputational barriers are likely to be greater in sectors where:

- Quality is more tacit, and *ex ante* determination of quality of the product or service is consequently more difficult. Most tradable services fall into this category—software is a good example.
- The risk of extreme adverse outcomes associated with poor quality is high. Food products and health care are good examples. The cost of a cataract operation in India (even including travel costs) is substantially less than in Europe in comparable facilities, but the poor reputation of Indian health care in general means that this segment will have to offer price discounts to attract customers.
- It is more difficult to design contractual mechanisms to mitigate information asymmetries.
- The importance of timely, reliable supply is great.

Diasporic networks help facilitate trade and investment in several ways. First, they help strengthen international contract enforcement by deterring opportunism. The Chinese diaspora uses co-ethnic business societies to keep knowledge of network members' characteristics "fresh," and thus enables the threat of "collective punishment" to dissuade opportunistic behavior by any network member.[4] Furthermore, the Chinese trade diasporic network, like many others, encouraged the formation of a "moral community," a group of individuals bound together by mutual trust and social and familial ties, which is thus less likely to engage in opportunistic behavior. Second, they promote further trade by matching providers with demand for products or services. Network members' unique knowledge of the situation on both sides of the trade route proves crucial in this respect. Third, they extend to the international market information (such as foreign consumer preferences or supplier information) that is otherwise available to nonmembers only on a domestic level, and thereby they serve as an informational conduit for communicating investment and trading opportunities to both producers and consumers.

It would seem, however, that the "private" informational advantages of being members of diasporic networks may be less important in the information age. Furthermore, improvements in international contract

[4] James E. Rauch, "Business and Social Networks in International Trade," *Journal of Economic Literature* 39, no. 4 (December 2001), 1186.

enforcement mechanisms have reduced the need for the "moral communities" that diasporic networks provided. This turns out not to be true for several reasons.

One, the abundance of market information is offset by the increasing share of differentiated products in international trade—that is, nonhomogeneous commodities without commonly known reference prices and thus whose value cannot be determined by market price alone.[5] With differentiated products, the need for diasporic networks still exists because only network members possess an intimate knowledge of producers, suppliers, and product marketability.

Second, the supply side of diasporas' informational role has expanded, not only because of greater migration, but also because of the sharp decline in communication costs. Frequent communication with co-ethnic partners helps members stay in touch with their diasporic roots despite a dominant host country culture or language.

Third, the explosive growth in the availability of information creates a new problem. Information is context-invariant, while knowledge is contextual. Knowledge and technology continue to have a tacit element, and their social contexts continue to be critically important in how knowledge is transmitted and received.[6] Moreover, the problem facing economic agents today is not one of a lack but one of a deluge of information. And as with all deluges, agents create dikes and embankments to provide some way to control the flood. Consequently, social networks continue to be important in modern economic life, and hence, diasporic networks still have a role to play, both in interpreting the credibility of information as well as in serving as reputational intermediaries. The reputational aspect might be even greater in the current context, as most countries have liberalized, and a multinational corporation (MNC) potentially has several equally viable investment locations to choose from. In this case, diasporas within firms can act as champions for their country of origin in internal management battles. Note that the need to protect their *internal* reputation within the firm ensures that they will only do so if their country of origin is indeed a viable candidate to begin with. Last, as a few MNCs locate investments in these countries, it is the reputation of the MNCs themselves that will signal to other MNCs the locational viability of that country. Thus, the reputational role of diasporas may have its greatest leverage in advancing the timing of investment, thereby acting as a "tipping point" with possibly far-reaching consequences.

[5] James E. Rauch and Victor Trindade, "Ethnic Chinese Networks in International Trade," *Review of Economics and Statistics* 84, no. 1 (February 2002): 116–30.

[6] John Seely Brown and Paul Duguid, *The Social Life of Information*, 4th ed. (Cambridge, MA: Harvard Business Press, 2002).

The evidence also suggests that immigrants increase bilateral trade between the country of residence and country of origin due to deeper tacit knowledge about their home countries' markets and institutions, rather than business connections or personal contacts with their home countries. A study of UK trading patterns from 1981 to 1993 found that foreign-born entrepreneurs' deeper knowledge of markets in their countries of origin lowered their transaction costs, thereby increasing trade.[7] However, the authors also found that the trade-enhancing information premium of immigrants from non-Commonwealth nations was greater than those from the Commonwealth. While a 10 percent increase in non-Commonwealth immigrants increased exports to those countries by 1.6 percent, the effect of immigrants from Commonwealth countries was "statistically insignificant." The former were more "foreign" from the perspective of the United Kingdom, when compared to its erstwhile colonies, and consequently brought new information. Other studies also find the trade-enhancing effects of immigration.[8] However, the greater the cultural differences between immigrants and natives, the larger the impact of immigration on the structure and volume of trade flows. This would suggest that Indian migration to non–Anglo Saxon countries is likely to yield the greatest marginal impact on India's trade.

A human-capital-rich diaspora can be an international business asset. The combination of preference, knowledge, and ability to pay may make members of the diaspora willing customers, investors, and purveyors of information. Their knowledge of the needs and capabilities of both host- and home-country-based firms make them potentially useful intermediaries in the search and matching process. The following section will examine the economic effects of the diaspora in the Indian context. Specifically, it will demonstrate that the diaspora has enhanced trade and investment in a range of Indian sectors, but especially in IT and diamonds.

India's Economy and the Diaspora

Empires have historically served as a springboard for the diffusion of trade diasporas. The British colonial expansion in Asia allowed a number of ethnic groups such as Armenians, Parsees, and Baghdadi Jews to operate within India as well as across the Indian Ocean in Hong Kong and

[7] S. Girma and Z. Yu, "The Link between Immigration and Trade. Evidence from the U.K.," *Weltwirtschaftliches Archiv* 138, no. 1 (2002): 115–30.

[8] K. Head and J. Ries, "Immigration and Trade Creation: Econometric Evidence from Canada," *Canadian Journal of Economics*, 31 (1998): 47–62; J. V. Blanes, "Does Immigration Help to Explain Intra-industry Trade? Evidence for Spain," *Review of World Economics* 141, no. 2 (2005): 244–70.

Southeast Asia. It also greatly increased the commercial presence of Indians abroad, especially after around 1880. According to one estimate, there were about 2.5 million Indians outside India around 1930, of which about 1.5 million were employed.[9] Region, rather than religion, was the key to the social groups from which these overseas business communities came: Gujarat and Tamil Nadu were the two most important areas, while the remaining migrants came mainly from Punjab, Sindh, and Kerala. The bulk of the Gangetic plain was unaffected by these outflows (although there was substantial migration of indentured labor). Nearly one-sixth of those employed (about 0.25 million) were involved in trade and finance, from a low of 3 percent in Fiji to about half in Uganda. Three countries under the British empire—Burma, Ceylon, and South Africa—accounted for three-quarters of the Indian migration.

The Chettiars of Tamil Nadu exemplified the commercial and financial reach of the Indian diaspora in India's "near abroad." From their origins as salt traders in the seventeenth century, they adapted to the colonial economy and became the leading merchant-banker caste of south India during the period of British rule. Under the imperial umbrella, they established banking houses in Ceylon, Malaya, and Burma, which financed agriculture, plantation crops, and mining. At one point, the Chettiars owned one-fourth of the land in the rice growing regions of Burma. The Great Depression led to a decline in this community's business fortunes, but it was its "foreigner" status after these countries became independent that proved to be its death-knell. A few of the wealthiest Nakarattars moved into industry, and others moved into clerical and bureaucratic jobs, but mainly within India and not outside.[10]

Interestingly, the umbrella of the British empire, while helpful, was not always necessary for the global expansion of the Indian merchant diaspora, which was active in developing modern commercial relations between India and Central Asia from the sixteenth until the beginning of the twentieth century. This diaspora consisted of tens of thousands of Indian merchant-moneylenders living in communities dispersed across Central Asia, Afghanistan, Iran, the Caucasus, and much of Russia.[11] Caste-based Indian family firms financed this transregional trade and complex systems of rural credit and industrial production. The diaspora eventually became

[9] Claude Markovits, *The Global World of Indian Merchants, 1750–1947: Traders of Sind from Bukhara to Panama* (Cambridge, UK: Cambridge University Press, 2000).

[10] David Rudner, *Caste and Capitalism in Colonial India: The Nattukottai Chettiars* (Berkeley: University of California Press, 1994); Sean Turnell, *Fiery Dragons: Banks, Moneylenders and Microfinance in Burma* (Copenhagen: NIAS Press, 2009), 13–52.

[11] Scott Levi, *The Indian Diaspora in Central Asia and Its Trade 1550–1900* (Leiden, The Netherlands: Brill Academic Publishers, 2002); Markovits, *The Global World of Indian Merchants* (2000).

a victim of the Russian colonial administration's policies toward the Indian merchants.

Those segments of the overseas Indian community that were engaged in trade, industry, and finance had little impact on India until the 1980s. For one, as the aforementioned examples illustrate, most of them were based in the newly independent countries and faced severe restriction on their activities. Just as trade diasporas based in India gradually disappeared, so did those of Indian origin located outside India, the result of economic nationalism and skepticism of the benefits of trade. But even when opportunities beckoned, India was not having any of it. When the government of Idi Amin expelled members of the Indian diaspora from Uganda, the Indian government insisted that the British government honor their UK passports, thus giving little weight to the entrepreneurial acumen of this small community. When the UK government reluctantly agreed, India claimed a diplomatic victory. But over time as this community emerged among the wealthiest communities in the United Kingdom, it was Britain that had the last laugh. Similarly, when Hong Kong reverted to China, the Indian government did little to try and attract the small but economically powerful Indian diaspora back to India.

Matters began to change in the 1990s, because of both economic changes within India as well as the manifest economic success of the Indian diaspora in high-tech industries in Silicon Valley. In the case of the Indian American diaspora, their ongoing relationships with both U.S. and Indian firms (and with other members of the diaspora) make them well situated to use their reputations to support complex transactions when legal contracting is difficult. In addition, their success as technologists, managers, and entrepreneurs in Silicon Valley has had broader externalities in terms of improved perceptions of Indian technology businesses in general.[12]

As discussed earlier, diasporic networks act as reputational intermediaries and as credibility-enhancing mechanisms, which may be particularly important in economic sectors such as software, where knowledge, especially *ex ante* knowledge of quality, is tacit. The Indian diaspora's success in Silicon Valley influenced how the world began reevaluating its beliefs about India, reflecting the reputational spillover effects of success in a leading sector in a leading country. It has created a "brand-name," wherein an "Indian" software programmer sends an *ex ante* signal of quality, just as a "made in Japan" label sends an *ex ante* signal of quality

[12] Devesh Kapur and John McHale, "Sojourns and Software: Internationally Mobile Human Capital and High-Tech Industry Development in India, Ireland and Israel," in *From Underdogs to Tigers: The Rise and Growth of the Software Industry in Some Emerging Economies*, eds. Ashish Arora and Alfonso Gambardella (Oxford, UK: Oxford University Press, 2005), 236–74.

in hardware. Of course, the positive reputation externality simply opens the door; after that, the quality of home-country firms and human capital will have to deliver to update the priors of buyers. Indeed, once the new member has established its own reputation—as is the case with Indian IT today—the diaspora's role in this respect becomes less important. In the case of IT, it is likely that this role was amplified by the sector's spatial clustering, despite it being the one industry where, theoretically, production can be decentralized the most (since there is very little physical movement of intermediate goods). This allowed groups like The Indus Entrepreneur (TIE—a high-technology networking organization) to flourish—a cause and consequence of the roughly quarter million Indians in Silicon valley. This clustering effect in turn helped nurture networks between the U.S. cluster and Indian clusters, especially in Bangalore, Hyderabad, Pune, and Delhi. Furthermore, the combination of money and ideas emanating from a technology hothouse—the archetypal Silicon Valley success story—had greater influence in the country of origin as well. [13]

Annalee Saxenian found that Indians were running 9 percent of Silicon Valley start-ups from the period 1995 to 1998, almost 70 percent of which were in the software sector.[14] In a later study based on her survey of members of TIE, she painted an optimistic picture of the role played by the Indian diaspora in facilitating international business for home-country firms.[15] More than three-fourths of the Indian-born respondents had one or more friends who returned to India to start a company, while half traveled to India on business at least once a year. Another quarter reported regularly exchanging information about jobs/business opportunities with those back home, while a third regularly exchanged information about technology. In terms of the potential role of Silicon Valley Indians as reputational intermediaries, 46 percent had been a contact for domestic Indian businesses. On the investment side, 23 percent claimed to have

---

[13] To take an illustrative example: when Rakesh Mathur, a graduate of IIT-Bombay, sold off his comparison-shopping service called Junglee to Amazon in 1998 for $241 million, he had both the money and a worldview, or "model." Mathur's particular overseas experience led him to believe that "a lot of huge economic growth comes out of nuclei. Silicon Valley, for example, is a nucleus, and the heart of that nucleus is Stanford. A lot of these companies have been born out of Stanford. And as a result of these ideas flowing out and becoming companies, we've got this powerhouse called Silicon Valley. . . . My vision is to replicate that in IIT." This led him to fund an IT incubator at his alma mater, as well as a venture capital fund for Indian companies. Lakshmi Chaudhry, "The Great Indian Dream," *Wired Magazine*, April 4, 2000, available at http://www.wired.com/culture/lifestyle/news/2000/04/35308.

[14] Annalee Saxenian, *Silicon Valley's New Immigrant Entrepreneurs* (San Francisco: Public Policy Institute of California, 1999). The 70 percent figure is based on all Indian-run start-ups from the period 1980 to 1998.

[15] Annalee Saxenian, *Local and Global Networks of Immigrant Professionals in Silicon Valley* (San Francisco: Public Policy Institute of California, 2002).

invested their own money into Indian start-ups, representing a 10 percent increase (although the amounts were unspecified). The answers also painted an optimistic picture about augmented human capital returning home: 45 percent report returning as somewhat or quite likely.

Saxenian's results, while suggestive of strong connections between the Silicon Valley–resident Indians and those in India, should, however, be treated with caution. There are strong problems of self-selection into membership of these associations and in the choice to respond to the survey. There is also reason to believe that diasporas will exaggerate their contribution to the country of origin. For instance, the optimistic picture about investment is belied by actual figures of investment from the Indian diaspora. Even though the propensity to invest is comparable for the Chinese and Indian diasporas in Saxenian's survey, actual flows from the Indian diaspora are only about 5 percent of its Chinese counterpart. Similarly, the finding that 45 percent would consider returning is belied by reality. While aggregate data on return migration are unavailable, segment-specific data such as National Science Board longitudinal data on PhD students suggest that the percentage of Indians obtaining PhDs in science and engineering who had "definite plans to stay" in the United States increased from 56.3 percent in 1994–1997 to 62.7 percent in 2002–2005, even as the number of Indians obtaining PhDs in these fields declined by 30 percent (from 5014 to 3587).[16]

Data from the SAIUS survey, which is a representative sample of the Indian American population, paint a more modest picture of the intermediary and network role of the Indian American community. People of Indian origin in the United States indeed help mediate informational flows between India and the United States about jobs and business opportunities in both countries. Between 7.7 percent and 14.7 percent of respondents reported having links with India about job and business opportunities several times a year or more, considerably less than in the self-selected sample of Saxenian (table 4.1). The vast majority of those who invested in India did so through passive investments, in real estate (33.1 percent) or bank accounts (28 percent). Another 5.6 percent invested through direct purchase of stocks, while 2.9 percent did so indirectly through mutual funds (table 4.2).

Although this emphasizes the need for caution and the limited scale of engagement of Indian Americans, random surveys often undersample wealthy entrepreneurs. Consequently, this data may in turn underestimate more direct financial and technical engagement of Indian Americans in entrepreneurial activities in India. Another study found that of an

---

[16] National Science Board, *Science and Engineering Indicators 2008* (Arlington, VA: National Science Foundation, 2008).

TABLE 4.1
Business/Job Links of Indian Americans with India

Frequency of Exchanging Information With Anyone In:	Several Times/ Month (%)	Several Times/Year (%)	Once a Year (%)	Less Frequently (%)	Don't Know (%)
India about job opportunities in the United States	1.8	12.9	5.4	45	35
India about business opportunities in the United States	1.5	11.2	4.6	45.5	37.2
United States about job opportunities in India	1.9	6.7	2.7	45.4	43.3
United States about business opportunities in India	1.7	6	2.8	45.6	44

Source: Author's survey. *N* = 2132.

TABLE 4.2
Investment Links of Indian Americans with India

Investments in India	Yes (%)	No (%)
Land/property/real estate	33.1	66.9
Bank accounts	28	72
Shares/stock	5.6	94.4
Mutual funds	2.9	97.1
Other investments	1	99

Source: Author's survey. *N* = 2132.

estimated 7300 U.S. tech start-ups founded by immigrants between 1995 and 2005, 26 percent have Indian founders, CEOs, presidents, or head researchers—more people than from the four next biggest sources (United Kingdom, China, Taiwan, and Japan) combined. A comparison with Saxenian's 1999 findings shows that while the percentage of firms with Indian or Chinese founders increased from 24 percent to 28 percent, Indian immigrants outpaced their Chinese counterparts as founders of engineering and technology companies in Silicon Valley. Saxenian reported that 17 percent of Silicon Valley start-ups from 1980 to 1998 had a Chinese founder and 7 percent had an Indian founder. Subsequently, from 1995 to 2005, Indian immigrants were key founders of 15.5 percent of all Silicon Valley start-ups, and immigrants from China and Taiwan were key founders in 12.8 percent. From 1995 to 2005, almost 90 percent of India immigrant-founded companies were within just two business fields: software (46 percent) and innovation/manufacturing-related services (44 percent).[17]

The success of the Indian American community has had considerable economic effects on India. Their association with a large number of start-ups in Silicon Valley and the venture capital industry gave them credibility in India. They have played a crucial role in shaping the regulatory structure of India's private equity and venture capital sector. Perhaps most importantly, just as returning Israeli entrepreneurs helped create the world's second-largest venture capital industry in Israel, returning Indian entrepreneurs are doing the same to replicate Silicon Valley at home.[18]

The steering of outsourcing—what one might call "insourcing"—is another example where the diaspora, through its overseas network and reputation, has enhanced trade and investment into India. Expectedly, this has particularly been the case with those firms owned or operated by Indian Americans, especially in periods when the firms are facing intense cost pressures and are looking to cut costs.[19] Another, albeit more modest, example can be seen in India's apparel industry, which exports a significant fraction of its annual output. However, most of those sales are at the cheaper end of the market, where margins are in single digits. While margins are much higher for the more high-end items, it is much harder to break into this segment. But going up the value chain requires much greater efforts on design, quality control, and delivery schedules. Exporting Indian

[17] Vivek Wadhwa and others, "America's New Immigrant Entrepreneurs: Part I," Duke Science, Technology and Innovation Paper No. 23 (January 2007), available at SSRN: http//ssrn.com/abstract=990152.

[18] For an illustration of this phenomenon, Helion Venture Partners, a venture capital firm with a first fund of $140 million, see "Delhi Dreams—Face Value," *The Economist*, December 23, 2006.

[19] An illustrative story is that of Javad Hassan, an Indian-born American. In 1998, he became CEO of AM Communications (AM), a small, publicly held company based in Pennsylvania, that developed and owned software used by cable TV operators to monitor their systems. The company was in financial trouble, having seen sales decline from $16 million the previous year to around $9 million, due to the loss of several key customers. Hassan sought to turn around the fortunes of the company by outsourcing programming and other tasks to India while steering the company into high-margin services. To this end, AM entered into an agreement with a firm located in India in which Hassan had a stake. In the next few years, the company moved first engineering jobs and then all of its manufacturing and development services; last even its knowledge competencies about how to do things—software, engineering savvy, and development expertise—had moved to India. David Gumpert, "An Unseen Peril of Outsourcing," *Business Week*, March 3, 2004.

designers, who from "inside" the foreign firm begin to source more from India, however, appears to increase the likelihood of greater demand for Indian apparel.[20]

Trade-enhancing effects of diasporas can also be attributed to "taste" effects.[21] Ethnic foods and media are consummate examples of taste effects. By and large, India has not taken advantage of business opportunities by using a captive ethnic food market created by a diaspora with substantial purchasing power as the launching pad for wider exports. Despite the growth of Indian restaurants and Indian cuisine overseas, there has been relatively modest sourcing of goods from India, and Indian brands in particular have made little headway. In all likelihood, this is a reflection of the weakness of the Indian agro-industry sector, which continues to be heavily regulated by state governments in India.

A more promising ethnic "taste" market has been Indian films, particularly those from Bollywood. While these films had been popular in many developing countries for a long time, their business potential only became apparent from the 1980s as new technologies, first the VCR and then DVDs, began to reshape the economics of the industry. In 2007, while domestic box office revenues of Bollywood films were $1.8 billion, export revenues were $214 million.[22] In addition, regional films in Tamil, Telugu, and Punjabi have begun to carve out a home video niche in the Middle East and Southeast Asian markets.[23]

The new finances of Bollywood had two major effects. First, content began following money, and the "diaspora" theme emerged as an important facet of Indian films—these films have been major money makers. As one commentator noted, the diaspora's "sense of homesickness and a conservative, sentimentalised nationalism gave filmmakers a new theme—and foreign currency revenues."[24] Second, the growth of Bollywood's overseas markets, driven in large part because of demand from the diaspora (coupled with domestic demand driven growth), made the sector more attractive to FDI. As with IT, the diaspora brought business "back home."

The wealth of a diaspora alone may have little effect on trade and investment in the country of origin; skill complementarities between the

[20] For instance, when Ritu Beri, a designer from Delhi, moved to Paris to head design at the couture house Scherrer, she began sourcing many of the fabrics and embroidery for her collection from India because of her intimate knowledge about the quality and cost. *Financial Times*, October 7, 2002, 12.

[21] Indeed the biggest global brand in Indian cuisine is British-Indian (Patak's).

[22] Estimates by Credit Suisse, cited in Joe Leahy, "Bollywood Dreams On," *Financial Times*, May 27, 2009.

[23] Kaajal Waalia, "Indian Diaspora Renews Love Affair with Bollywood," *Times of India*, July 18, 2002.

[24] Khozem Merchant, "I Make Films for Every Indian Everywhere," *Financial Times*, February 10, 2004, 12.

diaspora and the country of origin are also important. For instance, immigrants from India, almost all with ties to Gujarat, own about half of the U.S. economy lodging facilities and about 37 percent of all hotel properties in the United States (nearly 20,000 hotels—about 1 million rooms—in 50 states).[25] As with many ethnic businesses, this happened more by accident than by design. In the 1960s and 1970s, U.S. immigration laws granted residency for new arrivals who were willing to invest at least $10,000 in a new or an existing business. At that time, East African Indians (mainly of Gujarati origin) were looking for safer havens for their wealth, and with India in the economic doldrums this sector offered a viable option. They first began to buy into lower-end U.S. hotels, which provided them with a place to live on the premises; in return, the family had to be on call at all times to ensure smooth operations. But the wealth and expertise of this community has had relatively little direct trade or investment impact on India. Motels are a nontradable sector, and given Indian highways and driving habits, the expertise had virtually no market in India until quite recently.

Health is another sector where Indian physician migration has had a significant impact, although perhaps less positive than in other sectors. The most important health effect is, of course, on the population arising from the absence of some of India's best trained physicians (largely educated at public expense). In some cases, as with Indian physicians who go to work for the United Kingdom's National Health Service, their absence is temporary, and they are likely to return with augmented human capital. In other cases, such as migration to the United States, return rates are much lower. In 2005, about one-fifth of all doctors in the United States who had received their first medical degree abroad (more than 40,000 doctors) were trained in India. Their contribution to the Indian economy has been modest, although it appears to be growing. The American Association of Physicians from India (AAPI) and the AAPI Foundation in India have been working with India's health authorities (health ministry officials, ministers, and the Indian Medical Council) to improve regulation of physicians education. This includes compulsory continuing medical education (CME) for practicing physicians, three-year renewal of practicing licenses based on completing annual CME of 50 hours, peer review in all teaching hospitals and others with a capacity of 100 or more beds, and hospital management.[26] There have also been other efforts ranging from philanthropy of individual doctors, returning nonresident

[25] Asian American Hotel Owners Association (AAHOA), "Fact Sheet," available at http://www.aahoa.com/Content/NavigationMenu/MediaKit/FactSheet/default.htm.

[26] This group helped broker a collaboration between Hinduja Hospital and Johns Hopkins to start a Hospital Management Institute in Hyderabad in order to produce the professionals needed to manage Indian hospitals.

Indian (NRI) doctors starting private hospitals (the Apollo chain of hospitals being a prominent example), to programs whereby visiting NRI doctors conduct refresher courses. The overseas Indian medical community is also playing a role in outsourcing some segments of laboratory and diagnostic testing. In general, Indian laboratories are 70 to 80 percent less expensive than the U.S. ones.[27] This business is likely to come mainly from the United Kingdom and the United States, as well as the Middle East—the regions with the largest number of overseas Indian doctors.

Given the myriad health challenges that India faces, however, these efforts, although notable, have not been particularly significant. The principal health needs in India are in the realm of public health (i.e., vaccinations and inoculations and pre- and post-natal services), access to clean water and sanitation, maternal and infant mortality, and child nutrition. If anything, the skill sets of the Indian diaspora health community have amplified the bias toward tertiary and curative health care and away from preventive and primary care.

The relative benefits of diaspora networks vary across sectors. If the benefits for health care in India have been mixed, in another sector—India's diamond cutting and polishing sector—the results have been unambiguously positive. We turn to this sector next.

Diasporas and Diamonds

In 2003–2004, India's largest source of imports was the United States, followed by China.[28] The third largest was Belgium.[29] The large growth of trade between Belgium and India has been dominated by one commodity—diamonds (figure 4.1). And underlying this substantial trade is an unheralded reputational and brokering success of the Indian diaspora: its important role in the global diamond industry.

The global diamond industry has three major segments: the upstream rough mining segment; the intermediate step in which the roughs are cut and polished; and the final stage—namely, the jewelry market. In 2005, the upstream segment made about $10 billion annually. Of this market, De Beers controlled about half; Russia, Angola, Canada and Australia, another third. The market-size of the intermediate step, in which the roughs are cut and polished, was approximately $14 billion, including dealers and

[27] American Association of Physicians of Indian Origin (AAPI), "About AAPI—President's Message," available at http://aapiusa.org/about/president-message.aspx (accessed June 12, 2009).

[28] This section is based on fieldwork carried out in Antwerp in summer 2004. I am grateful to Mihir Sheth for his invaluable help in this regard.

[29] Reserve Bank of India, *Handbook of Statistics on the Indian Economy* (Direction of Foreign Trade, 2004), table 135.

Figure 4.1. Belgian–Indian trade and diamond trade.

manufacturers. And the final stage, the jewelry market, was worth about $57 billion.[30]

In 1968, India exported $40 million in cut and polished diamonds. By 2005, India had emerged as the largest exporter of cut and polished diamonds (whether measured in terms of value, pieces, or caratage) in the world. Its exports of cut and polished diamonds had skyrocketed to $11.9 billion, accounting for 55 percent of world net exports of cut and polished diamonds in value terms, 90 percent in terms of pieces, and 80 percent by caratage.[31] Polished diamond exports constituted 17 percent of India's exports in 2002–2003. Over 90 percent of these diamonds were processed in Gujarat, employing over 1 million people in that state. Concomitant with India's rising status as a world leader in the diamond industry over the past 35 years has been the ascent of Indian émigrés (mostly Gujarati Palanpuri Jains) in the world diamond trade. But what role have the Indian émigré diamantaires (as diamond traders are called) in Antwerp and other cities across the world played in the success of India's diamond industry?

To address this question, I document the major role that the Indian diaspora (in particular, Palanpuri Jains) plays in the global diamond trade, as well as India's leading role as an exporter of cut and polished

[30] Figures for 2002–2003. Ettagale Blauer, "The Diamond Industry," New York Diamonds 77 (July 2003): 62–63.

[31] Data from Gem and Jewelry Export Promotion Council (GJEPC), www.gjepc.com.

diamonds. I then trace the historical trajectory of Indian émigrés' and India's involvement in the global diamond trade since the early 1960s. The initial modest success in India's export of diamonds led a few Jain traders to move to Antwerp, Belgium (the hub of the global diamond trade), giving them greater access to capital and an opportunity to become major market players. Once in Antwerp, these traders first established themselves in extremely small rough diamonds, a segment that the established diamond trading community there regarded as too small to be cut and polished and hence of little value. Taking advantage of their knowledge of very low-cost cutting and polishing skills in India, they began exporting these tiny rough diamonds to India, where they were cut and polished and then reexported through the same distribution channels—namely, the Antwerp-based Jain diamond community. The community established itself as a market intermediary and, in a virtuous circle of development, boosted both its own fortunes as well as India's diamond exports.[32]

By the late 1990s, Indian émigré diamantaires had emerged as a significant force in the global diamond trade, with their share of diamond revenues in Antwerp growing from 2 percent in 1968 to 25 percent in 1980 to 65 percent in 2003.[33] During this period, they gradually replaced the Hasidic Jewish community in Antwerp's diamond trade and gained representation on Antwerp's High Diamond Council, the powerful body that regulates the city's diamond industry.[34] With Antwerp's $26 billion-a-year diamond industry accounting for 60 percent of the global diamond trade,[35] Belgian Indians (who are "really Belgian"[36]) control about two-fifths of the world diamond trade.[37]

---

[32] For a careful analytical investigation of the role played by the community network, see Kaivan Munshi, "From Farming to International Business: The Social Auspices of Entrepreneurship in a Growing Economy," NBER Working Paper No. 13065 (Cambridge MA: NBER, April 2007).

[33] *Wall Street Journal*, May 17, 2003, available at http://www.stefangeens.com/wsj .html.

[34] Ibid.

[35] From http://www.hrd.be/newscenter/newscenter/key_figures.aspx, website of HRD (Antwerp Diamond High Council).

[36] The following quote from Charlie Bornstein, regarding the importance "of the Indian community in Antwerp" is telling: "They are a fabulous part of the Antwerp industry. But you know it's unfair to say Indians, because these people and their companies are really Belgian. I believe that our vision must be that we are all Antwerp people today. I see the young generation of Indians who have become all Belgian. They speak very good French, Flemish, and English and they are a new generation of Belgian diamantaires." Source: www. diamonds.net/news, posted 12/9/2003.

[37] This number of 39 percent is likely an underestimation, because it is often cited that PIOs now have a large market share of the diamond trade in many other cities, including London, New York, Tel Aviv, and Hong Kong.

TWO CASE STUDIES

Brief capsule histories of two of the largest Jain-owned diamond companies in Antwerp—Eurostar and Rosy Blue—illustrate the linkages between the successes of the Indian diaspora and India's place in the global diamond trade.[38] Eurostar's antecedents lay in a Surat diamond merchant named Kirtilal Mehta. One of his sons moved to Bombay and started a company called Dimexon, which operated a diamond cutting and polishing plant in Bombay and exported most of its output. In 1975, Dimexon received a manufacturers' sight from the Diamond Trading Company (DTC), the selling arm of De Beers.[39] In 1977, encouraged by Dimexon's growing manufacturing output and exports, another son (who had been working with his father and brother), traveled to Antwerp and set up a local company there, Eurostar Diamond Traders N.V. Initially, Eurostar served as a selling office for the output of the Mehta family plants and for buying polished stones for the Mumbai office needs. However, in 1981, when a crisis occurred in the global diamond business, prices of both polished and rough goods dropped significantly. The manufacturing operations of the surviving Belgian companies were plagued by high labor costs, and many companies were going out of business. At this point, Eurostar expanded rapidly, its Antwerp marketing operations complementing its India manufacturing operations, bolstered by a cheap and experienced labor force and managerial experience.[40]

The trading family (the Mehtas—but a different Mehta family from the Mehtas of Eurostar) of Rosy Blue, which emerged as Belgium's largest diamond house by 2004, followed a historical trajectory from Palanpur to Mumbai to Antwerp similar to that of Eurostar's Mehta family.[41] Rosy Blue's antecedents can be traced to the establishment of B. Arunkumar & Co. in Mumbai, India, in 1960. In 1963, the company began to export, and in 1969 the firm became a De Beers-DTC sightholder. In 1973, it established an overseas operation, Rosy Blue, in Antwerp, to serve as a satellite office for rough procurement and polished distribution. Two years later, Rosy Blue also became a De Beers-DTC sightholder. In the next decade, the company opened offices in New York, Tokyo, Hong Kong, and Tel Aviv, and then in South Africa and Russia, giving Rosy Blue a presence in all major diamond manufacturing and distribution centers.

[38] The CEOs of these two companies (Dilip Mehta of Rosy Blue Group and Kaushik Mehta of EuroStar) were the only two Indians on Antwerp's 20-person Diamond High Council Board.

[39] Sightholders is an exclusive club through which De Beers sells rough diamonds.

[40] http://www.eurostardiamond.com/Content/aboutus/History.asp.

[41] On Rosy Blue's history, see also Matthew Hart, *Diamond: The History of a Cold-Blooded Love Affair (or) A Journey to the Heart of an Obsession* (New York: Walker Publishing, 2001), 223–40.

By 2004, the firm generated sales of $1.4 billion and employed more than 10,000 people worldwide, 7000 of them in India.

From the short histories of these two firms, it is possible to infer a general mechanism by which the Indian diaspora and India fed off one another in the diamond trade. In the 1960s, the Jain diamond community, consisting of cutters, polishers, and traders, started to export cut and polished diamonds. This early (albeit modest) export push seems to have resulted from two factors. In the aftermath of the war with China, diamond prices in India declined by about 20 percent, while they remained stable globally. Enterprising merchants saw arbitrage opportunities to purchase diamonds cheaply in India and resell them overseas. Beset by mounting foreign exchange woes, the Indian government facilitated the import of rough diamonds and more diamond cutting and polishing machines. Supply of roughs increased, and so did exports. The rupee's devaluation (36 percent in nominal terms) further increased the competitiveness of Indian cutting and polishing operations.[42]

India's modest increase in exports of cut and polished diamonds was boosted in the 1970s as entrepreneurial Jain diamond traders from India set up companies in Antwerp as selling outposts for the cut and polished diamonds produced in Mumbai and also to source rough diamonds for their India operations. During this period, there was a transition from using their Antwerp divisions as satellite offices to bolster the Mumbai base toward establishing Antwerp as the locus of the Indian diamond traders' business. Jain diamantaires in Antwerp began buying so-called Antwerp rejects (small and brown diamonds passed up by established traders) and sending them to India to be polished.

A worldwide diamond crisis in 1981–1982 gave Indian diamond exporters a break. It led De Beers to drastically slash prices on larger rough diamonds, forcing many companies out of business. This crisis, however, did not affect the Indian diamantaires' trade, which was based on small diamonds. It did, however, open up the market to newcomers, and the Jain traders capitalized on the opportunity. Their expertise in small, less expensive diamonds was given a further boost with the opening of the giant Argyle diamond mine in Australia in 1986. (Forty percent by weight of that year's world production of diamonds came from this mine.) Nearly all of the diamonds in the Argyle mine were small and brown, and the Indian diamond industry, with its cheap and inexpensive labor force, was well-positioned to benefit from this discovery.

It is important to keep in mind the centrality of small diamonds to India's diamond trade. This foundation allowed it to cater to the rapidly growing mass-consumption market in diamonds as well as to weather the

[42] Ibid., 232.

1981 crisis and thereby make a major move into the world diamond trade, and in addition to also capitalize on the new findings in Australia's Argyle mines. Although India has gradually moved up the value chain, cutting and polishing larger stones, it still remains the only country in the world with such an enormous, low-wage, skilled workforce of cutters and polishers of small diamonds (although China seems to pose a threat for the future, as it begins to enter the diamond trade). Indeed, India faces a growing problem in the loss of its technical diamond polishing and cutting talent as skilled workers are being sought to set up shop outside India—especially in markets like South Africa and China. Both countries have approached Indian diamond traders with attractive incentives to move shop—and expertise.[43]

The evidence is strongly suggestive of the synergies between the Indian émigré diamantaires and the Indian diamond industry. As Jain diamantaires have prospered, they have expanded their businesses globally, to places including Tel Aviv, Antwerp, China, New York, California, and Tokyo, but their manufacturing base remains in India, with its low-wage, skilled workforce. The diamantaires themselves remain critical market intermediaries to source roughs and find markets.[44] Furthermore, the strong family ties that permeate and in many ways define the diamond world (among both Jewish and Indian Jain traders) have meant that there remain extremely close connections between India and the Indian émigrés, despite growing global competition. The "boundedness of the interlinked families offered by the community of Jains" ensured that "the creditworthiness of the traders could be guaranteed."[45] The Jain diamantaires of Antwerp rely on the large, cheap, skilled workforce in India to cut cheap diamonds, and the Indian industry relies on Jain traders in Antwerp and other world centers of rough diamond trade to get their roughs and find markets. With Antwerp's US$29 billion-a-year diamond trade accounting for 80 percent of the world's uncut and half of its polished diamond trade,[46] the dominance of the Belgian Indian community has been critical. De Beers has only 85 sightholders today, and nearly 60 percent of

---

[43] *Economic Times*, November 28, 2001.

[44] Of course, other factors have also contributed. The Indian government helped establishment crucial infrastructure. These include the Gem Testing Laboratory at Jaipur, the Indian Gemological Institute at Delhi, and Jewellery Product Development Centers at Delhi and Mumbai. India's industrial base has meant that new technologies developed elsewhere to save on labor costs (such as laser diamond-cutting machines) have been adapted and are now made domestically in India.

[45] Sallie Westwood, "A Real Romance: Gender, Ethnicity, Trust and Risk in the Indian Diamond Trade," *Ethnic and Racial Studies* 23, no. 5 (2000): 857–70.

[46] Source: Website of HRD, the Antwerp Diamond Council, retrieved November 24, 2006, from http://www.hrd.be/index.php?id=20.

them are of Indian origin. In May 2006, diamantaires from India gained a historic political victory when for the first time they won five of the twelve seats on the board of the industry's key body in Antwerp, the Diamond High Council. The diamond trade has meant that Belgium is one of India's largest trading partners. (India's imports from Belgium totaled US$4.8 billion in 2005–2006.)

It is possible to come up with a rough estimate of the impact of the Indian diaspora in Belgium on the Indian economy. In 2002, for example, Belgium supplied India with $2.5 billion worth of rough diamonds (out of a total of $4.5 billion). Since Belgian Indian Jains control two-thirds of this trade (and conservatively assuming that Belgian Indian and non-Indian diamantaires in Belgium export in equal proportions to India), the Jain emigrant diamantaires supply India with roughly 36 percent of their rough diamonds. It is very likely that a considerable fraction of the rest of India's rough diamond imports are also being sourced from Jain émigré diamantaires based in Hong Kong, New York, London, and even Israel. Since cut and polished diamond exports constitute 17 percent of India's exports, the Jain émigrés are involved in at least 6.2 percent of India's exports. There is 42 percent value added to the rough diamonds imported, so the Jain émigrés and their Indian counterparts contributed around $0.7 billion valued added. Of course, these figures need to be compared with a realistic counterfactual, but they are illustrative of the economic impact of the diaspora.

The interplay between the Indian diaspora and India in the diamond trade illustrates the significant impacts of global networks resulting from migration. The Indian diaspora has been (and continues to be) a crucial intermediary between India and this global industry.

Financial Flows: Investment and Remittances

The two principal mechanisms of financial flows are either through unrequited transfers (remittances) reflected in the current account in a country's balance of payments or investments reflected in the capital account. The latter, in turn, can occur either through equity, mainly foreign direct investment (FDI) but portfolio flows as well, or debt flows, especially bank deposits. Indian diaspora financial inflows have been largely through remittances and bank deposits, with only modest amounts of FDI—quite different from Chinese diaspora inflows, which are largely FDI, with less remittances or bank deposits.

FOREIGN DIRECT INVESTMENT

Prior to the opening of the Indian economy in 1991, FDI into India was paltry. Subsequently, it increased modestly, averaging around $3 billion annually between the mid-1990s and 2005–2006, and rapidly thereafter. Between 1991–2004, total FDI into India was Rs 1,368 billion, while NRI-FDI was just Rs 95 billion (or $2.8 billion)—less than 7 percent.

A state-wise comparison of NRI investments in India reveals one surprising feature. Despite the Gujarati diaspora's size, wealth, and entrepreneurial characteristics (and whatever its other effects on Gujarat), it has been quite cautious of investing in Gujarat. Between 1991 and 2003, the state received Rs. 188 billion of foreign direct investment, of which the NRI share was a mere 4 percent. Andhra Pradesh and Maharashtra have received the highest NRI-FDI, followed by Karnataka, Delhi, and Tamil Nadu (table 4.3).

An often-made comparison between the Chinese and Indian diasporas is that FDI from the former into China exceeds FDI from the latter into India by 20–25 to one. During the 1990s, annual average FDI flows as a share of gross fixed capital formation into China exceeded 10 percent, while in India's case they have barely been above 2 percent. Nearly 60 percent of Chinese FDI (between 1978 and 1999) came from three ethnically Chinese economies (ECEs)—Hong Kong, Macao, and Taiwan.[47] As stated earlier, the diaspora's share in FDI in India has been under 7 percent, although as I argue later, it has been a source of large financial infows into India, but through other channels.

If the question is posed somewhat differently—what are the differences between overall financial inflows (i.e., remittances, portfolio flows, and diaspora FDI) from the Chinese diaspora into China and the Indian diaspora into India—the story is rather different. The two countries are more comparable, with inflows into China being about twice as large compared to India in absolute terms but somewhat less as a fraction of GDP (see table 4.4). The stark contrast between diaspora FDI into the two countries is offset to some degree by portfolio and remittance flows— except that in this case inflows into India are greater. These differences are in part the result of significant differences in the characteristics and location of oversize migrants from the two countries, differences in incentives (especially tax policies), the relative health of the financial sector in the two countries, as well as economic opportunities in the two countries. Given that a large fraction of FDI in China—about a quarter—is invested in real estate,[48] and since this type of investment is common to the deployment of remittances as well, it reinforces the suspicion that

[47] Yasheng Huang, *Selling China: Foreign Direct Investment during the Reform Era* (Cambridge, UK: Cambridge University Press, 2003), 37.

[48] Wanda Tseng and Harm Zebregs, "Foreign Direct Investment in China: Some Lessons for Other Countries," IMF Policy Discussion Paper PDP/02/3 (Washington, DC: IMF, 2002).

TABLE 4.3
NRI-FDI into India

State	Number of NRI Projects	Value of NRI Investment (Rs. millions)	Total Foreign Direct Investment (Rs. millions)	Nonresident FDI/total FDI (%)
Andhra Pradesh	190	19,058		
Maharashtra	273	18,907	503,330	3.7
Karnataka	163	13,330	239,700	5.6
Delhi	140	9595	346,360	2.8
Gujarat	88	7565	187,950	4.0
Tamil Nadu	192	6833	247,630	2.8

Source: Times of India, 4 February 2004.

TABLE 4.4
Financial Flows to China and India, 2000–2007 (Annual Average, Billions of Dollars)

	Portfolio Flows		FDI		Remittances		Total Financial Inflows	
	2000– 2005	2006– 2007	2000– 2005	2006– 2007	2000– 2005	2006– 2007	2000– 2005	2006– 2007
China	6.8	39	52	81	14.1	24.5	72.9	144.5
India	6	21.75	5.3	19.25	17.3	26.2	28.6	67.2

Source: Global Development Finance, 2008.

there is a not inconsiderable statistical overlap between remittances and FDI.[49]

However, even though FDI by the diaspora has been quite limited, the diaspora members' overseas professional success has positioned them to steer greater FDI and outsourcing to India. By filling what Ronald Burt calls "structural holes"[50] between two very different networks and acting as internal champions, the diaspora, at least at the margin, steered investment and trade into India. Thus, when Yahoo! decided to set up shop in India, its cofounder and chief Jerry Yang stated, "We've been wanting to

[49] India's improving economic prospects (compared to countries where the diaspora with an investible surplus is based) and a rapid increase in the number of diasporic Indians with an investible surplus are likely to change this behavior. According to recent estimates by Citigroup, there are 150,000 Indian millionaires overseas, with total investible surplus of $360 billion.

[50] Ronald Burt, Structural Holes: The Social Structure of Competition (Cambridge, MA: Harvard University Press, 1992).

come to India for some time now. In fact, a lot of Yahoo's employees are Indian and they felt it was long overdue that we came here. There is a tremendous excitement in India surrounding the Internet."[51]

There are a number of reasons why there was little foreign direct investment by the Indian diaspora. The diaspora was not seriously wealthy, since it was comprised largely of blue-collar labor and white-collar professionals rather than entrepreneurs. Additionally, the investment climate in India was hostile, further limiting the prospect of direct investment into the country. For instance, in the mid-1980s, when the NRI industrialist Swaraj Paul tried to invest in India by acquiring shares in two Indian companies (DCM and Escorts), the ensuing furor among Indian industrialists forced Paul to sell the shares back "without loss."[52]

However, subsequent changes in economic policies in India coincided with the emergence of Indian entrepreneurs and financiers abroad, particularly in Silicon Valley, New York, and London. Even then, many of the insvestments were in service-related sectors like IT, which were not capital intensive. By 2008, Paul's $1.5-billion Caparo Group had established sixteen plants for auto components in India with investments of nearly $250 million (and plans for $250 million more). But by now, his investment plans were modest compared to his two NRI peers in England, Anil Agarwal of Vedanta and Laxmi Mittal of ArcelorMittal. The former had built an international mining and nonferrous metals empire, and by 2009 his investments in India (existing and planned) were nearly $20 billion. Mittal meanwhile was planning to put up two steel plants in Orissa and Jharkhand.[53] Meanwhile, a different effect of the rise of overseas Indians was manifest when VodaFone, led by its Indian CEO, Arun Sarin, made the largest telecom investment in India—$10.9 billion in Hutch-Essar in 2007.

India's attractiveness as an investment destination coincided with the increasing financial prowess of overseas Indians, and this conjunction led to a sharp increase in financial flows to India (table 4.4). Between 2000 and 2005, FDI in India averaged around $5 billion annually (about one-tenth of China), but jumped to about $19 billion in 2006 to 2007 (about one-fourth of China). Portfolio flows to the two countries were similar between 2000 and 2005; while they jumped in both countries in 2006 to 2007, China received almost double compared to India. Remittances, however, have been somewhat greater in the case of India. Contrary to conventional wisdom, by 2006–2007, even though total financial flows into China were more than double that of India, as a share of

[51] *Business Standard,* June 29, 2000.

[52] Swaraj Paul, *Beyond Boundaries: A Memoir* (New Delhi: Viking-Penguin India, 1988), especially chapter 8, "Investing in India."

[53] At the time of this writing, however, these plans appear to have stalled.

gross domestic product (GDP) they were greater in India's case (about 6 percent) than in China's (about 4.5 percent).

DEPOSITS AND DEBT FLOWS

An important channel of capital flows from overseas Indians has been NRI deposits. These deposits have amounted to between one-sixth and one-third of India's external debt (figure 4.2). (By the end of 2008, NRI deposits exceeded $40 billion.) Unlike virtually any other country that receives substantial remittances, about half of India's remittances are local withdrawals from NRI deposits, and nearly a third of NRI deposits are withdrawn for local expenditures.

For nearly half a century, India's economic model, based on import substitution industrialization, meant that Indian policymakers operated under conditions of foreign exchange scarcity. Attracting inflows from NRIs has been part of official thinking since 1970, when the first scheme to attract NRI flows was discussed. Inflows from NRIs have come through the current account (remittances) and the capital account (NRI deposits). Although schemes to attract the latter were introduced in 1970, a decade

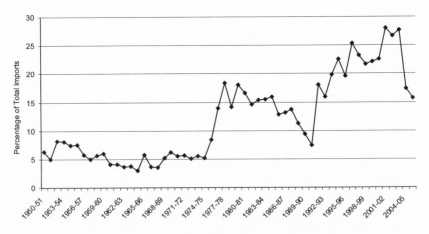

Figure 4.2. Share of total NRI deposits in India's total external debt. Source: "NRI Deposits Outstanding (1990–91) Onwards," from *Table 160: NRI Deposits Outstanding—US Dollars (Handbook of Statistics on Indian Economy)*, and "NRI Deposits Outstanding (1975–76 to 1989–90), from *Table 149: Key Components of India's Balance of Payments—US Dollars (Handbook of Statistics on Indian Economy)*, pp. 253–54; and *India's Total External Debt from Reserve Bank of India and Ministry of Finance, Government of India*. Available at http://www.rbi.org.in/scripts/AnnualPublications.aspx?head= Handbook%20of%20Statistics%20on%20Indian%20Economy.

later, in March 1980, deposits barely exceeded one billion dollars. During the 1980s, deposits accelerated, growing to $12.4 billion by March 1990. Following the onset of the 1991 liberalization reforms, deposits and remittances grew rapidly throughout the 1990s, with the latter exceeding $40 billion by the end of 2008. Earlier, India had been losing substantial inflows because of links between gold smuggling and remittances. To address this, tariffs on gold imports were lowered and gold imports gradually liberalized, which led to a shift of a substantial foreign exchange market from the *hawala* (underground) channels to the open market. Both remittances and NRI deposits surged in this period, and by the end of 2003 NRI deposits totaled $32.5 billion, about one-sixth of the total deposits by resident Indians in commercial banks and 26 percent of India's total external liabilities, just a shade less than the 27 percent share of multilateral loans.

These inflows have been an important source of insurance, significantly contributing to India's burgeoning foreign exchange reserves, allowing the Government of India (GOI) to retire multilateral debt prematurely, and permitting Indian companies to refinance costly external borrowings.

In recent years, the steady accretion of NRI deposits to India's burgeoning reserves poses a different problem—how to manage the country's growing reserves (which passed $200 billion by 2007). One estimate, based on data from the Reserve Bank of India's (RBI) 2005–2006 Annual Report, is that while the nominal rupee denominated rates of return on India's foreign currency assets (FCA) for 2005–2006 was 3.9 percent, inflation in India was about 5 percent, leading to a real rate of return on India's FCA around negative 1.1 percent.[54]

Although India is hardly alone in facing this embarrassment of riches from burgeoning reserves, it is unique in one respect. Since part of its reserves are due to the substantial NRI deposits, these deposits have a financial cost. Table 4.5 gives a basic summary of costs of NRI deposits. By this calculation, these schemes have cost the RBI $2.7 billion between 2002–2003 and 2005–2006. Of course, the costs depend on which benchmark interest rates are used. These costs must be balanced against the benefits of larger reserves. In the past, these inflows have allowed the GOI to retire costlier debt prematurely. Today, these could be seen as an insurance payment that gives assurances to markets, thereby reducing the international cost of borrowings by Indian corporates.

In principle, it is unwise to have schemes that are based on sources of capital, since they fracture capital markets. There has to be a compelling reason why resources and capital received from a country's diaspora should

[54] Jaimini Bhagwati, "Return on FCA," *Business Standard*, December 14, 2006.

TABLE 4.5
Costs of NRI Deposits

	2002–2003	2003–2004	2004–2005	2005–2006
RBI foreign currency assets (US$ millions)	71,890	107,448	135,571	145,108
Earnings on RBI investments (US$ millions)	1835	2115	3014	4520
Yield on RBI investments (%)	2.55	1.97	2.22	3.12
NRI deposits (US$ millions)	28,529	33,266	32,975	35,134
Interest payments on NRI deposits (US$ millions)	1413	1642	1353	1497
Yield on NRI deposits (%)	4.95	4.94	4.10	4.26
Difference in yields (%)	2.4	2.97	1.88	1.14
Costs to RBI (US$ millions)	684.8	987.2	619.9	402.6

Data source: RBI Bulletin, November 2006.

be treated differently than those from any other source. But the schemes are seen as politically important for India's engagement with its diaspora, even though the ability to invest in relatively high yielding risk-free assets may be one reason why NRIs (unlike their Chinese counterparts) invest less though FDI.

NRI capital flows appear to be relatively stable and are comparable to portfolio equity flows. They are influenced by standard risk and return variables, economic and political risk in the first case and the interest rate differential between deposit rates and the London Interbank Offer Rate (LIBOR) in the second.[55] The only significant behavioral difference between NRI capital flows and foreign portfolio investors is that the latter are much more sensitive to India's credit risk as assessed by foreign ratings

[55] Poonam Gupta, "Macroeconomic Determinants of Remittances: Evidence from India," International Monetary Fund Working Paper WP/05/224 (Washington, DC: IMF, 2005). LIBOR is a benchmark interest rate at which banks borrow unsecured funds from each other in the London money market.

agencies, while the former are more blasé about sovereign risk when they put money into India. The one clear case when NRI withdrawals amplified India's balance of payments (BOP) crisis (in 1991) appears to have been driven by the perception of an impending devaluation rather than credit risk per se. When storm clouds threatened, as in the aftermath of the Asian financial crisis in 1997 and India's nuclear tests in 1998, India raised funds from its diaspora: US$4.2 billion from the Resurgent India Bonds (RIBs) issued in 1998 and another US$5.5 billion from the India Millennium Deposit (IMD) scheme in 2000.

FINANCIAL REMITTANCES

Remittances are both a cause and a consequence of migration. Much of the recent excitement regarding international migration and diasporas stems from the resulting substantial financial flows to the "home" country.[56] The importance of migration for livelihoods has long been recognized. Both intranational and international migration has been increasing in recent years, and with it the importance of remittances has grown too. There is a large literature on the determinants of household transfers,[57] as well as on the uses of remittances. A substantial literature on the motives underlying remittances points to remittances as a form of altruism, as an implicit intrafamily contractual arrangement or as an implicit family loan with the relative importance of motives appearing to vary with the institutional setting.

External remittances have become an increasingly important source of financial flows for developing countries and have emerged as the single largest source of net financial flows to these countries. The total volume of financial remittances to developing countries rose from $57.5 billion in 1995 to an estimated $240 billion in 2007.[58] Financial remittances have emerged as an important part of India's balance of payments as well since the oil-boom-induced Gulf migration in the 1970s. If the foreign exchange inflows from remittances were entirely used to finance imports, they would account for between a sixth and a quarter of India's imports over the last three decades (figure 4.3).

[56] Devesh Kapur, "Remittances: The New Development Mantra?" in *Remittances: Development Impact and Future Prospects*, eds. S. M. Maimbo and Dilip Ratha (Washington, DC: World Bank, 2005).

[57] Andrew D. Foster and Mark R. Rosenzweig, "Imperfect Commitment, Altruism, and the Family: Evidence from Transfer Behavior in Low-Income Rural Areas," *Review of Economics and Statistics* 83, no. 3 (August 2001): 389–407. Reena Agarwal and Andrew W. Horowitz, "Are International Remittances Altruism or Insurance? Evidence from Guyana Using Multiple-Migrant Households," *World Development* 30, no. 11 (2002): 2033–44.

[58] Dilip Ratha and Zhimei Xu, *Migration and Remittances Factbook 2008* (Washington, DC: World Bank, 2008).

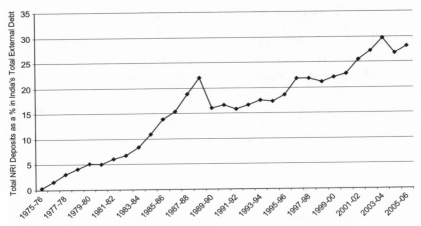

Figure 4.3. NRI remittances as a percentage of India's total imports. Source: *NRI Remittances from Table 151: Invisibles by Category of Transactions—US Dollars (Handbook of Statistics on Indian Economy)*, pp. 257–59; *Imports from Table 149: Key Components of India's Balance of Payments—US Dollars (Handbook of Statistics on Indian Economy)*, pp. 253–54. Available at http://www.rbi.org.in/scripts/AnnualPublications.aspx?head=Handbook%20of%20Statistics%20on%20Indian%20Economy.

In 1970, remittances were virtually negligible; in 1975, they had risen to $0.43 billion, and by 1980, they had jumped to $2.8 billion.[59] Following this rise, they stagnated in the 1980s, and even dropped slightly (to $2.4 billion) in 1990. These figures, however, underplay the extent of remittances during this period. Exchange rate controls and foreign exchange scarcities resulted in a foreign exchange black market premium, creating incentives for Indian workers in the Middle East to remit their earnings through unofficial *hawala* channels. Since then, remittances have climbed steeply, to $12.9 billion in 2000, $21.3 billion in 2005 and an estimated $52 billion in 2008. As a percentage of India's GDP, remittances have grown from 1.2 percent in 1991 to more than 3 percent in the 2000s. Other than merchandise exports, remittances are the least volatile source of foreign exchange inflows into India (table 4.6).

These figures reflect both the degree to which the stock of Indian citizens residing abroad (especially in North America) has jumped as well as the degree to which their earning power has increased. Policy changes including the large devaluation of the rupee and liberalization of gold imports and exchange rate convertibility in the current account have also

[59] All cited data on remittances are from the World Bank.

TABLE 4.6
Relative Volatility of Workers' Remittances and Financial Flows to India
(Coefficient of Variation of Annual Flows)

	1976–1991	1992–2004
Current account		
Private transfers	33.1	49.1
Services	41.7	56.5
Income	42.1	66.1
Merchandise exports	38.5	37.5
Capital account		
NRI deposits	94.4	62.8
FDI		57.6
Portfolio flows		98.9
Total foreign investment	48.1	72.6

Source: RBI Bulletin, November 2006.

made a difference, especially in bringing remittances from the Middle East
through official channels, rather than underground (*hawala*) markets.

MICRO-LEVEL EFFECTS

Remittances expectedly have important economic implications at the
household level. They finance consumption of staples, provide liquidity for
small enterprises (in the absence of well functioning credit markets) and
housing, and are an important source of social insurance. They have distributional consequences for income inequalities across states and households; and they also finance capital investments, both in physical capital
(equipment, land, irrigation works, and housing) and human capital (education), with longer-term implications for economic development. To take
an example, it has long been recognized that capital and liquidity constraints are critical for small enterprise development, especially in poorer
communities with imperfect capital markets; this is the case with India as
well.[60] As a result, remittances may be critical to alleviate liquidity constraints of small enterprises. For instance, an analysis of capital constraints

[60] Results of the 56th round of the National Sample Survey, which covered the unorga-
nized manufacturing sector in India in 2000–2001, indicate that the single biggest constraint on small enterprises is availability of capital. Nearly half of the enterprises surveyed
cited shortage of capital as the single biggest problem faced in day-to-day operations, followed by 19 percent who said that marketing of products was a problem.

on investment levels of microenterprises in Mexico found that remittances from migration by the owner or family members working in the United States were responsible for almost 20 percent of the capital invested in microenterprises throughout urban Mexico—an additional cumulative investment capital of nearly \$2 billion. Within the ten states with the highest rate of migration from Mexico to the United States, almost a third of the capital invested in microenterprises is associated with remittances.[61]

Although there is a body of literature that has examined some of the macroeconomic effects of remittances, given the large magnitude of these flows, the sources and consequences of remittances on the Indian economy have been surprisingly underanalyzed. The National Sample Survey (NSS) has been conducting surveys on migration through its quinquennial employment–unemployment schedules. Its quinquennial survey of consumer expenditure also gets at remittances through its schedule on the sources of household income. However, in line with the NSS's philosophy of not directly collecting data on household income, the questionnaire instead asks whether a sample household received any income in the last year from remittances. While this allows for non-sampling error–free estimates of the proportion of households receiving income from remittances, it does not give any information about their magnitude, the degree of dependence on remittances, or their uses.[62] Similarly, the Reserve Bank of India's data on remittances does not have a robust way to cross-check the reported data, nor can it identify clearly the country sources of these flows. There also appears to be reporting confusion between inflows into the current and capital accounts. Even at the local level, the impacts of remittances are hard to measure because of the interaction of the inflows with other mechanisms. A good example is the state of Punjab. Punjab is one of India's richest states and has experienced high rates of international migration, which contributed to rural development and the Green Revolution in the state (especially in the Jullundur Doab). Kessinger's detailed ethnographic account of one village (Vilayatpur) highlights the many channels through which this occurred. Remittances led to both investments in the land and the acquisition of more land, while the migration (especially of young men) reduced the pressure to subdivide the land into smaller plots.[63] Arthur

[61] Christopher Woodruff and Rene Zenteno, "Remittances and Microenterprises in Mexico," unpublished paper (University of California—San Diego, 2001), available at http://papers.ssrn.com/sol3/papers.cfm?abstract_id=282019.

[62] Even the limited questions on remittances from outside the country and out-migration were dropped in the 55th round (reportedly due to lack of interest in this data). The 64th Round of the NSS (under way at the time of this writing) is expected to address some of the data gaps in understanding migration-related issues in India.

[63] Tom Kessinger, *Vilayatpur 1848–1968: Social and Economic Change in a North Indian Village* (Berkeley: University of California Press, 1974).

Helweg's study of the village Jandiali corroborates this view, further arguing that the remittances were "responsible for a large increase in yields. Money enabled local residents to live better, invest in machinery, obtain and use new varieties of seed, and gain new ideas about farming from abroad. Furthermore, with the outflow of people, the pressure on the land decreased so that there was more production for less people."[64]

However, the absence of a viable counterfactual makes it difficult to come to a firm judgment on the overall welfare consequences of migration, even in this region alone. Some dispute the impacts of remittances on the Green Revolution, arguing that at best they had a modest effect, that they were the icing on the cake, not the cake itself.[65] A considerable portion of remittances appear to have been deployed to buy land, and the resulting rise in land asset prices appears to have had a distortionary impact on Punjab's political economy. Moreover, remittances appear to have become a form of rents and have established a culture of migration, used primarily to pay the large fixed costs to finance further migrants (individual estimates range around US$20,000 in recent years).

Remittances have been much more important for some states than others (figure 4.4). Given the large volumes of remittance inflows and the fact that international migration is concentrated in certain groups and regions, it is not suprising that there are large interstate variations in remittance receipts that have amplified inter-regional inequality in India (figures 4.4 and 4.5).

POLITICAL ECONOMY CONSEQUENCES OF REMITTANCES

The large inflows from remittances have had important political economy consequences. On the one hand, they have significantly enhanced India's external autonomy; on the other, they may have also relaxed pressures on fiscal discipline. In 1991, a combination of external shocks and internal weaknesses pushed India into a balance of payments crisis, forcing it to seek a $4 billion structural adjustment loan from the IMF.[66] Seventeen years later, amid the biggest global economic and financial meltdown in 2008, India's economy proved surprisingly resilient. While in part this was due to its much larger foreign exchange reserves (about

[64] Arthur Helweg, *Sikhs in England* (New Delhi: Oxford University Press, 1986), 4.
[65] Roger Ballard, "Emigration in a Wider Context: Jullundur and Mirpur Compared," *New Community* 11, no. 1 (1983): 117–36.
[66] In January 1991 the IMF approved a 552 million SDR Standby Agreement (which expired in April); and in October 1991 it approved another Standby Agreement for 1,656 million SDR (which expired in June 1993).

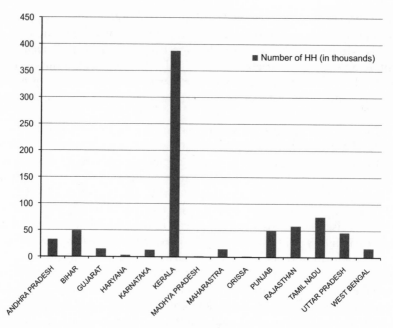

Figure 4.4. Interstate distribution of remittances from abroad. Source: National Sample Survey.

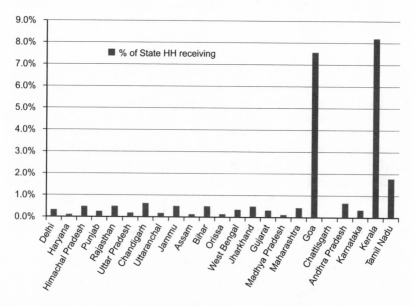

Figure 4.5. Percent of state households (HH) receiving remittance from overseas. Source: National Sample Survey.

$250 billion by the end of 2008), the large reserves accumulation was itself (at least in part) a result of the large remittance inflows since 1991. Between 1992–2008, remittances totaled $278 billion (in contrast, in the seventeen years preceding the 1991 crisis [1974–1990], remittance inflows totaled $32 billion), about the same order of magnitude as India's reserves at the time of the global crisis.

However, it could be argued that if financial remittances contributed to India's burgeoning reserves, the latter had internal political economy consequences as well.[67] High reserves have engendered a form of moral hazard, easing pressures to rectify India's fiscal mismanagement. In the past, when reserves were much more modest, India's policy makers were quite aware that large deficits sustained over a long time period would either inevitably spill over into higher levels of inflation (if the deficit was monetized) or a balance of payment crisis (if the country drew increasingly on external savings). Since both outcomes had harsh political repercussions, this forced policy makers to act with due caution (most of the time). The large increases in reserves have eased these pressures on policy makers. Trade liberalization has eased supply-side weaknesses, and monetization has not yet been seriously resorted to, thereby attenuating inflationary pressures.

Given the large number of international migrants from Kerala, the state is a good example of the political economy consequences of remittances. The number of emigrants from Kerala living outside India in 2003 was 1.84 million (up from 1.36 million in 1998), of which 17 percent were females, roughly 27 emigrants per 100 households.[68] The number of emigrants increased eightfold between 1982 and 2003, while the number of *Videsha Malayalikal* or nonresident Keralites (NRKs—emigrants plus return emigrants) increased from just above 1 percent of the population to nearly 9 percent during this period. By 2008, the number of international migrants from Kerala had climbed to 2.19 million, more than 10% of the state's population.[69]

Kerala's large investment in human capital, proximity, and historical links to the Middle East, as well as the stagnation of the economy, all contributed to extensive international migration.[70] Over time, migration,

[67] Devesh Kapur and Urjit Patel, "Large Foreign Currency Reserves: Insurance for Domestic Weakness and External Uncertainties?" *Economic and Political Weekly* 38, no. 11 (March 15, 2003): 1047–53.

[68] K. C. Zachariah and S. Irudaya Rajan, "Economic and Social Dynamics of Migration in Kerala, 1999–2004: Analysis of Panel Data," Working Paper No. 384 (Trivandrum: Centre for Development Studies, 2007).

[69] These estimaes are from Zachariah and Irudayarajan, cited in "Emigration, Remittances in Kerala Not Hit by Meltdown: Study," *Economic Times*, August 14, 2009.

[70] Internal, pan-India migration from Kerala is also very substantial, but that is not the subject of this book.

remittances, and return migration have transformed the state's economy. The Center for Development Studies in Kerala has been analyzing international migration from Kerala and its manifold effects. The studies indicate that remittances accounted for between a fifth and a quarter of state net domestic product.[71] Remittances have been critical in underpinning the Kerala model of economic development and have contributed "more to poverty alleviation than any other factor including agrarian reforms, trade union activities and social welfare legislation."[72]

However, even as Kerala has emerged as the most globalized of India's states, the ideological climate has changed less markedly. Reflecting the strong left traditions in the state, its intellectual culture is quite hostile to "globalization," and this has shaped the economic impact of remittances. Like most Indian states, Kerala grew steadily in the last two decades, with some acceleration in the 1990s. However, an inhospitable labor culture in industry has meant that remittances have not been channeled into the primary and secondary sectors. The declining credit-to-deposit ratio in Kerala is one of the lowest in India, meaning that investment has been stymied less by the lack of access to credit than the lack of perceived profitable opportunities. Consequently, much of the demand boom for consumer durables has spilled over to other states. Kerala itself has gotten slimmer pickings in the form of trade and transport and repair and maintenance services to service these goods. Instead, remittances have fueled a consumption boom, and the resulting demand has driven growth in the service sector, which consists mainly of nontradables such as transport, trade and telecommunication.[73] However, one sector that has grown on the back of investments is the hospitality industry (i.e., tourism, transport, hotels, and restaurants) and a mushrooming of private institutions in health and education. The feedback mechanisms—high human development indicators and industrial stagnation leading to migration, remittances, and service sector growth in Kerala—have led to a new equilibrium: industrialization is unlikely to be important for Kerala's economy in the forseeable future.

In 2003, remittances were 1.74 times the revenue receipts of the state, seven times the transfers to the state from the Central Government, and

[71] K. Kannan and K. Hari, "Kerala's Gulf Connection: Emigration, Remittances, and Their Macroeconomic Impact, 1972–2000." Working Paper Series No. 328 (Trivandrum: Centre for Development Studies, 2002); K. C. Zachariah and S. Irudaya Rajan, "Migration, Remittances, and Employment: Short Term Trends and Long Term Implications," Working Paper Series No. 395 (Trivandrum: Centre for Development Studies, 2007).

[72] J. T. Mathew, S. Irudaya Rajan, and K. C. Zachariah, "Impact of Migration on Kerala's Economy and Society," International Migration 39, no. 1 (2001): 63–85.

[73] K. Pushpangadan, "Remittances, Consumption and Economic Growth in Kerala: 1980–2000," Working Papers No. 343 (Trivandrum: Centre for Development Studies, 2003), available at http://www.cds.edu/download_files/343.pdf.

1.8 times the annual expenditure of the Kerala government. Household remittances used for education were 40 percent of total state government expenditure on education. Estimates of remittance inflows to Kerala in 2008 were Rs. 433 billion, about one-third of gross state domestic product (GSDP). Remittances reduced the pressures on the state both on the revenue and expenditure fronts. As a Kerala government report put it, the own tax component of government revenues has been a steady 9 percent of GSDP in the three years leading up to 2004–2005. Although this tax effort is similar to that in other Southern states, the fact is that remittances are not recorded in the GSDP figures, which are calculated at factor cost, while taxes are levied on expenditure, which is funded out of household disposable income inclusive of external remittances. Consequently, Kerala's own tax revenue to GSDP ratio should be higher than for other states not receiving remittance income.[74]

There have been other effects as well. With emigrant households more likely to send their children to private schools and use private health facilities, the pressures on government facilities also lessened. Importantly, in 2003, the largest number of emigrants (about 63 percent) was in the 20–29 age group. The incidence of migration in this age group was 20 percent (approximately double for males aged 20 to 29). This age group is politically volatile, but a painless exit strategy has increased the opportunities for those left behind while reducing pressures for change.

HUMAN-CAPITAL EFFECTS

International migration has impacted human-capital formation in India in several ways. It is useful to draw on the migration channels explained earlier in chapter 2. First, as mentioned before, the *prospect* of migration current affects behavior by changing forward expectations. For instance, at the individual level, the possibility of emigration leading to a higher expected return to human capital could lead to greater human capital investments. There are some indications that the burgeoning demand for private engineering, IT, and medical education in India and for English-language education is at least in part being fueled by the prospects of higher returns from working abroad. Traditionally, nurses in India have come from the Kerala Christian community. In recent years, the growing international demand for nurses—especially in Organisation for Economic Cooperation and Development (OECD) countries—is leading women

[74] Kerala Public Expenditure Review Committee, First Report, May 2006.

from other communities in Kerala to also join nursing schools, and new private nursing schools have sprung up to meet this demand.[75]

On the other hand, the consequences of the *absence* of scarce human capital resulting from the so-called brain drain are likely to be negative. As you saw in chapter 3, India has one of the most positively selected emigration rates in the world. Around 2000, one estimate by the United Nations put the total number of expatriates from India in OECD countries at 1.93 million, of which more than half (51 percent) were "highly skilled," i.e., with a graduate degree.[76] Among persons with tertiary education, the former USSR ranked first (1.3 million), with India having the second-largest expatriate community (1 million). How does this compare with skill availability in India? As per the 2001 census, of the total population of 1.0286 billion, the total number of graduates was 37.67 million, while the number with a technical degree (or diploma equal to degree) or postgraduate degree was 5.054 million.[77] Thus, high-skilled Indian expatriates (in OECD countries) were just 2.7 percent of graduate degree holders in India, which at first glance seems like a modest number.

While the total number of graduates in India was barely 3.7 percent of the population in 2001, the number with a technical graduate or postgraduate degree was just 0.5 percent of the population. In contrast, more than half of Indian expatriates had a graduate degree. Even more, while about one-eighth of the total stock of graduates in India had degrees in engineering and technology, this figure is closer to half among Indian expatriates, and even this is drawn from the upper tail of the talent distribution. According to the U.S. National Science Board estimates, of the estimated 1.5 million foreign-born U.S. residents with a science and engineering (S&E) highest degree in 1999, the largest number (14 percent, or 210,000) was from India. This number can be compared to China with 10 percent, and Germany, Philippines, United Kingdom, Taiwan, and Canada with 5 percent each. Of the foreign-born S&E doctorates, India ranks second, with 16 percent of the total (after China with 20 percent).[78]

The story has been similar in medicine. Around 2000, Indian-born doctors and nurses were the largest expatriate medical personnel in OECD countries, representing about 15% of all immigrant nurses and doctors.

---

[75] Irudaya S. Rajan and Marie Percot, "Female Emigration from India: Case Study of Nurses," *Economic and Political Weekly* 42, no. 4 (January 27–February 2, 2007): 318–25.

[76] Jean-Christophe Dumont and G. Lemaître, "Counting Immigrants and Expatriates in OECD Countries: A New Perspective," United Nations Secretariat, Department of Economic and Social Affairs, UN/POP/PD/2005/09 (July 1, 2005; see table A6 in Annex 2).

[77] http://demotemp257.nic.in/httpdoc/Census_Data_2001/Census_data_finder/B_Series/Educational_Level.htm.

[78] Source: National Science Board, "Science and Engineering Indicators," 2004, figure 3-32, available at http://www.nsf.gov/sbe/srs/seind04/.

These consisted of 22,883 nurses and 55,794 doctors and an expatriation rate of 2.6 and 8 percent, respectively.[79] According to another estimate, nearly 60,000 Indian physicians (more than 10 percent of the stock in India) practice abroad, and by all indications these come from the upper tail of physician quality.[80] Since there are additional Indian medical workers (especially nurses in the Middle East), the actual numbers would be considerably higher. The majority of Indian doctors are in the United States (approximately 40,000). About 90 percent of these were trained in public institutions, while the rest were trained in private medical colleges.[81] In part, this reflects vintage effects, since the majority of India-trained doctors in the United States came in the period when most Indian medical colleges were state-supported. In recent years, the majority of doctors coming to the United States from India are from the private sector, reflecting changes in the supply of medical education in India. By 2005, private medical schools accounted for more than 40 percent of the total number of medical students, down from less than a sixth in the mid-1960s, when the medical brain drain to the United States commenced.[82]

The implications of this loss are manifold, including negative effects on higher education institutions in India, the quality of health care, and innovation. An indication of the severity of the flight of scientific and engineering talent can be gauged by the fact that the ratio of patents filed by Indians in North America to that by Indians in India (when normalized by population) is about 28,000:1 (see chapter 3). Furthermore, since this group is precisely the one that pays taxes, the public exchequer loses not only because many have been trained at public expense, but also in terms of the loss of tax revenues.[83] But the most severe long-term impact has been the loss of potential high-quality faculty in Indian higher education, and thereby on the human capital of the next generation.[84]

[79] Table III.A2.1 in "Expatriation Rates for Doctors and Nurses, circa 2000," in OECD 2007, *International Migration Outlook*. Organisation for Economic Cooperation and Development, 2007.

[80] Fitzhugh Mullan, "Doctors for the World: Indian Physician Emigration," *Health Affairs 25*, no. 2 (2006): 380–93.

[81] This is based on my analysis of the membership data of the American Association of Physicians from India (AAPI), the largest organization of doctors of Indian origin in the United States in 2004. Of the 27,021 members for which data was available, 20,832 had degrees from Indian public institutions and another 2051 from Indian private medical colleges.

[82] Mullan, "Doctors for the World" (2006).

[83] Mihir A. Desai, Devesh Kapur, John McHale, and Keith Rogers, "The Fiscal Impact of High Skilled Emigration: Flows of Indians to the U.S.," *Journal of Development Economics* 88 (2009): 32–44.

[84] This issue is examined in greater detail in Devesh Kapur, "Indian Higher Education," in *American Universities in a Global Market*, ed. Charles Clotfelter (Chicago: University of Chicago Press, forthcoming).

However, the brain drain has had a more positive side as well. As mentioned in chapter 2, recent literature has argued that the prospect of emigration affects decisions to acquire human capital since the returns on skills are greater abroad than at home. Since only a fraction can actually emigrate, it is at least possible that the country will end up with a greater stock of human capital. This phenomenon has been referred to in the literature as "brain gain."[85] Although the basic brain gain story has some plausibility, given the clearly forward-looking nature of the demand for skills, it has been strongly criticized since the highest-ability individuals will invest in skills regardless of the prospect of emigrating, but these individuals will be particularly prone to being recruited away when the prospect of emigration is opened up.[86] In the Indian case, a good example of this phenomenon is with regard to nurses: in contrast to earlier years, the prospect of migration—especially to OECD countries—is even persuading women from upper-caste and Muslim households (and not just Christian, the earlier dominant social group) to take up nursing as a profession.[87]

Another area where the economic effects of the brain drain have been positive is in the flow of ideas both from the diaspora as well as from return migrants. Some of India's most distinguished economists residing abroad have long been active participants and contributors to debates on India's economic policies, and a younger generation appears to be following suit. Increasingly, a large number of Indian-origin faculty in business schools abroad advise Indian firms. Return migration has augmented human capital through additional training, experience, and networks. I discuss these effects in the next chapter.

Conclusion

International migration from India has had four principal economic effects on the sending country. One, the reputation and network capital of the diaspora has played an important catalytic role in the development of India's IT and diamond cutting sectors, both among the largest sources

[85] Michel Beine, Frédéric Docquier, and Hillel Rapoport, "Brain Drain and Economic Growth: Theory and Evidence," *Journal of Development Economics* 64, no. 1 (2001): 275–89.

[86] Simon Commander, Mari Kangasniemi, and Alan L. Winters, "The Brain Drain: Curse or Boon? A Survey of the Literature," in *Challenges to Globalization: Analyzing the Economics*, eds. Robert E. Baldwin and L. Alan Winters (Chicago: University of Chicago Press, 2004), 235–78.

[87] Marie Percot and S. Irudaya Rajan, "Female Emigration from India: Case Study of Nurses," *Economic and Political Weekly* 42, no. 4 (2004): 318–25.

of foreign exchange. Two, the diaspora has been an important source of foreign exchange for India for a nearly a quarter century, from the mid-1970s through the end of the twentieth century. Three, financial flows from the diaspora have been regionally concentrated in the Southern and Western states. These states have been growing faster in any case than their poorer counterparts in the North and East, and, consequently, international migration has amplified interstate inequalities in India. Last, migration abroad has reinforced two trends in the Indian economy—the bias toward skill-intensive services and capital-intensive manufacturing—since these are the sectors where the diaspora has the most expertise. While the net economic impact of international migration on India is mixed, this chapter has demonstrated that the economic effects, while complex, are significant.

This chapter has focused on the direct economic effects of international migration on India. However, it is at least plausible that the indirect effects may have been of equal or greater import. There are several ways that this could be possible. The diaspora could have significant political impact on India and thereby affect political stability, which of course would have an affect on investment and growth. This issue is addressed in chapters 6 and 8. In addition, international migration may have affected the direction and quality of economic policy-making in India. In the context of a book review on the Indian economy, the *Economist* quipped, "One cannot escape the conclusion that although India is a net exporter of economists, its policies still suffer from a deficit of economic logic."[88] But what if the causality was reversed, and one substituted "because" for "although"? Has international migration adversely affected the quality and content of India's economic policies? More broadly, just how has it affected the flow of ideas and how did these ideas in turn impact the country's political economy? We turn to this issue in the next chapter.

[88] *The Economist* June 26, 2008. The book in question, *India's Turn*, was a collection of essays by the Indian expatriate economist Arvind Subramanian.

CHAPTER 5

Social Remittances: Migration and the Flow of Ideas

INTRODUCTION

IN JANUARY 2003, the Indian Government organized the first *Pravasi Bharatiya Divas*—a celebration of overseas Indians that mixed emotion and sentimentality with business and economic opportunities. In his inaugural address, the Indian prime minister Atal Bihari Vajpayee inevitably asked for help from the distinguished "alumni" of his country in building the country. But the "ask" was not for money:

We do not want your investments, we want your ideas.
We do not want your riches; we want the richness of your
experience.[1]

With financial remittances having emerged as the largest source of net financial flows to developing countries, it is natural that the buzz around international migration and development has focused on the financial benefits to the country of origin. But the Indian prime minister's request focused on something less tangible and less visible: the expertise, ideas, and experiences of a country's diaspora. Might these, rather than money, have greater impacts on the country of origin?

A major focus of the postwar history of economic development has been to enhance financial flows from capital-rich industrialized countries to capital-poor developing countries, whether through foreign aid, multilateral institutions, or market mechanisms. Given this historical context, it is not surprising that remittances have emerged as the latest "development mantra."[2] However, insofar as the "software" of development—ideas—matter,[3] the most significant impact of remittances could well be occurring through the transmission of ideas from return migrants and

---

[1] Atal Bihari Vajpayee, Prime Minister of India, Pravasi Bharatiya Divas (Overseas Indians Day), New Delhi, January 9, 2003.

[2] Devesh Kapur, "Remittances: The New Development Mantra?" in *Remittances: Development Impact and Future Prospects*, eds. S. M. Maimbo and Dilip Ratha (Washington, DC: World Bank, 2005).

[3] Paul Romer, "Idea Gaps and Object Gaps in Economic Development," *Journal of Monetary Economics* 32, no. 3 (1993): 543–73.

diasporas overseas. In this chapter, I examine the impact of these "social remittances" on the political economy of India.[4]

The transmission of ideas through international migration, especially studying and working abroad, has had a significant impact on sending countries historically as well as in the recent past. Governments have long recognized the potential for human capital flows to serve as a mechanism for the diffusion of skills and technologies. In the early nineteenth century, Britain, in an effort to thwart French and Russian efforts to recruit its skilled workers, sharply limited these workers' mobility abroad: emigrant workers who failed to return home within six months of being warned could lose their land, property, and even citizenship. And if, before the end of the Cold War, Western countries were always trying to get Soviet scientists to migrate (defect), in the aftermath of the Soviet Union's collapse, they were equally concerned with ensuring that these scientists—especially those with expertise in weapons of mass destruction (WMD) technologies—did *not* leave. And with good reason. The United States had brought back Wernher von Braun from Germany after World War II to develop its missile program. In the mid-1950s, amidst the "Red Scare," the United States deported one of its most distinguished rocket scientists, Qian Xuesen (then at Caltech), who went on to father China's missile and space program. And A. Q. Khan's knowledge of uranium enrichment technologies, while working in Holland, allowed him to play a key role in the development of Pakistan's nuclear weapons program.

Returning and circulatory elites, embedded in international "epistemic communities" have long served as conduits for the diffusion of new ideas and paradigms within both domestic and international spheres.[5] In early twentieth-century Europe, the great cities of Europe—particularly, London, Paris, and Berlin—provided an ecumene for exiles from all over the world. Some of strongest votaries and intellectual articulation of Indian nationalism prior to World War I centered around "India Houses" in London, New York, and Tokyo.[6] And in the interwar period, Berlin, standing at the crossroads of the ideological movements—communism, fascism, and nationalism—sweeping Europe at the time, was an important hub for Indian exiles, from M. N. Roy to Subhas Chandra Bose.

[4]The term "social remittances" was first used by Peggy Levitt, albeit in a somewhat different sense.

[5]Haas (1992) defines epistemic communities as networks of professionals and experts with an authoritative claim to policy-relevant knowledge and who share a set of normative beliefs, causal models, notions of empirical validity, and a common policy enterprise.

[6]Harald Fischer-Tiné, "'Indian Nationalism and the World Forces': Transnational and Diasporic Dimensions of the Indian Freedom Movement on the Eve of the First World War," *Journal of Global History*, 2 (2007):325–44.

Returning elites also serve as an intangible source of influence of the sort that underlies Joseph Nye's concept of "soft power."[7] To take an example, the more than 50,000 Soviet Union cultural, scientific, and intelligence elites who came to the United States between 1958 and 1988 as part of cultural exchange programs (and the even larger number of Americans who went to the Soviet Union) were an important source of influence and persuasion that paved the way for Gorbachev's "glasnost," "perestroika," and the end of the Cold War.[8]

Foreign education, especially in Western universities, has been a key mechanism for the transmission of ideas of modernity, be it political regimes or economic systems. Although foreign-educated individuals are a very small fraction of their native populations, there is evidence to suggest that they promote democracy in their home country, but only if the foreign education is acquired in democratic countries.[9] In the early part of the twentieth century, Chinese students who had studied in U.S. universities played "pivotal roles in Chinese intellectual, economic, and diplomatic life upon their return to China."[10] A century later, the reemergence of Chinese science has been attributed to the return of overseas scholars—81 percent of the members of the Chinese Academy of Sciences and 54 percent of the Chinese Academy of Engineering are returned overseas scholars.[11] It should be emphasized that this influence is not a one-way street. U.S. President Barack Obama's childhood years in Indonesia and in racially diverse Hawaii (away from mainland United States) potentially "gave him a sense of the world that was enriching."[12]

The ideational effects of international migration on decision-making behavior are manifest at multiple levels of society. The migration and education abroad of Latin American elites, for instance, has been a contributing factor in explaining the sharp shift in macroeconomic policies in that region.[13] A country's "ownership" of World Bank and International

[7] Joseph Nye, *Soft Power: The Means to Success in World Politics* (New York: Public Affairs, 2004).

[8] Yale Richmond, *Cultural Exchange and the Cold War: Raising the Iron Curtain* (University Park, PA: Penn State University Press, 2003).

[9] Antonio Spilimbergo, "Democracy and Foreign Education," *American Economic Review* 99 (March 2009): 528–43.

[10] Weili Ye, *Seeking Modernity in China's Name Chinese Students in the United States, 1900–27* (Stanford, CA: Stanford University Press, 2001).

[11] P. Zhou and L. Leydesdorff, "The Emergence of China as a Leading Nation in Science," *Research Policy* 31, no. 1 (February 2006): 83–104.

[12] Edward Luce and Demetri Sevastopulo, "Obama's Journey: He Gets It," *Financial Times*, November 5, 2008.

[13] Sarah Babb, *Managing Mexico: Economists from Nationalism to Neoliberalism* (Princeton, NJ: Princeton University Press, 2001); Jorge I. Domínguez, *Technopols: Freeing Politics and Markets in Latin America in the 1990s* (University Park, PA: Penn State Press,

Monetary Fund (IMF) programs is greater when its economic decision makers have studied in similar graduate schools as their fund counterparts or have worked in that institution.[14] Even at the micro level, controlling for household characteristics, Mexican households with family members in the United States have more neoliberal economic views than those who do not; accordingly, the former are the households that increasingly form the electoral support for neoliberal economic policies.[15]

Emigrants are also agents of familial, social, and demographic changes in their communities of origin. An important reason for the greater fertility declines in Morocco than Egypt since the 1970s has been attributed to the different destinations of migrants from the two countries: to France and Spain from Morocco, and to Saudi Arabia and the Gulf countries from Egypt. Emigrants from both countries (and their wider family networks back home), have adopted the habits of their new societies: antinatalist in the former and pro-natalist in the latter.[16]

Of course, it is one thing to acknowledge that ideas and influence arising from international migration matter, and quite another to demonstrate precisely how much they matter. My goal in this chapter is modest. I note that developing countries have certain structural characteristics, such as a narrow middle class, weak higher-education institutions, "thin" markets for talent, and few organized interest groups that constitute the pluralist vision of democratic politics. Above all, an intrinsic feature—indeed, one may say the very definition—of a developing country is that it has weak institutions. Consequently, individuals, leaders, and elites simply matter more, particularly in designing and shaping the institutional landscape. With this as background, in this chapter I argue that the patterns of elite circulatory migration and the U.S.-based diaspora in particular have reshaped the preferences of Indian elites and, as a result, significantly impacted the political economy of India.

Throughout this chapter, I focus on the role of elites as decision makers rather than as a class. Thus, insofar as elites matter, so will the ideas shaping their preferences. The causal chain I posit describes how elites get exposed to new ideas that shape their policy preferences and how such

---

1997); Judith A. Teichman, *The Politics of Freeing Markets in Latin America: Chile, Argentina, and Mexico* (Chapel Hill and London: University of North Carolina Press, 2001).

[14] Devesh Kapur and Moises Naim, "The IMF and Democracy," *Journal of Democracy* 16, no. 1 (January 2005): 89–102.

[15] Devesh Kapur and John McHale, *The Global War for Talent: Implications and Policy Responses for Developing Countries* (Washington, DC: Center for Global Development, 2005).

[16] Youseff Courbage, "Fertility Transition in the Mashriq and the Maghreb," in *Family, Gender, and Population in the Middle East*, ed. Carol Obermeyer (Cairo: American University in Cairo Press, 1995).

preferences get institutionalized, ultimately critically affecting a country's political economy. The chapter first examines the role of ideas and elites. It then examines broad trends in the overseas education of key Indian decision-making elites—political, business, bureaucratic, and scientific— spanning the last half-century. This analysis is based on a database developed specifically for this purpose.

Subsequently, I examine in greater detail two key turning points in recent Indian history and the role of foreign-educated elites in shaping the country's future trajectory. The first of these moments occurred when the country became independent and the blueprints for independent India's future were being drawn up; the second was in 1991, when the country's balance of payments crisis brought it to a crossroads in deciding on future economic choices. In the first historical moment, at the time of independence, members of India's political elite had an unusually extensive exposure to liberal democratic ideas due to their overseas education; this exposure, I argue, affected the institutional choices the elites made, and, accordingly, had critical long-term effects on the country. Likewise, in the second moment, during the 1991 balance of payments crisis, Indian decision-making elites had significant exposure to liberal economic ideas, again stemming from their overseas education; this exposure once again impacted their policy choices and had a significant impact on India's political economy. Thus, I argue that temporary migration—particularly the overseas education of key Indian decision-making elites—played a critical role in influencing the course of events during two historical junctures in modern Indian history.

This analysis reveals three broad trends. First, in the decades following Indian independence, the number of India's decision-making elites being educated abroad declined steadily, as new political elites representing hitherto marginalized social groups came to the fore through democratic processes. Thus, even as India's political elites became more socially representative vis-à-vis India, they became more parochial relative to the earlier elite profile. Second, since the 1990s there has been a reversal: just as India became more "open" to international trade and finance, the international exposure of its elites has also grown. Third, the source of ideas to which Indian policy elites were exposed has shifted markedly from the United Kingdom to the United States. The chapter concludes by examining some implications of these trends.

IDEAS AND ELITES

Max Weber famously argued that ideas have profound effects on the course of events, because they serve as "switchmen" directing interest-based action down one track or another.[17] What actors believe in may be just as important as what they want, insofar as these beliefs influence interests, priorities, and preferences. Ideas give content to interests, and new ideas can profoundly change an agent's interests. Understanding the exchange of ideas can help us to understand how interests are formulated.

However, the extent to which ideas exert long-term effects depends on whether they are institutionalized in administrative procedures, programs, and bureaucracies. The notion that ideas and interests are mutually constituted, even the stance that ideas are often a cloak camouflaging material interests, is not particularly contentious. But ideas cannot be reduced solely to material interests, a point conceded even by arch-materialist Karl Marx: "The materialist doctrine that men are products of circumstances and upbringing, and that therefore, changed men are products of other circumstances and changed upbringings, forgets that it is men who change circumstances and that it is essential to educate the educator himself."[18]

A different view on the role of ideas is that they act more as lubricants that help reduce friction, making possible the collective action that is necessary for institutional supply.[19] My point is not to argue whether ideas or interests are more important in shaping policy per se, but rather to focus on how they interact and how changing ideas can affect the ways in which actors redefine their interests. In either case, once they become programmatic and paradigmatic, ideas are institutionalized and can generate constituencies to later defend these ideas. Consequently, the concept of institutionalized ideas helps us understand the prolonged stability or path-dependent nature of public policy.

In recent years, a growing literature has emphasized the causal role of norms and ideas in explaining political outcomes.[20] However, the study of the role of ideas has been handicapped by two methodological weaknesses: how to measure norms and ideas and how much causal weight to

---

[17] Max Weber, *Essays in Sociology*, ed./trans./intro. H. H. Gerth and C. Wright Mills (Oxford, UK: Oxford University Press, 1946), 280.

[18] Karl Marx, "Theses on Feuerbach," in *The Marx-Engels Reader*, ed. Robert C. Tucker (New York: W. W. Norton, 1978).

[19] Douglas North, *Institutions, Institutional Change and Economic Performance* (Cambridge, UK: Cambridge University Press, 1990).

[20] P. Hall, *The Political Power of Economic Ideas* (Princeton, NJ: Princeton University Press, 1989); J. Goldstein and R. O. Keohane, "Ideas and Foreign Policy: An Analytical Framework," in *Ideas and Foreign Policy*, ed. Keohane Goldstein (Ithaca, NY: Cornell University Press, 1993); K. R. McNamara, *The Currency of Ideas* (Ithaca, NY: Cornell University Press, 1998); Hilary Appel, *A New Capitalist Order: Privatization and Ideology in Russia and Eastern Europe* (Pittsburgh, PA: University of Pittsburgh Press, 2004).

assign them.[21] Ideas are inherently intangible and, therefore, not directly observable. Attempts at analyzing the role of ideas by focusing on behavioral outcomes—i.e., whether an actor's behavior complies with norms and ideas—risk being tautological and circular. A different methodological approach has been to use content analysis to measure what actors say and write about their actions. This approach, too, is problematic in that it is difficult to distinguish how much of this is for public consumption rather than being genuine, deeply held, personal beliefs.

In this chapter, I argue that higher education is a key source of ideas. The socializing role of education has been long recognized, and the type of education people receive leads them to value things differently. It is hardly controversial to say that anthropologists and economists put different weights on similar situations; nor is it controversial to suggest that there will likely be a difference in policies when "technocrats" in developing countries are primarily lawyers and engineers (as was the case a half-century ago), or largely economists (as is the case today).

There is, of course, a key analytical conundrum here: to what extent are choices regarding the "what" and "where" of higher education exogenous or endogenous? In general, for nationals of developing countries, both choices are relatively exogenous, primarily because of the large financial barriers. Until the 1990s, most Indians who went abroad to study could do so only through scholarships, whose availability varied with the field and country of study. Even in the rare cases where a student could afford it, India's central bank did not permit foreign exchange for undergraduate overseas education except to three institutions (Cambridge, Oxford, and Harvard). The decision by the Thatcher-led conservative government in the early 1980s to sharply increase fees for overseas students led to a significant drop in Indian students going to the United Kingdom. That drop was more than compensated by an increase in Indians going to the United States due to the greater availability of financial aid there. However, this aid was available only in some areas (especially science and technology fields) and rarely in professional fields like law, medicine, or business. All these exogenous factors affected who could go abroad, where they could go, and what they could study.

For most students with middle-class backgrounds, the choices of what and where to study are relatively more exogenous, whereas for elites the choices are endogenous, for the simple reasons that they do not face resource constraints. However, even in this case, the choice of what to study—e.g., law—determines where a course of study was pursued. The legacy of the British legal system in India had very strong selection effects

---

[21] Craig Parsons, "Showing Ideas as Causes: The Origins of the European Union," *International Organization* 56, no. 1 (winter 2002): 47–84.

on the "where" to study, when it came to the pursuit of an overseas law degree. There was simply no question that in this field the choice would be the United Kingdom; this was exogenously determined. Even today, the one area where the United Kingdom dominates over the United States in the matter of overseas education is law. Meanwhile, the legal professions in the United States and India still do not recognize each other's degrees.

In all societies—but more so in democracies—politicians need to frame policies in particular ways in order to make them politically acceptable. At one level, they may need overarching cognitive paradigms of how the world works, but they will definitely also need precise programmatic guidelines that can affect the political acceptability of one set of policies being adopted over another. Returning human capital carries with it new ideas, ideas that may be deployed in policy-making. These actors are often academics and other intellectuals. There is considerable evidence in a variety of contexts of the role of university-trained professionals and technocrats as valuable state-building resources.[22] Of course, actors do not operate in a vacuum. The formal rules and procedures governing policy-making affect which ideas penetrate the policy-making process and are adopted and implemented as policy. In other words, institutions influence the degree to which academics and other intellectuals can access policy-making arenas. Indeed, the ways in which idea-producing institutions, such as professions and universities, are linked to the state helps determine which ideas affect policy-making. This sort of institutional filtering has affected economic policy.[23] While our understanding of the informal channels through which this occurs is weak, insofar as intellectuals and policy makers travel in the same social circles, social institutions can act as filters affecting policy.

The ideational effects of international migration are manifest in business, as well as in the state and civil society. They may occur through the diaspora or the act of return migration. In many cases, people go abroad, augment their human capital through education and work experience, and then return. But the type of education, the country of education, and the specific experiences in the workplace and broader environment may also matter. The differences between an education at the London School of Economics and the University of Chicago, or experiences working at the International Labour Organization (ILO) compared to the IMF, do make

[22] In the context of the United States, Stephen Skowronek has argued that an intellectual vanguard of university-trained professionals and other progressive thinkers were among America's most valuable state-building resources during the early twentieth century. Skowronek, *Building a New American State: The Expansion of National Administrative Capacities, 1877–1920* (New York: Cambridge University Press, 1982).

[23] Hall, *The Political Power of Economic Ideas.*

a difference; whether this is due to the selection effect (preexisting skills and values of the individual) or the transformative effects of the institution is exceedingly hard to distinguish. The ideational effects of migration will depend on the migrant population's size, socioeconomic characteristics, country of location, and access points in the power structure of the country of origin. Reentry points—whether in academia, business, politics, or policy-making—will influence policy agendas back "home."

Drawing on survey responses of the U.S. resident Indian-origin population, I tested the ideational effects of an overseas education by specifically examining the prejudice of members of this group against Muslims.[24] Using a technique developed to examine racial prejudice (specifically anti-black prejudice among whites in the American South), the survey established differential anti-Muslim prejudice by different respondent characteristics. While I examine this issue in detail in chapter 8, here I present the results of the effects of the country where the respondent received his or her last degree (table 5.1). If there is something to the socialization effects of education, we might expect the U.S. resident Indian-origin population who received at least some of their education in the United States to be less prejudicial than those who did receive any education in the United States because prevailing social norms in the United States are less receptive to interpersonal prejudice than those in India. This is indeed the case—on average, those having a U.S. degree are less prejudiced against Muslims (by 9.5 percent) than those who do not have this profile. Other factors such as length of stay or country of birth are not significant (see chapter 8), pointing to the important ideational effects of higher education. Of course, there is the possibility of a selection bias if individuals interested in pursuing higher education in the United States are more liberal in their outlook to begin with.

Does an outside education privilege a person when she returns more than if that person had completed a similar level of education in the home country? Insofar as the student goes from a developing to an industrialized country, and the average educational institutional quality is greater in the latter, then a foreign degree is likely to have, at a minimum, a positive signaling effect. But does it also change the individual's worldview or, in addition, give her greater domestic leverage as well? Does a degree obtained abroad provide decision-making elites greater impartiality in making judgments pertaining to the group from which they are drawn, or does it simply leave them less grounded in local realities? If it is the former, the normative case is favorable. For instance, Sen distinguishes between cases where only members of the focal group are involved with ones where an "impartial spectator" from outside the group is also involved (and one

---

[24] Details of this survey (the SAIUS survey) are provided in chapter 2 and appendix II.

TABLE 5.1
Difference in Prejudice by Place of Last Degree

Where Last Degree Received	Observations	Mean	Standard Error	95% Confidence Interval	t-value	Significant	Level of Anger
0 = Elsewhere	1171	2.462	0.0258	[2.411, 2.512]	2.4855	Yes	−9.53%
1 = United States	919	2.366	0.028	[2.311, 2.422]			

Note: For further details on methodology, see chapter 8.

whose very impartiality derives from being outside the group).[25] Cautioning that the former arrangement can lead to a "procedural parochialism," Sen argues that the "impartial spectator does indeed have something to tell us—even more vocally today than in the world that Smith knew." Last, even if externally educated elites are not more impartial, the exposure they have gained might equip them with the skills of "boundary-spanning individuals," identified as playing a particularly important role in organizations.[26]

An outside education and experience might also enhance internal power. Organizational theorists have analyzed why managers prefer external knowledge.[27] Thus, despite the general bias for ingroup favoritism, external knowledge may be sought because it lowers status costs. Because the successes of ingroup members can be more threatening than the successes of outgroup members, knowledgeable ingroup members may be ignored in order to avoid the painful implications of social comparisons with them. These status threats are less when the knowledge source is external. Thus, in internally competitive organizational settings, internal knowledge may be at a disadvantage relative to external knowledge. A second mechanism is informational, whereby the scarcity and uniqueness of external knowledge heighten its value. Because internal knowledge is more readily available than external knowledge, it is subject to greater scrutiny and more critical evaluation, while scarce external knowledge retains its uniqueness and scarcity and, hence, heightened value. Additionally, like many scarce

[25] Amartya Sen, "Open and Closed Impartiality," *Journal of Philosophy* 99, no. 9 (2002): 445–69.

[26] M. L. Tushman and T. J. Scanlan, "Boundary Spanning Individuals: Their Role in Information Transfer and Their Antecedents," *Academy of Management Journal* 24 (1981): 289–305.

[27] Tanya Menon and Jeffrey Pfeffer, "Valuing Internal versus External Knowledge: Explaining the Preference for Outsiders," *Management Science* 49, no. 4 (2003): 497–513.

goods, external knowledge might be subject to overvaluation, in part because it requires greater expenditures of time, effort, and financial resources. Thus, internal knowledge often comes to be seen as familiar and flawed, while external knowledge is venerated because of its scarcity and uniqueness. In either case, this would privilege an external education.

Recent studies suggest a different mechanism to explain why an overseas education might be empowering.[28] These studies have found a positive relationship between living abroad and creativity. Time spent living abroad (but not time spent traveling abroad) appears to have a positive relationship with creativity. Experiments in which respondents were primed about their foreign living experiences temporarily enhanced creative tendencies for participants who had previously lived abroad. The degree to which individuals had adapted to different cultures while living abroad mediated the link between foreign living experience and creativity. And individuals who have lived abroad or who identify themselves with multiple national cultures seem to be more likely to become entrepreneurs or come up with new product ideas at work.

Who Are Elites?

The study of elites and the role of ideas has fallen on hard times, partly a casualty of self-inflicted methodological weaknesses and partly a victim of the vicissitudes of intellectual cycles. Notwithstanding the rich traditions of European political sociology represented by stalwarts such as Pareto, Mosca, and Marx, as well as the North American debates sustained by C. Wright Mills, Dahl, Lasswell, Bachrach, Bottomore, and Putnam, claims that the scholarship on elites potentially displayed "abounding vigour" have been found wanting.[29]

The shift in what drives politics—from class to cultural and identity issues—has also contributed to the decline of a field where the key variable was conceived of in class terms. Thus, Lasswell's classic definition of elites basically encompasses the popular notion of elites as "people at the top": "The study of politics is the study of influence and the influential . . . the influential are those that get the most of what there is to get. . . . Those who get the most are elite; the rest are mass."[30] Marxist

---

[28] A. K. Leung, W. W. Maddux, A. D. Galinsky, and C. Chiu, "Multicultural Experience Enhances Creativity: The When and How," *American Psychologist* 63 (2008): 169–81; W. W. Maddux and A. D. Galinsky, "Cultural Borders and Mental Barriers: The Relationship between Living Abroad and Creativity," *Journal of Personality and Social Psychology* 96, no. 5 (2009): 1047–61.

[29] Dankwart Rostow, "The Study of Elites," *World Politics* 18, no. 4 (1966): 696.

[30] Harold Lasswell, *Politics: Who Gets What, When, How* (New York: McGraw-Hill, 1936), 13.

and neo-Marxist scholarship in particular has seen elites as a social class where history is conceived as the rise and fall of elites who represent the "ruling class," which is present in all societies and "performs all political functions, monopolizes power, and enjoys the advantages that power brings."[31]

An analysis of elites can examine their social composition (in India, caste, ethnicity, and religion), functional skills, recruitment and replication processes, cohesiveness, and reasons for decline. For instance, in India the privileges of high ritual caste status had a strong impact on the constitution of post-independence elites because they had historically held a monopoly of administrative and literary skills. In this chapter, however, I focus only on elites as *decision makers whose actions have political economy consequences*. While this is a much narrower definition, it is not inconsistent with the usual understanding of elites as a small dominant group enjoying a privileged status within a larger society.

DATABASE OF NATIONAL ELITES

For the purposes of this study, I have focused on national elites who may have a potential impact on the political economy of India in some direct way. Consequently, the analysis focuses on political, business, bureaucratic, and scientific elites while excluding cultural elites (such as experts in the performing arts and literature). Such a definition is clearly open to debate. Surely, in all countries writers, playwrights, and musicians shape politics. Art is often considered subversive precisely because of its presumed political effects, and, if so, we should perhaps include all those whose works have been banned. For the most part, however, the influence of a litterateur on political economy is quite diffuse and indirect. The political impact of literary figures such as Aleksandr Solzhenitsyn or Václav Havel, while considerable, is undoubtedly greater in authoritarian systems, because of the lack of alternative avenues for protest. Although India has periodically banned films and books, and governments have harassed individual artists, there is no significant case of blanket proscription or jailing resulting in a Havel-like figure. In general, for cultural figures—be it actors, artists, or literary figures—higher education plays little role as a filtering and signaling device, and consequently an overseas education is not particularly germane in the construction of an individual's elite status. However, cultural figures, ranging from actors to authors, do parlay their public persona into politics. Indeed politics in

[31] Gaetano Mosca, *The Ruling Class*, trans. H. D. Kahn (London: McGraw Hill, 1939).

several southern Indian states (especially Tamil Nadu and Andhra Pradesh) has been dominated by such figures. In this study, any person who has been directly active in politics (by heading a political party or being elected to Parliament) is included in the database, regardless of the route of access to politics. This also includes several influential personalities in cultural fields who are nominated to the upper house of Parliament (the Rajya Sabha).

Overseas exposure can encompass a range of experiences, from tourism to pilgrimages, education, and work. The database focuses on education for several reasons. Education has been the "hallmark of the elite," as state-building and the imperatives of modern economy created the demand for new bureaucratic and managerial elites.[32] Whether in Meiji Japan or nineteenth-century Europe, academic training and education were central to the creation of new bureaucratic elites and more elaborate state structures.[33] Historically, overseas education was actually usually the first overseas experience for many, and therefore, it was likely to have had an especially lasting effect. Moreover, this overseas experience often occurred in a person's formative years and was thus more likely to have had long-term effects. Using survey data in Italy, Putnam et al. found that the coherence and temporal stability of belief systems of political elites, especially on fundamental issues of political culture and ideology, are relatively high whether compared to those of the general population or segmented by individual characteristics such as religion and demographic traits.[34] Insofar as this finding is true more generally, it increases the importance of understanding the processes that shape the beliefs of political elites since, once formed, they are likely to persist. Third, and importantly for the purposes of this study, elites are educated to govern. Education has been the key mechanism for constructing new elites. Unlike most other developing countries, Indian politics has been characterized by an unusual regime stability, which meant that elite mobility took place gradually but steadily through democratic politics. Hence, overseas education may matter even more. Last, as a practical matter, this is the one overseas experience for which data are most precise and comparable over time.

The database of Indian elites covers four critical decision-making groups: politicians, bureaucrats, scientists, and industrialists. Education was measured on two dimensions: the level to which the individual studied and the place from which the degree was obtained. The time period

[32] Frederick Frey, *The Turkish Political Elite* (Cambridge, MA: MIT Press, 1965).

[33] For Europe, this point is elaborated by Hilde de Ridder-Symoens, "Training and Professionalization," in *Power Elites and State building*, ed. Wolfgang Reinhard (New York: Clarendon Press, 1996).

[34] Robert Putnam, Robert Leonardi, and Raffaella Nanetti, "Attitude Stability among Italian Elites," *American Journal of Political Science* 23, no. 3 (1979): 463–94.

covered was 1950 to 2000. Since elites do not change annually, the data covers three points in time: 1950, 1980, and 2000. (For the groups comprising politicians and scientists, the data covers all three time periods, while for industrialists and bureaucrats the data covers only 1980 and 2000.) A wide range of sources was consulted to ensure the robustness of the data. The methodology, in particular problems of consistency over time, and sources for the database are elaborated in appendix IV.

Political Elites

In a parliamentary system, members of Parliament constitute a self-selective national political elite. The following criterion was adopted for including an individual in the database: all members of both houses of the Parliament, the Lok Sabha (the lower house of Parliament) and Rajya Sabha (the upper house), and all Cabinet ministers were included. This criterion, however, does not hold for 1950, since the Rajya Sabha came into existence only after 1952. Instead, the data for 1950 covers members of the Indian Council of States, supplemented with members of the newly formed Rajya Sabha. The logic for including the latter is that any individual who was part of the first Rajya Sabha was probably in a position to be included in an elite list for 1950. However, while such a criterion is attractive from the point of view of consistency, it does suffer from one limitation. For a country of India's size, there have always been regional power brokers who have never been members of Parliament. While this was less of an issue in earlier years, the growing importance of regional parties since the 1990s makes this more problematic for 2000.[35]

The data are presented in table 5.2. While one of ten parliamentarians after independence had an overseas education, by 1980, this figure had declined to 6.2 percent. Two decades later, the figure had dropped further: one out of twenty-five had an overseas education. While in 1950, India's political elites who were educated abroad predominantly studied in the United Kingdom, by 2000 the United States had emerged as the principal destination. The decline in overseas education of India's political elites reflects the significant selection effect regarding who studies abroad. Either the student came from a family that had enough wealth to send him abroad (and it was usually "him"), or the family background allowed access to educational institutions that could then be leveraged into overseas scholarships. In both cases, these were usually members of India's upper-caste social elites. The gradual entry into political power of

[35] Thus, leaders such as Jyoti Basu (CPM, West Bengal), Bal Thackeray (Shiv Sena, Maharashtra), Karunanidhi (DMK, Tamil Nadu), Jayalalitha (AIDMK, Tamil Nadu), and Chandra Babu Naidu (Telugu Desam, Andhra Pradesh), all of whom have national influence, were not members of Parliament in 2000.

TABLE 5.2
Political Elites

Year	1950	1980	2000
Percent studying abroad	10.4	6.2	4.0
By location			
• In UK	74.6	61.4	42.9
• In U.S.	12.7	24.6	45.7
• Elsewhere	14.3	15.8	11.4
Education level			
• High school or less	21.2	21.4	14.9
• Bachelor's degrees	21.7	24.9	28.6
• Professional degrees	39.5	31.0	28.3
• Other master's and PhD degrees	16.2	15.8	22.2
• More than one degree	0.0	1.0	4.7
• Diplomas in the arts, etc.	1.7	1.4	1.4
Sample size (N)	605	915	879

Source: For data sources, see appendix IV.

Note: The percentages do not precisely add up to 100 because in some cases a person has studied in more than one country and several others have more than one type of degree.

members from hitherto marginalized social groups (often rural) and non-Anglicized elites changed the social basis of India's political elites. The very success of India's democracy resulted in Indian political elites becoming more parochial and less cosmopolitan and "open." This was inevitable: nationalist movements were invariably led by Western-educated elites, whose education empowered them both within their societies as well against the colonizing power. However, universal franchise in such a socially heterogeneous society meant that sooner or later, voters would select representatives that better reflected their social group and were less drawn from urban, Western-educated, Anglicized elites.

Scientific Elites

The modernizing role of science and technology was a major preoccupation of Nehru's India. Consequently, scientific elites played an important role in shaping Indian development strategies.[36] Relative to other colonies, by independence India had already begun to develop a basic infrastructure

---

[36] For a good account, see Baldev Raj Nayyar, *India's Quest for Technological Independence* (New Delhi: Lancer Publishers, 1983).

of science and technology (S&T) institutions, which was especially impressive when compared to its average income levels. External recognition was an important validation of the legitimacy of this enterprise. Thus, while the mathematical genius of Srinivasa Ramanujan was innate, the corpus of his contributions (and recognition) was significantly enhanced by his collaboration with the great British mathematician, G. H. Hardy in Cambridge.[37] The key protagonists who laid the foundations of independent India's S&T infrastructure—Homi Bhabha, P. C. Mahalanobis, Vikram Sarabhai, Shanti Swarup Bhatnagar, D. S. Kothari, Raja Ramanna—all did their doctoral work abroad.

However, it is one thing to argue that scientists mattered; it is quite another to systematically examine which ones mattered, particularly given the range of scientific disciplines. Again, the sources and methodology for inclusion in the database are elaborated in appendix IV. As might be expected, scientific elites have a greater exposure to foreign education than seen among political elites (table 5.3). Although the sample size is smaller than in the case of political elites, the trends remain similar. As with political elites, there is a sharp decline in overseas education of scientific elites, from 61 percent in 1950 to 34 percent in 2000.

At first glance, this appears surprising given the sharp increase in the overseas consumption of higher education by Indians, especially in science and technology. There are two reasons for this. First, there was a sharp decline in the return of Indians with education degrees from the United States (the preferred destination), from the late 1960s to at least the late 1990s. According to National Science Board estimates, of the estimated 1.5 million foreign-born U.S. residents with science and engineering as their highest degree in 1999, the largest number (14 percent, or 210,000) was from India. (China with 10 percent, and Germany, Philippines, UK, Taiwan and Canada followed with 5 percent each.) Among countries of origin for foreign-born science and engineering doctorates, India ranked second (30,100 PhDs) with 16 percent of the total (after China with 20 percent).[38] Second, while the enrollments of Indians in overseas science and engineering programs has increased (in 2007, there were 66,535 graduate students from India in the United States—one-fourth of the total)[39] and the rate of return appears to have also increased as a consequence of greater opportunities in India, it will be a while before some of this cohort makes it to the top.

[37] Hardy famously called their collaboration "the one romantic incident in my life." Robert Kanigel, *The Man Who Knew Infinity: A Life of the Genius Ramanujan* (New York: Pocket Books, 1991).

[38] Source: National Science Board, "Science and Engineering Indicators," 2004, figure 3-32, available at http://www.nsf.gov/sbe/srs/seind04/.

[39] National Science Foundation, "Science and Technology Indicators," 2008, appendix table 2–24, available at http://www.nsf.gov/statistics/seind08/append/c2/at02–24.xls.

TABLE 5.3
Scientific Elites

Year	1950	1980	2000
Percent studying abroad	61.2	48.0	34.0
By location			
• In UK	65.6	35.0	36.1
• In U.S.	15.8	56.7	56.9
• Elsewhere	18.6	7.0	11.1
Education level			
• High school or less	0.3	0.0	0.0
• Bachelor's degrees	7.7	4.9	3.8
• Professional degrees	17.7	9.2	7.1
• Other master's and PhD degrees	71.6	86.5	88.2
• More than one degree	0.3	0.6	1.4
• Diplomas in the arts, etc.	2.3	0.0	1.9
Sample size (N)	299	327	212

Source: For data sources, see appendix IV.

Bureaucratic Elites

In examining bureaucratic elites, I took two different approaches. In the first case, I followed an approach similar to that for other elites, for 1980 and 2000. (Data for 1950 were not available from this source.) As shown in table 5.4, in a trend similar to the other types of elites, as time passes, there is a decline in overseas education as well as in the importance of the United Kingdom as a source for education. However, in contrast to the other elites, the share of the United States does not grow; instead, other countries (notably Australia and several Asia countries) become more important.

In the second approach, another database was compiled from the list of all current (as of mid-2004) serving officers of the Indian Administrative Service (IAS), based on the records of the Ministry of Personnel, Government of India. These records help track different cohorts of the India's bureaucratic elite over the past thirty-five years. Given the source of the database, the accuracy and consistency of this data are very high. The oldest cohort in this database was from 1965 and the youngest from 2003.

The total number in the database was 4791. Of these, 542, or 11.3 percent, had some form of global exposure—either in terms of education, foreign training, or foreign posting. (More precisely, 438 had foreign

TABLE 5.4
Bureaucratic Elites

Year	1980	2000
Percent studying abroad	17.7	13.7
By location		
• In UK	55.0	45.0
• In U.S.	45.0	40.0
• Elsewhere	0.0	15.0
Education level		
• High school or less	0.0	0.0
• Bachelor's degrees	18.6	8.2
• Professional degrees	15.0	16.4
• Other master's and PhD degrees	49.6	49.3
• More than one degree	15.9	25.3
• Diplomas in the arts, etc.	0.9	0.0
Sample size (N)	113	146

Source: For data sources, see appendix IV.

training, 195 a foreign posting and 26 foreign education.) Some have had both foreign training as well as a foreign posting. The bulk of the training courses (248 out of a total of 552) were after 1995 (i.e., in the last 10 years). Nearly half of all training programs were in the United Kingdom, but while the United Kingdom still holds a dominant position, its share has been declining since 1999. This decline has been offset by the emergence of Australia and other Asian countries as destination sites, while the relative share of the United States and Canada has remained unchanged (although in terms of absolute numbers, there has been an increase).

A substantial number of officers are of too recent vintage to have had foreign training or a foreign posting. In general, 12 to 15 years of service are required before being eligible for selection for overseas training/posting. Indeed, in analyzing the data we see a significant drop in the percentage of officers getting foreign training starting from the 1989 cadre (14 years of service). Thus, while the percentage of officers with foreign training or posting was 13.1 percent for the 1987 cadre, it drops to 12.3 percent by 1988 and then sharply to 5.6 percent for the 1989 cadre and just 2.2 percent for the 1990 cadre. If we confine the analysis to the IAS cohorts until 1988, 497 out of 2706 have a global exposure—or just under one out of five. If we take an average of the percentage of officers who have gone abroad in the 1970–1974, 1975–1979, and 1980–1984 cadres—we see a clearly rising trend. This suggests that just as India's economy opened up, its bureaucracy also began to put a greater emphasis on "openness," at least in the sense of being more open to foreign ideas. This is true even for older cohorts of the IAS (those who joined the service in the 1970s) who appear to have participated in overseas courses recently, while younger cohorts (those who joined in the 1980s) are now being exposed to overseas programs earlier in their careers.

Business Elites

The importance of overseas experience to business acumen is perhaps best described in the story of Indian nationalism's capitalist hero—Jamsetji Nasserwanji Tata. From his early experiences in China, where he spent four years, to his later ones in England, where "he gained first-hand knowledge of manufacturing in the world's most developed country," the greater international exposure of the key protagonists of the House of Tata, compared to its more insular counterpart, the Birlas, appears to have shaped the very different imaginations and styles of the two giants of Indian business.[40] Even the idea of setting up the Indian Institute of Science (IISc), the most well regarded research university in India, came about during a conversation that Tata had with one of India's most influential spiritual leaders, Swami Vivekananda, when they were fellow travellers on a ship from Japan to Chicago in 1898.

The most readily apparent way to rank individuals in this category is to use a money metric scale. Since nearly half of the names in the 2000 ranking were repeats of the 1980 list, the data are presented in both ways, both including and excluding individuals common to both years. Consistent data were not available for 1950. There is again a modest decline in overseas education as time passes. Meanwhile, the United States dominates in both periods, largely because of the importance of business degrees for this group and the fact that business schools in the United States are highly coveted (table 5.5).

THE INSTITUTIONALIZATION OF ELITE IDEAS

The Institutions of Independent India

The hallmarks of preindependence India's urban elites were international migration, education, and *return*. As I noted in chapter 2, return skilled

[40] Interview, Dwijendra Tripathi, June 2004. As India's foremost business historian, Tripathi himself had been sent to Harvard Business School, to train under the renowned Alfred Chandler, so that he could return and start a program in business history at India's first (and most well known) school of business, Indian Institute of Management at Ahmedabad.

TABLE 5.5
Business Elites

Year	1980	2000	2000 (With Some Repeat Names from 1980 List)
Percent studying abroad	34.3	28.6	29.9
By location			
• In UK	46.0	40.4	43.5
• In U.S.	54.8	57.7	57.6
• Elsewhere	2.4	13.5	7.6
Education level	0.0	0.0	0.0
• High school or less	3.0	1.6	2.3
• Bachelor's degrees	28.2	22.5	26.6
• Professional degrees	29.8	36.3	32.1
• Other master's and PhD degrees	30.7	28.0	28.9
• More than one degree	8.0	11.5	9.4
• Diplomas in the arts, etc.	0.3	0.0	0.3
Sample size (N)	362	182	308

Source: For data sources, see appendix IV.

migration is likely to be more selective on those who are more intensely nationalist. Indian national elites had considerable overseas exposure, be it through education or work experience. Indeed, what stands out is just how disproportionately India's elites—in politics in particular, but also in science, business, and the bureaucracy—were educated and/or lived abroad at the time the country became independent. K. N. Raj, the development economist; K. R. Narayanan, a member of India's elite foreign service and, later, during the 1990s, president of India; S. Gopal, an eminent historian; and Raja Ramanna, a nuclear physicist and father of India's first nuclear test in May 1974, were all students in London when India became independent. As Ashish Nandy put it, "[T]he greatest of Indian social and political leaders built their self-definitions as Indians over the past two centuries on liminality."[41]

This is not to say that only elites were exposed to an overseas experience. Even at a much humbler level where formal education was not an option, experience abroad made a difference. Letters written by sepoys of the British Indian army serving at the Western front in World War I are revealing in the cognitive effects of this experience on the soldiers, from greater gender

[41] Ashish Nandy, *The Intimate Enemy* (Delhi: Oxford University Press, 1988), 104.

equality to the absence of bargaining in local stores.[42] For the *lascar,* or Indian seafarer, the effects of having foreign-returned seamen in their midst, while not "Conradesque," were "not inconsiderable."[43] Their interactions with British (shipping) trade unions led them to deploy the latter's "idioms and techniques." Balachandran argues, "Foreign-returned seafarers would also have been more democratic and direct vehicles for new ideas, values and influences than the local elite and middle classes who are generally thought to have monopolized these mediatory and transmitting roles."

Indeed, as these examples show, the adoption of new ideas resulting from migration can be deployed strategically by socially marginal groups in hierarchical societies, especially when yoked to material and symbolic resources. In India, given the importance of religious practices in the construction of social hierarchies, it is not surprising that changes in religious practices play a key role in reordering these hierarchies. Thus, Simpson shows how low-status Muslim sailors and ship owners in the port of Mandvi in Gujarat have used their access to international Islamic networks to engage in a more orthodox form of Islam and challenge local Muslim practices—and, thereby, the social hierarchy among local Muslims. Hence, conflicts between rival versions of Islamic orthodoxy are primarily expressions of the types of migration and the economy that forms and sustains them.[44]

In Kerala, migration to the Gulf has accelerated ongoing processes of commoditization of ritual practices, allowing newly moneyed low castes, who had hitherto lacked the symbolic and financial capital necessary to conduct "traditional" rituals, to use their new wealth to introduce innovations in public rituals that challenge the traditions and symbolic power of high-caste elites.[45] And for Malayali Muslims, Gulf migration has strengthened ties with Arab religious scholars: "[M]any contemporary *ulema* hold post-graduate degrees from Saudi Islamic Universities. Arab *ulema* are regularly invited to address public religious meetings and local doctrinal conflicts are sent to Saudi religious scholars for adjudication. Saudi, Kuwaiti and Bahraini religious organisations provide financial

[42] David Omissi, *Indian Voices of the Great War: Soldiers' Letters, 1914–18* (New York: St. Martin's Press, 1999).

[43] G. Balachandran, "Circulation through Seafaring: Indian Seamen, 1890–1945," in *Society and Circulation: Mobile People and Itinerant Cultures in South Asia 1750–1950,* eds. Claude Markovits, Jacques Pouchepadass, and Sanjay Subrahmanyam (New Delhi: Permanent Black, 2003), 93.

[44] Edward Simpson, "Migration and Islamic Reform in a Port Town of Western India," *Contributions to Indian Sociology* 37 (2003): 83–108.

[45] Filippo Osella and Caroline Osella, "Migration and the Commoditisation of Ritual: Sacrifice, Spectacle and Contestations in Kerala, India," *Contributions to Indian Sociology* 37 (2003): 109–39.

support and ideological legitimation to the movement."[46] Gulf migration has shaped—and been shaped—by local religious reform movements, which consciously seek a "modern"outlook through promotion of education. This has gone hand-in-hand with seeking to privilege the more "authentic" Islamic practices from the Middle East, in contrast to the prevalent orthopraxy resulting from local influences.

Nonetheless, there is no evidence on the *systemic* effects of these international experiences in these examples; historically, that narrative was confined to the elites. In politics, for example, the giants of India's freedom movement equipped themselves with a knowledge of British legal mores and the constitutional processes of that country both to confront the colonizing power as well as to design India's own constitutional norms and structures. Gandhi obtained his legal education in England and work experiences in South Africa; Nehru attended Cambridge; Patel studied law in England; and Ambedkar was a student of economics at Columbia University and law at the London School of Economics (LSE).[47]

As table 5.1 indicates, an astounding 10 percent of India's first Parliament had degrees abroad, virtually all of them in law. The most significant institutional impact of the overseas education of India's elite was on the character and content of the Indian constitution, which proved to be its "cornerstone."[48] During the same period, a sizable number of India's intellectual elites, particularly those who would be involved in policy debates as well as train the next generation of students who would become the mainstay of the bureaucracy, also went abroad to get advanced training in economics. Unlike the post-independence period (especially after the late 1960s), most of those who went abroad returned, and in turn trained an emerging new generation of economists at Calcutta University, Gokhlae Institute, Bombay University, and Allahabad University well until the 1960s.[49]

---

[46] Filippo Osella and Caroline Osella, "Islamism and Social Reform in Kerala, South India," *Modern Asian Studies* 42, nos. 2/3 (2008): 331.

[47] One might add the brilliant but mercurial Subhas Chandra Bose. However, his premature death in 1945 meant that he did not leave any institutional legacy. Interestingly, overseas education also appears to have been a spur to subnationalism. Sachidanad Sinha, Gandhi's classmate in the law college in London and the first from Bihar to travel to England to study law, led the movement for the creation of Bihar out of Bengal in 1911 soon after his return from England.

[48] Granville Austin, *The Indian Constitution: Cornerstone of a Nation* (New Delhi: Oxford University Press, 1966).

[49] These included P. N. Banerjea, Gyan Chand, Jehangir Coyajee, D. R. Gadgil, P. S. Lokanathan, John Mathai, Radhakamal Mukherjea, J. P. Niyogi, P. P. Pillai, P. J. Thomas, and C. N. Vakil. S. Ambirajan, "Ambedkar's Contributions to Indian Economics," *Economic and Political Weekly*, November 26, 1999.

In the early decades of post-independent India, the LSE was widely viewed to have played an influential role in shaping Indian economic policy. As Ivor Jennings remarked, "The ghosts of Sidney and Beatrice Webb [the founders of the LSE] stalk through the pages of the text" of the Directive Principles of the Indian Constitution.[50] One possible reason may be that Dr. B. R. Ambedkar, the Chairman of the Drafting Committee of the Constitution, had been a student at the LSE. While Nehru himself was a graduate of Cambridge and Indira Gandhi studied at (but did not graduate from) Oxford, their key advisors were LSE alumni (V. K. Krishna Menon in Nehru's case and P. N. Haskar and B. K. Nehru in Mrs. Gandhi's case).[51] The impact of the LSE on the policies and politics of independent India was allegedly so great that it was said "in every meeting of the Indian Cabinet there is a chair reserved for the ghost of Professor Harold Laski."[52] No doubt, the LSE's stellar connections to the Labor Party and socialism notwithstanding (this category includes stalwarts like Harold Laski and Beveridge), it also hosted some of the strongest opponents of socialism, such as economist Frederick Hayek, political theorist Michael Oakeshott, and philosopher Karl Popper. Nonetheless, the prevailing gestalt of the LSE was clearly the former and not the latter.

The Indians in British India's elite bureaucracy (the Indian Civil Service), the "steel frame" that administered India and played an important role in independent India's early years, were also largely educated in the United Kingdom.[53] Ramchandra Guha sheds some light on the effects of an LSE education in the case of Sardar Tarlok Singh, who studied economics there before joining the Indian Civil Service in the 1930s. After partition, Tarlok Singh was appointed Director-General of Rehabilitation in the Punjab and managed "the biggest land resettlement operation in the world." As against approximately 2.7 million hectares abandoned by Hindus and Sikhs in West Punjab, there were only 1.9 million hectares left behind by Muslims in East Punjab. The shortfall was made more acute by the fact that the areas in the west of the province had richer soils and were more abundantly irrigated. Using the sort of progressive tax schema that was part of the worldview of an LSE education, Tarlok Singh developed the idea of a "graded cut," which helped overcome the massive discrepancy between the land left behind by the

[50] The quote is attributed to Ivor Jennings. Cited in Ramchandra Guha, "The LSE and India," *The Hindu*, November 23, 2003.

[51] Much later, President K. R. Narayanan, also a BSc in economics (1948) from the London School of Economics, was also less than an ardent supporter of liberalization.

[52] Cited in Ramchandra Guha, "The LSE and India."

[53] Despite the expansion of the civil service after independence, even by the 1990s, its total strength—about 5000—was a tiny sliver of the 17 million federal government employees.

refugees and the land now available to them—a gap that was close to a million acres.[54] It was precisely this relatively egalitarian allocation of land that resulted in East Punjab (which had been agriculturally backward) catching up to, and then overtaking, West Punjab in a few decades.

Three other examples of key institutions that shaped independent India and that, in turn, were shaped by overseas experiences, were the Indian Constitution, the Finance Commission, and the Planning Commission. The antecedents of the Finance Commission lay in a visit made by B. K. Nehru and B. P. Adarkar to Australia; in 1946, they were sent by Liaquat Ali Khan's finance department to frame policies to strengthen provincial autonomy and improve provincial finances. Their tract, "Report of the Australian System of Federal Finance and its Applicability to Indian Conditions," became the basis of India's Finance Commission— a statutory body that became the cornerstone of India's fiscal federalism. P. C. Mahalanobis, a distinguished professor of physics at Cambridge, returned to India on Nehru's urging and set up the Planning Commission. Arguably, he had a greater impact than almost any economist on India's economic policies, be it through the second Five-Year Plan, the establishment of the Indian Statistical Institute, or the Planning Commission.

Colonial links usually meant that those of India's political elite who went abroad to study did so in the United Kingdom (table 5.1). In his elegant summary of Indo-U.S. relations, Jairam Ramesh asked, "what might have happened to Indo-American relations had an earlier generation of public personalities and political figures crossed the Atlantic and had been educated in the Cambridge by the Charles and not by the Cam or had been exposed to Ford, not Oxford."[55] The exceptions were notable. Given Ambedkar's seminal role in the drafting of the Indian constitution, his own overseas influences (at Columbia University and the LSE), assume greater importance. According to Eleanor Zelliot, Ambedkar used his "knowledge of American culture to analyse his own country's social situation." Thus, according to her, the value of Ambedkar's experience in America "seems to be chiefly in developing his commitment to a pragmatic, flexible democratic system."[56] The period of Ambedkar's stay at

[54] For the first 10 acres of any claim, a cut of 25 percent was implemented—thus, one got only 7.5 acres instead of 10. For higher claims, the cuts were steeper: 30 percent between 10 to 30 acres, and on upward, until those having in excess of 500 acres were taxed at the rate of 95 percent. By November 1949, Tarlok Singh and his men had made 250,000 allotments of land.

[55] Jairam Ramesh, "Yankee Go Home, But Take Me with You: Yet Another Perspective on Indo-American Relations," *Economic and Political Weekly*, December 11–17, 1999.

[56] Eleanor Zelliot, *From Untouchable to Dalit* (New Delhi: Manohar, 1988).

Columbia University (1913–1916) coincided with the Harlem Renaissance, and Columbia University, where Ambedkar was based, is adjacent to Harlem. However, it is unclear if Ambedkar's view that capitalism was one of the two principal obstacles (the other being brahminism) to the liberation of oppressed groups was because of or despite his American experience.[57] Sardar Pratap Singh Kairon, who dominated post-independence Punjab's politics, "returned determined to make Punjab a Kansas or an Iowa-clone in farming at least."[58] The only other notable politicians who went to America and returned in the pre-independence years were Lala Lajpath Rai and Jayaprakash Narayan, but "unfortunately" the latter "went to Wisconsin during the Depression and returned a Marxist to begin with."[59] Lala Lajpath Rai died in 1928 (as a result of injuries inflicted by police action in a protest), but Jayaprakash Narayan played a prominent role as the focal point of protests against Mrs. Gandhi in the mid-1970s that resulted in the Emergency and the historic defeat of the Congress in the 1977 general elections.

The 1991 Reforms

It is quite evident to any observer of Indian policy-making that there has been a paradigmatic shift in economic policies since the launch of economic liberalization in 1991. The reasons for this shift are varied and complex, ranging from economic crisis to manifest inimical effects of existing policies, broader political and ideational changes in the outside world, and external pressure from international financial institutions. But to what extent was the subterranean shift in ideas influenced by international migration and return?

Few would argue that exposure to a different worldview at a young age does not have any consequences on an individual's thinking. Palaniappan Chidambaram, who received his MBA from Harvard Business School and served as finance minister in the United Front Government from 1996 to 1998 and again in the Congress-led United Progressive Alliance (UPA) government of 2004, had this to say: "Let me tell you very frankly, when I went to the Harvard Business School I was more or less a committed socialist. Even in the Harvard Business School I don't believe I quite gave up my admiration for socialism, although remaining in the U.S. for two years exposed me to another model, which appeared to be more successful,

---

[57] According to Teltumbde, "although there cannot be any doubt that he stood against capitalism, he could not articulate a sound theoretical basis for doing so." Anand Teltumbde, *Ambedkar in and for the Post-Ambedkar Dalit Movement* (Pune, India: Sugawa Prakashan, 1997), 55.

[58] Jairam Ramesh, "Yankee Go Home."

[59] Ibid.

which appeared to have brought jobs and incomes and prosperity to a much larger proportion of people. But I must confess that I still remained quite pink when I was there."[60]

But the mere fact of a change in an individual's worldview may say little about the broader economic and political consequences, unless we can demonstrate the mechanisms that institutionalize these views. The flow of ideas embedded in the diaspora or in return migration depends on three critical factors; first, the institutional configurations in the country of origin and its relative receptivity to accepting new ideas and returning human capital; second, the willingness of individuals to return; and third, the reputation and credibility of the destination to which the individual goes abroad. These are, of course, interrelated, but, nonetheless, they are also distinct. Despite the supposed hegemony of the Indian Administrative Service (IAS) in Indian policy-making, the fact is that economic policy-making in India has been also been shaped by returning economists who had studied and worked abroad. As might be expected, they have worked most in the economic ministries—the Finance Ministry and the Commerce Ministry—but also the Reserve Bank and the Prime Minster's Office. While this phenomenon has been especially marked in the last few decades, it was present earlier as well. And of course, key IAS personnel in important economic ministries have also usually had overseas exposure.

Khatkhate sheds light on some of the principal actors, their academic and institutional backgrounds, and their contributions to Indian policy-making.[61] Unlike their predecessors in the period prior to the mid-1960s, in subsequent decades many of the country's brightest young minds who went abroad to study did not return. The Planning Commission, which had been an intellectually stimulating and politically powerful institution, lost both attributes after Nehru's death. India's economic (and increasingly political) travails also made return less attractive, and indeed, many who had returned left again. Despite the fact that several notable economists doggedly remained in academia (Mrinal Datta Chaudhuri, B. S. Minhas, Suresh Tendulkar, Amartya Sen, and K. N. Raj, to name a few), the lower rate of replenishment, as well as selective out-migration, led economic thinking in Indian academia to become more dogmatic. In some cases, those who left India—like Jagdish Bhagwati, Padma Desai, and T. N. Srinivasan—became voices in the wilderness dissenting from the

[60] Palaniappan Chidambaram, interview, "Commanding Heights: The Battle for the World Economy," PBS, 2002, available at http://www.pbs.org/wgbh/commandingheights/shared/pdf/int_palaniappanchidambaram.pdf.
[61] Deena Khatkhate, "Looking Back in Anger," *Economic and Political Weekly* 38, nos. 51–52 (December 27, 2003). Of course, Khatkhate has himself played an important if subtle role, whether through the *Economic and Political Weekly* or championing young Indian economists and academics.

then-dominant view of the state-led economic strategy. Their departure meant that a generation of India-trained economists, as well those who joined the bureaucracy, continued to be skeptical of international trade.

Other economists joined the International Monetary Fund (IMF) and the World Bank, especially the latter, which during the 1970s had emerged as one of the most intellectually vibrant places for research in economic development. These included Montek Singh Ahluwalia, a Rhodes scholar who, perhaps more than any other technocrat, shaped Indian economies policies over nearly two decades, first in the Prime Minister's Office, then as Finance Secretary (the youngest ever) in the crucial early years of liberalization, and after a hiatus in the IMF from 2001–2004, again as Deputy Chairman of the Planning Commission; Arun Shourie, whose doctoral dissertation from Syracuse University castigated India's controls and licensing regimes; Rakesh Mohan and Suman Bery from Princeton (both of whom later headed National Council of Applied Economics Research (NCAER); Arvind Virmani from Harvard; Shankar Acharya from Oxford and Harvard; and Bimal Jalan, from Oxford, who had a brief stint at the World Bank and later served as India's Executive Director, both at the IMF and the World Bank. Starting in the early 1980s, although only a few returned (including all of the preceding), there was enough strength in numbers for them to matter.

Several key actors in economic policy-making, while they spent extended periods of time both studying and working outside the country, did not work for an extended period for the Bretton Woods institutions. This path was tread by I. G. Patel, who was educated at Cambridge and Harvard, worked briefly in the IMF during the 1950s, and then played an important role in Indian economic policy-making during the next few decades. As governor of the Reserve Bank of India (RBI) during the late 1970s, he played a key role in changing India's exchange rate regime, engineering an effective devaluation that, unlike the infamous 1966 one, went unnoticed by India's politicians. The RBI's gradual resurrection in Indian monetary, financial, and exchange rate policy-making can be dated to his tenure and was continued by his successors at the institution, nearly all of whom had studied and worked outside India. The most prominent of them was of course Manmohan Singh (Cambridge and Oxford), who went on to play a preeminent role as the architect of India's economic liberalization in 1991and became India's prime minister in May 2004. The other two were S. Venkitaramanan, who as head of India's central bank played a critical role in the early years of liberalization and had done his doctoral work at Carnegie Mellon (however, unlike the others he was a member of the IAS), and S. Rangarajan, who received his PhD at the University of Pennsylvania and taught at Carnegie Mellon University. Vijay Kelkar, India's first finance secretary to receive his PhD in the United States (at Berkeley), served in a variety of senior government positions, including petroleum secretary, and subsequently laid the blueprint of a major overhaul of India's tax system as well as a rehaul of the country's center-state fiscal relations.

Virtually all of the aforementioned individuals had worked in, or with, international financial institutions. Khatkhate argues that, in their case, working on diverse countries at the World Bank "enriched" their insights and, more importantly, that

> the lack of insularity in their thinking enabled them to see India's problems in a broader perspective and real world context and counter some of the ingrained habits of many Indian economists, both in academia and the government, brought up in the interventionist environment. They became an elite intellectual force to counteract the influence of the entrenched but starry-eyed interventionist economists who held sway until 1990s.

Acharya asks whether these economists and civil servants, who at one time or another worked in international financial institutions like the IMF and the World Bank and then returned to shape policy in India, "were heroes or villains" and whether their association with these bodies "posed problems of ideology or loyalty." His verdict is that they were neither villains nor heroes but "just competent professionals who have gone through the rigorous screening of both national and international competitive recruitment procedures and have (hopefully) tried to be useful and productive in both arenas." Their efforts laid the analytical foundations that underpinned India's liberalization and adjustment.[62]

However, I want to emphasize that there is no isomorphic mapping between working with the Bretton Woods institutions and support for liberalization. Several economists and senior civil servants who had served in the Bretton Woods institutions and subsequently held senior positions in the Indian government were much more hostile to these institutions and their viewpoint. These included Ashok Mitra, who was in the Economic Development Institute (EDI) of the World Bank and former chief economic adviser to the Government of India; K. S. Krishnaswamy, who was a director of EDI and deputy governor of the RBI and economic adviser to the Planning Commission; and Arun Ghosh, who was in the IMF and economic adviser to the Commerce Ministry and a member of the Planning Commission.[63] There were, of course, other policy-oriented academics who had studied abroad (such as Deepak Nayyar, at Oxford, who became chief economist) who were much less enamored of liberalization.

[62] Shankar Acharya, *India's Economy: Some Issues and Answers* (New Delhi: Academic Foundation, 2003), 176.

[63] I am grateful to Deena Khatkhate for pointing this out.

Technocrats have played an important role in economic reforms around the world in the last few decades. During this period, India's reforms have borne richer fruit in comparative terms. I would argue that this is the case in part because India's reforms were "home-grown"—they reflected the global experience of its key architects, but with a keen eye on domestic political realities. India's institutional setup—a strong bureaucracy and a parliamentary system—means that a returning technocrat has to spend time in an advisory capacity before he or she can move to decision-making roles. This both creates trust as well as gives the returning technocrat a better sense of the political nuances that are critical if policies are to be adopted and implemented. The fact that one has to pay one's dues to the system ensures that the technocrat becomes a stakeholder. No matter how confident the theorists of reforms may sound, in practice, there is always considerable uncertainty. Politicians are understandably wary of advisors who will cut and run if things go wrong. This is an important reason why individual Indians living abroad, no matter how prominent they may be, have far more limited influence than those who return and work from within the system.

The extension of human capital with international experience in influencing economic policy-making, from the federal government in Delhi to the subnational level, is an emerging trend. The underlying cause is India's resurgent federalism, which has given states greater policy agency. Furthermore, unlike the reforms in the aftermath of 1991, "second generation" reforms, such as those affecting social sectors or power, are constitutionally the prerogatives of states. Regional diasporas are also trying to influence policies at the state level. Organizations such as the Telugu Association of North America (TANA) and U.S.-based Telugu professionals were active in shaping Chandrababu Naidu's ideas for Andhra Pradesh. The new Congress-led government, which came into power in 2004, continued the cultivation of the overseas Telugu diaspora.

Again, however, the degree of influence is critically mediated by institutional structures. For instance, neither the *Biswa Banga Sammelan* nor return talent appears to have had any influence in West Bengal. No state in India has produced as many eminent economists as West Bengal, and, with the exception of Bihar, no state has hemorrhaged as much human capital. India's only Nobel Laureate, Amartya Sen, is deeply respected, but even in his home state his emphasis on primary health and education has had at best a modest impact. An article proposing an economic strategy for West Bengal and written by some of the most respected Bengali economists was striking in that none of the nine authors were actually located in West Bengal—indeed, eight of the nine were part of the great intellectual migration from Bengal outside the country.[64] The possibility that any of them could become part of the official policy-making apparatus in West Bengal is quite remote. The contrast between New Delhi and West Bengal, with respect to the receptivity to the diffusion of ideas through migration, reflects the greater institutional porosity in the former compared to the latter. In turn, this is due to what has become a near-monopoly of the Communist Party of India (Marxist) in West Bengal and its strong ideological control in vetting appointments in that state. This means that fealty to the party is much more critical in economic policy-making in West Bengal than in Delhi.[65] It is also the reason why, as alluded to earlier, the *Biswa Banga Sammelan* has had little influence (given the lack of access points) in West Bengal, while the Telugu Association of North America (TANA) and U.S.-based Telugu professionals have played a greater role in shaping policies within Andhra Pradesh.

Diaspora Effects

In addition to return migration, the diaspora itself has become a source of influence on public policy. The many Indian academics abroad tend to have relatively easy access to policy-makers and business groups. Despite being abroad for decades, some of India's most distinguished economists have long been active participants and contributors to debates on India's economic policies, and a younger generation appears to be following suit.[66] The greater receptivity—indeed hunger—for business *gurus* has also increased the influence of the large number of Indian-origin faculty in marquee business schools (especially in the United States, but also elsewhere).[67]

Meetings with the wealthy nonresident Indian community, especially U.S. NRIs, have become *de rigueur* for politicians from India on their overseas visits. S. Venkitaraman, the former governor of the Reserve Bank, cites his interactions with the diaspora when he accompanied finance ministers V. P. Singh, N. D. Tiwari, and Manmohan Singh abroad. At a meeting attended by V. P. Singh in New York, NRIs had come forward

[64] Abhijit Banerjee, Pranab Bardhan, Kaushik Basu, Mrinal Datta Chaudhuri, Maitreesh Ghatak, Ashok Sanjay Guha, Mukul Majumdar, Dilip Mookherjee, and Debraj Ray, "Strategy for Economic Reform in West Bengal," *Economic and Political Weekly* 37, no. 41 (October 12, 2002): 4203–18.

[65] An analogy can be drawn with the fealty to the BJP when it was in power in the center, for appointments to central government bodies dealing with history and culture.

[66] Examples include Pranab Bardhan, Jagdish Bhagwati, Vijay Joshi, Amartya Sen, and T. N. Srinivasan, to name a few.

[67] For instance, Professor Krishna Pallepu of Harvard Business School was an advisor to Chief Minister Chandra Babu Naidu in Andhra Pradesh.

"with a constructive point of view." V. P. Singh realized that in a permit and license *raj*, a quick response was not possible. But this interaction led him to pay more attention to the operations of the India Investment Centre at its branches at London, New York, and Tokyo in order to bolster NRI investments in India. At another meeting with NRIs in Bangkok in 1991–1992, "Manmohan Singh was all ears as the NRIs told him of how easy it was to set up business in Thailand, obtain finances and carry on financial transactions. Their arguments for convertibility did seem to have an impact on the fertile mind of the finance minister." The same year, at an NRI meeting in Singapore (primarily designed to canvas support for the State Bank of India bonds), "Manmohan Singh heard a mouthful regarding the delays in clearance of foreign direct investment proposals. This led to his announcing the automatic clearance scheme, under which a proposal would be deemed to be cleared if it did not receive a negative response from the Reserve Bank of India within a short period of time."[68] In some areas, the diaspora even has formal access points to influence policy. For instance, in 2000 the GOI constituted a group comprising select NRIs to formulate a global strategy for promoting India as a prominent investment destination.[69] The group advised the ministry in formulating IT policies, strengthening telecommunications infrastructure, and providing guidelines on venture capital funds as well as issues related to IT education.

However, for the most part examples of members of the diaspora shaping sectoral policies are uncommon. A rare example of the member of the diaspora returning twice to do so was Sam Pitroda, a successful inventor and entrepreneur who returned to India in 1984 at the invitation of then Prime Minister Indira Gandhi and played a major role in reforming India's telecommunications policies. He returned to the United States in 1989 following disagreements with the then government but returned again in 2004 to head the National Knowledge Commission, a body set up to reform India's higher education policies.

Sons, Socialists, and Swadeshis

An important, albeit informal and subtle, mechanism for the transmission of overseas economic ideas has been occurring through the progeny of India's governing elite, who are returning to India after studying and

[68] S. Venkitaramanan, "The Prodigals Return," *The Telegraph*, February 3, 2003.

[69] The eight-member group chaired by then Union IT minister Pramod Mahajan included IT secretary P. V. Jayakrishnan, TIE group president Kanwal Rekhi, KPCB group partner Vinod Khosla, Cirus Logic chairman Suhas Patil, Exodus chairman K. B. Chandradshekhar, Sabeer Bhatia of Arzoo.com, and Devendra Chaudhary of MIT. *Economic Times*, 21 January 2000.

working abroad. Even if their fathers (or mothers) are not in power, India's political culture continues to give them access to the corridors of power. Consider the career paths of Ajeya Singh, son of former Prime Minister V. P. Singh, and Jayant Sinha, son of former Finance Minister Yashwant Sinha in the Bharatiya Janata Party (BJP)–led government. After working for a small merchant bank in London, Ajeya Singh joined Grindlays and returned to India in 1984. Since his father had been appointed India's minister of finance, the potential conflict of interest led him to leave India and join Citibank in New York. Then in 1989, Ajeya joined Merrill Lynch, jumped to Bear Stearns after three years, and in 1995 joined Lehman Brothers, where he "quickly helped Lehman punch well above its weight in India. It's little wonder he got the deal—his connections are impeccable."[70] Ajeya Singh was "well known for his connections. He has been responsible for gaining the U.S. firm some of the choicest mandates to come out of the subcontinent such as a $370 million global depositary receipt (GDR) issue for State Bank of India in 1996."[71] Yashwant Sinha's son worked at McKinsey in Boston, and his daughter-in-law worked at Oppenheimer (an investment bank). During the late 1990s, V. P. Singh emerged as an opponent of liberalization, and Yashwant Sinha was under pressure from *swadeshi* (partisans of indigenous industry and culture) stalwarts in his party. While one cannot construct a counterfactual, it is surely at least plausible that the position of the two men was tempered by the influence of their children's personal and professional economic views.

Sinha's predecessor as finance minister, Palaniappan Chidambaram (who, again, assumed that post when the Congress-led government came to power in 2004), put it aptly when he was questioned about the role of NRIs in the United States and Britain on policy-making in India:

At a subliminal level, two things played an important role upon administrators, both political and civil service. First, the phenomenal success achieved by Indians abroad by practicing free enterprise meant that if Indians were allowed to function in an open market, they could replicate some of that success here. Secondly, by 1991 sons and daughters of political leaders and senior civil servants were all going abroad and studying abroad and living and working abroad. I think they played a great part in influencing the thinking of their parents. I know a number of political leaders, a number of civil servants, who were shuttling

[70] Steve Irvine, "Ajeya Singh: Head of India, Lehman Brothers," *Euromoney*, September 1998, 39. As a former prime minister's son, he gets protection from Special Protection Group, which is "a business traveler's dream." Steven Irvine, "Seen from India's Ivory Tower," *Euromoney*, December 1998, 38.

[71] Steve Irvine, "Ajeya Singh: Head of India, Lehman Brothers," *Euromoney*, September 1998, 39.

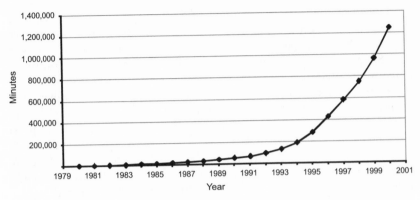

Figure 5.1. Telephone traffic between the United States and India, 1979–2001.

between one ideology at home and one ideology at the workplace. They had been challenged by their children. "What are you talking about when we are doing the exact opposite thing?"[72]

In chapter 3, I provided empirical evidence of the extensive overseas networks of India's elite. The probability that a household in India has members abroad sharply increases with socioeconomic status, defined in terms of income level and professional background. As demonstrated earlier, nearly 32 percent of households in SEC A—largely India's urban professional elites—know someone abroad (see figure 3.6).

The effects of the extensive overseas networks of Indian elites are amplified by the ease of travel and communication. The exponential growth in telephone traffic between India and the United States in the last two decades (figure 5.1) is likely to have resulted in a substantial increase in the flow of ideas as well.

For example, even if just one percent of the telephone conversations between professionally successful children abroad and their parents in India concerned substantive issues of economic policy or approach, the huge increase in communications would have intensified the diffusion of ideas. The triple combination of a wealthy, educated diaspora, embedded in networks that give them access to policy-relevant institutions in India, and lubricated by easy and relatively inexpensive communication technology has amplified the policy influence of international migration.

A somewhat different mechanism arises from an overlap between two factors: the "dynastic" structure of Indian politics and the tendency of politicians' progeny to study abroad. The first factor stems from the

[72] Palaniappan Chidambaram, interview, "Commanding Heights," available at http://www.pbs.org/wgbh/commandingheights/shared/pdf/int_palaniappanchidambaram.pdf.

institutional weakness of Indian political parties, with politics being treated as a family business, the second from the poor quality of Indian higher education. In the 2004 national elections, the children of several major political figures from a wide range of political parties stood for elections. A considerable number were educated abroad, and all of them won comfortably (table 5.6). Two of them, Dayanidhi Maran and Anbumani Ramadoss, became ministers (of information technology and health and family welfare, respectively). Even if this does not imply a predictable process of ideational osmosis, whereby the child's preferences are transmitted to the powerful parent, it is suggestive of the likely preferences of the rising generation of India's politicians—and India's future economic policies.

TABLE 5.6
Political Dynasties with Overseas Education: Overseas Educational Background, Party Affiliation, and Electoral Constituency of Children of Prominent Politicians in the 2009 General Election

Name	Son of	Education	Candidate's Party and Constituency	Whether Reelected
Jayant Chaudhary	Ajit Singh, Rashtriya Lok Dal leader and grandson of Charan Singh (former PM)	London School of Economics	RLD, Mathura, UP	No
Milind Deora	Murli Deora, Maharashtra Congress MP and cabinet member	Boston University (bachelor's degree in business administration)	Congress–Mumbai South	Yes
Rahul Gandhi	Rajiv Gandhi, former PM of India	Enrolled at Harvard	Congress–Amethi	Yes
Varun Gandhi	Maneka Gandhi (BJP leader); grandson of Indira Gandhi	BSc (economics), University of London External System	BJP, Pilibhit, UP	No

TABLE 5.6 (continued)

Name	Son of	Education	Candidate's Party and Constituency	Whether Reelected
Deependra Hooda	Bhupinder Singh Hooda, Congress CM of Haryana	MBA, Kelley School of Business, Indiana University	Congress, Rohtak, Haryana	Yes
Naveen Jindal	O. P. Jindal, steel magnate and MLA and former Lok Sabha member	MBA from University of Texas, Dallas	Congress candidate–Kurukshetra (Haryana)	Yes
Dayanidhi Maran	Murasoli Maran, DMK and former cabinet member	Owner/President Management (OPM) Program at Harvard Business School	DMK–Madras Central	Yes
Sachin Pilot	Rajesh Pilot, Congress leader	MBA from Wharton School of Business, University of Pennsylvania	Congress–Ajmer (Rajasthan)	Yes
Jyotridaya Scindia	Madhav Rao Scindia, Congress leader	Harvard undergraduate; Stanford MBA	Congress–Guna (Madhya Pradesh)	Yes
Dushyant Singh	Vasundhara Raje, former BJP chief minister of Rajasthan	Boston University	BJP–Jhalawar (Rajasthan)	Yes
Akhilesh Yadav	Mulayam Singh Yadav, leader of the Samajwadi Party	Master's degree in environmental engineering, University of Sydney, Australia	Samajwadi Party–Kannauj (UP)	Yes

Note: Deependra Hooda was first elected in a by-election in 2005; Sachin Pilot was elected from Dausa in 2004.

Conclusion

Much of the literature on international migration has focused on direct consequences arising from increased cross-border flows of human capital, ranging from remittances and foreign direct investment to "brain drain" effects and long-distance nationalism. This chapter highlights a more subtle mechanism of impact arising from migration—namely, the flow of ideas embedded in human capital, both through returning migrants as well as from diaspora members living abroad.

In the context of migration for the purpose of education, it is of course entirely possible that the transformative effects of overseas experience were not the result of higher education alone. Rather, the very dislocation from one's habits, ingrained routines, and assumptions may force a deeper introspection, one informed by varied experiences—the "life experience" as it were. Gandhi himself once remarked, "I have thankfully copied many things from [the English]. Punctuality, reticence, public hygiene, independent thinking and exercise of judgment, and several other things I owe to my association with them."[73] It may even be the encounter with other members of the diaspora that explains the value of overseas experience. For instance, it has been suggested that Gandhi's manifesto for nonviolent action in fostering a Hind Swaraj directed against imperialism (and banned by the British) was not the product of either his experiences in South Africa or with the British; it was instead the outcome of his encounters with Hindu extremism in London and was designed, in other words, to contain nationalist Hindu sentiment.[74]

Ambedkar's experiences in the United States and Europe arguably erased his consciousness of being a Dalit, which meant that the discrimination he experienced after returning was all the more searing. More than a half-century later, a prominent India economist, Sukhdeo Thorat (also a Dalit) similarly found that a sustained absence from India enabled him to emerge more confident. A three-year trip to Iowa's International Food Policy Research Institute recharged him: "My esteem among . . . colleagues grew. There was newfound respect."[75]

But are there any downsides of the overseas experience? Ideas, after all, need not have unambiguously positive effects. There are good reasons to question whether some of these ideas are necessarily "beneficial" for India (even if one could agree on what "beneficial" means in this case). To the extent that diasporas have a greater knowledge of their countries of origin,

[73] Quoted in *Young India*, June 3, 1930, 80.
[74] Sumit Sarkar, "Meanings of Nationalism in India," Nehru Memorial Lecture, 2005.
[75] Siriyavan Anand, "Caste on the Couch," *Himal*, April 2003.

are the technologies transferred "appropriate"? While this may seem intuitively likely, caution is warranted. Three examples from India are illustrative. The flight of physicians from India, trained largely at public expense,
has been a considerable brain drain for the health sector in India. Its impact has already been commented on in chapter 4. Here, I want to emphasize that the human capital of this professional group, as well as those who
return, is likely to be centered around cutting-edge curative technologies.
Ideas flowing home from this group could well amplify the tertiary bias in
India's health system, which is not unimportant in a country where the
health system is already weakest in primary, preventive, and public health
care.

Bollywood provides another example. As mentioned earlier, exports
constitute an increasingly important component of the market for Hindi
films, catering in considerable part to the Indian diaspora. In addressing
to this more technologically sophisticated market, the technical quality of
Hindi films has improved markedly—an analog to the technological up-
grading that occurs through feedback effects when developing country
firms enter global export markets. However, at the same time, the content
of Hindi films has also changed—even though India is still largely a rural
country, rural India is barely visible in Hindi films, since that does not
"sell" in the export markets that the industry is aiming at. The increasing
cognitive dissonance between Indian cinema and the country's realities
may or may not matter in a material sense, but it may perhaps be indicative of the dangers of a weakening of a shared sense of citizenship. I will
revisit the question of how international migration has affected conceptions of citizenship in India in chapter 9.

Last, social science research on India carried out by Indian academics
from within India and from abroad might respond to different incentives
and audiences. The historian Ramchandra Guha has argued that the former responds to a much greater extent to questions thrown up by the
society in which the scholars are embedded. In contrast, the latter responds much more to the professional incentives to publish in North
American journals, which means that intellectual cues and fashions demanded by these journals dominate their work.[76] But if scholarship responds to incentives, there is also the harsh reality that (as the editor of
one of Indian's leading national dailies has put it) the study of the liberal
arts in India has got so politicized that "history has become our most
contentious social science and professional historians our most ideologi-
cally polarised academics." Consequently, he argues that "most of the
good research is done by foreigners, or Indians safely based at foreign

[76] Ramchandra Guha, "The Ones Who Stayed Behind," *Economic and Political Weekly*
38, nos. 12 and 13 (March 22, 2003): 1121–24.

institutions."[77] Without taking a strong position on the debate between quality and relevance, it is certainly the case that professional incentives will affect research output—both for better and worse, in India as well as outside the country. But arguments as to the normative implications cannot belie the reality that international migration and the Indian diaspora have been important mechanisms for the diffusion of ideas that have shaped India's institutions and policies.

[77] Shekhar Gupta, "Masters in Illiberal Arts," *India Express*, August 23, 2009, available at http://www.indianexpress.com/news/masters-in-illiberal-arts/505446/0.

CHAPTER 6

International Migration and the Paradox of India's Democracy

> By almost any theory, India in 1947 appeared to be among the
> least likely country to sustain democratic institutions.
>
> —*Myron Weiner*[1]

INTRODUCTION

WHILE THE PREVIOUS chapters examined migration's economic and cognitive impact on India, this chapter examines its effects on India's democracy. As the preceding observation by the late Myron Weiner suggests, the endurance of India's democracy has been an exception to Western theories of democratic government. More than sixty years after independence, India continues to remain a vigorous democracy, despite the predictions of many scholars. In this chapter, I argue that emigration from India has had a significant impact in sustaining India's democratic tradition. In a country of limited resources, emigration has allowed social groups constituting the "old" political elite to diversify their economic portfolio by moving abroad without sacrificing economic privileges. This has created space for the mobility of "new" political elites drawn from numerically larger but historically marginalized communities, without provoking the sorts of intense intraelite conflict that have led to the breakdown of democracies.

In this chapter, I argue that any understanding of the domestic impact of international capital mobility needs to move beyond the current narrow conceptualization in its financial sense to include human capital as well. Through empirical evidence and historical analysis, I demonstrate the impact of international migration on India's national politics in general and democracy in particular: elite "exit," fueled by the endowments of Indian elites in mobile human capital (rather than immobile land assets), has played an important role in ensuring India's democratic stability.

[1] Myron Weiner, *The Indian Paradox: Essays in Indian Politics* (New Delhi: Sage Publications, 1989), 320.

THE PARADOX OF INDIAN DEMOCRACY

India's emergence in 1947 as a nation with functioning democratic institutions that have (with some qualifications) continued to flourish was in many ways considered an unlikely outcome. Many observers, not least India's former colonial masters, thought it improbable that the diverse and seemingly contentious mosaic of religions, languages, and traditions that marked this sixth of humanity could ever be woven into a modern nation. It was thought even less likely that democracy could take root and flourish in this part of the world. There was, and still is, no articulate thinking in Western social theory that would have led one to expect this outcome. India did not have what many took to be the essential conditions for a functioning democracy. Its multiple social cleavages and social heterogeneity—lacking even a national language—were a major handicap.[2] It was an agrarian country, with a weak middle class and a comparatively small bourgeoisie. Its population was overwhelmingly poor and illiterate, seemingly lacking the socioeconomic prerequisites for the survival of a democracy.[3] Its cultural antecedents did not appear propitious either. It was (and remains) one of the more deeply hierarchical societies in the world, which according to some, had little conception of the egalitarianism and individualism thought to be necessary for a functioning liberal democracy.[4]

While India's experience with democracy since 1947 has been complex and decidedly mixed, there is little doubt that it has brought about an extraordinary politicization of Indian society. There has been a perceptible shift in the balance of political power in favor of historically socially marginalized groups—the backward and scheduled castes—which given the entrenchment of caste in India society, is nothing short of a social revolution. Indeed, with regard to two criteria—participation and contestation in elections—that are critical to any democracy, India's performance has been particularly noteworthy. While voter participation in established

[2] The classic formulation on why heterogenous societies were ill-suited for democracy is John Stuart Mill, *Considerations on Representative Government* (New York: Liberal Arts Press, 1958).

[3] Seymour Martin Lipset, "The Social Requisites of Democracy Revisited," *American Sociological Review* 59, no. 1 (February 1994), 1–22; Przeworski et al., *Democracy and Development* (Cambridge, UK: Cambridge University Press, 2000).

[4] India's "parochial subject" political culture was far from the "civic culture" thought to be essential for democracy. See Gabriel Almond and Sidney Verba, *The Civic Culture: Political Attitudes and Democracy in Five Nations Culture* (Boston: Little, Brown, 1963). Similarly, the divergence in authority patterns between state and society in India were predicted to lead to democratic breakdown. See Harry Eckstein, *Division and Cohesion in Democracy* (Princeton, NJ: Princeton University Press, 1966).

Organisation for Economic Cooperation and Development (OECD) democracies has declined in recent years, it has increased in India (from around 45 percent in the first two general elections to around 60 percent in more recent ones). And while voter turnout rates in OECD countries are generally higher for higher income and more educated groups, in India, voter turnout rates are marginally higher among the poor and illiterate.[5] Furthermore, while incumbency in OECD democracies confers an electoral advantage (in the United States as a result of gerrymandering), incumbency has been virtually a disadvantage in Indian elections.[6]

As expressed by the opening quote of this chapter, attributed to one of the most distinguished scholars of Indian politics, India's democracy has belied all predictions. Likewise, for Dahl, given that India "lacks all the favorable conditions," the fact that it "could sustain democratic institutions seems, on the face of it, highly improbable."[7] Political scientist Pradeep Chibber adds that if a vibrant civil society is critical for democratic durability, then India's "democracy without associations" again does not fit conventional wisdom.[8] Recently, in trying to explain why the Middle East has been an exception to global democratizing trends, political scientist M. Steven Fish puts the onus on the dominance of patriarchical norms in these societies. However, he finds that the large literacy gaps, lopsided male-dominated sex ratios, and scarcity of women in high politics are also evident in India and concludes that while "India's open politics would seem to challenge the arguments advanced in this article . . . , the Indian experience shows that the problems of patriarchy analyzed here do not necessarily spell doom for open government. India has a well-established reputation for violating social scientific generalizations; perhaps it is unsurprising that it is also exceptional in terms of the link between societal patriarchy and political regime." He concludes, however, "Nonetheless, the findings of this article furnish grounds for skepticism regarding the viability of democracy in India."[9]

India is similarly an outlier in the numerous quantitative analyses of democratic durability. In their extensive empirical analysis of the relationship between democracy and development in 135 countries, Przeworksi

[5] Yogendra Yadav, "Electoral Politics in the Time of Change: India's Third Electoral System, 1989–99," *Economic and Political Weekly* 34, nos. 34–35 (1999): 21–28.

[6] Leigh Linden, "Are Incumbents Really Advantaged: The Preference for Non-Incumbents in Indian National Elections," Draft 2004, available at http://econ-www.mit.edu/graduate/candidates/download_res.php?id=89 (accessed December 12, 2005). Nirmala Ravishankar, "Voting for Change: Turnout and Vote Choice in Indian Elections," PhD Dissertation, Harvard University, 2007.

[7] Robert Dahl, *On Democracy* (New Haven, CT: Yale University Press, 1998), 158.

[8] Pradeep Chibber, *Democracy without Associations* (Ann Arbor: University of Michigan Press, 1999).

[9] M. Steven Fish, "Islam and Authoritarianism," *World Politics* 55 (October 2002): 4–35.

et al. found that India was a major outlier, given its low levels of income and literacy and high levels of ethnic and religious unrest: "India was predicted as dictatorship during the entire period ... the odds against democracy in India were extremely high."[10] Explaining this puzzle—the resilience of India's democracy (not its initial inception but its ongoing endurance) contrary to the predictions of political science—is the focus of this chapter.

The conventional argument about democratic breakdown usually centers on some variant of distributional conflicts. In traditional societies, the "propertied classes" (landed elites) dominated society by means of their hold on land, control of the military, and through the religious and educational indoctrination of the population.[11] Elites deployed a variety of mechanisms to preserve their privileges and resist the incorporation of new actors into the political arena, including a gradual expansion of the franchise, institutional design with checks and balances, preservation of a weak state, and guarantees for the maintenance of their dominance over a procedurally democratic society.[12] Of course, when all else failed, outright subversion, especially through repression and military coups, was always an option. In India's case, meanwhile, universal franchise was granted overnight, and the constitutional design gave the state a preeminent role in socioeconomic transformation, even as it withheld any guarantees to extant elites.

However, in the repertoire of elite strategies, one option is highly discounted (if at all considered) in the literature: that of elite "exit." Elite exit has been taken into account only in the face of successful, violent revolution, and then not as a long-term strategy but as the inevitable short-term response to military defeat.[13] The bottom line seems to be that elites "voice" but do not "exit," unless by force and violence.

In this chapter, I posit that elite "exit," which is the result of the limited hold of Indian elites (relative to elites in Latin America or Pakistan or Philippines) on immobile physical capital and their relatively greater hold

[10] Adam Przeworski, Michael E. Alvarez, José Antonio Cheibub, and Fernando Limongi, *Democracy and Development: Political Institutions and Well-Being in the World, 1950–1990* (New York: Cambridge University Press, 2000), 83, 87.

[11] Benedict Anderson, *Imagined Communities: Reflections on the Origin and Spread of Nationalism* (New York: Verso, 1991).

[12] See for instance Jorge Dominguez, *Democratic Politics in Latin America and the Caribbean* (Baltimore: Johns Hopkins University Press, 1998); Seymour Martin Lipset and Aldo Solari, eds., *Elites in Latin America.* (New York: Oxford University Press, 1967); Scott Mainwaring, Guillermo O'Donnell, and J. Samuel Valenzuela, eds., *Issues in Democratic Consolidation: The New South American Democracies in Comparative Perspective* (Notre Dame, IN: University of Notre Dame Press, 1992).

[13] H. Chehabi and J. J. Linz, eds., *Sultanistic Regimes* (Baltimore, London: Johns Hopkins University Press, 1998).

on mobile human capital, has played an important role in ensuring India's democratic stability. This is not to say that the traditional elites of India did not want to have the voice capability. As it was, however, they lacked the physical resources available to the landed oligarchy in many other countries and were dependent on the state to a substantially greater degree than their typical Latin American counterparts. My argument is that the "option value" of exit (i.e., the fact that elites could exit spatially and relocate the locus of their privilege from the political to the economic realm) facilitated democratization in India by allowing for a relatively smooth integration of new actors into the polity. The possibility of (relatively) peaceful relocation allowed Indian elites to reconstitute their power away from traditional sectors. Access to education played a critical role. Limited access to primary and secondary education went hand in hand with a large and relatively sophisticated higher-education sector, both limiting competition to incumbent elites and providing them with the human capital essential for mobility. The availability of exit mitigated the distributional conflicts that were inevitable following the introduction of universal franchise and produced a less hostile environment that fostered the eventual deepening of democracy, much in the way that empires provided colonial powers with an escape-valve for displaced domestic actors.[14] In short, these elites abandoned their monopoly on social and political prerogatives and leveraged their human capital to succeed in the modern market economy. By reconstituting their power in the economic arena, they began to operate relatively independently of the reach of a state that was no longer (if it had ever been) the traditional elites' instrument to control society. There is of course the prior puzzle on why Indian elites designed a system that would sooner or later undermine their power, necessitating exit. That is a different question from the one in which I am interested in this chapter, but I briefly discuss it later.

In the next section, I first summarize the principal explanations for democratic breakdown and then review some of the arguments that have been advanced to explain the Indian paradox. Subsequently, I draw upon empirical evidence on international migration from India presented earlier in chapter 3 and demonstrate that this migration is exceptional in its elite composition. I next examine some key political events in post-independence India and their relationship with emigration trends. Last, I consider some implications of international migration for national politics in general and democratic governance in particular, concluding that an understanding of the domestic impact of international capital

[14] J. G. Darwin, "Civility and Empire," in *Civil Histories: Essays Presented to Sir Keith Thomas*, eds. Peter Burke, Brian Howard Harrison, and Paul Slack (Oxford, UK: Oxford University Press, 2000), 321–36.

mobility needs to move beyond the current narrow conceptualization of capital in its financial sense to include human capital as well.

CONVENTIONAL EXPLANATIONS: DEMOCRATIC BREAKDOWN AND INDIAN EXCEPTIONALISM

The history of the expansion of the franchise, both in Western democracies as well as in many developing countries (especially in Latin America and East Europe), is a story of countless local struggles to widen the voting franchise and gradually chip away at entrenched privileges. While today it is taken for granted as an almost natural political law, a reading of history offers a stark reminder of how new democracy's habits and institutions are. That these habits and institutions require "enormous reversals of traditional assumptions about power and legitimacy" is one reason why they have often proven fragile.[15] In all Western democracies, the franchise was extended only gradually. In part, this was to ensure that elites—in particular, the propertied classes—continued to sustain their monopoly on the levers of government and retain their hold on decision-making powers. But it also reflected a fear among elites everywhere—namely, that democracy implied mob rule, or as one Federalist leader put it in 1804, "the government of the worst."[16] Even when property ownership ceased to be a prerequisite for voting, the franchise continued to be withheld from marginalized social groups, whether by gender or ethnic status. Additionally, elites deployed a variety of strategies to check the erosion of their power, from erecting a system of institutional checks and balances (such as the House of Lords in England) to ensuring that the state was weak (as in the United States), so that even if "the people" did achieve control over the state, that achievement was limited. When all else failed, outright subversion—democratic breakdown, especially through coups—was in many cases a possible last resort.

The endurance (or lack thereof) of "new" democracies has long preoccupied analysts of democracy, from the seminal study by Linz and Stepan to more recent work by Przeworski et al., Boix, and Bermeo.[17] Debates

[15] Sean Wilentz, *The Rise of American Democracy: Jefferson to Lincoln* (New York: W. W. Norton, 2005).

[16] Wilentz, *The Rise of American Democracy*. In the United States, it was only by 1828, a half-century after independence, that even all white males could exercise their franchise.

[17] Przeworski et al., *Democracy and Development: Political Institutions and Well-Being in the World, 1950–1990* (New York: Cambridge University Press, 2000); Nancy Bermeo, *Ordinary People in Extraordinary Times: The Citizenry and the Breakdown of Democracy* (Princeton, NJ: Princeton University Press, 2003); Carlos Boix, *Democracy and Redistribution* (Cambridge, UK: Cambridge University Press, 2003); Juan Linz and Alfred Stepan, eds.,

on democracy versus authoritarianism are conventionally posited as a redistributional game, where ruling elites strive to preserve the status quo and lower classes seek to change the distributional equilibrium. Przeworski et al. argue that the answer lies in economic development, which, while it may not explain the transition to democracy, explains democratic stability (i.e., more economically developed countries, once they become democratic, are less likely to revert to authoritarian rule than less developed countries). For Boix, relative equality, capital mobility and high costs of repression ensure democratic stability. Bermeo provides wide-ranging evidence in support of her view that "the culpability for democracy's demise [lies] overwhelmingly with political elites."[18] This view is echoed by Bunce, who argues that the "termination of democracy is very much a matter of what elites choose to do—and not to do."[19] In the end, according to these views, ordinary people are powerless in the face of elites determined to end the democratic experiment. As Hagopian (in her review of Bermeo's book) puts it, "If past is prologue, the destiny of many a democracy may still lie in the hands of the few."[20] While elites may be just one actor on the *path* to democratization, they appear to be critical in explaining the *breakdown* of democracy.

Consequently, it is hard to underestimate just how big a leap of faith the Indian decision to extend the franchise to all adults without any exceptions entailed. That faith in democracy, exemplified in Nehru, helped lay the foundations for democratic endurance.[21] Actor-centric approaches to Indian history emphasize the role of India's elites in establishing democracy, but what was their role in ensuring the stability of democracy? As Khilnani notes, "[T]he elite who introduced it was itself surprisingly insouciant about the potential implications of its actions."[22] It should be emphasized that this decision was not in response to demands from the masses, but initiated independently by a group completely unrepresentative of Indian society—a group that was predominantly highly educated,

---

The Breakdown of Democratic Regimes: Crisis, Breakdown and Reequilibrium (Washington, DC: Johns Hopkins, 1978).

[18] Bermeo, *Ordinary People in Extraordinary Times: The Citizenry and the Breakdown of Democracy*, 221.

[19] Valerie Bunce, "Comparative Democratization: Big and Bounded Generalizations," *Comparative Political Studies* 33 (2000): 6.

[20] Frances Hagopian,"What Makes Democracies Collapse?" *Journal of Democracy* 15, no. 3 (2000): 166–69.

[21] As Dahl puts it, "Democracy, one might say, is the national ideology of India." Robert Dahl, *On Democracy,* 162.

[22] Sunil Khilnani, *The Idea of India* (New York: Farrar, Straus and Giroux, 1999), 34. The promise of universal franchise was first proposed by the Radhakrishnan Committee at the annual meeting of the Indian National Congress in 1931.

high caste, and male. And whose views, as I argued in chapter 5, were informed by their overseas educational experience.

The decision appears to have been driven by a complex amalgam of rational calculus and idealism. Mass-mobilization was needed both to confront the repressive apparatus of the colonial power as well as to address the "moral" arguments put forward by colonial powers that portrayed themselves as champions of self-determination and responsible government.[23] Thus, Indian nationalist elites had to a priori grant what only decades of strife forced upon their Latin American counterparts: universal franchise. But there was a trade-off between Indian elites' need to initiate mass-mobilization to confront the colonial "other" and the degree to which these elites could control the state. That is, the more the elites promoted mass-mobilization, the greater became their risk of losing control over the state post-independence.

Another explanation, meanwhile, places the onus on the structural weakness of India's elites—that is, they possessed a limited command over material resources, unlike elites elsewhere. In contrast to Latin American landed elites who exercised power at the national level, India's landed elites were essentially local, and at best, their power extended to the provincial level. Land concentration was lower, although in a context of pauperism,[24] and domestic power structures were extremely localized. Critically, linkages between the landed elite and the army were weak. Many of the largest landlords in Northern and Eastern India, where land concentration was highest, were Muslims who left for Pakistan. In 1954, when the first comprehensive data on landholding are available, 87 percent of all Indian rural households had less than 10 acres of land, while the upper 13 percent controlled 41 percent of all land.[25] Yet this "upper 13 percent or so of rural households could be considered 'large' landowners only from the perspective of their size relative to the mass of landless and subsistence cultivators—fewer than 1 percent owned holdings of 50 acres or more. Even then, there were many fewer large farms than large landowners . . . [for] 'large' holdings of 10 acres or more were commonly separated into seven or eight parcels of 2, 3 and 4 acres."[26] Thus, even if

[23] David Abernethy, *The Dynamics of Global Domination: European Overseas Empires, 1415–1980* (New Haven: Yale University Press, 2002).

[24] Jean Dreze and Amartya Sen, *India: Economic Development and Social Opportunity* (New Delhi: Oxford University Press, 2002).

[25] Francine Frankel, *India's Political Economy, 1947–1977: The Gradual Revolution* (Princeton, NJ: Princeton University Press, 1978), 97.

[26] Frankel, *India's Political Economy, 1947–1977: The Gradual Revolution*, 97–98. By comparison, Robustiano Costas, vice-presidential candidate in the 1943 elections in Argentina, had land holdings equivalent to half the size of his province of origin, Salta. The province of Salta has an area of 154,775 square kilometers (about 38,000 acres).

they had held a "conventional" preference for social dominance, the Indian ruling elites "could not formulate any new social and cultural policies or launch mobilizational campaigns to demonstrate a majority support to such policies or a "cause," without taking interest of these various conglomerations of communities into account, even if such acts sometimes went against the ruling elites' own perceived interests."[27]

Another set of explanations for the persistence of India's democracy seeks recourse to institutional factors. Foremost among these was the institution of the Congress Party, which was clearly an exceptional political party in its scale, scope, and democratic culture. The institutional legacy of the British, including the establishment of civilian control of the army, a strong bureaucracy and civil service, and the possible "socializing" effects of British rule, arguably permeated into the Congress Party, and consequently into the Indian state. Or else, perhaps India developed consociational institutions, deemed to be the hallmark of stability for multiethnic states.[28]

While all these explanations have merit, in the end they are inadequate in explaining the paradox of Indian democracy. Actor-centric theories, while providing compelling explanations about the reasons for the initial adoption of universal franchise, do not explain long-term democratic stability. British colonial rule extended across many countries where democracy did not survive. Moreover, the institutional legacy of British rule in South Asia was shared by India's neighbors, many of whom have had much less success with democracy. Although over the years, India had acquired variegated experiences with British conceptions of law, the breadth and depth of these experiences is doubtful. India had some experience with representative government prior to independence, but even that was confined to less than 4 percent of the population. If India did not have the sort of landed elites that Latin America or the Philippines had, neither did most African countries. As for India's alleged fealty to consociationalism, this is more the result of an expansive view of consociationalism and a selective interpretation of India's realities.[29]

Boix has argued that "authoritarianism predominates in those countries in which both the level of inequality and the lack of capital mobility are high" and the costs of repression relatively low.[30] Boix further argues

[27] D. L. Sheth, "Caste, Ethnicity and Exclusion in South Asia: The Role of Affirmative Action Policies in Buislind Inclusive Societies," Background paper for *Human Development Report*, 2004.

[28] Arend Lijphart, "The Puzzle of Indian Democracy: A Consociational Interpretation," *American Political Science Review* 90 (June 1996): 258–68.

[29] Steve Wilkinson, "Consociational Theory and Ethnic Violence," *Asian Survey* 40, no. 5 (October 2000): 767–91.

[30] Boix, *Democracy and Redistribution*, 3.

that while his insights do not "completely" solve the "Indian paradox ... the big stumbling block of modernization theory," they approximate the case much better since income and land inequality in India is "mild" and redistributive pressures have been "softened" by the country's federal structures.[31] However, this explanation is questionable. By Boix's criteria (the share of agriculture in GDP or GDP per capita, which he argues can be thought of as a "first approximation of asset specificity"), India has had high asset specificity. Yet given the strictness with which India controlled its capital account, international capital mobility was not an option for India's commercial and industrial elites, in sharp contrast to many other developing countries.[32] Furthermore, while federal structures may soften horizontal redistributive pressures (i.e., across subnational governments), it is unclear that they have any effect on vertical redistributive pressures (between elites and masses).

In the conventional story, universal franchise pits masses against elite interests in a zero-sum game, and the resulting conflict precipitates democratic breakdown. In the next section, I argue that the Indian case was different. Specifically, the opportunity to spatially relocate abroad allowed old elites to recalibrate their portfolios, whereby they retained their economic privileges while enabling aspiring domestic actors to capture state organs (figure 6.1).

In chapters 1 and 2, I had drawn attention to the complex political effects of international migration and the multiple mechanisms through which they operate. In some cases, as in Western Europe in the nineteenth century, international migration offered a way to get rid of potential troublemakers and subversive elements, which might have given greater confidence to elites to cautiously expand the franchise. Likewise, in the United States, the contested but influential "Turner thesis" postulates that westward expansion was critical to American political development and, in particular, promoted the unique trait of individualistic democracy that characterized the United States.[33] As the new states in the Northwest

[31] Ibid.

[32] Although firm data are hard to come by, prior to economic liberalization at least, financial capital flight from India was less than most other developing countries, even though India had one of the highest marginal tax rates. According to one estimate in 1990, among developing country regions, South Asia (in which India dominates) had the lowest share of private portfolios held overseas (3 percent), lower even than East Asia (6 percent). Not surprisingly, the countries of the Middle East and Africa had the highest share (in both cases, 39 percent) with Latin America at 10 percent. Paul Collier, Anke Hoeffler and Catherine Pattillo, "Flight Capital as Portfolio Choice," World Bank Working Paper No. 2066 (2000).

[33] Migrants to the frontier usually ended up becoming pioneer farmers. Their isolation forced them to become self-reliant and skeptical of any form of centralized political authority. Frederick Jackson Turner, *The Frontier in American History* (New York: Dover Publications, 1996).

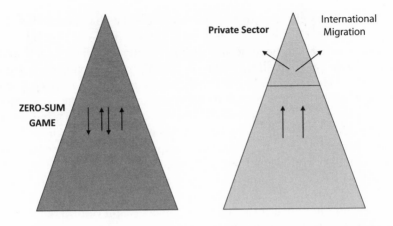

Figure 6.1. Universal franchise and elite mobility.

liberalized voting laws to attract new settlers, states along the Atlantic coast were forced to follow suit to check the emigration rate.[34]

In more recent times, forced migration has allowed authoritarian regimes like Cuba and Zimbawe to get rid of potential challengers and further entrench themselves. Many post-colonial states expelled ethnic minorities, which often meant losing a good part of their small middle class. However, where international migration is voluntary, exit can undermine totalitarian regimes—one reason why Communist regimes have tightly controlled "exit." Indeed, in the rare case that these restrictions were lifted—as when migrants fled from East to West Germany (via Czechoslovakia) in mid-1989—regime stability was rapidly undermined by exit.[35]

REPRESENTATION AND CONTESTATION IN INDEPENDENT INDIA

Contemporary India has many glaring failures, including its abysmal human development indicators, the weak accountability of state functionaries, and its poor record in providing physical security to religious minorities and socially marginalized groups. It is easy to see and critique

[34] Wilentz, *The Rise of American Democracy*.

[35] In the East German case, it forced the government to allow free movement directly to the West later that year, eventually leading to the pulling down of the Berlin Wall, a key event in ending the Cold War.

the gap between the lofty objectives the Indian state set for itself in its constitution and the prosaic reality. It is equally easy to identify the negative consequences this overgrown Indian state has had on the well-being of a sixth of humanity.[36] Those obvious limitations should not, however, prevent us from recognizing just how exceptional the Indian experience has been in holding together a society with extremely limited material resources, a society that comprises countless ethnic, linguistic, and religious divisions, all within a democratic polity.

Drawing on comparative data and analysis from the World Values Surveys, Linz et al. argue that India is "one of the world's democracies that scores most highly on three key state nation indicators: identification, trust and support."[37] Indians appear to strongly identify with the country ("being Indian") and have strong trust in key state and political institutions, more than in many long-standing Western democracies. Furthermore, citizens' support for democracy continues to be higher than in most other developing countries. Even among India's potentially alienated social groups—its largest religious minority (Muslims), the social group lowest in the caste hierarchy (the Dalits), and the lowest income group (the "very poor")—the percentage who answer that "democracy is preferable to any other form of government" is more than ten percentage points higher than the average for Latin American countries in 2001.[38]

While India still has a long way to go in improving the quality of its democracy, there can be little doubt that social groups that were historically marginalized have significantly increased their representation in organs of the Indian state, be they Parliament or the bureaucracy. Additionally, while the old high-caste elites continue to be economically privileged, they are much less politically and socially hegemonic. India's national political elites at independence were dominated by individuals who had privileged social origins to be sure, but they drew their stature from their human capital. They comprised an intellectually outstanding group of persons, trained abroad (usually in law) and relatively independent of domestic landed interests. It was this group that formed the country's leadership after independence. Although India was an overwhelming rural society at the time of independence (the urbanization

---

[36] Jagdish Bhagwati, *India in Transition* (Oxford, UK: Clarendon Press, 1995); Jean Dreze and Amartya Sen, *India: Economic Development and Social Opportunity* (New Delhi: Oxford University Press, 2002); Pranab Bardhan, *The Political Economy of Development in India* (New Delhi: Oxford University Press, 1999).

[37] Juan Linz, Alfred Stepan, and Yogendra Yadav, "Nation State or State Nation: Conceptual Reflections and Some Spanish, Belgian and Indian Data," Background paper prepared for the *Human Development Report*, 2004.

[38] Linz et al., "Nation State or State Nation: Conceptual Reflections and Some Spanish, Belgian and Indian Data," 37.

rate was less than 15 percent in 1951), 55 percent of the members of the provisional Parliament (which was based on a very limited franchise) were urban professionals (especially lawyers), and just 6 percent listed their occupation as agriculture.[39] Following the first general elections in 1952, when universal franchise came into effect, 35 percent percent of the Lok Sabha (the lower house equivalent to the House of Commons) were lawyers. By the time the fourth general elections were held in 1967, this figure had declined by half (to 17.5 percent) and was paralleled by a concomitant increase in agrarian interests from 22 to 31 percent. And by the Twelfth Lok Sabha, "political and social workers" and "agriculturists" emerged as the largest occupational groups. While one in ten parliamentarians after independence had an overseas education, by 1980 this figure had declined to 6.2 percent. Two decades later, the figure had dropped further: one out of twenty-five had an overseas education, reflecting the emergence of politicians from historically socially marginalized groups.

The shifts in representation are evident in the arena where redistributional conflict has been most intense: employment in public institutions. Table 6.1a shows the increasing share of scheduled caste (SC) appointees in the federal bureaucracy. It should be noted that the more elite the category of employment (Class I is the most elite and Class IV the least), the greater has been the increase in representation. The story is similar in employment in state-owned enterprises, where both SC and scheduled tribes (ST) representation has increased much faster in more elite categories (Groups A and B) than lower rung occupations (see table 6.1b).

Not surprisingly, these efforts met strong resistance. According to Heller, "efforts to develop and democratize local institutions for community development and democratization, such as village councils and cooperatives, were defeated by elite capture . . . [as] the state enmeshed itself in a matrix of accommodations and patronage networks."[40] Nonetheless, the large mass of Indian "have-nots" was "acutely aware of its new political value, [and it] became the most coveted political object of appeasement as well as of manipulation even as it became available for all manners of campaigns for social and political mobilization."[41]

In fact, this mobility was outpaced by that observed among the numerically dominant middle-caste groups known as other backward castes (OBCs). As a consequence of their numbers, the OBC representation in

---

[39] David Rosenthal, "Deurbanization, Elite Displacement and Political Change in India," *Comparative Politics* 2, no. 2 (1970): 169–201.

[40] Patrick Heller, "Degrees of Democracy: Some Comparative Lessons from India," *World Politics* 52 (July 2000): 505.

[41] D. L. Sheth, "Caste, Ethnicity and Exclusion in South Asia: The Role of Affirmative Action Policies in Building Inclusive Societies," Background paper for *Human Development Report*, 2004.

TABLE 6.1A
SC Representation in the Federal Bureaucracy, 1953–2000
(% of total employees)

	1953	1967	1980	1991	2000
Class I	0.53	2.08	4.95	9.09	10.77
Class II	1.29	3.1	8.54	11.82	12.13
Class III	4.52	9.33	13.44	15.65	15.84
Class IV	20.52	18.18	19.46	21.24	19.72

Source: For 1953–1987, Jaffrelot, 2003, 92. For 1991–2000, Sheth, 2004, part II, tables 1 and 3.

TABLE 6.1B
SC/ST Representation in State-Owned Enterprises

	Percent Scheduled Caste		Percent Scheduled Tribe	
	1971	2001	1971	2001
Group A	0.52	10.8	0.17	3.0
Group B	0.54	11.5	0.16	4.6
Group C	5.59	18.9	1.3	8.8
Group D	16.0	22.9	5.9	11.3
Total	8.2	18.8	2.2	8.16

Source: Department of Public Enterprises, Annual Report, 2001–2002.
Note: Group D data excludes Safai Karamcharis (or cleaners).

legislatures increased remarkably, which eventually allowed them to achieve mandated reservations in 1990. Even the upper-caste-dominated BJP, which vociferously opposed reservations for OBCs in 1991, had by 1996 promised "the continuation of reservations for the Other Backward Castes till they are socially and educational [sic] integrated with the rest of society."[42] This followed its losses in state elections in Uttar Pradesh and Madhya Pradesh, largely because of Dalit and OBC voters, forcing the BJP to promote more low-caste members within the party hierarchy. Thus, even this high-caste-led Hindu nationalist party had to eventually bow to the logic of electoral competition.

India's state organs have undergone a significant shift in their social representation. While the old high-caste elites continue to be economically privileged, they are much less politically and socially hegemonic. That this "silent revolution" (in Jafferlot's vivid characterization) could occur without precipitating systemic instability is a singular achievement

[42] Christophe Jaffrelot, *India's Silent Revolution: The Rise of the Lower Castes in North India* (New York: Columbia University Press, 2003), 464.

of India's democracy. How did it occur? I address this question in the next section.

Migration and Indian Democracy

The impact of international migration on India's democracy must be understood in the context of the history and characteristics of emigration from India. As noted in chapter 3, the first hundred years of migration from colonial India since the 1830s largely comprised unskilled and low-caste workers, whereas in its more recent decades emigration has been more human-capital intensive and upper-caste dominated. International migration from India in the late nineteenth and late twentieth centuries has been starkly different in its selection characteristics. While migrants in the nineteenth century came from poorer socioeconomic groups and from poorer parts of the country and went to (relatively poor) Southern countries, a century later virtually the opposite was true—they came from richer socioeconomic groups and from wealthier parts of the country and, with the significant exception of the large migration to the Middle East, went to industrialized countries. This more recent migration stream has been notably defined by high-skilled migration to the United States following the liberalization of U.S. immigration law in 1965. This migrant stream has been the most highly educated, compared both to other immigrants into the United States as well as to other Indian migrant streams abroad. Since the 1990s, increasing numbers of skilled emigrants from India have also been moving to Australia, Canada, New Zealand, and Singapore—English-speaking industrialized countries whose higher-education systems are an important mechanism to attract and screen potential immigrants. The fact that over this century-long historical period Indian politics has concurrently become more democratic raises the question of whether the two phenomena may be interlinked.

As discussed in chapter 3, the political impact of migration depends critically on the selection characteristics of the migrant, including factors such as ethnicity, religion, caste, education, and income. Although statistically robust data on migrant characteristics vis-à-vis these dimensions simply do not exist, the two principal surveys underlying this study, the Survey of Emigration from India (SEI) and the Survey of Asian Indians in the United States (SAIUS), go some way in providing robust data on international migrant characteristics from India.

The results of the SEI survey reveal that barely 1.7 percent of households in India have immediate family members abroad and 2.9 percent have extended family abroad (table 3.1). While this is not surprising for a country of India's size, at first glance the very modest levels of international migration might give pause about its possible political effects. However, as I argued in chapter 3, a striking feature of recent Indian migration is its extreme selection bias: Indian elites have extremely high migration rates compared to the general population. The key trends of Indian migration include the following: (1) There is a strong urban bias in households that have global links through migration. (2) The likelihood of households having family members abroad increases with income, but much more sharply at the highest end (figure 3.2). As one would expect, the number of members abroad also increases with income (figure 3.3), in both urban and rural areas. (3) The richest rural households (R1) have a greater likelihood of members abroad than poor urban households (SEC C and SEC D).

The data underscore a key point: the more "elite" the social group, the greater the selectivity of international migration from India. (This point was further illustrated in chapter 3 by the survey of the locational choices of children of senior officers of the Indian army [table 3.6]). As mentioned in chapter 3, the survey evidence on Indian emigration is complemented by survey evidence on Indian immigration to the United States, the primary destination of India's elites. Sources include the Current Population Survey (CPS) and the U.S. Census, which confirm that among ethnic groups in the U.S., Indian Asians have the highest median family income, a function of the highest levels of education (nearly two-thirds have a college education or better), the highest labor participation rates (71 percent), and the highest fraction engaged in a high-skill occupation (more than half) (table 3.7).

Given the selectivity of Indian migration with respect to the U.S. population, it should not be surprising that the selectivity is an order of magnitude greater compared to the Indian population from which it is being drawn. While 71 percent of Indian immigrants to the United States had some college education, just 3.42 percent of Indians in India were college educated—a more than twentyfold difference (figure 3.16). This feature masks another striking characteristic that has long defined cleavages in Indian society, but which in more recent years has emerged as a key mobilizing feature of democratic politics: caste.

As discussed in chapter 3, while there is a strong correlation between caste and class, it is by no means isomorphic. Although respondents in the SEI and SAIUS surveys did not directly provide information about their caste status, the latter survey did allow for an estimation of the caste composition of the people of Indian origin living in the United States. The results are given in figure 3.19. While the use of names to impute caste can be only an indicative (rather than a precise) guide to the composition of the population, the data are strongly suggestive of underlying trends. To reiterate, high castes are predominant, with dominant castes as the second largest group. (The dominant caste data include only those who are not high castes.[43]) Access to resources in India significantly increases the probability of emigrating to the United States. Members of scheduled castes and scheduled tribes—more than one-fifth of India's population—comprise at best two or three percent of the Indian-origin population in the United States However, underlying political trends in India are likely to change this in the medium term. The increasing political clout of the lower castes within India is likely to result in their children having greater mobility—both vertical (within the country) as well as spatial (outside the country).

THE IMPACT OF MIGRATION ON INDIAN DEMOCRACY

The first major impact of migration on India's democracy occurred just prior to, and in the immediate aftermath of, partition, when a large part of India's Muslim elite migrated to Pakistan. Muslims comprised about one-third of the British Indian army prior to independence, a number that dropped to just 2 percent by 1953.[44] A majority of the Muslims in the elite Indian Civil Service and Indian Police cadres had opted for Pakistan as independence loomed, and many more senior government officials left soon after partition. Middle- and lower-ranking employees continued to emigrate in large numbers into the early 1950s. In the state of Uttar Pradesh (UP), the heartland of Muslim separatism, the proportion of Muslim employees in the UP civil service and police fell precipitously (in the case of the police, from nearly 46 percent to less than 15 percent a decade later).[45] Other government departments where the Muslims previously occupied between 40 and 50 percent of the positions suffered a similar decline in Muslim employment. In Delhi, the literacy rate of Muslims prior to partition was nearly 50 percent and dropped to barely 5 percent in the 1951 census. Although the exodus of the Muslim elite may have had severely inimical consequences for the largely less educated Muslim community left behind (and in that sense adversely affected the quality of India's democracy), it removed at a stroke a critical potential source of

---

[43] Dominant castes (e.g., the Jats in Northwestern India, Patels in Gujarat, Vokkaligas and Lingayats in Karnataka, Kapus and Kammas in Andhra Pradesh, and Marathas in Maharashtra) were upper or intermediate cultivating castes that controlled large areas of land and were numerically large; hence, they held a preeminent position in the rural economy (Srinivas, 1995). They were often not ritualistically high caste.

[44] Mahavir Tyagi, Minister of State for Defense, quoted in Omar Khalidi, *Khakhi and Ethnic Violence in India* (New Delhi: Three Essays, 2003), 11.

[45] Steven Wilkinson, *Votes and Violence: Electoral Competition and Ethnic Riots in India* (Cambridge, UK: Cambridge University Press, 2004), 112.

destabilizing intraelite conflict on religious lines and shifted elite conflict to other cleavages—region and caste.

In contrast, the migration of the Hindus and Sikhs from the western districts of (Pakistan) Punjab had little effect on social and political relations in Pakistan. If anything, "the transfer of population saw the landed elites tightening their grip over rural society further," with many of the big landowners grabbing the land abandoned by non-Muslims.[46] Consequently, the average landholding of large family estates still averaged over 11,000 acres in the 1950s, cementing the alliance between landed elites and the military that would prove fatal to Pakistan's democratic prospects.[47]

In post-independence India, the first major instance of universal franchise affecting upper-caste elites occurred in Tamil Nadu in the 1950s. Tamil Brahmins, who constituted barely 5 percent of the state's population but had a tight grip on politics and society, were ousted when the lower-caste Dravidian parties captured power—reflecting the iron law of numbers. As a result, Tamil Brahmins left that state in large numbers for major metropolitan cities including Calcutta and Bombay, to work in the private sector, and Delhi, to work in the federal government. The high human capital of Tamil Brahmins made them easily mobile. The ability to exit was amplified by economic opportunities in other parts of the country. If one were to pose the counterfactual (i.e., if Tamil Nadu were a closed system where out-migration was not possible), would the degree of political conflict in that state have been much greater? The relatively painless exit of Tamil Brahmins from Tamil Nadu also foreshadowed another feature of Indian elite migration. The loss of economic privilege at the local level could be more than regained through nonlocal opportunities, first national and then international. While the Dravidian movement was successful in undermining the hegemony of the upper castes in Tamil Nadu, it did not achieve equality and justice for everyone else. It shifted power to the numerically largest "backward castes." In turn, these new elites, rather than the "upper castes," emerged as the main source of oppression for the lowest castes, the Dalits. Only very recently has the latter begun to emerge as an independent political force, emphasizing that the "democratization of democracy" is an incomplete and ongoing process.[48]

The exit option was initially provided by the federal government, particularly through the All India Services. Employment in the federal

---

[46] Ayesha Jalal, *The State of Martial Rule* (Cambridge, UK: Cambridge University Press, 1990), 79.

[47] A. Hussain, "Pakistan: Land Reforms Considered," in *Sociology of Developing Societies of South Asia*, eds. H. Alavi and J. Harris (London: Macmillan Press, 1989), 61.

[48] Hugo Gorringe, *Untouchable Citizens—Dalit Movements and Democratisation in Tamil Nadu* (New Delhi: Sage Publications, 2005).

bureaucracy provided an initial haven for displaced elites in the provinces, which were the first sites of voice exercised by numerically larger subordinate social groups. The peaceful realization of a "silent revolution" would have been much less so otherwise.

The second phase in India's democratic transition occurred in the decade following the 1967 elections and was concurrent with a period marked by growing elite emigration from India. This was the first time since independence that the Congress Party lost power in many states and regional lower-caste parties began to make their presence felt, a result of the rising agency of lower-caste voters. E.P.W. da Costa, India's pioneer pollster, termed this election as "the second Non-Violent Revolution in India's recent history" because of "the disintegration of the monolithic exercise of power by the Congress party."[49] The political hegemony of upper castes was no longer secure. At the same time, India's economy stagnated. This combination of economic malaise and democratic upsurge due to mass mobilization in general poses severe challenges to democratic stability. Indeed, India was faced with the most potent threat to its democracy during this period. Distributional conflicts intensified, and the then Prime Minster Indira Gandhi imposed an "Emergency" in the mid-1970s, the one period when democratic rights in India were most seriously threatened. Nonetheless, as the elections of 1977 demonstrated, India's democracy survived these pressures.

This period coincided with the first substantial elite "exit" from India, primarily to the United States. The U.S. Immigration and Nationality Act of 1965 abolished the nationality quotas established in 1924 that had effectively shut out immigration from India. This change in U.S. immigration policy gave preference to immigrants with high levels of human capital—thus opening the door to the immigration of doctors, engineers, and scientists from India. Yet, notwithstanding the fact that this human capital was a scarce resource that had largely been educated at public expense and India's socialist policies imposed high taxes on anything that would seem "progressive," it took no steps to curtail this hemorrhaging of talent—no "brain-drain" tax or any attempt to recover scarce public money spend on building this human capital. This inaction is consistent with my argument that the old elite continued to dominate the policymaking apparatus and consequently was loathe to check the overseas opportunities available to its kith and kin at a time when these opportunities were diminishing within the country. At the same time, the rising new political elites, of course, had little interest in curbing the flight of a

[49] An excellent analysis of the long-term systemic importance of the 1967 elections can be found in Yogendra Yadav and Suhas Palshikar, "From Hegemony to Convergence: Party System and Electoral Politics in the Indian States, 1952–2002," *Journal of Indian School of Political Economy* 15, nos. 1 and 2 (2003): 97–122.

possible source of competition and conflict. It was a "social safety valve" for all concerned—and indeed was argued so at the time.[50]

The third key period in the democratic transition of post-independence India occurred in 1989–1990. At that time, the minority V. P. Singh government issued a report (known as the Mandal Commission Report), which advocated a major increase in reservations in education and jobs for the lower castes over and above the statutory provisions in the Constitution for the scheduled castes and scheduled tribes. Numerous anti-reservation riots followed, especially in Northern India, throwing the country into tumult. Yet barely a couple of years later, the Mandal Commission Report had become a political nonissue. Although in part this was the result of a successful strategy by the Hindu nationalist BJP to shift political cleavages from caste to religion, it was also because of two singular factors that rendered the bite of reservations moot for a large number of upper castes. The first was the rapid expansion of private higher education and private sector job opportunities following economic liberalization, even as state educational institutions and jobs stagnated.[51] The second was a massive expansion of high-skilled emigration, especially to the United States. Thus, even as Indian politics became more democratic, at least in the narrow sense where legislators were more representative of society, the older elites, while losing their social and political hegemony, did not lose their economic privileges. The locus of economic privileges simply shifted from the Indian state to the private sector and, through emigration, to global networks and opportunities.

International migration—and in particular, its specific selection characteristics—also helps to explain a particular paradox of India's political economy. India is to educational inequality what Brazil is to income inequality: both are outliers in their respective domains. Why has a country whose national elites have been committed to poverty eradication and whose intellectuals profess deep concern about the welfare of the poor done so poorly on one of the most basic tools for empowering the poor—literacy?[52] For instance, although a Marxist government has ruled the state of West Bengal for nearly three decades, its rhetorical pretensions

[50] Deena Khatkhate, "Brain Drain as a Social Safety Valve," *Finance and Development* 18, no. 1 (1971): 34–39.

[51] Total employment in the public sector (including central government, state government, local government, and quasi government) increased rapidly in the 1970s and 1980s from 10.7 million in 1971 to 15.95 million in 1981 and 19.06 million in 1991. It barely inched upward in the 1990s to 19.14 million in 2001 before declining to 18.58 million in 2003. Source: "Employment Statistics in India," *Economic and Political Weekly*, May 3, 2003 for 1971–2001, and Ministry of Labour, Government of India, Annual Report 2004, for 2003.

[52] For an elegant discussion on this issue more broadly, see Myron Weiner, *The Child and the State in India* (Princeton, NJ: Princeton University Press, 1990).

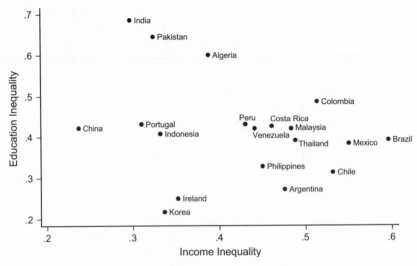

Figure 6.2. Income inequality versus education inequality, 1990.

notwithstanding, the state has performed worse in educational indicators than neighboring Bangladesh, which shares a similar culture but is poorer and has a weaker state. The crucial factor that facilitated Indian elite migration was its human capital. This meant that the only substantive distinction between this group and the masses was access to education; "pedagogic suppression" was one way to maintain this distinction.[53] This may in turn explain why, although India has had relatively low level of inequality in income and physical assets, it has the dubious distinction of having one of the highest levels of inequality in human capital (figure 6.2).

CONCLUSION: INTERNATIONAL MIGRATION AND INDIA'S DEMOCRATIC STABILITY

This chapter offers a new explanation for understanding a major lacuna in our understanding of democratic stability: the endurance of India's democracy, which has defied the predictions of democratic theory. Since the Indian democracy encompasses nearly a fourth of the world's voters, its importance goes beyond just that of a single-country study. I have argued that the conventional story of conflict leading to democratic breakdown did not occur in India because of the spatial mobility of

[53] Professor Surajit Sinha, cited in Weiner, *The Child and the State in India*, 189.

India's elites. Indian elite migration, first domestic and then international, created space for the vertical mobility of new elites drawn from India's historically marginalized communities, who became new "stakeholders" in India's political system. Unlike elites in many other poor developing countries, India's elites could exit because their assets were relatively greater in mobile human capital than in immobile land assets. International migration allowed Indian elites to shift (and diversify) their portfolios, making it easier to accommodate newer social groups. Thus, the international spatial mobility of one set of actors created space for the domestic vertical mobility of another set.[54]

This chapter does not claim that international migration is the sole explanation for the persistence and stability of India's democracy. How would this story have been different if the leadership of India's nationalist struggle had been Nkrumah or Mao instead of Gandhi or Nehru? Or if the French rather than the British had been the colonizers? Or if Partition had not occurred? History is invariably more complex than parsimonious social science explanations allow for. The chapter does, however, highlight a previously neglected variable that is important in understanding several characteristics of India's democracy. My argument is that elite emigration has helped democratic stability in India. It is not an assessment of the quality of that democracy. However, it is important to recognize that while the analysis and data presented is consistent with the argument advanced in this chapter, it does not support a causal argument. The latter would require systematic time series data showing asset specificity, caste competition, and political competition around income and caste in order to really assess the causal role between migration and political and caste conflict within India. It needs a viable counterfactual on what the levels of conflict and stability would have been absent migration rates.

The contrasting examples of the democratic experience in the Indian states of Bihar and Tamil Nadu offers partial counterfactual evidence. Bihar has long been the poster child of the weaknesses of India's democracy, with high levels of political violence, while Tamil Nadu by comparison has had a much better track record. The assets of upper-caste elites in Tamil Nadu (almost entirely Brahmins) were in both land and human capital, but by the time of independence the Brahmins did not dominate land ownership in that state. In contrast, in Bihar upper castes were large landlords. As the lower castes gained power in Tamil Nadu, the Brahmins took advantage of their mobile human capital (and relatively lower stakes in immobile land) and migrated to urban centers in India or abroad, attenuating

[54] The links between spatial and social mobility within India have been made by Myron Weiner, *Sons of the Soil: Migration and Ethnic Conflict in India* (Princeton, NJ: Princeton University Press, 1978), 293–94.

conflict in that state. In Bihar, however, upper castes were much more vested in an immobile asset (land) and hence fought the democratic upsurge of the lower castes. The distributions conflicts were more vicious, resulting in greater political violence and more tenuous democratic stability.

If the pattern of international migration from India at least partially explains India's democratic stability, it also raises questions regarding whether a factor that has contributed to the country's democratic stability has also been the source of some of its weaknesses. As I noted earlier, the very factor that made elite migration possible—human capital—also skewed incentives to supply this critical resource more broadly. The loss of talent could not but have had negative effects on domestic capabilities. It would be hard to argue that the fact that more than a tenth of India's medical professionals—drawn from the upper end of the medical talent pool—are abroad has not negatively affected the quality of health care in India. The broader negative effects of the exit of considerable numbers of India's talent pool are discussed in chapter 4.

In contrast to Hirschman's classic formulation, however, in today's world exit does not necessarily imply a loss of voice. As the Indian case reveals, the exit of elites simply changed the locus of privilege from political power in the state to economic power in the private sector and outside India. By gaining access to external resources and networks, groups can amplify their voice through international migration. Indeed, with the rise of dual nationality/citizenship, the "voice" effects may be even greater. However, if elite exit does not necessarily undermine elites' "voice," it may adversely affect their "loyalty." This may be one reason why even though international migration has strengthened the procedural aspects of Indian democracy (increased participation and contestation), it may have negatively affected the substantive aspects.

Last, this chapter draws attention to the neglected leg of the globalization triad, international migration, in the context of its political consequences for democratic regime stability. While the effects of capital mobility on democracy have been well analyzed,[55] this chapter emphasizes the need to broaden the conception of capital beyond solely its financial manifestation. Just as human capital has become increasingly important in economic growth models, human capital mobility needs to be incorporated in analytical conceptions of capital mobility and specificity—and its political consequences.

[55] For instance, Boix (2003).

CHAPTER 7

The Indian Diaspora and Indian Foreign Policy: Soft Power or Soft Underbelly?

INTRODUCTION

INTERNATIONAL MIGRATION HAS played an important role in shaping various aspects of India's political economy. Previous chapters have examined a range of these effects on India's economy and domestic politics, focusing on several channels through which emigration influences the sending country, including *absence* and *return*. In this chapter, I turn to the implications of another channel, *diaspora*, for India's foreign policy. Emigration from India prior to its independence created a large diaspora in regions ranging from the Caribbean to Southeast Asia. After independence, and particularly since the 1970s, an upsurge in migration from India—first to the Gulf and later within the industrialized world to Anglo-Saxon countries and Singapore—has created a diaspora of more recent vintage. As demonstrated in chapter 3, India has one of the largest pools of skilled labor in the world and will also be one of the largest sources of emigrants in the foreseeable future. What relevance does this large and growing diaspora have for India's foreign policy? Can the diaspora be a strategic asset for the country, or might it actually become a constraint?[1]

DIASPORAS AND INTERNATIONAL RELATIONS

The global movement of peoples across borders poses some conceptual conundrums for traditional models of international relations that are based on territory and the state system. International migration is making borders and citizenship more fluid and permeable, as formal institutions mingle with informal ethnic networks, creating a "politics of belonging" that is not territorially bounded.[2] Moreover, this movement is creating "competition among segments of the overall 'people' inside

[1] Devesh Kapur, "The Indian Diaspora as a Strategic Asset," *Economic and Political Weekly* XXXVIII, no. 5 (February 1–7, 2003): 445–48.

[2] Yossi Shain, *Kinship and Diaspora in International Affairs* (Ann Arbor: University of Michigan Press, 2007).

and outside 'homelands' for legitimate authority."[3] A certain duality about diasporas—residing outside their kin-state yet claiming a legitimate stake in it—inherently challenges the traditional boundaries of nation-states. Furthermore, as actors that straddle national boundaries, diasporas have recourse to autonomous resources and values. Unlike most domestic actors, they can more easily interact with other actors across state boundaries. These intrinsic attributes of diasporas suggest that they are likely to have an impact on a country's foreign policy. But how?

The attempt to understand the effects of a diaspora on a country's foreign policies poses several conceptual problems. Are diasporas independent actors or simply instruments deployed by other actors? Under what conditions are they mobilized, and if so, by whom? What characteristics of the diaspora, the country of origin, and the country of settlement matter? Under what conditions are diasporas a mechanism of a country's "soft power"? To the extent that diasporas are autonomous actors that engage in long-distance nationalism, as with all nationalisms, this role can be a mixed blessing—for both source and destination country.

A nation's "soft power," a term much in vogue since it was coined by Joseph Nye, represents the state's ability to shape the preferences of other states in accordance with its own. Soft power flows from the ability of a state to "attract" others based on its institutions, values, culture, and policies—"in behavioral terms [it] is attractive power."[4] Nye suggests that attractiveness flows in part from having values that accord with prevailing global norms.[5] This attractiveness then enhances the legitimacy of the state's preferences.

If diaspora members can be instruments of soft power, what motivates them? Most explanations center on long-distance nationalism with cognitive explanations that emphasize identity as the driving force. However, these theoretical explanations are of little help in understanding the intensity of a diaspora's nationalism relative to that in the country of origin, the intensity of one diaspora's nationalism relative to others, or what form this long-distance nationalism takes: whether ethnic or civic. Diasporas engage in civic nationalism, ranging from lobbying the government of their adopted country on foreign policy to sending funds during a natural calamity. Yet they also support, to varying extents, ethnic nationalism, whose consequences can be deeply inimical (but also easily exaggerated).

By their very nature, diasporas are particularly well placed to exercise "network power"—the tendency for social networks to grow as time

---

[3] Ibid.
[4] Ibid, 6.
[5] Ibid, 31–32.

progresses—which is a driving force of globalization.[6] Although conceptually distinct, network power could potentially be viewed as a component of a nation's soft power. As an analytical category, soft power is problematic in that it can be so expansive, making it hard to be precise. Nonetheless, Nye's argument—that in today's world, power is not just about economic and military strength but also comes from a "contest of competitive credibility"[7]—points to the importance of persuasion, reputation, and credibility in a hyper-information age. As Nye argues, "Countries that are more credible are more likely to be believed and then followed. When a country gets very popular with the American public it gets somewhat harder for Washington to follow a hard line against them."[8]

But how does a country persuade a skeptical potential partner of the validity of its preferences? Even if it does not hope to convince broader public opinion, how does it persuade key foreign policy, security, and business elites?[9] In all countries, even those with deep-rooted democratic structures, elites (and especially the executive branch) dominate foreign policy decisions.[10] Elites have greater influence in this policy domain, using their power in "cueing public opinion" for agenda setting and "policy initiation."[11] Thus, if diasporas are to influence the foreign policy of the country of residence in favor of the country of origin, it is critical that they are in a position to shape the opinions of elites in the former. Of course, this will be easier if the diasporas are from states that are not adversaries of the country of residence. But the power of the diaspora to influence the degree and pace of convergence of views between the country of residence and country of origin will crucially depend on its own attributes—its ability to undertake collective action either as a concentrated bloc of voters or

[6] For a lucid analysis of the phenomenon, see David Grewal, *Network Power: The Social Dynamics of Globalization* (New Haven, CT: Yale University Press, 2008).

[7] Joseph Nye, *Soft Power: The Means to Success in World Politics* (New York: Public Affairs, 2004), 106.

[8] Ibid.

[9] On the importance of persuasion in international relations, see Martha Finnemore and Kathryn Sikkink, "International Norm Dynamics and Political Change," *International Organization* 52, no. 4 (1998): 887–917; Alastair Iain Johnston, "Treating International Institutions as Social Environments," *International Studies Quarterly* 45, no. 4 (2001): 487–515.

[10] Much of the comparative foreign policy literature focuses on elites or on bureaucracies (perhaps because it is easier to show relationships between elite preferences and beliefs and foreign policy) as key decision makers in foreign policy. Examples include Margaret Hermann and Charles Hermann, "Who Makes Foreign Policy Decisions and How: An Empirical Inquiry," *International Studies Quarterly* 33, no. 4 (December 1989): 361–87; Daniel L. Byman and Kenneth M. Pollack, "Let Us Now Praise Great Men (and Women): Restoring the First Image," *International Security* 25, no. 4 (spring 2001): 107–47.

[11] John Zaller, *The Nature and Origins of Mass Opinion* (Cambridge, UK: Cambridge University Press, 1992), 97–117.

with financial heft as election financiers or with the "cultural capital" to act as opinion makers.[12]

The idea of soft power has had considerable appeal in policy circles, especially in India. This, after all, is one area in which India can claim to stand out among players in the international arena, as the source of diffusion of culture and religion to all corners of the world. From business gurus to religious gurus, Buddhism to yoga, Bollywood to bhangra-rap, classical music to cuisine, there seems to be a cornucopia of Indian "soft power." Furthermore, with scholarship in international relations in India dominated by a variety of theoretical strands all critiquing realism from a variety of perspectives (Marxist, constructivist, feminist, postcolonial, critical theory), the concept of soft power has been intuitively attractive in Indian international relations thinking.[13] But the attraction of soft power may not just be to the outside world. There is a danger of narcissistic delusion, the possibility that one becomes more enamored of one's own attractive qualities than others really are. Indeed if there is any substance to "civilizational soft power," it should be most evident in India's neighbors, where its limits have been all too apparent over the past six decades.

The more probable mechanism of India's soft power is arguably less the export of its culture and more the export of its people. Raja Mohan has argued that "the biggest instrument of our soft power is the Indian Diaspora."[14] India's former External Affairs Minister Yashwant Sinha similarly pointed out, "People of Indian origin are extremely important sources of support for the Indian Government in the execution of its policies through the influence and respect they command in the countries in which they live."[15]

But this recognition of the Indian diaspora as a strategic asset among India's foreign policy elites is relatively new. For decades, India neglected the strategic possibilities of its diaspora, in part because of its regional preoccupations (especially with China and Pakistan) on the one hand and its fixation with the Great Powers on the other. Consequently, India's diplomatic vision focused little on countries where the diaspora was settled—Africa, the Caribbean, and Southeast Asia. There was hardly any

---

[12] Stephen M. Walt and John Mearsheimer, *The Israel Lobby and U.S. Foreign Policy* (New York: Farrar, Straus and Giroux, 2007).

[13] On the absence of the dominant Anglo-American paradigm of structural realism in Indian international relations theorizing, see Kanti Bajpai and Siddharth Mallavarapu, eds., *International Relations in India: Bringing Theory Back Home* (New Delhi: Orient Longman, 2005).

[14] C. Raja Mohan, "Indian Diaspora and 'Soft Power,'" *The Hindu*, January 6, 2003.

[15] Cited in Raja Mohan (2003).

government-to-government contact (let alone government-to-people contact) between India and those countries.

This seems particularly surprising, given the fact that prior to independence, the nationalist movement made very active efforts to forge bonds with the diaspora. Inspired by Gandhi's efforts on behalf of the Indian community in South Africa, the leadership of the Indian National Congress took up the cause of overseas Indians as an extension of anti-imperialist struggle in other parts of the empire and even set up an Overseas Department under Jawaharlal Nehru in 1929.[16] Shortly after independence, in a communication addressed to "Heads of Indian Missions and Posts Abroad," the then Foreign Secretary K.P.S. Menon wrote what reports he expected from them on a regular basis. Among the items was: "Where there is any large body of persons of Indian descent, a report, once year, on their number, employment, economic and political position, treatment, all relevant matters as well as on consular work generally. This should be sent in January."[17]

But this attention was short lived, as the shockwaves of partition quickly congealed notions of citizenship and sovereignty. In 1948, large numbers of North Indian Muslims, who had gone to Pakistan, began to return, and the Indian government rushed an emergency permit system to stem the tide.[18] Post-independent India adopted a civic, territorial nationalism and a secular, inclusive state. In this vision, émigrés were no longer considered nationals, and thus, there was no need to maintain official ties with them. The official view, as articulated by Nehru, was that, "[i]t is the consistent policy of the Government that persons of Indian origin who have taken foreign nationality should identify themselves with and integrate in the mainstream of social and political life of the country of their domicile."[19]

With India becoming a "sovereignty hawk," Nehru's views were consonant with the fierce protection of sovereignty common to newly independent countries at the time, which precluded taking a strong stance on protecting the rights of the Indian diaspora who were now citizens of other sovereign countries. Moreover, insofar as supporting the rights of people of Indian origin in other newly independent countries might

[16] For a succinct account, see Gyanesh Kudaisya, "Indian Leadership and the Diaspora," in *The Encyclopedia of the Indian Diaspora*, ed. Brij V. Lal (Singapore: Editions Didier Millet, 2006), 82–89.

[17] Foreign Secretary KPS Menon to All Heads of Indian Missions and Posts Abroad, September 10, 1949.

[18] Vazira Fazila-Yacoobali Zamindar, *The Long Partition and the Making of Modern South Asia: Refugees, Boundaries, Histories* (New York: Columbia University Press, 2007).

[19] M. C. Lall, *India's Missed Opportunity* (Aldershot, UK: Ashgate, 2001), 88.

weaken India's relations with them, it also risked Nehru's ambitions of Indian assuming a leadership role of the nonaligned countries. Therefore, it was perhaps not just coincidental that India's emerging rival for leadership in Asia, the People's Republic of China (PRC), adopted a similar stance. Initially, the PRC sought to leverage the privileged position of the overseas Chinese in Southeast Asia to the country's political and economic advantage. This, however, ran counter to the attempts of Southeast Asian countries to integrate the Chinese into their own polities and weaken their economic grip. The growing importance of Southeast Asian goodwill to China's foreign policy prompted a new line, whereby overseas Chinese were encouraged to acquiesce to Southeast Asian nationalist aims without appealing to Peking for protection. China gradually began to distance itself from the several million persons of Chinese descent and even to forgo much of the overseas Chinese contribution to China's economy.[20]

Since Nehru was also the principal architect of India's foreign policies at the time, this view prevailed and would remain dominant until the 1980s, when Rajiv Gandhi came to power. Gandhi's tenure as prime minister marked the beginning of a rethinking of a range of policies that had become entrenched over the previous few decades. The changing attitude toward the diaspora was reflected in the stark contrast between India's lack of response to the 1972 Ugandan crisis, in which almost all people of Indian origin (about 70,000) were expelled from that country following a coup that brought Idi Amin to power, and its more vociferous reaction to the 1986 Fiji crisis, when Indo-Fijians were ousted from government in the aftermath of a military coup, leading to an exodus of Indo-Fijians from the country. In the latter case, the Indian government pressed for the isolation of the Fijian government in various international fora.

Additionally, the then-prevailing wisdom in India paid little attention to international trade. As a result, the importance of leveraging its diaspora for overseas trade networks was simply ignored early on. This is an important reason why Indians in East Africa and Hong Kong were not courted by the Indian government and business, despite the potential payoffs. India's fear of the outside world was reflected not only in its policies toward international trade and foreign direct investment (FDI) but also in its apathy (bordering on resentment) toward its more successful diaspora (especially in the West). Since the policy changes of the 1990s, there has been a transformation of the ideological climate in India. Its growing economic confidence, and the success of the diaspora, especially in the United States, has instilled much greater self-confidence vis-à-vis

[20] G. William Skinner, "Overseas Chinese in Southeast Asia," *The Annals of the American Academy of Political and Social Science* 321, no. 1 (1959): 136–47.

both the international community and the diaspora. The resulting lack of defensiveness has been an important reason for the growing links and stronger bonds between India and its diaspora. Nowhere has this been more manifest than in the case of the Indian diaspora in the United States.

THE INDIAN DIASPORA'S SOFT POWER: INDO-U.S. RELATIONS

"In the diffuse system of American politics, an effective lobbying apparatus acts as a magnifying glass. A narrow electoral beam, properly focused, can ignite a blaze of influence. The Poles and the Jews were both expert political arsonists."[21] With these dramatic (and contentious) words, Martin Weil offers one perspective on the impact of Jewish and Polish Americans on American foreign policy in the 1940s and the tactics deployed by these groups to achieve their goals. He highlights how Polish Catholic voters and activists pushed for a hard-line anti-Russian, anti-Communist stance as World War II came to an end. The Jews, meanwhile, not only demanded political support for a Jewish state, but also used their extensive connections and influence to run their own clandestine operations in support of Israeli military action against British-backed Arabs in the 1940s. More recently, Yossi Shain argues that the legitimacy of "multiculturalism, when official America no longer imposes cultural assimilation upon its members," combined with a polity built on "political rather than ethnic criteria for inclusion and loyalty," has made members of diasporas in the United States freer to pursue transnational political ties.[22] But just as the country of origin can manipulate the diaspora, so, too, can the country of settlement. As Shain concludes, "the vulnerability of diasporas to the charge of dual loyalty is a lever that either home or host country can use to motivate or stymie diaspora political activity." Thus, diasporas "may function as pawns used to send messages between the United States and their native countries."[23]

Studies on the factors driving American foreign policy-making concur that influence over American foreign policy requires a combination of an electoral threat, a lobbying apparatus, and a successful appeal to the country's national interests and American symbols and values, such as democracy and freedom.[24] Does the Indian American community

[21] Martin Weil, "Can the Blacks Do for Africa What the Jews Did for Israel," *Foreign Policy* 15 (1974): 109–30, 117.
[22] Yossi Shain, "Ethnic Diasporas and U.S. Foreign Policy," *Political Science Quarterly* 109, no. 5 (winter 1994–1995), 812.
[23] Ibid., 815.
[24] See Weill (1974), 109–30; Samuel Huntington, "The Erosion of American National Interests," *Foreign Affairs* 76, no. 5 (1997); and Tony Smith, *Foreign Attachments: The*

meet these criteria? As you saw in chapter 3, Indian migration to the United States stands out in its exceptional nature. The point is not just that it is an outlier among immigrant groups, but that its success has been achieved within a single generation. The stylized story of immigrants entering the United States typically involves relatively poor and uneducated individuals coming to the country and gradually working their way up the socioeconomic ladder over several generations. The great waves of migrants from Ireland and Italy in the late nineteenth century, and the more recent wave of migration from Mexico and Central America, are often cited as archetypal examples of this phenomenon. However, in the case of Indian Americans in the United States, the triple combination of economic success in the country of residence, their temporal proximity, and their close links with Indian elites, gives them the *ability*, *willingness*, and *access to mechanisms* to influence policies in the countries of origin and settlement.

The influence of the Indian American diaspora on Indo-U.S. relations should be placed within the historical context of bilateral relations between the United States and India. Both the tenor and strategic importance of this volatile relationship have fluctuated over time—usually in tandem—and can broadly be divided into three periods: (1) between India's independence and the late 1960s, when the relationship was cautiously amiable and of moderate strategic importance to both countries; (2) between the early 1970s and the end of the Cold War, when the relationship was estranged and was of minimal strategic importance to both countries; and (3) from the early 1990s through the present, when the relationship has become both significantly deeper and broader and stands on a foundation of common (but by no means identical) economic and security interests.

The reasons for the closer relations between the two countries since the early 1990s are certainly overdetermined: the end of the Cold War and the demise of the Soviet Union, threats from Al Qaida and Islamic terrorism, the rise of China, India's economic opening and the role of business in both countries, and the rise of the pro-U.S. Bharatiya Janata Party (BJP) in India have all played a role. Consequently, isolating the role of the diaspora, independent of these other factors, is simply not possible. Nonetheless, I will argue that the growing affluence and visibility of the Indian American community in the United States, together with the strength of its bonds with India, has led it to play an influential bridging role in persuading both U.S. and Indian elites on common interests between the two countries.

Power of Ethnic Groups in the Making of American Foreign Policy (Cambridge, MA: Harvard University Press, 2000).

The Diaspora's Mobilization Post-1990: Pushing on an Open Door?

Not surprisingly, the changing nature and import of Indo-U.S. relations over the past several decades has affected the Indian American diaspora's ability to influence bilateral ties. Prior to the early 1990s—when bilateral relations were characterized by apathy or antipathy—the diaspora's influence on U.S. foreign policy was circumscribed both by its own limitations as well as by the exogenous constraint of estranged relations between the United States and India. As former U.S. Secretary of State Madeleine Albright remarked, "There really was a sense among U.S. policymakers during the Cold War that they [Indian Americans] weren't a part of our team."[25] Furthermore, given India's minimal importance to U.S. strategic interests, as a former co-chair of the India Caucus remarked, "There was virtually no recognition of the Indian-American community amongst the United States foreign policymaking elites until the 1980s."[26]

The pendulum in relations between the two countries began to swing the other way in the mid-1980s, when Rajiv Gandhi became prime minister. He was less beholden to the shibboleths of the past and began to rethink India's economic and foreign policies. His first visit to the United States in 1985 saw the beginnings of the identification of the Indian American diaspora as a potentially valuable bridge-builder between the two countries. In a speech at a state dinner held in Rajiv Gandhi's honor, President Ronald Reagan proposed "a toast to Indo-American friendship. Perhaps your most precious gift to us has been the many Indians who have become proud citizens of our country . . . they embody the human bond that is between us."[27]

Since the early 1990s, the diaspora's capability to influence Indo-U.S. relations increased for two principal reasons. First, given the rising stakes and growing optimism underlying bilateral relations, Indian Americans had more to gain instrumentally from mobilizing. Earlier, there were limited instrumental gains for the diaspora from mobilization, since the two countries held little strategic significance for one another. Second, the size and economic clout of the Indian American community increased tremendously in this period. The diaspora's size grew sharply, with the number of Indian-born residents in the United States growing from less than thirteen thousand in 1960 to 206,087 in 1980 to nearly 1.5 million in 2007 (nearly 2.8 million if one includes the second generation). Its recent vintage (by 2006, nearly 70 percent of the Indian-born U.S. population

[25] Interview by Manik Suri, October 12, 2004, Washington, DC. I am grateful to Manik Suri for sharing with me interview materials that have been used in this section.
[26] Jim McDermott (US Congressman and former co-chair of India Caucus), phone interview by Manik Suri, November 18, 2004.
[27] Joy Cherian, *Our Relay Race* (New York: University Press of America, 1997), 16.

had arrived after 1990) suggests that it has closer ties to India—in the chronological sense at the very least. As described earlier, this group is also unusually educated (table 7.1), with a very large fraction (76 percent) in the working age group of 25–64. Among immigrant groups (and indeed even compared to the U.S.-born population), this group is an outlier in terms of its education and wealth—the traditional parameters of influence. Furthermore, Indian Americans are less assimilated in the mainstream than most other immigrant groups in the country. Indian immigrants to the United States score below the overall average in an "assimilation index" compiled by Vigdor. While Indian-origin immigrants show above-average levels of economic assimilation, they (along with emigrants from China) show the greatest degree of cultural distinction from native-born Americans.[28]

In the past two decades, the Indian American community has become increasingly visible within the United States. Its members have achieved professional success in a variety of fields, ranging from information technology and medicine to management and finance. Concurrent with their rising socioeconomic status, Indian Americans are becoming increasingly politically mobilized, evidenced by their significant financial contributions to recent political campaigns, the growing size of Indian American political organizations, and (to a lesser extent) a rising number of Indian American political candidates. Furthermore, Indian Americans have also become increasingly prominent in elite American business circles—taking on senior management positions in American firms, becoming key players in U.S. financial markets, and contributing a disproportionate number of entrepreneurs to drive innovation in the United States.

The rise of the Indian American community in the United States has fortuitously coincided with major changes in the geopolitical context. As a result, both countries' governments have been more willing to engage with this community, as bilateral relations become more strategically important; consequently, the diaspora has been able to "push on an already-open door." In all this, as former U.S. Assistant Secretary of State for South Asian Affairs Karl Inderfurth put it, "Indian Americans have unquestionably influenced the development of Indo-U.S. relations."[29]

One mechanism of influence has been the Congressional Caucus on India, established in 1993. The establishment of this body is widely attributed to the efforts of a small group of members of the Indian American Forum for Political Education (IAFPE), who as staffers to key policymakers convinced these officials of the importance of forming a congressional

[28] Jacob L. Vigdor, "Measuring Immigrant Assimilation in the United States," Manhattan Institute, Civic Report No. 53 (May 2008).
[29] Interview by Manik Suri, November 12, 2004, Washington, DC.

TABLE 7.1
Education Attainment of Foreign-Born Population in the United States,
Age 25 and Over, 2000

Percent	Africa	Asia	Europe	Latin America	India
Bachelor's degree	24.3	25.5	14.7	5.7	31.1
Graduate or professional degree	18.3	17.7	14.5	3.8	38.0

Source: U.S. Census, 2000.

caucus on India.[30] Indeed, one of the cofounders of the Caucus, Congressman Jim McDermott (D-WA), acknowledges that when "Congressman Frank Pallone and I started the Congressional Caucus on India and Indian Americans . . . Indian Americans on our staff were largely responsible for the launch [of the caucus]."[31] The formation of the Congressional India Caucus was hailed as a milestone in Indo-U.S. relations, and over time it emerged as the largest country caucus in Congress (see table 7.2).[32] This has led one Indian American political leader to call it "the biggest single thing the Indian American community has done to affect the U.S. political system."[33]

A former senior Congressional staffer has noted that the caucus is "more a cheerleading organization than a serious policy oriented adjunct to Congressional work" with at least some members regarding it "as an opportunity to shake down the Indian American community for political donations."[34] Nonetheless, the caucus has been a useful coordinating mechanism in promoting Indo-U.S. relations in a number of instances. As mentioned earlier, the formation of the India Caucus in the House of Representatives was initiated by strong lobbying from Indian Americans. While the idea for a Friends of India Caucus in the Senate was considered

[30] Specifically, the concept of a Congressional India Caucus was proposed by an Indian American congressional staffer, Kapil Sharma, who also conducted much of the initial lobbying while working for Congressman Frank Pallone (D-NJ) representing the district with the heaviest concentration of Indian Americans in the United States. Amberish Diwanji, "The India Caucus Still Has a Long Distance to Go," *Rediff,* September 18, 2000.

[31] Jim McDermott (US Congressman and former co-chair of India Caucus), phone interview by Manik Suri, November 18, 2004.

[32] US-India Friendship.net, "Congressional Caucus on India and Indian Americans," available at http://www.usindiafriendship.net/congress1/housecaucus/caucusonindia.htm.

[33] Christopher Dumm (former Executive Director, India Abroad Center for Political Awareness), interview by Manik Suri, August 13, 2004, Washington, DC.

[34] Robert Hathaway, quoted in "Aziz Haniffa Reports on the First Conference to Gauge the Group's Effectiveness," *India Abroad,* May 6, 2005, A6.

TABLE 7.2
Congressional Country Caucuses

Country	Number of Members	Partisan Breakdown	Year Founded
Armenia	157	107 Democrats, 50 Republicans	1995
China	34	9 Democrats, 25 Republicans	2005
Greece	140	98 Democrats, 42 Republicans	1996
India	176	115 Democrats, 61 Republicans	1993
Israel	n/a	50 Republicans	n/a
Mexico	28	15 Democrats, 13 Republicans	2003
Pakistan	72	39 Democrats, 33 Republicans	2004
Turkey	77	41 Democrats, 36 Republicans	2001

n/a = not available. Data valid as of May 2008.

by U.S. policymakers for some time before its creation in March 2004, the Indian American community played a key role—lobbying key senators in states with high concentrations of Indian American votes (notably New York, Texas, and California) to build a critical mass of support for the India Caucus. As one Indian American leader who was involved with the process notes, "you had 36 Senators join, mostly pooled in by members of the Indian American community."[35]

Another relevant example is the diaspora's role in encouraging then President Bill Clinton's trip to India in December 2000, an event widely seen as a significant step in improving Indo-U.S. relations.[36] In this instance, once again, the trip would likely have taken place even absent pressure from Indian Americans, given the many evident strategic reasons

[35] Sanjay Puri (Chairman, US–India Political Action Committee), interview by Manik Suri, August 13, 2004, Washington, DC. Tellingly, the formation of the Senate Caucus was announced by Senator Joe Cornyn (R-TX) at the Second Annual Capitol Hill Gala Dinner of the American Association of Physicians of Indian Origin (AAPI), a national organization representing the affluent Indian American physician community. At the dinner, the Indian Ambassador to the United States, Lalit Mansingh, recognized the key role played by the diaspora in lobbying crucial congressmen: "I have to commend all the Indian leaders of the Indian American community that finally made this happen." Aziz Haniffa, "US Senate India Caucus," US–India Friendship.net, March 31, 2004.

[36] Embassy of the United States of America, *Report on the Official Visit of Prime Minister Atal Bihari Vajpayee to the United States*, September 13–17, 2000.

for Clinton to go, but the pressure accelerated the timetable. Senior policymakers within the Clinton administration acknowledged the significant role played by Indian Americans in shaping the president's official visit to India. As former Secretary of State Madeleine Albright remarked, "As people were getting ready for Clinton's trip to India, Indian Americans were very important in working with President Clinton to change our attitudes about going to India . . . it was a deliberate effort."[37] By exerting pressure on both congresspeople and executive decision makers, Indian Americans helped to secure President Clinton's trip to India.

The Indian American community has also sought to strengthen Indo-U.S. relations by impeding the passage of policies that they believe would undermine relations between the United States and India. This influence was manifest, for instance, in the wake of the 1998 nuclear tests, when the U.S. government imposed a range of sanctions on India. The Indian American community responded with a targeted mobilization, aimed at its most influential supporters in Congress, to reduce the severity of these punitive measures. They were particularly successful in influencing Senator Jesse Helms (R-NC), then chairman of the U.S. Senate Foreign Relations Committee, and Senator Sam Brownback (R-KS), chairman of the Senate Foreign Relations Subcommittee on South Asia.

The Indian American community played a similar role in shaping the U.S. response to the terrorist attack against the Indian Parliament in 2001. In the wake of the attack, Indian Americans lobbied lawmakers for an amendment to the U.S. Congress's $3 billion aid package to Pakistan that pressured the country to stop Islamic militants from crossing into India. The newly formed U.S.-India Political Action Committee (USINPAC) led the effort to pressure Congressman Gary Ackerman (D-NY), then co-chairman of the India Caucus, and other senior members of the India Caucus to sponsor an amendment to the aid package which obligated the U.S. president to annually report on the Pakistani government's anti-terrorism initiatives.[38]

Beginning in the mid-1990s, the Indian government sought to persuade the United States to engage in high-technology transfers with India, yet these initiatives were stalled by the United States' unwillingness to

[37] Madeleine Albright (former U.S. Secretary of State), interview by Manik Suri, October 12, 2004, Washington, DC.

[38] Specifically, the amendment required that for the next two years, the president must prepare and transmit to Congress a report describing the extent to which the government of Pakistan closed all known terrorist training camps operating in Pakistan and Pakistan-held Kashmir, has established serious and identifiable measures to prohibit the infiltration of Islamic extremists across the Line of Control into India, and has ceased the transfer of weapons of mass destruction, including any associated technologies, to any third country or terrorist organization.

negotiate prior to reaching an agreement with India on the issue of nuclear proliferation. Indeed, in the wake of India's 1998 nuclear tests, senior U.S. officials seemed unlikely to consider the topic of high-technology transfers at any point in the near future.[39] Members of the Indian American diaspora, particularly a group of notable scientists and businessmen, mobilized in 1999 and approached the U.S. Commerce Department to reconsider high-technology transfers to India in order to assist in the development of its space program.[40] The diaspora's efforts facilitated the opening of a dialog between Washington and New Delhi to discuss the possibility of revising U.S. export licensing policies.[41] Four years later, in September 2004, the United States and Indian governments culminated ongoing negotiations by issuing a joint statement, the "Next Steps in Strategic Partnership" (NSSP), in which the United States agreed "to make modifications to U.S. export licensing policies that will foster cooperation in commercial space programs . . . including removing the Indian Space Research Organization (ISRO) Headquarters from the Department of Commerce Entity List," thereby loosening export restrictions on numerous high-technology exports to the ISRO.[42]

The informational and reputational role of Indian Americans in senior management positions in U.S. firms was an important factor in promoting U.S. investment in India.[43] Many U.S. firms lack accurate information regarding the business climate in India, and Indian Americans in senior management are well-positioned to "boost the confidence of overseas investors about India's potential, despite its innumerable problems."[44] An analysis of 40 large services-oriented U.S. companies where an Indian American served as the chief executive officer, chief financial officer, or chief information officer revealed that more than half commenced operations in India between 1984 and 2003. As Montek Singh Ahluwalia, one of India's preeminent policy makers, put it, "It is true, NRIs gave

[39] Ajay Kuntamukkala (former Senior Advisor to Under Secretary of Commerce Kenneth Juster), interview by Manik Suri, December 14, 2004, Washington, DC.

[40] Kenneth Juster (former US Under Secretary of Commerce), interview by Manik Suri, December 14, 2004, Washington, DC.

[41] Ibid.

[42] The Department of Commerce Entity List is a "list of foreign end users involved in proliferation activities. These end users have been determined to present an unacceptable risk of diversion to developing weapons of mass destruction or the missiles used to deliver those weapons. Publishing this list puts exporters on notice of export license requirements that apply to exports to these parties." State Department Press Release, "United States–India Joint Statement on Next Steps in Strategic Partnership," September 17, 2004, available at http://www.state.gov/r/pa/prs/ps/2004/36290.htm (accessed February 4, 2005).

[43] For an example of a well-publicized article, see Amit Shankardass, "Ask the Expert," *CIO Magazine*, September 24, 2003.

[44] Devesh Kapur, "The Causes and Consequences of India's IT Boom," *India Review* 1, no. 2 (April 2002): 99.

[business investment] a push. I've had very senior Americans in U.S. corporations, when I ask them why they became more aggressive in India, point to one of their top guys who was Indian American and say 'he was really sold.'"[45]

To be sure, the activities of this group were more important in lowering the *initial* reluctance of U.S. firms to invest in India; after that, financial returns were what mattered. But by promoting the U.S. business community's engagement in India, the diaspora's activities in the private sector have allowed the much larger and more powerful U.S. business community (and groups such as the U.S.-India Business Council) to become a lobbying force for strengthening relations between the two countries; thus, the diaspora's activities have indirectly exerted influence on policy-makers.

The U.S.-India nuclear deal offers a good example of the intermediary role of the diaspora (and its limitations). The Indian American community's efforts were important in pushing the deal forward, especially in the U.S. Congress, where it was nearly derailed by anti-proliferation skeptics. Indeed, one account has referred to this community as "India's U.S.-based lobby" and "the only lobby in Washington likely to acquire the strength of the Israel lobby."[46] That the deal went through despite the opposition of many members of the U.S. foreign policy establishment (mainly on nonproliferation grounds but also those anxious to avoid offending China and Pakistan) may seem to vindicate the power of the Indian American lobby.

However, such an explanation ignores the many other powerful forces at work in support of the deal, beginning, first of all, with President George W. Bush, who saw this deal and its concomitant consequences for U.S.-India relations as one of his legacies. Powerful commercial interests, ranging from the U.S.-India Business Council and the U.S. Chamber of Commerce to large corporations, such as General Electric and Westinghouse, that produce nuclear reactors and saw enormous sales potential for these products, were also strong supporters. Subsequently, when the Indian American lobby tried to put in riders in the U.S. aid bill for Pakistan and the Executive Branch opposed it, the limits of its influence became all too apparent.

If direct lobbying alone matters, then any group with money can sway U.S. foreign policies. However, the influence of the Indian American community has resulted from more than just its financial clout. It enjoys a considerable degree of "network power," exercised as much by informal

[45] Montek Singh Ahluwalia (Deputy Chairman of the Indian Planning Commission), interview by Manik Suri, August 23, 2004, New Delhi.

[46] John Newhouse, "Diplomacy, Inc. The Influence of Lobbies on U.S. Foreign Policy," *Foreign Affairs*, May/June 2009.

and personalized channels as by formal institutional mechanisms, a consequence of its overrepresentation in key power nodes—particularly U.S. business—whose interests play an important role in influencing American foreign policy. These nodes are akin to "structural holes," and filling them gives this community a comparative advantage.[47] Within U.S. business circles, key influence nodes include major management consulting firms, key financial institutions, and top-tier business schools, in addition to senior management and entrepreneurs. Indian Americans are disproportionately overrepresented in each of these nodes.

In India, the diaspora's deep "network power" is largely a consequence of personal relationships and professional ties with Indian elites in business and media and key Indian policymakers. However, since the Indian diaspora in the United States is largely drawn from upper-caste elites, its networks with the new Indian political elites, who are largely drawn from lower-caste parties, are much more limited. Additionally, the very source of the diaspora's network power in the United States—its significant presence in U.S. business and finance—is a liability with many leftist politicians in India, especially the Communists. As mentioned, the nuclear deal serves as an illustrative example. Although the BJP also opposed the nuclear deal, the reason was at least in part simply to deny the Congress any victory; the Communists, however, were less opposed to the intrinsic merits of the deal than the possible strategic implications of closer Indo-U.S. ties. With the Congress-led ruling coalition relying on their support to stay in power, the Communists effectively had veto power on the deal. For reasons mentioned earlier, the diaspora's Indian network power does not extend into this group. (The few diaspora members who did have access to this group—especially in nongovernment organizations (NGOs) and academia—were themselves opposed to the deal.)

The diaspora's overall influence on Indo-U.S. relations, although perceptible, should not be exaggerated. It does not set the policymaking agenda; its influence has been on the pace rather than the direction of change. To put it differently, it does not have its hands on the steering wheel, but its feet can press on the accelerator or the brakes. The varying impact of the diaspora on bilateral relations can be explained as a function of the nature of its "network power" in both countries: it has exerted greatest influence where its representation in key nodes has been significant and limited influence in other nodes, where its representation has been minimal. Overall, the diaspora's influence on bilateral relations can perhaps best be characterized as facilitative rather than causal, acting at

[47] Ronald S. Burt, *Structural Holes: The Social Structure of Competition* (Cambridge, MA: Harvard University Press, 1992). In Burt's model, a "structural hole" represents a gap between two entities with complementary resources. An entrepreneur, who connects the two, fills the gap and gains competitive advantage.

times as a catalyst and at others as a force multiplier; impacting the pace rather than the direction of Indo-U.S. relations over the past two decades.

THE INDIAN DIASPORA: A SOFT UNDERBELLY?

Diasporas have long been known to engage in long-distance nationalism. Indeed, nationalism as a modern phenomenon of imagined communities is one that has often grown in the minds of diasporic elites. Diasporic identities range from the cosmopolitan to the virulent ethnic nationalist. It should therefore not be surprising that the actions of a diaspora toward the country of origin manifest themselves in complex ways.

The role of diasporas in ethnic violence and civil wars in the country of origin has drawn particular attention given its serious implications. The charge that a diaspora has supported a hard-line ultranationalist group in the country of origin is a familiar one. Does India also face similar threats from its diaspora? While I have just argued that the diaspora is a key component of India's soft power, could it also constrict India's strategic space? The large number of Indians (approximately three and half million) working in the Middle East represent a key element of India's soft power in that region. But they are also hostage to any adverse events in the region—as was the case in the 1991 Gulf Crisis, the 2003 Iraq War, and the 2006 Lebanese Crisis. Consequently, these crises had serious implications for Indian foreign policy. The Iraqi invasion of Kuwait in 1991 stranded very large numbers of Indian workers, who had to be evacuated. The subsequent loss of remittances, plus the substantial costs of evacuation, contributed to India's balance of payments crisis. During the 2005 Lebanese Crisis, the Indian government suddenly realized that that there were many Indians in Lebanon, including numerous farmers. The Indian Navy sent three ships to Beirut to evacuate them to Larcana and then transported back to India on special flights.

The treatment of Indian workers overseas and calculated violence directed against them (such as hostage takings in Iraq or killings in Afghanistan) certainly pose episodic challenges to Indian diplomats. However, I posit that the *systemic* challenges are caused by three different streams of the Indian diaspora: those supporting separatist movements, majoritarian ultranationalists, and "beached diasporas" stuck in neighboring countries. It is these three streams that I turn to next.

Separatist Diasporas

Separatist groups that (for whatever reason) want to challenge the authority of the Indian state have relied to a considerable extent on support from the ethnonationalism of their diasporas. There is an array of diasporic groups that have been, and continue to be, involved in a range of insurgencies in India.[48] India's Northeast has been wracked by insurgencies for nearly a half-century, and the leaderships of the numerous insurgent groups have operated from India's neighborhood (Bhutan, Bangladesh, Myanmar, Pakistan, and Thailand).

During the 1980s, conflicts within Punjab led elements of the Sikh diaspora (whose homeland is primarily concentrated in that state) to actively support armed separatist groups. Several Sikh groups in Canada, the United Kingdom, and the United States provided men and money to the Khalistan movement, particularly after Operation Bluestar and the massacres that followed the assassination of Mrs. Gandhi. Some of the most hardline militants fled to Pakistan, which then actively supported their violent campaign. The involvement of Sikh militants based in Canada in the bombing of an Air India flight in 1985, which killed all 329 people aboard, cast a pall on Indo-Canadian relations. In an apparent bid to limit civil damages, Canada concealed a key report from the Indian government on the 1985 bombing, which suggested that the plot was "planned and orchestrated" entirely in the country.[49]

Despite the fact that Indians are the third largest immigrant group in Canada (after the United Kingdom and China),[50] many of whom have also done well in that country's politics (perhaps more than in any other industrialized country), relations between the two countries have been less strong than would otherwise have been warranted, offering contrasting effects of the Indian diaspora based in Canada and the United States on relations between these countries and India. There are several explanations for this difference: the dominance of one community in the Indian immigrant population in Canada (almost half by some estimates), some of whose members have been estranged from India; the spatial concentration of this community in one province (British Columbia) and its electoral implications; and their lower education and income (relative to the community in the United States), with concomitant weaker economic links to India.[51] While external support for the most lethal separatist movement and insurgency in India—in Kashmir—has come from

---

[48] Chapter 8 gives more details about these groups.

[49] CBC News, "Mulroney Adviser Tried to Hide Air India Bombing Facts, Memos Suggest," 2009, available at http://www.cbc.ca/canada/story/2009/05/08/air-india.html.

[50] India immigrants accounted for 7.2 percent of the immigrant population in 2006. Source: Statistics Canada, available at http://www40.statcan.gc.ca/l01/cst01/demo24a-eng.htm.

[51] Emerging intergenerational conflicts may also be playing a role. See Timothy Taylor, "Showdown on Scott Road," *The Walrus*, September 2009, available at http://www.walrus magazine.com/articles/2009.09-religion-sikh-youth-daaku-Indo-Canadian-timothy-taylor/.

Pakistan, overseas Kashmiri Muslim groups (particularly in the United Kingdom) have also been active supporters of the separatist movement there. In the wake of the communal pogrom in Gujarat, news reports indicate that Lashkar-e-Taiba stepped up recruitment among Indian expatriates in Kuwait and Saudi Arabia, who appear to have been "central to a welter of terrorist attacks that took place in India through 2003."[52] Investigations into the Students Islamic Movement of India (SIMI) and the Indian Mujahideen (both of who have been implicated in terrorist attacks within India) indicate that they have been "fed and watered by transnational financial networks: networks linked both to diasporic Islamists living in west Asia and Pakistan-based organisations like the Lashkar."[53]

As I note in the next chapter, support from overseas for groups in India who are party to violence also comes from the majoritarian community. The difference, however, is that the latter is directed against minority groups in Indian society, while the former is directed against the Indian state. The reason is obvious: state oppression and egregious miscarriages of justice in India (such as the 1984 anti-Sikh and 2002 anti-Muslim riots) are not directed against the majority community and can result in some members of the affected communities to seek recourse from abroad.

Majoritarian Ultranationalists

The growth of Hindu nationalism in India in the 1980s and 1990s gave rise to charges that the Indian diaspora (particularly those based in Western countries) was supporting Hindu militant groups implicated in anti-Muslim violence within India. The anti-Muslim violence in the state of Gujarat in 2002 led to further charges that diasporic philanthropy has been financing the groups responsible for the violence, particularly those groups linked with the Sangh Parivar.

The next chapter examines the extent and intensity of support for militant Hindu right-wing groups by the Indian diaspora and the effects of this in promoting ethnic violence in India. The question became particularly urgent following the savage communal violence in Gujarat in 2002. Given the substantial international migration from that state, questions arise as to whether this is more than just a correlation. While international migration from Gujarat has been an ongoing phenomenon, spanning centuries, it began accelerating from the late nineteenth century onward, when migrants from Gujarat went to East and South Africa and

[52] Praveen Swami, op. cit.
[53] Praveen Swami, "Diaspora Cash Fed Domestic Jihad," *The Hindu*, May 8, 2009, available at http://www.hindu.com/2009/05/08/stories/2009050861131500.htm.

parts of the Gulf. After independence, and especially after the 1960s, the migrants went north, particularly to Britain and North America. Those who migrated included many of those who were forced to leave East Africa after independence. Since the 1980s, overseas Gujaratis began to cast their shadow over the state through their support of the BJP and related political and social groups. In 2002, there were unprecedented anti-Muslim riots in Gujarat, and a chorus of voices claimed that overseas Indians of Gujarati origin were implicated through their financial support for Narendra Modi, the BJP Chief Minster of Gujarat at the time.

While I examine this claim in the next chapter, I focus here on the implications of the Gujarat riots for India's foreign policy. Given the lack of accountability in India, a range of civil society actors domestically and abroad (especially in the United States and Britain) mounted a campaign to ostracize Narendra Modi as the "merchant of death" and eventually succeeded in persuading the U.S. government to refuse a visa to Modi to enter the country. This forced the Congress Party–led Indian government to criticize the denial of the visa, on the one hand, and to mollify angry Muslim countries, on the other.

Within Gujarat, these intense criticisms were cleverly turned around by Modi as an attack on Gujarati *astitva* (pride). The attacks on Modi led to a "rally around the leader" effect among Gujaratis, both in India and abroad, and in 2007 he led the BJP back to power in that state.[54] Denied permission to travel to the West, Modi began traveling to the East (China and Singapore) and Russia, cultivating business and selling his vision of the state's future. Building on an Indo-Russian agreement signed in 2000, Modi pushed through a protocol of cooperation between Gujarat and Russia's Astrakhan region (Russia's gateway to the Caspian) and pushed for Ahmedabad's sister-city link with Astrakhan.[55] The choice built upon the Gujarati diaspora's two-century-long links with that region, and it offers the prospect of the shortest trade route between India and Russia (from Okha port to Astrakhan's Olya port). The large Gujarati diaspora, one of the most entrepreneurial communities across the globe, allowed Modi to launch his own brand of commercial diplomacy on behalf of Gujarat, independent of the federal government and Ministry of External Affairs. This link between regional diasporas

[54] Christophe Jaffrelot, "Gujarat: The Meaning of Modi's Victory," *Economic and Political Weekly*, April 12, 2008, 12–17.

[55] "The Agreement between the Government of the Republic of India and the Government of the Russian Federation on the Principles of Cooperation between the Governments of the States and Union Territories of the Republic of India and the Bodies of Executive Authority of the Constitutional Entities of the Russian Federation." K. P. Nayyar, "Masks of Conquest," *The Telegraph*, December 26, 2007, available at http://www.telegraphindia.com/1071226/jsp/opinion/story_8707952.jsp.

and regional nationalism could pose an increasing challenge for Indian foreign policy.

Beached Diasporas

The foreign policy and international security implications of "beached diasporas"—people left outside the borders of their titular states—were highlighted by King and Melvin in the case of the successor states of the former Soviet Union.[56] Diasporic identity and the feelings of members of a "kin state" toward their co-ethnics in other countries are constructed and varied according to political exigencies. The policies of Russia, Ukraine, and Kazakhstan to reach out to their diasporas since 1991 have been largely driven by the compulsions of domestic politics and as a means to coalesce nationalist sentiment. For example, in Russia "the discovery— or, more accurately, the invention—of a solidly and self-consciously 'Russian' ethnic community beyond the new Russia's borders became the basis for developing a consensus about Russia's new identity."[57] Shortly after independence, Kazakhstan began encouraging diaspora "return" as a way to address the disadvantageous demographic position of ethnic Kazakhs within their own republic. By the late 1990s, as the demographic balance began to look more favorable after the out-migration of Russians, Kazakhstani policy toward the diaspora turned lukewarm, demonstrating that just as diasporas use states, they themselves are used by governments as political resources whenever they are useful (as overseas Italians were to Mussolini).

As with the demise of the Soviet Union, the breakdown of the British Empire left many Indian migrants "beached" all over the world, but especially in India's neighborhood. A good example is the case of Indian Tamil workers who went as indentured labor to the Caribbean, Malaya, Burma, Ceylon (now Sri Lanka), and Fiji. In the case of Ceylon, the problems began to fester with the enactment of citizenship laws by that country in 1948 and 1949, laws that disenfranchised nearly 900,000 people, mainly descendents of Indian Tamils who had gone to Ceylon as indentured labor in the latter half of the nineteenth century. Between 1947 and 1963, periodic discussions between Ceylon and India failed. While the Ceylon government insisted that India accept all rejected persons, arguing that they had at one point been its citizens, India rejected that view, claiming that they were "really and in fact the residents of Ceylon."[58] At the same time, Ceylon argued that while this was a domestic

---

[56] Charles King and Neil J. Melvin, "Diaspora Politics: Ethnic Linkages, Foreign Policy, and Security in Eurasia," *International Security* 24, no. 3 (1999): 108–38.

[57] King and Melvin, 120.

[58] Jawaharlal Nehru, March 31, 1955, Lok Sabha Debates, Part II, 2 (1955), col. 3904.

issue, the Indian government's cooperation was needed for repatriation. The Indian government accepted Ceylon's right to pass any citizenship legislation, disclaiming any legal responsibility for this group and professing merely a "sentimental" interest in them because of their Indian origin.[59] Nehru was opposed to "forced repatriation," fearing that it would create a precedent for other overseas Indian communities.

Matters came to a head when, in 1963, only 134,187 people of Indian origin qualified as citizens of Ceylon.[60] After Nehru's death, the Sirimavo-Shastri Pact of 1964 began the process of resolving the stateless question. The agreement called for the repatriation of 525,000 persons together with their natural increase to India and the absorption of 300,000 as citizens of Ceylon. The two sides agreed to negotiate the fate of the remaining 150,000 at a later date. Indian and Sri Lanka Tamils constituted 15.2 and 11.3 percent of Sri Lanka's population in 1931 and 11.6 and 11.2 percent in 1971. By 1981, the former had dropped to 5.5 percent (a decline of more than 50 percent in a decade), largely because of repatriation to India and in some cases because people declared themselves as Sri Lankan Tamils (which increased to 12.7 percent of the general population). Last, in October 2003, the Sri Lankan Parliament passed the "Grant of Citizenship to Persons of Indian Origin Act," which in principle offered all stateless persons of Indian origin who had lived in Sri Lanka since October 30, 1964, and their descendants (estimated at 300,000) Sri Lankan citizenship.

The status of "Persons of Indian Origin" in Sri Lanka has been a perennial irritant between the two countries. The 1964 agreement ran aground because a new government came into power in Ceylon in 1965; and in 1967 the Dravida Munnetra Kazhagam (DMK), a regional party which had been a vociferous opponent of the pact, came into power in a landslide victory in Tamil Nadu. Since that time, regional parties have been in power in Tamil Nadu, and the DMK in particular (along with some other smaller chauvinist parties), has portrayed itself as the flag bearer of Tamil nationalism. National parties and the federal government have had to balance their electoral interests with larger national interests.

In the mid-1980s, a flood of refugees into India led the Indian government to use Tamil nationalism as leverage to press Sri Lanka to come to the table by providing arms and training to the Liberation Tigers of Tamil Eelam (LTTE), a militant Tamil separatist group, before the rupture with the group in 1987. India's relationship with Sri Lanka and later support for the LTTE was at least in part shaped by the treatment of people of

[59] Lok Sabha Debates, 56 (1961), col. 13. The conflicting views are evident in the various debates on the subject in Indian Parliament in the 1950s.

[60] Urmila Phadnis, "The Indo-Ceylon Pact and the 'Stateless' Indians in Ceylon," *Asian Survey* 7, no. 4 (April 1967): 226–36.

Indian origin, principally Tamilians, by that country.[61] When fighting flared up again in 2006, the Tamil Nadu Chief Minister M. Karunanidhi said, "Our brethren, our own race, are being killed, hunted down and victimised in Sri Lanka. This is no pleasant to news to us. It is like bombarding us with missiles. It is because of certain circumstances that we have to bear this sad news."[62] Subsequently in 2009, as the Sri Lankan army was crushing the LTTE, with elections looming and Tamil Nadu's thirty-nine parliamentary seats vital for the government, India's foreign policy mandarins were forced to spend vital time in Colombo, despite the vital interests at stake in the looming crisis in Afghanistan and Pakistan. And by late 2009, there were reports that "out of work" LTTE mercenaries were training India's Maoist rebels in guerilla warfare. The diaspora had come home.

Similar to the Sri Lankan case, Indians (again largely of Tamil origin) migrated to Malaya as indentured laborers in the late nineteenth century. After Malaysia achieved independence, the country's dominant Malaya polity instituted a series of ethnically discriminatory policies, and even as the country became an enviable economic role model, the Indian-origin minority languished as the poorest underclass. When people of Indian ethnicity protested against their ill treatment in 2007, the ensuing police action (beating up the supporters of the Hindu Rights Action Force), brought protests again from Karunanidhi.

The Indian high commissioner in Kuala Lumpur met with Malaysian officials to assert that New Delhi "remains deeply solicitous for the welfare of people of Indian origin living abroad."[63] His counterpart in India was also quietly summoned. India's external affairs minister, Pranab Mukherjee, initially gave a diplomatic statement in the Lok Sabha. But before he could give an identical statement in the Rajya Sabha, Malaysia's justice minister, Nazri Aziz, attacked Karunanidhi's efforts to champion the cause of the Malaysian Tamils: "This is Malaysia, not Tamil Nadu," Aziz said, "This has got nothing to do with him . . . lay off. His place is in Tamil Nadu, not Malaysia. He should worry about his own state. His own state has got problems." Since a key member of the ruling

[61] J. N. Dixit, then India's high commissioner in Colombo, reportedly informed the Sri Lankan president that "India would not watch idly Tamil civilians being oppressed by Sri Lanka's security forces in Jaffna or in the eastern province." J. N. Dixit, *Assignment Colombo* (New Delhi: Konark Publishers, 1998).

[62] "Vaiko's Visit Pre-empted Solution to Sri Lankan Tamil Issue," *The Hindu*, August 20, 2006, available at http://www.hindu.com/2006/08/20/stories/2006082013360100.htm. At the time, the DMK was a coalition parter in the federal government in Delhi and held several lucrative ministerial portfolios.

[63] Special correspondent, "Manmohan Voices Concern over Unrest in Malaysia," *The Hindu*, December 1, 2007, available at http://www.hinduonnet.com/2007/12/01/stories/2007120155721400.htm.

United Progressive Alliance coalition had been given a dressing down, the Indian external affairs minister now had to make a tougher statement, adding, "Certain observations have been made against a highly respected Indian leader, Dr. K. [*sic*] Karunanidhi, in this context. We are in touch with the Malaysian authorities and the matter is being taken up." But in being forced to go public, this action merely exposed the limits rather than the effectiveness of India's options. India's relations with Malaysia had been delicate during the Mahathir era, with Malaysia opposing India's attempts to join various East Asian fora. In the end, the U.S. Commission on International Religious Freedom (USCIRF) issued a statement in support of Malaysian Indians that was stronger than anything New Delhi was prepared to say.

If the power of national parties in India wanes, regional parties, particularly those with strong subnationalist roots, will have greater sway in foreign policy decisions on issues affecting that region's diaspora; this is especially true if these regional parties form part of the coalition government at the Center. There is a corresponding risk that India's national interest may well become hostage to regional pressures.

Conclusion

If, as appears likely, international migration from India increases in the next few decades, how will these greater levels of migration (flows) and a larger diaspora (stock) affect Indian foreign policy? This chapter argues that the principal determinants of the impact will be the nature of insertion of the diaspora in host countries and factors endogenous to India, in particular the cleavages and extent of fragmentation in Indian politics.

In the world's established industrialized democracies, the Indian diaspora has strong links to India's elites, enjoys full citizenship rights, and is also in a privileged economic position in those countries. In these countries, but especially in the Anglo-Saxon countries (where this group of the Indian diaspora is concentrated and is of more recent vintage), the diaspora is likely to facilitate Indian foreign policy goals in a unique role as a "bridging power" that "provides the essential connective tissue, the connectivity, that a fragmenting world requires."[64] In sharp contrast, there is another group of countries—concentrated in the Middle East and the Gulf—where the Indian diaspora, while also of relatively recent vintage, has much more limited rights and forms a mix of an economic

[64] Sunil Khilnani, "India as a Bridging Power," in *India as a New Global Leader* (London: Foreign Policy Centre, 2005).

underclass, middle-class professionals, and businesspeople. In this case, the diaspora's role in influencing India's foreign policy will be narrower, but it is likely to continue to weave a web of ties between India and the Middle East and play a stabilizing role in the region. The third group of countries, where the Indian diaspora is of older vintage, and where citizenship rights are contested with other ethnic groups, will pose the greatest problems. These include countries in India's neighborhood ("beached diasporas") and in countries ranging from Guyana to Fiji to Malaysia. While in the first two categories of countries there is relatively little uncertainty about the status of the diaspora, this is not the case in the third group, and this uncertainty is bound to lead to unpleasant surprises and pose greater challenges to Indian foreign policy.

In 2009, a series of attacks on Indian students in Australia preoccupied India's chattering classes, forcing the Indian foreign minister to spend time on this issue with his Australian counterparts. Similarly, intrareligious conflict within the Sikh community leading to a shootout in a Vienna *gurdwara* (a Sikh temple) sparked major riots in Punjab, threatening to open up new tensions in the state. Ironically, at least some of the attackers were Austrian residents of Indian origin who had asked for asylum.[65] These incidents (as well as events in Fiji, Malaysia, and Sri Lanka) all exemplify the reality that while the diaspora could certainly leverage Indian foreign policy, it could also be distractive and impose high opportunity costs.

But the most serious challenge for India's foreign policy is the support from members of the diaspora for India's separatist movements and insurgencies. And the key to minimizing this lies within India. There is strong evidence today that the problems faced by countries with internal strife are amplified if they have substantial diasporas abroad. India's experiences support this argument, especially its treatment of minorities, be it during the 1984 anti-Sikh riots in Delhi or, more recently, in the 2002 anti-Muslim riots in Gujarat. It cannot be overemphasized that, increasingly, a country's minorities living abroad will press their claim to justice not in the country of origin but in the country of settlement. And when that happens, it is bound to adversely impact bilateral relations between the country of origin and the country of settlement.

The reality is that the more India cultivates its diaspora, the more its foreign policy becomes hostage to the well-being of its diaspora. It remains to be seen whether India's foreign policy will be influenced more by the geography that it is part of (Asia) or by countries overseas where the influential parts of its diaspora are settled (Anglo-Saxon countries).

[65] James Lamont, "Vienna Sikh Attack Sparks Punjab Riot," *Financial Times*, May 25 2009.

Civil or Uncivil Transnational Society? The Janus Face of Long-Distance Nationalism

> You ask me about that country whose details now escape me,
> I don't remember its geography, nothing of its history
> And should I visit it in memory,
> It would be as I would a past lover,
> After years, for a night, no longer restless with passion, with no
>   fear of regret.
> I have reached that age when one visits the heart merely as a
>   courtesy.
>
> —*Urdu poet Faiz Ahmed Faiz*[1]

INTRODUCTION

EARLIER IN THIS book, I presented an analytical framework for examining the impact of migration on the sending country. As I outlined in chapter 2, the political economy effects of migration can occur through four channels: the *prospect* of people leaving, their *absence, diaspora*, and *return*. In chapter 5, I examined the impact of the return channel on changing preferences and expectations. In chapter 6, I analyzed the effects of the absence channel on India's democratic tradition. In chapter 7, I shifted focus toward the *diaspora* channel, examining the impact of the Indian diaspora on India's foreign policy. This chapter continues to look at the diaspora's impact on Indian politics, but focuses on another dimension of impact: long-distance nationalism.

There is a long history of diasporas engaging in political activities in the country of origin, yet little evidence about the precise mechanisms and their impact. Indeed, one feature of the burgeoning literature on the phenomenon of "transnationalism" is the absence of rigorous empirical evidence.[2] This does not imply that the claims of this literature are necessarily

---

[1] "Sochne do," written in 1967 (in Moscow), reprinted in *Nushkhaha-e vafa* (Lahore, Pakistan: Maktaba-e Karvan), 417.

[2] For a notable exception, see Luis Eduardo Guarnizo, Alejandro Portes, and William Haller, "Assimilation and Transnationalism: Determinants of Transnational Political Action among Contemporary Migrants," *American Journal of Sociology* 108, no. 6 (2003): 1211–48.

wrong, but it does suggest that there may be a difference between the existence of this phenomenon and its relative importance.

Diasporas participate in the politics of the country of origin in a variety of ways, just as there are myriad forms of political participation in the domestic context. When President Felipe Calderón of Mexico toured the United States in early 2008, instead of meeting with the White House, Capitol Hill, and the presidential candidates, he spent time with Mexican immigrants in major U.S. cities; this move reflected the reality that Mexican migrants in the United States have become an extension of Mexico's own politics, and a Mexican politician can ill-afford to ignore them.[3] The reasons for this are manifold. In some cases, expatriates can vote. Perhaps more importantly, they influence the voting preferences of kin in the country of origin, and their influence may be amplified if they send financial remittances (which many diasporas, such as the Mexican one, do). In other cases, they return and run as candidates (or campaign for candidates if the former option is ruled out), sometimes successfully (e.g., Karzai in Afghanistan) and sometimes rather dismally (e.g., Chalabi in Iraq). Another mechanism through which a diaspora can affect the politics of the country of origin is through its influence on policy changes—in particular, on issues and areas where the diaspora has strong economic interests and if it enjoys legitimacy and points of contact with decision-making elites in the sending country, a subject I examined in chapter 4.

Additionally, diasporas can affect politics in the country of origin by way of financial contributions to parties and candidates. The impact of these contributions will depend both on their relative magnitude as well as on the groups and parties to which they are made. The general claim is that people in the diaspora have greater average incomes than those in the sending country (since one would be less likely to leave for a lower income), and this increased income gives them greater financial capacity vis-à-vis constituents in their country of origin. However, the possibility that diasporas might finance and support relatively more extremist organizations (i.e., groups or parties more prone to using violence) makes this aspect of diasporic involvement in the country of origin's politics both more significant and, potentially, more dangerous.

For a country of India's size, where nonresidents do not enjoy voting rights and international migration is a very small fraction of the resident population, direct or indirect participation in elections is unlikely to have significant consequences, with the exception of a few states (notably Gujarat, Kerala, and Punjab) where international migration is relatively

[3] James McKinley, "Mexican Leader to Visit U.S., Outside the Beltway," *New York Times*, February 9, 2008, A3.

larger.[4] Even in these cases, the effects are more influential at the local level, and their systemic impact is unlikely to be substantial.

Thus, the most significant direct political impact of the Indian diaspora on India is likely to be its engagement in "long-distance nationalism." In chapter 7, while analyzing the effects of international migration on the sending country's foreign policy, I examined one aspect of long-distance nationalism—namely, the diaspora lobbying the country of settlement on behalf of the country of origin (in that case, the Indian American diaspora and its activism in the United States). In this chapter, I examine further the nature of long-distance nationalism in the Indian context, analyzing the U.S.-based Indian diaspora's Janus-faced impact on domestic politics in India: fomenting political violence on the one hand and supporting philanthropy on the other. I first consider several theoretical explanations for why diasporas engage in long-distance nationalism, arguing that these theoretical explanations are of little help in understanding the *intensity* of the diaspora's nationalism relative to that in the country of origin, or what *form* this long-distance nationalism takes—whether ethnic or civic nationalism. Like other diasporas, Indian Americans engage in civic nationalism, ranging from lobbying the government of their adopted country on foreign policy or sending funds during a natural calamity. Yet they also distinctively support ethnic nationalism—for instance, by supporting a variety of ethnic nationalist groups in India—although to what extent they do so is a contentious issue.

I next discuss the links between the Indian diaspora and Hindu nationalism. This issue has received a great deal of attention in recent years, especially with the rise of the Bharatiya Janata Party (BJP) in Indian politics and the sharp increase in Hindu–Muslim violence in India (particularly in the decade bracketed by the destruction of the Babri Masjid in 1992 and the Gujarat riots in 2002). Much less attention has been paid, however, to support of violence by other groups of the Indian diaspora. While there are good reasons for the focus on Hindu nationalism—majoritarian violence is likely to be much more dangerous than that spawned by minority groups— violence has pernicious consequences, no matter who the sponsor.

The empirical focus in this chapter is on the U.S.-based Indian diaspora's support for Hindu extremist groups. As you will see in the following, activist groups and intellectuals have linked the diaspora to anti-Muslim violence in India. But to what extent has support from the Indian diaspora been causal, facilitative, or marginal to these developments? The evidentiary requirements are severe: one has to first demonstrate that

---

[4] At the time of writing, a bill pending in Indian Parliament would grant nonresident Indians (NRIs) voting rights. However, this privilege would not extend to members of the Indian diaspora holding foreign passports who had obtained Person of Indian Origin (PIO) cards or who had become Overseas Citizens of India (OCI).

the diaspora harbors prejudice of the sort that could provoke violence; second, that the intensity of this prejudice is strong enough that the diaspora actually acts on these prejudices; and third, that the extent of these actions are large enough to shift the status quo in India (i.e., that in the absence of financial support from the diaspora, Hindu–Muslim violence would have been significantly less intense). The last two steps of this "supply chain" require data that are exceedingly difficult to obtain. However, based on a novel survey technique presented here, one can at least better understand the first step: the degree of anti-Muslim prejudice within the U.S.-based Indian diaspora.

The key findings from the survey analysis are that while a significant minority of the U.S.-based Indian diaspora does indeed exhibit a high level of prejudice toward Muslims, this does not necessarily transfer into broad support for Hindu nationalism. In addition, there is little support for correcting historical wrongs or a uniform civil code, the pet projects of Hindu nationalism. On other issues, such as nuclear tests or affirmative action, the U.S.-based Indian diaspora is in general more liberal than public opinion within India. Thus, it would appear that contrary to the general impression, the Indian diaspora (at least that based in the United States) appears to be relatively more prone to civic than ethnic nationalism. I should emphasize that the evidence presented here cannot by itself rule out that individuals nor small groups within the diaspora may have provided funds to a specific group or individuals who have directly or indirectly instigated violence against religious minorities in India. The statistical evidence presented here is with regard to the beliefs and behavior of the broader group (the Indian diaspora in the United States) and its likely implications for the country of origin.

Additionally, I examine another face of Indian long-distance nationalism: the diaspora's support of philanthropic efforts in India. Based on the limited data available, I conclude that while there have been cases of the diaspora using the guise of philanthropy to support extremist organizations, there is no firm evidence that this is either of a relatively large magnitude or of a systemic nature. India has had, and continues to have, violence targeting minorities. The principal causes, however, are internal, and the role of the "foreign hand," whether a diasporic hand or any other, is marginal.

DIASPORAS AND LONG-DISTANCE NATIONALISM

In chapters 2 and 7, I discussed the many forms and historical cases of the engagement of diasporas in long-distance nationalism. While this engagement ranges from philanthropic to economic, the role of diasporas in ethnic violence and civil wars in the country of origin has drawn the most attention. The conventional wisdom is that diasporic nationalism is a consequence of the failure of immigrants to identify with the host society—it fills their identity "needs" in the host society primarily because of low levels of assimilation. Thus, Portes argues that the preoccupation with the country of origin is greatest among those immigrants who intend to return (e.g., political exiles and migrant laborers) and least among those immigrants who have made a long-term commitment to the host society (e.g., professionals and immigrant entrepreneurs).[5] Others argue that ethnic identity will be salient even among professionals if they experience discrimination.[6] A different view is that support for the country of origin is most deeply prevalent among assimilating ethnic, since it is the "cheapest" way for them to maintain their membership status within the immigrant community while eschewing any commitments (especially cultural practices) that might impede their upward mobility.[7] Another view argues that loss of status is a driving force behind diasporic transnational political activity. Latino males face a greater loss of status (compared to Latino women) upon migrating to the United States and consequently may be more likely to participate in political activities in the country of origin.[8] British women of Pakistani origin have greater earning power than their Pakistani husbands, upending traditional roles. In some cases, extremism (among some members of the UK-based Pakistani diaspora) may stem in part from male frustration that the old order is being subverted.[9] Salman Rushdie ruminates whether "exiles or emigrants or expatriates, are haunted by some sense of loss, some urge to reclaim." Speaking of Indian expatriates, he wonders if their "physical alienation from India almost inevitably means that we will not be capable of reclaiming precisely the thing that was lost; that we, in short, create fictions . . . imaginary homelands, Indias of the mind."[10] But even if distance alienates and leads a diaspora to look back at the country through "guilt-tinted" spectacles, does it necessarily imply a vengeful enthnonationalism supportive of violence or one that leverages its privileged position to help communities in the country of origin?

[5] Alejandro Portes, "Immigration Theory for a New Century: Some Problems and Opportunities," *International Migration Review* 31 (1997): 799–825.

[6] Ernest Gellner, *Nations and Nationalism* (Ithaca, NY: Cornell University Press, 1983).

[7] Michael Berkowitz, *Western Jewry and the Zioinist Project, 1914–1933.* (Cambridge, UK: Cambridge University Press, 1997).

[8] Michael Jones-Correa, *Between Two Nations: The Political Predicament of Latinos in New York City* (Ithaca, NY: Cornell University Press, 1998).

[9] *The Economist*, April 16, 2009.

[10] Salman Rushdie, *Imaginary Homelands* (London: Granta Books, 1991), 9–21, 10.

While these theories argue that diasporic nationalism is linked to levels and aspirations regarding assimilation, support for diasporic nationalism has also been a strategy adopted by particular groups within the immigrant community as a means of generating support for their own local goals in the host society.[11] According to this view, immigrants support homeland nationalism not because of their failure to assimilate, but because supporting nationalism in the homeland will advance their position in the host society.

However, although these theories attempt to explain the salience of long-distance nationalism among diasporas, they are weaker when it comes to understanding the form this nationalism takes. Although there is considerable suggestive evidence that diasporas are socially and politically reactionary, with conservative and often strongly nationalist views with regard to the country of origin, there are major weaknesses in this argument. Analytically examining why diasporas behave in this fashion is seldom clear. There are many assumptions with regard to the selection effects of who leaves and a perceived "identity crisis." It is not made clear what characteristics of emigrants would result in such behavior or why an "identity crisis" (even if that term can be clearly specified) would necessarily manifest itself in one direction and not another. Long-distance nationalism manifests itself in a variety of ways—economic, political, philanthropic, and reactionary. Just how important is the last in the U.S.-based Indian diaspora?

THE INDIAN DIASPORA AND LONG-DISTANCE NATIONALISM

Indian politics has witnessed much churning in recent decades, and the rise of Hindu nationalism—particularly in the quarter-century between the early 1980s and mid-2000s—has been one of the most singular features of the Indian polity. There has been a spate of analysis on the causes and consequences of the phenomenon—in particular, the dangers posed to India's secular fabric—although the defeat of the Bharatiya Janata Party (BJP) in the 2004 and again in the 2009 elections has abated fears of an inexorable expansion of *Hindutva* (Hindu religious nationalism).[12] A number of academic and popular commentators have argued that the Indian diaspora, particularly through its members residing in the United Kingdom and the United States, is a strong supporter and financier of

[11] John Kenny, "Mobilizing Diasporas in Nationalist Conflicts," PhD Thesis, University of Chicago, 2000.

[12] The BJP is a political party with strong support among sections of Hindu voters, which has evolved from the erstwhile Jan Sangh party. The BJP is a political arm of the so-called Sangh *parivar* (or family), which also includes the Rashtriya Swayamsevak Sangh (RSS), the Vishva Hindu Parishad (VHP), and the Bajrang Dal.

Hindutva. A reading of this material appears to suggest that the Indian diaspora settled abroad has developed what in another context has been termed as a "pathological identity"—"a pervasive hostility projected onto other ethnic groups."[13] Writing nearly two decades ago, Romila Thapar, one of the most respected Indian historians, cautioned against the diaspora's unhealthy yearning for Hindu nationalism.[14] Nearly a decade later, in the aftermath of the destruction of the Babri Masjid mosque by Hindu zealots in 1992, Shashi Tharoor (a writer and former UN functionary who became a minister in the Indian government in 2009) warned, "Expatriates are no longer an organic part of the culture, but severed digits that, in their yearning for the hand, can only twist themselves into a clenched fist."[15] Ashish Nandy, in an essay titled, "What Fuels Indian Nationalism?," confidently answered: "A deep sense of insecurity and fear. Among NRIs in the First World, I shall not be surprised if some survey finds that the support base of Hindu nationalism is more than 90 percent."[16]

Since then, many scholars have argued that the Indian diaspora has financed Hindu nationalism and, by implication, the anti-Muslim violence often instigated by Hindu nationalists.[17] In 2002, there was widespread anti-Muslim violence in Gujarat—one of the worst such cases in independent India—following the burning of a train coach in which returning Hindu pilgrims were killed. At least a thousand Muslims were killed, by official accounts (and perhaps double that, unofficially). The widespread condemnation that followed led to a close scrutiny of groups behind the violence that were linked to the Sangh Parivar,[18] and, in turn, to an array of charges that diasporic philanthropy had been financing the groups responsible for the violence. The philosopher Martha Nussbaum, for instance, charged, "*Highly significant* in the funding of the Gujarat violence were private donations organized through the American VHP [Vishva Hindu Parishad] and various charities that it has organized."[19] The general tenor of these arguments runs as follows: the Indian diaspora is largely

---

[13] Alexander Broth and Donald Rothschild, "Pathological Dimensions of Domestic and International Ethnicity," *Political Science Quarterly* 110, no. 1 (1995): 15.

[14] Romila Thapar, "Syndicated Moksha," *Seminar* 313 (September 1985): 14–22.

[15] Shashi Tharoor, "Growing Up Extreme: On the Peculiarly Vicious Fanatacism of [Indian] Expatriates," *Washington Post*, July 15, 1993, C5.

[16] http://www.tehelka.com/story_main.asp?filename=Fe021404fuels.asp.

[17] Arvind Rajagopal, *Politics after Television: Religious Nationalism and the Reshaping of the Indian Public* (Cambridge, UK: Cambridge University Press, 2001). See also Tambiah (2001) and Van Der Veer (2001).

[18] "Sangh Parivar" refers to the family of organizations linked to the Hindu nationalist movement.

[19] Martha C. Nussbaum, "Genocide in Gujarat: The International Community Looks Away," *Dissent*, Fall 2003, emphasis added.

pro-*Hindutva*, which leads it to finance the Sangh Parivar in India, and these resources, in turn, have empowered the Sangh Parivar and allowed it to engage in violence directed principally against Muslims but also at other religious minorities as well. But what is the analytical and empirical support for these arguments?

There are several claims embedded in these statements. The first concerns the political mind-set or beliefs of the diaspora. More than a few individuals in the diaspora certainly support the Sangh Parivar strongly. But to draw generalized conclusions about a population based on a visible sample requires strong analytical and empirical foundations. The second claim concerns the degree to which these beliefs are translated into actions. If actions speak louder than words, what is the evidence of the actions of the diaspora? The Indian diaspora engages in a range of actions directed toward the country of origin, from business to lobbying to financing civil society and political actors. As part of the portfolio of actions by which the diaspora engages with India, just how significant is the financing of the Sangh Parivar? And, last, how significant are the causal or contributory effects of these actions on violence in India? Has external funding been a marginal, considerable, or significant basis of financial resources for the Sangh Parivar? On this final issue rests the counterfactual: does ethnic violence take place in India due to, or in spite of, the diaspora? More generally, how dominant is the role of overseas Hindus in diaspora-supported violence in India?

The causal chain in these arguments appears to run as follows:

1. Indians in the United States (and perhaps elsewhere, especially the United Kingdom) have a strong anti-Muslim prejudice.
2. They act on this prejudice by sending money to Hindu extremist organizations.
3. The amount of money matters sufficiently in a relative sense—that is, it is large enough to overturn the counterfactual that in the absence of these financial flows the violence would not occur.

However, what is the evidence that the Indian diaspora in Western countries (which is of relatively recent vintage) is really any different from the pool from which it is drawn (namely, relatively higher educated Indians), which ranges from dedicated young men and women working with progressive nongovernment organizations (NGOs) to those who harbor rabid anti-minority sentiments and those preoccupied with making a quick buck? Periodically, Indian politicians and political commentators seek recourse to the "foreign-hand" argument to explain either their own or the country's failings, and this, more often than not, has served as a convenient bogey. Is this the case here, except in this case the charges are being leveled by politicians rather than civil society? To understand the nature of the long-distance nationalism of the Indian diaspora, we first need to have some understanding of its political beliefs.

Political Beliefs of the Indian Diaspora

As with any diaspora, the Indian diaspora's identities can be expected to range from a cosmopolitan identity that underpins a civic nationalism to the other extreme—namely, the espousal of an exclusionary ethnic nationalism—but the presumption that the latter is dominant (at least among the diaspora living in Western countries) is puzzling. Academic writings on the issue, much of them by diaspora members themselves, have a strong anti-*Hindutva* stance, a fact which seems to undermine the supposed dominance of *Hindutva* in the diaspora. But how would one more rigorously analyze a diaspora's political disposition toward the country of origin?

Confining the analysis to the Indian diaspora of recent vintage (i.e., post-independence emigrants), we can try to determine what characteristics of the diaspora are likely to impact their politics. A broad set of factors that shape a diaspora's views stems from who leaves—the so called selection bias. First, what are the diaspora's regions and states of origin? Based on conventional wisdom, if the migration has been much greater from North India than from Southern India, or much greater from Gujarat than from Bengal, it could result in greater anti-Muslim sentiment, given the relative degrees of polarization in these different regions of India. For instance, Ashutosh Varshney has argued that, "Gujarati Americans have been among the most, and South Indians among the least, anti-Muslim in their predispositions."[20] Of course, nonresident Gujaratis (NRGs) do not necessarily buy this line, with some of them arguing that they "know the essence of Hinduism which has a broader perspective. In India, Hinduism seems to be mired in the slush of bigotry."[21] Gujaratis indeed dominate Bengalis in the diaspora, but the large flows of Indian information technology (IT) workers (the so-called knowledge diaspora) to the United States in the 1990s had a significant (if not dominant) South Indian component, especially from Andhra Pradesh (see chapter 3).

However, the effect of the state of origin is qualified by a second factor: how migrants (even from these regions) select themselves. Who is more likely to leave: the more cosmopolitan Indians or those dripping in *Hindutva* (e.g., members of the apparently neofascist Bajrang Dal)? Three other factors come into play as well: the caste, education, and gender profile of the diaspora. International migrants from lower-caste groups and women may be less likely to support hard-line groups, perhaps

[20] http://www.rediff.com/news/2002/apr/23inter.htm.
[21] "Proud Hindu, Not a Proud Indian." *Times of India*, April 10, 2004.

because their own experience of marginalization and oppression makes them more sensitive to such afflictions on other groups. If so, since both of these groups are relatively underrepresented, the diaspora could be more prone to ethnonationalism. The dominance of science and technology in the educational profiles of Indian migrants (especially to the United States), may also make them more susceptible to the pro-*Hindutva* ideology (supposedly due to their lack of exposure to the humanities and social sciences). If the migration is male-dominated and if males are more prone to enthnonationalism, this too could lead to great support to groups supportive of violence. But whether this is the case, or whether, indeed, it is such postmodern narratives that create a more fertile ground for *Hindutva* is a moot point.[22] It is also possible that it is not the level or the type of education but the country of education that matters, since education may affect behavior through its socialization role. Thus, an Indian living in the United States may have a lesser anti-Muslim bias if she had a U.S. education as opposed to an Indian one.

In contrast to the effects stemming from the selection bias on who leaves India, the diaspora's own characteristics, in addition to "host-country" effects, further shape the political views of the diaspora. First, a diaspora's sense of identity—and resulting political views—depends on a cohort effect—i.e., when the diaspora members left the country of origin. Migrants who came from India to the United States in the 1970s did so at a time of economic stasis and political turmoil in India. Thus, they might tend to put the blame on the Congress Party and, to that extent, might be stronger supporters of an ideology that is anti-Congress (and, by default, more pro-BJP). In contrast, those who came in the 1990s left India at a time when India had greater self-confidence (at least among groups that form the potential pool of international migrants from India), but, at the same time, the country had also turned toward the right. How would this affect their political views? If a sense of insecurity and anxiety were the wellspring of prejudice, the earlier cohort would be more pro-*Hindutva*, since the more recent arrivals come from a country where levels of self-confidence are higher than in the 1970s.

Second, political views could reflect an age effect. A diaspora that is younger is likely to be much more engaged in economic activities, whereas retirees are supposedly searching for meaning beyond the stereotypical empty large home in New Jersey after their children have left home. If so, the latter might find some meaning to their lives in supporting hard-line groups.

[22] Meera Nanda, *Prophets Facing Backward: Postmodern Critiques of Silence and Hindu Nationalism* (New Brunswick, NJ: Rutgers University Press, 2003).

Third, views could also reflect a generation effect. The second (and later) generations are more likely to be influenced by the values of the countries in which they grew up and harbor the resentments of their parents to a lesser degree. For them, India is an experience of relatives and gatherings, food and family rituals, and visits to places of worship. While this cultural bond may be felt intensely, it is unlikely to be political in any significant sense, often because this generation has not encountered racism in the same way as earlier generations. In addition, the diaspora's views may also be different if its members have come via a third country. The East African Gujaratis in the United States and the United Kingdom are a case in point. Speculations apart, we simply do not have a firm sense as to whether there are systematic differences between those who came to the United States or Britain via a third country (e.g., East Africa or the Middle East) versus those who came directly.

Last, how important is the role of the Indian diaspora in ethnic violence in India? In this chapter, I argue that the diaspora's role *is* important, but in more complex ways than simply the presumption of its support for hard-line Hindu organizations. There have been many excellent analyses of Hindu—Muslim violence explained through a decline of social capital, electoral competition, or the (in)actions of state organs.[23] The Sangh Parivar's socioeconomic base as well as the fact that it has been in power in many states ensures that it has good access to domestic resources (and, ugly as it may seem, riots, murder and mayhem are not that expensive in India). By way of illustration, the financial needs of the Maoist insurgency in India—which is spread across a fifth of the country and which, in recent years, has been claiming even more lives than the conflict in Kashmir—is less than $5 million a year. According to Koteshwar Rao, a member of the politburo of the Communist Party of India (Maoist), the party "runs on an annual budget of Rs15–20 crore around $5 million. That's what we spend on our operations across the country, and it's almost the same amount that we raise through donations, seizures and heists."[24] Any self-respecting chief minister or cabinet member in India can raise that money within the country with ease.[25]

Consequently, as I argued in chapter 7, it is *weaker groups* that (for whatever reason) want to challenge the Indian state that rely to a relatively

[23] See for instance, Ashutosh Varshney, *Ethnic Conflict and Civic Life: Hindus and Muslims in India* (New Haven, CT: Yale University Press, 2002); Steven Wilkinson, *Votes and Violence: Electoral Competition and Ethnic Riots in India* (New York: Cambridge University Press, 2004).

[24] Romita Datta and Aveek Datta, "Mainstream Politics Not for Us, Says Koteshwar Rao," *Mint*, May 28, 2009.

[25] For instance, in late 2009, the former chief minister of Jharkhand state, Madhu Koda, had been charged in money laundering of around half a billion dollars.

greater extent on support from diasporas. While this argument depends on what constitutes "Indian," insofar as violence in India from overseas groups with origins within India's territorial boundaries is concerned, the ethnonationalism of overseas Hindus is just one aspect. An array of diaspora groups has—and continues to be—involved in a range of insurgencies in India; in the Northeast, Sikh groups in the 1980s, overseas Kashmiri groups, and even Indian Muslims overseas have all been involved to varying degrees.[26] Analysis of the activists of the Students Islamic Movement of India (SIMA, a proscribed terrorist group) revealed that most "were away from home for the first time, lonely and disconnected from their social context." And "many travelled abroad, encountering both religious discrimination as well as global Islamist causes and organisations in the process."[27] The critical difference of course between overseas Hindus who are party to violence and many other groups is that the former's actions are not directed against the Indian state, while the latter's are. The reason is obvious. State oppression and egregious miscarriages of justice in India are not directed against the majority community. (The majority community also suffers from the infirmities of the Indian state but that is out of indifference and venality rather than active organized violence). The 1984 anti-Sikh and 2002 anti-Muslim riots are the most blatant examples of state connivance in organized violence. But once violence erupts, the direction of causality becomes blurred. Does the diaspora cause or react to events in India? Does increasing communalism and violence in India make the diaspora more prone to directly or indirectly instigate violence in India? Are Hindus or ethnic minorities more militant in India or outside the country? While in all of these questions, we can make informed guesses, in the absence of stronger empirical foundations, they will remain just that.

Anti-Muslim Prejudice in the Diaspora

In trying to trace support for extremist groups, it is beyond our capacity to obtain evidence on the flow of money. Money flows through many channels, and even the combined resources of Western intelligence agencies have found it extremely difficult to track terrorist financing. The more extremist the cause, the more subterranean the financial flows, and extremist organizations do not (usually) keep transparent accounts for the convenience of researchers. However, it may be possible to get a sense

[26] Praveen Swami, "Lethal Remittance," *Frontline* 21, no. 1 (January 3–16, 2004). Available online at http://www.hinduonnet.com/fline/fl2101/stories/20040116003202600.htm.

[27] Praveen Swami, "Jihad in the Cyber City," *The Hindu*, March 8, 2008, available at http://www.hindu.com/2008/03/08/stories/2008030854911200.htm.

of the likelihood of such flows by measuring the characteristics of nationalism and prejudice of the Indian diaspora. I used data gleaned from the Survey of Asian Indians in the United States (SAIUS) to do just that.

Ethnic prejudice has been defined as "an antipathy based upon a faulty and inflexible generalization. It may be felt or expressed. It may be directed toward a group as a whole, or toward an individual because he is a member of that group."[28] A significant body of literature examines why people form group identities and discriminate against out-groups.[29] These works support an earlier view that individual-level prejudice is of secondary importance[30] and suggest that each group's sense of social position in relation to the others is more important in understanding the perpetuation of hierarchies. *Ethnocentrism* manifests itself "in a complex of attitudes including positive identification with one's own group and xenophobia expressed in varying degrees to outside groups." Prejudice can also be seen as a product of the extent to which a person endorses social hierarchies, a concept examined by *social dominance orientations*.[31] In both instances, prejudices directed at specific groups are treated as manifestations of more basic psychological orientations.

While direct instruction and reinforcement (especially by significant others in the group) matter in the building of prejudice, observation and experiences play an important role as well. Prejudice is thus both "taught" and "caught." Contact theory focuses on the effect of personal contact by individuals with outgroup members. If the experience was positive (or negative) the contact hypothesis on individual explanations of prejudice predicts this should reduce (or increase) prejudice.[32] However, the existence of prejudice per se does not necessarily imply support for violence, and conversely, even in the absence of hostility, "organizational roles and obedience may be sufficient to produce violence against out-groups even in the absence of hostility."[33]

The SAIUS survey used a technique first used by Kuklinski et al. to gauge the level of prejudice in a population.[34] In their study, the researchers

[28] G. W. Allport, *The Nature of Prejudice* (Cambridge, MA: Addison-Wesley, 1954), 9.

[29] M. B. Brewer, "The Psychology of Prejudice: Ingroup Love or Outgroup Hate?" *Journal of Social Issues* 55 (1999): 429–44.

[30] H. Blumer, "Race Prejudice as a Sense of Group Position," *Pacific Sociological Review* 1 (1958): 3–6.

[31] J. Sidanius and F. Pratto, *Social Dominance: An Intergroup Theory of Social Hierarchy and Oppression* (Cambridge, UK: Cambridge Univ. Press, 1999).

[32] T. F. Pettigrew, "Intergroup Contact Theory," *Annual Review of Psychology* 49 (1998): 65–86.

[33] Donald P. Green and Rachel L. Seher, "What Role Does Prejudice Play in Ethnic Conflict?" *Annual Review of Political Science* 6 (2003): 518.

[34] J. H. Kuklinski, M. D. Cobb, and M. Gilens, "Racial Attitudes and the 'New South,'" *Journal of Politics* 59 (1997): 323–49.

employed a "list experiment" to detect racial grievances while finessing the problem of extracting truthful answers from respondents who might otherwise conceal their prejudiced attitudes. The authors presented two groups of respondents with different lists of possible grievances and asked them to simply report the *number* of statements items (not *which* statements) on the list that they found objectionable. The two lists were identical except that the second list also contained a racial grievance. By comparing the difference in the average number of grievances reported by the two groups, the authors could gauge the level of prejudice, since in the absence of any prejudice the average scores across the two randomly selected groups should be equivalent.[35] In their study, Kuklinski et al. found that while blatantly prejudiced attitudes (about blacks) were pervasive among the white population in the United States, resistance to affirmative action was not simply an extension of this prejudice.[36] White resistance to affirmative action stemmed less from a lack of concern with racial equality than from a commitment to individual achievement and self-reliance.

In interpreting the results in the following, two caveats are in order. One, it is important to keep in mind that, for reasons discussed earlier, the survey respondents were overwhelmingly non-Muslim. Two, because the survey was only carried out among Indian Americans, and there are no comparative figures for India, one cannot make any firm judgment on how this sample's levels of prejudice compares with Indians in India.

In the phone survey, one half of the randomly assigned sample was asked the following question: "Now I am going to read out three things that sometimes make people angry or upset about India. After I read all three, just tell me *how many* of them upset you. I don't want to know which ones, just *how many*."

1. Politicians taking bribes in India.
2. Dirt and pollution in India.
3. The swarms of people and crowds (in India).

In their responses, they could agree with one, two, or all three statements.

---

[35] To calculate the "level of anger" against blacks, the authors calculated the mean number of statements that upset respondents from the first category (presented with three statements), subtracted it from the mean number of statements that upset respondents from the second category (those presented with four statements), and multiplied it by 100. This gave the percentage "level of anger" directed toward the fourth statement. Although there are potential "ceiling effects," the authors used a simulation to show that these are not significant.

[36] J. H. Kuklinski, M. D. Cobb, and M. Gilens, "Racial Attitudes and the 'New South,'" *J. Politics* 59 (1997): 323–49.

The second half of the randomly assigned sample was asked the following question: "Now I am going to read out four things that sometimes make people angry or upset about India. After I read all four, just tell me *how many* of them upset you. I don't want to know which ones, just *how many*."

1. Politicians taking bribes in India.
2. Dirt and pollution in India.
3. The swarms of people and crowds (in India).
4. The Muslim population is growing at a faster rate than the Hindu population in India.

In this case, respondents could agree with one, two, three, or all four statements. Note that the critical statement focuses attention on the differential growth rates of population across two religious groups and, therefore, is unlikely to get a positive response from those who get angry at population growth per se.

The results are given in table 8.1. Although the number of observations is not identical across the two groups, that does not materially impact on the results. The difference between the two means is statistically significant at the 1 percent level, indicating that some 43 percent of people of Indian origin in the United States express anger at the possibility that the Muslim population may be growing at a faster rate than the Hindu population.

However, this does not give us a sense of how the anger may vary across different characteristics of the Indian American population. To address this question, one may examine the subsample of the data where the respondents have been asked all four questions and look for statistically significant differences between the average anger shown by people exhibiting a particular characteristic (language, religion, etc.) and the rest of the population. However, since the anger measured here is the total anger across all the four statements, we cannot infer that differences represent only prejudice against Muslims; this could be accounted for by the fact that some groups might systematically be more upset about the other three statements as well. What we can do is look at the mean anger exhibited by a

TABLE 8.1
Level of Anger

Number of Statements	Observations	Mean	Standard Error	95% Confidence Interval	t-value	Significant	Level of Anger
3	1277	2.25	0.021	[2.213, 2.295]	−11.212	Yes	42.57%
4	813	2.68	0.034	[2.613, 2.747]			

particular group relative to the rest of the population in the subsample that was asked only three questions, and then in the subsample that was asked four questions. If there is no statistically significant difference in the means in the three-question subsample, but there is a statistically significant difference in the four-question subsample, then we can be more confident in interpreting this as an indicator of differential anti-Muslim prejudice.

The statistical tool used to evaluate prejudice against Muslims is a two-sample *t*-test in Stata, which performs a paired test of the hypothesis that *variable1–variable2* has a mean of zero. In this case, *variable1* is the rest of the sample, and *variable2* is the category of interest, whether ethnicity, religion, age, gender, or any other category that potentially affects anti-Muslim prejudice in the Indian American population.

The two-sample *t*-test was run twice for each category, once for the subsample that was presented with three statements and once for the subsample that was presented with four statements. I first compared the difference in means between a specified category and the rest of the sample in the three-statement subsample, and the difference in means between the same category and the rest of the sample in the four-statement subsample. If the difference in means was not statistically significant in the three-statement subsample, but it was statistically significant in the four-statement subsample, this basically means that respondents from a particular category are more prejudiced *specifically* against Muslims, as distinct from being *generally* more angry/prejudiced than the rest of the sample.

Regional Differences

Historically, Hindu–Muslim conflict has been much greater in Northern and Western India than in Southern India. We would therefore expect anti-Muslim prejudice to be least among South Indians. The results (in table 8.2) confirm this to some degree. North Indians (Hindi and Punjabi speakers) have the highest level of anger, and the result is significant at the 1 percent level.

TABLE 8.2
Regional Differences in Level of Anger

Combined Ethnicities	Observations	Mean	Standard Error	95% Confidence Interval	t-value	Significant	Level of Anger
0 = Other	538	2.611	0.0413	[2.530, 2.692]			
1 = Hindi,					−2.8304	Yes	20.30%
Punjabi	275	2.814	0.0593	[2.697, 2.931]			

Differences by Ethnicity

If we further disaggregate and examine differences across different states in India, two groups stand out: Punjabi speakers in Northern India and Tamil speakers in Southern India (table 8.3). The difference between the two means is statistically significant at 5 percent level in both cases. The high levels in the case of Punjabi speakers reflect the long memories of partition and refugees.[37] Pre-partition, Punjab had roughly equal numbers of Hindus, Muslims, and Sikhs. Partition divided Punjab, and the region witnessed the worst of the violence, with estimates of between one-half to one million people killed. The resulting ethnic cleansing left virtually no Hindus and Sikhs in West Punjab (which became part of Pakistan) and no Muslims in East Punjab (which became part of India). In the four-statement subsample, the difference in means is statistically significant at the 5 percent level for both Punjabi and Tamil speakers. Thus, Punjabi respondents are, on average, 26.1 percent *more* prejudiced against Muslims than the sample average, whereas Tamil speakers are, on average, 26.4 percent *less* prejudiced against Muslims than the sample average. As far as Marathi speakers are concerned, the difference in means is statistically significant at the 1 percent level only for the three-statement subsample, which tells us that Marathi speakers are, on average, 26.6 percent more angry/prejudiced in general, but not specifically against Muslims.

The most surprising result, in light of the hypotheses mentioned earlier, is the relatively low degree of prejudice among Gujaratis. Much of the argument about support for Hindu extremist organizations stems from the massive violence in Gujarat in 2002. While the evidence here does not necessarily negate this link, it certainly does not offer support for it either. The not-so-low level of prejudice among Bengalis is also somewhat surprising. Although Bengal has one of the highest percentages of Muslim populations of any state in India, its strong leftist tradition is one reason for its low levels of communal violence. The prejudice could be the result of a selection bias among Bengalis who leave that state.

Violence is a product of many factors. The question is whether the diaspora increases the likelihood of violence. It may do so without resulting in actual events of violence, just as one can increase the temperature of water without causing it to boil over. For instance, in Gujarat, a higher level of domestic proclivity to communal violence may be tipped over by a lower level of diaspora support, while a lower proclivity for communal violence in Bengal (for a variety of reasons, including, especially, the nature of the domestic political discourse) may still not cross the threshold,

---

[37] On the political affects of refugees, for example, as it applies in the Punjab or Rwanda-Burundi, see Steve Wilkinson (2004), chapter 2.

TABLE 8.3
Level of Anger by Individual Ethnicity

Individual Ethnicity	Observations	Mean	Standard Error	95% Confidence Interval	t-value	Significant	Level of Anger
0 = Other	1205	2.25	0.0218	[2.207, 2.293]	-0.7507	No	6.88%
1 = Bengali3	72	2.319	0.0811	[2.157, 2.481]			
0 = Other	776	2.679	0.0347	[2.610, 2.747]	-0.1441	No	2.35%
1 = Bengali4	37	2.702	0.1727	[2.352, 3.053]			
0 = Other	1000	2.259	0.0237	[2.212, 2.305]	0.4041	No	-2.07%
1 = Gujarati3	277	2.238	0.0463	[2.147, 2.329]			
0 = Other	607	2.703	0.0396	[2.625, 2.781]	1.1719	No	-9.18%
1 = Gujarati4	206	2.611	0.0669	[2.479, 2.743]			
0 = Other	921	2.258	0.0249	[2.209, 2.307]	0.2975	No	-1.40%
1 = Hindi3	356	2.244	0.0399	[2.165, 2.323]			
0 = Other	629	2.655	0.0384	[2.579, 2.730]	-1.3672	No	11.13%
1 = Hindi4	184	2.766	0.0733	[2.621, 2.911]			
0 = Other	1220	2.242	0.0217	[2.199, 2.285]	-2.6056	Yes***	26.61%
1 = Marathi3	57	2.508	0.0796	[2.349, 2.668]			
0 = Other	758	2.676	0.0352	[2.607, 2.746]	-0.3719	No	5.05%
1 = Marathi4	55	2.727	0.1334	[2.459, 2.994]			
0 = Other	1236	2.256	0.0214	[2.214, 2.298]	0.5114	No	-6.13%
1 = Malayalam3	41	2.195	0.122	[1.948, 2.441]			
0 = Other	790	2.682	0.0346	[2.614, 2.750]	0.3578	No	-7.36
1 = Malayalam4	23	2.608	0.1962	[2.201, 3.015]			

TABLE 8.3 (continued)

Individual Ethnicity	Observations	Mean	Standard Error	95% Confidence Interval	t-value	Significant	Level of Anger
0 = Other	1151	2.246	0.0221	[2.203, 2.290]	−1.1096	No	7.86%
1 = Punjabi3	126	2.325	0.0711	[2.184, 2.466]			
0 = Other	722	2.65	0.036	[2.58, 2.721]	−2.4227	Yes**	26.11%
1 = Punjabi4	91	2.91	0.1008	[2.711, 3.112]			
0 = Other	1137	2.263	0.0223	[2.220, 2.307]	1.2606	No	−8.53%
1 = Tamil3	140	2.178	0.0651	[2.049, 2.307]			
0 = Other	736	2.705	0.0359	[2.634, 2.775]	2.2705	Yes**	−26.36%
1 = Tamil4	77	2.441	0.102	[2.238, 2.644]			
0 = Other	1206	2.252	0.0217	[2.209, 2.294]	−0.4735	No	4.37%
1 = Telugu3	71	2.295	0.0927	[2.110, 2.480]			
0 = Other	763	2.673	0.0354	[2.604, 2.743]	−0.7494	No	10.63%
1 = Telugu4	50	2.78	0.1188	[2.541, 3.018]			
0 = Other	1225	2.253	0.0216	[2.210, 2.295]	−0.3308	No	3.54%
1 = English3	52	2.288	0.0964	[2.094, 2.482]			
0 = Other	785	2.68	0.0345	[2.612, 2.747]	0.009	No	−0.16%
1 = English4	28	2.678	0.2124	[2.242, 3.114]			
0 = Other	1242	2.258	0.0214	[2.216, 2.300]	1.1135	No	−14.41%
1 = Kannada3	35	2.114	0.1281	[1.853, 2.374]			
0 = Other	785	2.684	0.0349	[2.615, 2.752]	0.6025	No	−11.26%
1 = Kannada4	28	2.571	0.1493	[2.265, 2.877]			

* indicates significance at 10% level; ** indicates significance at 5% level; and *** indicates significance at 1% level.

even with higher levels of diasporic support. To put it differently, there may not be suitable domestic receptacles for diasporic anger in Bengal, while there may be many in Gujarat.

Alternatively, the situation may reflect concerns arising from the considerable influx of Muslims from neighboring Bangladesh. The results invite caution in making simple and direct links between prejudice in a diaspora and violence in the regions where it comes from.

The preceding analysis enables us to assess how a certain subgroup compares to the rest of the sample. For instance, it gives us an indication of how prejudiced Punjabi respondents are when compared to non-Punjabi respondents. However, it does not give us a clear indication of how prejudiced Punjabi respondents are relative to, for instance, Hindi or Gujarati respondents. In order to achieve this, the analysis can be further refined by conducting a Welch T-test (a *t*-test with unequal sample variances), which helps us compare all the subgroups within one particular group of interest. Tables appendix 8.1 through appendix 8.5, at the end of this chapter, summarize the results of this analysis for the ethinicity, religion, religiosity, education, and income subgroups.

As summarized in table 8.16, the Welch T-test for the ethnicity subgroup reveals five sets of statistically significant results. First, Gujarati-speaking respondents are less prejudiced against Muslims than Hindi-speaking and Punjabi-speaking respondents. Second, Hindi-speaking respondents are more prejudiced than Tamil- and Marathi-speaking respondents, as well as more than the sample average. Third, Marathi-speaking respondents are less prejudiced than Punjabi- and Telugu-speaking respondents, as well as less than the sample average. Fourth, Punjabi-speaking respondents are more prejudiced than Tamil-speaking respondents and the sample average. Last, but not least, Tamil-speaking respondents are less prejudiced than Telugu-speaking respondents and the sample average.

Differences by Religion

The fact that many members of the Indian diaspora in the United States are prejudiced against Muslims is already clear from table 8.1. It stands to reason that this result is significantly affected by the views of Hindus, given their predominance (more than four-fifths) in the sample. Hence, the *t*-test methodology is not helpful in saying anything more interesting about this group. Those who do not profess any religion should be less prejudiced, and the results show that that these respondents are, on average, 19.8 percent less angry compared to the general population (significant at the 10 percent level), and 28 percent less prejudiced against Muslims than the sample average, although the latter result is not statistically significant. While Jains are less prejudiced than the sample average (which is largely driven by views of Hindus), Christians are about same as the sample average, although in both cases the results are not statistically significant (table 8.4). As I explained in chapter 2, one consequence of my sampling methodology was that Muslims were largely excluded from the sampling frame. Consequently, while the SEI survey puts the number of Indian Muslims in the United States at 10 percent, in the SAIUS survey they are barely above 1 percent. However, since the question at hand is prejudice against Muslims, their absence from the sample frame will not materially affect the results.

An interesting result is the high levels of prejudice among Sikhs against Muslims. In the four-statement subsample, the difference in means is statistically significant at the 1 percent level for Sikh respondents, indicating that, on average, Sikh respondents are 49.2 percent more prejudiced against Muslims than the sample average.

As summarized in table 8.17, the Welch T-test for the religion subgroup reveals five sets of statistically significant results. First, Hindu respondents are less prejudiced against Muslims than Sikh respondents but more prejudiced than respondents of other religions. Second, Christian respondents are less prejudiced than Sikh respondents but more prejudiced than respondents of other religions. Third, Jain respondents are less prejudiced than Sikh respondents. Fourth, Sikh respondents are more prejudiced than the sample average, as well as more than respondents of other religions, respondents who claim no religion, and Muslim respondents.

In table 8.5, I report the results obtained when Punjabis are disaggregated by religion. Respondents whose ethnicity is Punjabi and whose religion is Sikh are, on average, 47.7 percent more prejudiced against Muslims than the sample average, and the difference in means is statistically significant at the 1 percent level. The interesting question is how prejudice differs across Punjabi Hindus and Punjabi Sikhs. It should be emphasized again that there is no evidence that the high level of prejudice of this subgroup of the diaspora has translated into anti-Muslim violence in India. This may be either because there are few Muslims in that region or that the methodology captures the extent but not the intensity of prejudice. However, the results appear to illustrate the persistence of historical memory. There is a large literature on the political incentives that drive ethnic violence. While these incentives are largely structured by the institutional setting, these results demonstrate that incentives unfold against a historical backdrop, which can amplify or attenuate incentives.

The *intensity* of religious preferences may have a greater effect on prejudice than religious preference per se, that is, it is not religion per se

TABLE 8.4
Level of Anger by Religion

Religion	Observations	Mean	Standard Error	95% Confidence Interval	t-value	Significant	Level of Anger
0 = Other	1230	2.261	0.0217	[2.219, 2.304]	1.7645	Yes*	−19.79%
1 = None3	47	2.063	0.0769	[1.908, 2.218]			
0 = Other	779	2.692	0.0347	[2.623, 2.760]	1.6471	No	−28.01%
1 = None4	34	2.411	0.1695	[2.067, 2.756]			
0 = Other	264	2.234	0.0454	[2.145, 2.324]	−0.4745	No	2.47%
1 = Hindu3	1013	2.259	0.0238	[2.212, 2.306]			
0 = Other	145	2.774	0.0811	[2.584, 2.905]	0.8834	No	−7.86%
1 = Hindu4	668	2.666	0.0375	[2.592, 2.739]			
0 = Other	1194	2.258	0.0218	[2.215, 2.300]	0.6195	No	−5.31%
1 = Christian3	83	2.204	0.0853	[2.035, 2.374]			
0 = Other	784	2.679	0.0347	[2.611, 2.748]	−0.0533	No	0.98%
1 = Christian4	29	2.689	0.1726	[2.336, 3.043]			
0 = Other	1259	2.256	0.0212	[2.214, 2.298]	0.8109	No	−14.54%
1 = Muslim3	18	2.111	0.1961	[1.697, 2.525]			
0 = Other	805	2.683	0.0342	[2.616, 2.750]	0.8926	No	−30.82%
1 = Muslim4	8	2.375	0.375	[1.488, 3.261]			

TABLE 8.4 (continued)

Religion	Observations	Mean	Standard Error	95% Confidence Interval	t-value	Significant	Level of Anger
0 = Other	1250	2.256	0.0214	[2.214, 2.298]	0.4817	No	−7.08%
1 = Jain3	27	2.185	0.1197	[1.939, 2.431]			
0 = Other	800	2.681	0.0343	[2.613, 2.748]	0.2423	No	−6.58%
1 = Jain4	13	2.615	0.2895	[1.984, 3.246]			
0 = Other	1205	2.248	0.0217	[2.205, 2.290]	−1.2329	No	11.29%
1 = Sikh3	72	2.361	0.0934	[2.174, 2.547]			
0 = Other	764	2.65	0.035	[2.581, 2.719]	−3.461	Yes***	49.23%
1 = Sikh4	49	3.142	0.1304	[2.880, 3.405]			
0 = Other	1260	2.25	0.0212	[2.209, 2.292]	−1.5112	No	27.86%
1 = Other3	17	2.529	0.1939	[2.118, 2.940]			
0 = Other	801	2.681	0.0344	[2.614, 2.749]	0.3477	No	−9.83%
1 = Other4	12	2.583	0.2289	[2.079, 3.087]			

* indicates significance at 10% level; ** indicates significance at 5% level; and *** indicates significance at 1% level.

TABLE 8.5
Level of Anger by Ethnicity and Religion

Ethnicity and Religion	Observations	Mean	Standard Error	95% Confidence Interval	t-value	Significant	Level of Anger
0 = Other	767	2.653	0.0349	[2.584, 2.721]	−3.2542	Yes	47.72%
1 = Punjabi and Sikh	46	3.13	0.1376	[2.853, 3.407]			

but *religiosity* that is more important.[38] The survey gets at this in two ways. First, respondents were directly asked, "How important is religion to the way you live your life? Would you say very important, somewhat important, not very important, or not at all important?" We would expect the degree of prejudice to increase the more important religion was to respondents; the results support this, albeit not very strongly (table 8.6). Thus, respondents for whom religion is "very important" are, on average, 11.8 percent more prejudiced against Muslims than the sample average. However, the results are significant only at the 10 percent level. Conversely, respondents for whom religion is "not very important" are, on average, 41.3 percent less prejudiced against Muslims than the sample average (significant at 1 percent level).

Religiosity can be inferred either as self-expressed intensity of belief or intensity of formal practice. The survey inferred the latter by asking respondents, "How often do you go to church, temple, or mosque for formal worship? Would you say you visit several times per week, several times per month, several times per year, once a year or less, or never?" Again we would expect a relationship between prejudice and intensity of religious practice. The results bear this out to a degree (table 8.7). Respondents attending a place of worship several times per month are, on average, nearly 24 percent more prejudiced against Muslims than the sample average, the result being statistically significant at the 1 percent level. Conversely, respondents attending a place of worship once a year or less are, on average, 35.8 percent less prejudiced against Muslims than the rest of the sample, the result being statistically significant at 1 percent level. However, for immigrants in particular, places of worship often serve as community gathering places, and therefore to infer religiosity from frequency of visits might be misleading, to the extent that for many Indians

[38] For evidence in the United States, see Bob Altemeye, *The Authoritarian Specter* (Cambridge, MA: Harvard University Press, 1997).

TABLE 8.6
Level of Anger by Intensity of Religious Beliefs

Importance of Religion	Observations	Mean	Standard Error	95% Confidence Interval	t-value	Significant	Level of Anger
0 = Other	422	2.623	0.0473	[2.530, 2.716]	−1.7388	Yes	11.84%
1 = Very important	391	2.741	0.0489	[2.645, 2.837]			
0 = Other	732	2.721	0.0354	[2.651, 2.790]	3.6539	Yes	−41.26%
1 = Not very important	81	2.308	0.1119	[2.085, 2.531]			

TABLE 8.7
Level of Anger by Frequency of Visits to Place of Worship

Frequency of Visits	Observations	Mean	Standard Error	95% Confidence Interval	t-value	Significant	Level of Anger
0 = Other	563	2.605	0.0413	[2.524, 2.686]	−3.3008	Yes	24.23%
1 = Several times per month	250	2.848	0.0589	[2.732, 2.964]			
0 = Other	700	2.73	0.0362	[2.658, 2.801]	3.6647	Yes	−35.83%
1 = Once a year or less	113	2.371	0.0934	[2.186, 2.556]			

going to a place of worship may be one of the few ways they can interact with other Indians.[39]

As summarized in table 8.18, the Welch T-test for the religiosity group reveals three sets of statistically significant results. First, respondents attending a place of worship several times per week are more prejudiced against Muslims than those attending several times per year or once a year or less. Second, respondents attending a place of worship several times per month are more prejudiced against Muslims than those attending several times per year or once a year or less, as well as than the sample average. Third, those attending a place of worship once a year or less are less prejudiced against Muslims than the sample average.

[39] I am grateful to Steve Wilkinson for this insight.

Demographic Differences: Age and Gender

Respondents' demographic characteristics might also affect prejudice. Younger respondents may be less prejudiced insofar as the shadow of the past is weaker. Female respondents could be less prejudiced if one believes that males are more prone to anger. However, work in Northern Ireland suggests that the young were more prejudiced, probably because of greater segregation and violence in past few decades, indicating that cohort effects rather than age effects may be more important. In this case, neither age nor gender effects were significant.

Place of Birth and Emigration Cohort

To the extent that prejudice can be both "caught" and "taught," place of birth might play an important role insofar as identities (and prejudices) are formed by the adolescent experience. More than 90 percent of the survey respondents were born in India. However, place of birth was not statistically significant. As discussed earlier, the emigrant's cohort may affect the relative degree of prejudice. Respondents who emigrated were asked when (which year) they first came to the United States. In this case as well, the results were not statistically significant.

Differences by Education

Respondents were asked about the highest degree they had received. The choices were, "less than high school," "high school," "some college," "bachelor's degree," "master's degree," "professional degree," and "doctoral degree." The surprising result is that those with high school or less education stand out—they are 23 percent less prejudiced against Muslims than the sample average. (The result is statistically significant at 5 percent level; see table 8.8.) It is possible that persons with lower levels of education work in service sectors, and as a result, have to interact with members of other communities more frequently. If so, this would appear to validate the predictions of contact theory.

As summarized in table 8.19, the Welch T-test for the education group reveals that respondents with a bachelor's degree are less prejudiced against Muslims than respondents with a graduate degree.

The effects of education lay not only in the *level* of education, but also the *place* of education, in that the latter may have a socializing role. Respondents were asked where they had received their last degree. Respondents who received their last degree in the United States were, on average, 13.23 percent less prejudiced against Muslims compared to those who

TABLE 8.8
Differences in Responses by Education

Education	Observations	Mean	Standard Error	95% Confidence Interval	t-value	Significant	Level of Anger
0 = Other	705	2.71	0.0359	[2.640, 2.781]			
1 = High school or less					2.2879	Yes	−22.91%
	108	2.481	0.1023	[2.278, 2.684]			

received their last degree elsewhere (primarily in India).[40] This result is statistically significant at 10 percent level (table 8.9).

Differences by Income and Wealth

Unlike the data used in reporting all prior results, the survey did *not* ask questions on income and wealth. In the testing phase of the survey, when asked about income and/or wealth, respondents were evasive and were less welcoming of the continuation of the survey thereafter. However, based on the respondent's address, I was able to obtain information about likely income and wealth.[41] Respondents with low estimated income were less biased against Muslims, which is consistent with the link between low levels of education and lower levels of prejudice reported in table 8.10. (The results were significant at the 10 percent level.)

As summarized in table 8.20, the Welch T-test for the income group reveals that respondents in the low-income category are less prejudiced against Muslims than respondents in the middle- and high-income category, as well as less than the sample average.

REGRESSION ANALYSIS

We can also have cases where the differences are significant in both the three-statement and four-statement subsamples, but where the magnitude of the difference is much larger in the four-statement subsample, which

[40] 45.5 percent of the sample received their last degree in the United States, 50.6 percent in India, and the rest from other countries.

[41] The data on wealth and income were collected by Donnelley Marketing. They matched the Zip + 4 code of each respondent with the respective wealth and income data in their database based on a proprietary program. I have grouped the breakdowns for family income into the following three categories: A–G, low income; H–O, middle income; and P–T, high income.

TABLE 8.9
Differences by Country of Last Degree

Place Last Degree Received	Observations	Mean	Standard Error	95% Confidence Interval	t-value	Significant	Level of Anger
0 = Other	458	2.738	0.0462	[2.647, 2.828]	1.9293	Yes	-13.23%
1 = United States	355	2.605	0.0502	[2.506, 2.704]			

TABLE 8.10
Differences by Income

Income	Observations	Mean	Standard Error	95% Confidence Interval	t-value	Significant	Level of Anger
0 = Other	611	2.718	0.0393	[2.641, 2.795]	1.9577	Yes	-15.41%
1 = Income < $40,000	202	2.564	0.0676	[2.431, 2.697]			

would suggest that differential prejudice exists even though general levels of anger are also higher for the concerned group. The most general statistical technique to isolate differential prejudice in this setting involves running a regression of the form:

$$Anger = \beta_0 + \beta_1 \cdot Statements + \beta_2 \cdot X_i + \beta_3 \cdot Statements \cdot X_i + \varepsilon$$

where X_i is a dummy variable that takes the value 1 if the individual has the particular characteristic being studied (say, a specific language or religion) and 0 otherwise. The *Statements* variable is a dummy that takes the value 1 if the respondent was presented with four statements and 0 if the respondent was presented with three statements. β_0 gives the average anger of someone was presented with three statements, β_1 provides an estimate of the average amount by which presenting the fourth statement raised the level of anger in the sample, β_2 tells us how much higher or lower the average level of anger across *all statements* is when a respondent exhibits characteristic X_i.

The key parameter of interest here is β_3 which is the coefficient on the interaction term *Statements* · X_i (this term takes the value 1 only when the individual exhibits characteristic X_i and was also presented with four statements) because this tells us how much the combination of belonging to a specific group and being presented with the fourth statements (regarding differential Muslim population growth) changed the average level of anger, which is exactly what we are looking to identify. The magnitude and significance of β_3 therefore provide an estimate of the differential prejudice of a specific group relative to the rest of the population.

The regression results are given in table 8.11. The regressions broadly support the results of the double t-tests shown earlier. As expected, in all cases, the coefficient for the "statements" dummy (i.e., whether a respondent was presented with three or four statements) is positive and statistically significant at the 1 percent level, indicating that, on average, being asked a greater number of statements leads to a higher level of anger.

In the case of respondent ethnicity, Marathi-speaking respondents were more angry in general (the coefficient for the ethnicity dummy is positive and statistically significant at the 1 percent level), but they are not more angry specifically against Muslims (the coefficient for the interaction term is not statistically significant).

Respondents who do not hold religious beliefs were less angry in general (the coefficient for the religion dummy is negative and statistically significant at the 5 percent level), but not less angry specifically against Muslims (the coefficient for the interaction term in not statistically significant). On the other hand, Sikh respondents were not angrier in general (the coefficient for the religion dummy is not statistically significant), but they were more prejudiced specifically against Muslims (the coefficient for the interaction term is positive and statistically significant at the 5 percent level). Respondents who were both Punjabi and Sikh were more prejudiced specifically against Muslims (the coefficient for the interaction term is positive and statistically significant at the 5 percent level).

The religiosity variable is measured in two ways. Respondents considering religion not very important are less prejudiced against Muslims. The coefficient for the interaction term is negative and statistically significant at the 1 percent level. If, on the other hand, religiosity is measured by the frequency of visits to a place of worship (church, gurdwara, mosque, temple), respondents attending a place of worship several times a month are not only more angry in general (the coefficient for the frequency of visits dummy is positive and statistically significant at the 10 percent level), but also more prejudiced against Muslims (the coefficient for the interaction term is positive and statistically significant at the 10 percent level). On the other hand, respondents attending a place of worship once or less per year are less angry in general (the coefficient for the frequency of visits dummy is negative and statistically significant at the 5 percent level), and at the same time, are less prejudiced against Muslims (the coefficient for the interaction term is negative and statistically significant at the 5 percent level).

The only other variable that seems to play a role in prejudice is income. Respondents with *low* income appear *less* prejudiced against Muslims

TABLE 8.11
Anti-Muslim Prejudice

	Statements	Independent Variable	Interaction Term	Constant
		Religion		
None				
Coefficient	0.43	−0.198	−0.082	2.261
t-value	[10.49]***	[−2.50]**	[−0.44]	[104.04]***
Sikh				
Coefficient	0.402	0.113	0.379	2.248
t-value	[9.76]***	[1.18]	[2.31]**	[103.57]***
		Ethnicity		
Marathi				
Coefficient	0.434	0.266	−0.215	2.242
t-value	[10.47]***	[3.25]***	[−1.35]	[103.00]***
		Religiosity: importance of religion		
Not very important				
Coefficient	0.471	0.033	−0.446	2.25
t-value	[11.18]***	[0.54]	[−3.37]***	[98.95]***
		Religiosity: frequency of visits		
Several times/month				
Coefficient	0.376	0.077	0.165	2.229
t-value	[7.78]***	[1.68]*	[1.93]*	[88.39]***
Once or less/year				
Coefficient	0.455	−0.1308	−0.2275	2.275
t-value	[10.58]***	[−2.28]**	[−1.98]**	[98.65]***
		Ethnicity and religion		
Punjabi and Sikh				
Coefficient	0.405	0.135	0.342	2.248
t-value	[9.85]***	[1.32]	[1.96]**	[103.98]***
		Income		
Low income				
Coefficient	0.467	0.019	−0.173	2.25
t-value	[10.20]***	[0.36]	[−1.83]*	[95.83]***

(the coefficient for the interaction term is negative and statistically significant at the 10 percent level). None of the other variables—education
(level and place), age, gender, immigration cohort, wealth—appear to significantly affect the level of prejudice.

Long-Distance Nationalism: Civic or Ethnic?

The results indicate that a substantial minority of Indian Americans are
prejudiced against Muslims. But the variance across categories does
not correspond with the record of anti-Muslim violence in India, suggesting that domestic rather than diasporic factors are predominant.
The survey included two additional questions that shed some light on
the degree to which individual-level prejudice translates into support
for Hindu nationalism.

Correcting Historical Wrongs

One of the most emotive issues pressed by the Hindu religious right is to
"correct historical wrongs"—in particular, by erecting temples in places
where mosques that are claimed to be built on the sites of destroyed
temples currently stand. The 1992 storming of the Babri Masjid, a mosque
in Northern India that is claimed to be the birthplace of the Hindu god
Ram, is an example of attempts in that direction.

Respondents were asked, "There are certain issues that everyone agrees
are important. I will read out two statements at a time, and then I'd like
you to tell me which one is more important to you personally. Do you
think it is more important to correct historical wrongs or to promote
harmony and equality between Muslims and Hindus in India?"

Of the respondents, 85.8 percent preferred promoting harmony, while
just 4.9 percent were for correcting "historical wrongs." The only variable that was significant was religiosity (at the 5 percent level), albeit in a
modest way. Respondents attending places of worship several times per
week were 3.5 percent less likely to support promoting harmony than the
sample average. On the other hand, respondents attending places of worship just several times per year were 2.8 percent more likely to support
promoting harmony than the sample average. Thus, a pet project of
Hindu nationalism finds little support among the diaspora.

Uniform Civil Code

Unlike most Western democracies, India does not have a uniform civil
code. Under the British, different communities had separate personal laws,

and this phenomenon has persisted after independence. The issue has been politicized by Hindu religious nationalists, who see it as symptomatic of India's "pseudo-secularism" "pandering" to Muslims, and they have long demanded that the country implement a uniform civil code. The issue also divides those strongly committed to secularism, since it violates the principle of "one law for all citizens."

Respondents were asked, "Currently in India, different religions have different laws on marriage and divorce. Do you think that the Indian government should impose a uniform law for everyone?" Of the respondents, 57.6 percent were in favor of everyone having the same law, 31.6 percent were opposed, and 10.8 percent responded "Don't know." Among linguistic groups, English speakers stood out. They were 16.6 percent less likely than the sample average to support a uniform marriage law for everyone (the result was statistically significant at the 1 percent level). Hindu respondents were 6 percent more likely to support a uniform marriage law for everyone than the sample average (the result was statistically significant at the 5 percent level). Religiosity also affected differences in views. Respondents attending places of worship several times per week were, on average, 7.4 percent less likely to support a uniform marriage law for everyone than the sample average (the difference in means is statistically significant at the 5 percent level). While respondents with a high-school education were 8.4 percent less likely to support a uniform marriage law for everyone compared to the sample average, those with a postgraduate degree were 4.6 percent more likely to support a uniform marriage law for everyone than the sample average (the difference in means was statistically significant at the 5 percent level in both cases).

The survey also asked two questions that shed light on the diaspora's civic nationalism. The first relates to India's controversial nuclear tests; the second bears on India's affirmative action policies, which have been resisted by India's upper castes (who dominate the Indian American community) in India.

India's Nuclear Tests

Respondents were asked, "When you first heard about the 1998 nuclear tests conducted by India, what was your reaction?" In general, the tests did get strong support from the U.S.-based Indian diaspora.

Of the respondents, 44.2 percent expressed strong support, and another 19 percent "somewhat strong support." 7.8 percent were somewhat strongly opposed, while 5.8 percent were strongly opposed. A significant number, 23.3 percent, responded, "Don't know." In contrast, a survey conducted in India in the immediate aftermath of the nuclear tests found that an overwhelming majority (91 percent) of the respondents approved of India conducting the nuclear tests, while just 7 percent disapproved (the remaining two percent did not offer any opinion).[42] Although the two surveys are not strictly comparable, since the passage of time might make for more considered opinions, again it offers little support that overseas Indians are more nationalist than those living in India.

How did support for the tests vary with different characteristics? As before, I used the two-sample *t*-test to determine whether the responses of a subgroup were different from the sample average. With one exception, there was no difference across different linguistic groups. Those who reported themselves as English speakers (about 2.5 percent of the sample) were 77 percent less likely to support Indian nuclear testing than the sample average. (The result was statistically significant at the 1 percent level; see table 8.12.)

The responses were markedly different depending on the religious beliefs of the respondents. Those who reported themselves as not believing in a religion, Christians, and "other religions" were, on average, 42 percent, 42.4 percent, and 78.6 percent less likely to support Indian nuclear testing than the sample average. Conversely, Hindu respondents were 34.4 percent more likely to support Indian nuclear testing than the sample average. In all cases, the results are significant at the 1 percent level.

The intensity of religious preferences also appears to make a difference in opinions. Those respondents for whom religion is "very important" are 17.8 percent more likely to support Indian nuclear testing than the sample average. On the other hand, respondents for whom religion is "not at all important" are 42.4 percent less likely to support Indian nuclear testing than the sample average (table 8.13). In both cases, the results are statistically significant at the 1 percent level.

If intensity of religious preferences is measured by formal religious practice, support for nuclear tests appears to grow with this practice. Respondents attending a place of worship several times per month are 23.5 percent more likely to support India's nuclear tests than the sample average. Conversely, respondents who visit a place of worship several times a year and once a year or less are 10 percent and 19.5 percent less likely to support Indian nuclear testing than the sample average (table 8.14). The difference in means is statistically significant at the 5 percent level if attendance is several times per year and at the 1 percent level if attendance is several times per month and once a year or less.

Last, those who received their last degree in the United States were 25.5 percent *less likely* to support India's nuclear tests than the sample average (the difference is statistically significant at the 1 percent level). As

---

[42] The survey was conducted by the Indian Market Research Bureau (IMRB) on May 12, 1998, less than 24 hours after the tests. (The sample was 1007 adults.)

TABLE 8.12
Differences in Views on Nuclear Tests by Religious Group

Religion	Observations	Mean	Standard Error	95% Confidence Interval	t-value	Significant	Difference from Sample Average
0 = Other	1570	1.656	0.0232	[1.611, 1.702]			
1 = Do not believe in religion	65	2.076	0.1357	[1.805, 2.348]	−3.5773	**Yes**	−42.02%
0 = Other	302	1.953	0.0598	[1.836, 2.071]	5.8494	Yes	34.37%
1 = Hindu	1333	1.609	0.0244	[1.562, 1.658]			
0 = Other	1557	1.653	0.0233	[1.607, 1.699]	−3.9383	Yes	−42.37%
1 = Christian	78	2.077	0.115	[1.847, 2.306]			
0 = Other	1615	1.663	0.023	[1.618, 1.709]	−3.7669	Yes	−78.62%
1 = Other religions	20	2.45	0.245	[1.935, 2.964]			

TABLE 8.13
Differences in Views on Nuclear Tests by Intensity of Religious Preferences (by Importance of Religion)

Importance of Religion	Observations	Mean	Standard Error	95% Confidence Interval	t-value	Significant	Difference from Sample Average
0 = Other	888	1.754	0.0313	[1.623, 1.816]			
1 = Very important	747	1.577	0.0336	[1.51, 1.643]	3.8554	Yes	17.75%
0 = Other	1538	1.648	0.0232	[1.602, 1.693]			
1 = Not at all important	97	2.072	0.1156	[1.842, 2.301]	−4.3715	Yes	−42.39%

TABLE 8.14
Differences in Views on Nuclear Tests by Intensity of Religious Preferences (by Frequency of Visiting Place of Worship)

Frequency of Visiting Place of Worship	Observations	Mean	Standard Error	95% Confidence Interval	t-value	Significant	Difference from Sample Average
0 = Other	1096	1.75	0.0289	[1.694, 1.807]			
1 = Several times per month	539	1.515	0.0366	[1.443, 1.587]	4.8314	Yes	23.51%
0 = Other	1161	1.644	0.0277	[1.589, 1.698]			
1 = Several times per year	474	1.744	0.0408	[1.664, 1.825]	−1.9804	Yes	−10.04%
0 = Other	1392	1.644	0.0244	[1.596, 1.692]			
1 = Once a year or less	243	1.839	0.065	[1.711, 1.967]	−3.0204	Yes	−19.51%

with anti-Muslim prejudice, place and not level of education seems to be significant.

Affirmative Action

Affirmative action, or "reservations," has long been a politically contentious issue in India. They were originally put into the constitution as a temporary measure to help the most socially disadvantaged groups overcome the historically cruel practice of caste discrimination. Since then, they have expanded as more and more social groups in India claiming to be disadvantaged have clamored to be included in affirmative action programs. As you saw in chapter 2, most Indians in the United States (more than 90 percent) are from privileged higher and dominant castes, groups that perceive themselves to have been adversely affected by affirmative action. Survey respondents were asked:

> Some people say that because of discrimination in the past, an extra effort should be made to ensure that qualified minorities are considered for university admissions in the United States. Some say that this is wrong because it discriminates against other groups. How do you feel? Are you in favor or opposed to such policies? Would you say you favor such policies, oppose such policies, or are indifferent to them?

Of the respondents, 37.3 percent were in favor of such policies, and 22 percent opposed such policies. 25.6 percent were indifferent to such policies, and another 15.1 percent responded, "Don't know." Tamil and Kannada respondents were, on average, 20.1 percent and 23.7 percent more likely to favor affirmative action policies than the sample average (table 8.15). On the other hand, English speakers are, on average, 21.8 percent more likely to *oppose* affirmative action policies than the sample average. The means are statistically significant at the 5 percent level if respondents are English or Kannada speakers and at the 1 percent level if respondents are Tamil speakers.

TABLE 8.15
Differences in Views on Affirmative Action

Ethnicity	Observations	Mean	Standard Error	95% Confidence Interval	t-value	Significant	Difference from Sample Average
0 = Other	1616	1.84	0.0203	[1.800, 1.880]	3.2531	Yes	20.11%
1 = Tamil	194	1.639	0.0553	[1.529, 1.748]			
0 = Other	1739	1.81	0.0196	[1.771, 1.848]	−2.2082	Yes	−21.79%
1 = English	71	2.028	0.0873	[1.854, 2.202]			
0 = Other	1749	1.826	0.0195	[1.788, 1.865]	2.2285	Yes	23.66%
1 = Kannada	61	1.59	0.0974	[1.395, 1.785]			

Views on affirmative action are also affected by intensity of religious preferences. Respondents who consider religion very important are, on average, 12.7 percent more likely to support affirmative action policies than the sample average (the result is statistically significant at the 1 percent level). Similarly, respondents who attend places of worship several times per month are 12.7 percent more likely to support affirmative action policies than the sample average, while respondents whose attendance is once a year or less are 19.4 percent less likely to support affirmative action policies than the sample average (the difference in means is statistically significant at the 1 percent level).

TRANSFORMING BELIEFS INTO ACTIONS: DIASPORIC PHILANTHROPY

It is one thing to have beliefs about something; it is quite another to act upon them. Long-distance nationalism can take many forms, such as lobbying in the country of residence or raising funds for philanthropy in the country of origin. Philanthropy offers an individual the opportunity to both network as well as raise his or her status within the community. The latter could be narrowly defined (ethnicity or a sect within a religious group) or more broadly defined.[43] But it is also a convenient cover for extending support to extremist groups. With regard to the last, there is well-documented evidence on three organizations: one in the United States, (the India Development and Relief Fund [IDRF]) and two that are UK-based (Hindu Sewa Sangh [HSS] and Sewa International).[44] Of the $18 billion that flowed into India in 2003 as remittances, the combined flows from these organizations was less than 0.05 percent, or $9 million.

Official data, at least, are not supportive of the claim that diasporic philanthropy provides a cover for support of religious extremism in India, but this data itself has its limitations. The only available source of official data on foreign inflows to nongovernment organizations (NGOs) in India is that maintained by the home ministry under the statutory Foreign Contributions Regulation Act (FCRA). An analysis of these data also does not provide support for diaspora flows to Hindu religious

[43] A parallel is Michael Berkowitz's argument that the success of Zionism lay in its ability to offer upwardly mobile secular Jews a social outlet to express their Jewishness through philanthropy (1997).

[44] See "The Foreign Exchange of Hate: IDRF and the American Funding of Hindutva," available at http://stopfundinghate.org/sacw/; from Awaaz: South Asia Watch, "In Bad Faith? British Charity & Hindu Extremism," 2004, available at http://www.awaazsaw.org/ibf/ibflores.pdf; as well as the report of the International Initiative for Gujarat (IIJ), available at http://www.onlinevolunteers.org/gujarat/reports/iijg/.

groups, but again, that could be due to the coverage and classification of the data. These data exclude contributions by nonresident Indians (NRIs) but includes data from naturalized citizens and persons of Indian origin (PIOs). However, it is not possible from these data to desegregate that fraction of FCRA funds originating from the diaspora, from that emanating from other sources—namely international NGOs and non-diaspora foreign citizens. The data maintained by the home ministry on its website give a breakdown of the FCRA organizations by purpose. classifying them into five principal purposes: cultural, economic, educational, religious, and social. Slightly more than one-quarter of FCRA organizations have a religious purpose. There is a further breakdown by religious denomination. The majority of FCRA organizations that have "religion" as one of their purposes are Christian (84 percent), while Hindu and Muslim organizations are roughly similar in number (6 and 5 percent, respectively). The stark difference between the number of Christian and Hindu organizations—virtually in inverse proportion to their share in the population—is puzzling and may be due to three factors. Hindu organizations either raise their money domestically, and very little from the diaspora. Alternatively, they get their money from the diaspora through informal channels and since NRI flows are not covered by FCRA requirements, they are largely undocumented. Or alternatively, organizations that are ostensibly "social" and "cultural" might be more sectarian, while those that impart education might be much less so, even though they might be religiously motivated. Again, we simply do not have the empirical basis to draw firm conclusions.

On the sending-country side, I surveyed more than one hundred Indian American diaspora organizations. They reveal a range of activities and engagement with India—but religion (and especially support for Hindu organizations) was marginally, if at all. But again, this could be because it support is indeed low or because those who support extremist organizations are unlikely to give information about the same. I want to emphasize that all of this *does not* necessarily mean that the Indian diaspora is not a significant financier of the Sangh Parivar—it could be, but we simply do not have the evidence to hang such a claim upon.

CONCLUSION

This chapter examined an important consequence of international migration on sending countries arising from the *diaspora* channel: the ability of a diaspora to engage in long-distance nationalism and influence politics within the country of origin. It is important to point out what the data and analysis presented in this chapter can tell us, and what it cannot.

The survey data examined here directly measures the diaspora's social and political attitudes. It also allows us to address the argument laid out earlier—namely, to what extent the diaspora's support for political violence is consequential, in the sense that the violence would not occur without these flows. In that case, one should expect, at a minimum, that there would be a close correlation between those language/regional groups that are more biased relative to their peers and the incidence of political violence in the home regions from which these groups are drawn. Yet our data do not support this argument—the rough parity in anti-Muslim prejudice between Gujaratis and Bengalis (indeed, with the latter being somewhat greater than the former), does not correlate with the incidence of communal violence in those regions. Neither is there any evidence that the high level of anti-Muslim prejudice among overseas Sikhs has any implications for anti-Muslim violence in India.

Most of the discussion of these issues—the degree to which sponsorship of communal violence can be laid at the door of the diaspora—has tended to be speculative, with little recourse to data on either financial flows or diaspora attitudes. The survey data underlying the preceding analysis allows us to contribute to this discussion by directly examining diaspora attitudes. As argued previously, these results suggest a degree of caution, both in ascribing political violence to the financial fuel provided by the diaspora, and in drawing facile links between the degree of prejudice in subgroups among the diaspora and violence in the region from which that subgroup is drawn. Indeed, if the diaspora were such a strong supporter of the BJP, the party should ostensibly have pressed for the inclusion of voting rights of overseas Indians when it introduced the Overseas Citizens of India Bill in 2003. However, despite the fact that some 60-odd countries allow expatriates to vote in home-country elections (either by mail or by visiting a consulate or embassy), the BJP (in a seemingly selfless act to keep its supporters at bay) insisted that the diaspora would not be granted the right to vote (or hold Constitutional Offices or be appointed to government jobs). This is hardly what one would expect from a political party seeking to reward its supposedly loyal supporters.

With the defeat of the BJP in mid-2004, when the Congress-led United Progressive Alliance (UPA) government took power, India was led by a Sikh prime minister, a Muslim president, and a naturalized Catholic as the driving force of the Congress Party, and with it the specter of the juggernaut of Hindu nationalism taking over the country ebbed. The even worse performance of the BJP in 2009 suggested that Hindu nationalism, while certainly having the power to do considerable mischief in different parts of the country, was not as strong a national force as some commentators had feared. If the Indian diaspora's funding had indeed been so important for Hindu nationalism, the electoral outcomes certainly provided little evidence of that claim. In this case at least, blaming the "foreign hand" may simply be barking up the wrong tree, and it detracts from understanding the primacy of domestic political variables in explaining communal violence in India.

In conclusion, the many commentaries on the proclivities of the diaspora in fomenting ethnic violence in India appear to be somewhat exaggerated. The normative concerns that arose consequent to the emergence of Hindu nationalism as a significant political force in India during the 1990s were understandable, given its potential to inflict severe damage to India's polity. However, these concerns appeared to have been more a projection of the anxieties of the commentators than based on careful empirical analysis.[45] In the 2000s, even as the diaspora grew in numbers and wealth, Hindu nationalism's power waned in India, underscoring the limitations of the Indian diaspora's presumed role as the force-multiplier of Hindu nationalism.

---

[45] See for example the contributions to the special issue of *Ethnic and Racial Studies* 23, no. 3 (2000).

APPENDIX: TABLES

TABLE 8.16
Welch T-Statistics for Subgroups by Ethnicity

Group	1	2	3	4	5	6	7	8	9	10
Bengali										
English	-0.036									
Gujarati	-0.024	0.023								
Hindi	-1.229	-0.986	2.048**							
Kannada	-0.404	-0.332	-0.475	0.594						
Malayalam	-0.156	-0.110	-0.166	0.812	0.212					
Marathi	1.013	0.933	1.367	2.681***	1.355	1.037				
Punjabi	-1.556	-1.303	-2.225**	-0.668	-0.957	-1.135	-2.846***			
Tamil	0.832	0.756	1.263	2.925***	1.217	0.872	-0.328	2.996***		
Telugu	-0.634	-0.520	-0.826	0.519	-0.157	-0.382	-1.757*	0.951	-1.681	
Average	-0.441	-0.316	-0.824	1.794*	0.139	-0.155	-1.945*	1.966**	-2.064	0.432

* indicates significance at 10% level; ** indicates significance at 5% level; and *** indicates significance at 1% level.

TABLE 8.17
Welch T-Statistics for Subgroups by Religion

Group	1	2	3	4	5	6	7
Hindu							
Christian	−1.155						
Jain	−0.083	0.538					
Sikh	−3.618	−1.722*	−1.774*				
Muslim	0.564	0.995	0.509	1.952*			
Other	1.704*	2.083**	1.325	3.259***	0.623		
None	0.516	1.198	0.359	2.868***	−0.288	−1.208	
Average	−0.587	0.960	−0.038	3.433***	−0.654	−1.820	−0.704

* indicates significance at 10% level; ** indicates significance at 5% level; and *** indicates significance at 1% level.

TABLE 8.18
Welch T-Statistics for Subgroups by Religiosity

Group	1	2	3	4	5
Several times per week					
Several times per month	−0.262				
Several times per year	2.073**	2.910***			
Once a year or less	3.086***	3.826***	1.556		
Never	0.269	0.352	−0.348	−0.809	
Average	1.244	2.076**	−1.486	−2.803***	0.059

* indicates significance at 10% level; ** indicates significance at 5% level; and *** indicates significance at 1% level.

TABLE 8.19
Welch T-Statistics for Subgroups by Education

Group	1	2	3
High school			
Bachelor's degree	−0.502		
Graduate degree	−1.580	−1.759*	
Average	−0.974	−0.775	1.335

* indicates significance at 10% level; ** indicates significance at 5% level; and *** indicates significance at 1% level.

TABLE 8.20
Welch T-Statistics for Income Subgroups

Group	1	2	3
Low Income			
Middle Income	−2.793***		
High Income	−2.264**	0.616	
Average	−2.016**	1.476	0.736

* indicates significance at 10% level; ** indicates significance at 5% level; and *** indicates significance at 1% level.

CHAPTER 9

Spatially Unbound Nations

> A country is not territorial, but ideational.
>
> —*Rabindranath Tagore*[1]

"[P]EOPLE HAVE MOVED across India's borders over thousands of years, enriching India as well as the rest of the world."[2] Amartya Sen's observation about India could plausibly be made for any country. After all, the history of humanity is a history of migration and material progress, starting from its antecedents in Africa. The wider the historical canvas, the more likely a transformative force of history will have an affirmative ring to it. But if the historical canvas is more limited, as in this study, the colors appear more muted—and the doubts somewhat greater.

The first great migrations from India occurred approximately a millennia ago, when groups now known as the Roma left what became India and ended up in Europe. Even now it is exceedingly difficult to say how this substantial migration from India affected either of the parties: those who moved, those living in the areas where they moved (mainly Europe), and those who remained behind. To whatever degree the Roma may have enriched Europe, the fact is that they have been one of the most persecuted groups in that continent. Yet in the millennia that they have been wandering, the regions they came from (the Northwestern parts of the Indian subcontinent) have also been beset by turmoil, conflicts, and low standards of living. What if they had never left?

The expectations of contemporary social science are that, at the end of an extensive research, there should be a categorical bottom line and a parsimonious causal explanation. This book does not meet either of these expectations. What this study does demonstrate, however, is that the answer to the seemingly simple question "How has international migration affected the political economy of India's development?" is not so

---

[1] Quoted in the preface of Ashish Nandy, *The Illegitimacy of Nationalism: Rabindranath Tagore and the Politics of Self* (New Delhi: Oxford University Press, 2004). I am grateful to Sunil Khilnani for this reference. The original quote is from Rabindranath Tagore, *Rabindra-Rachnabali*, vol. 1, p. 1: "A country is not territorial (*mrinmaya*); it is ideational (*chinmaya*)."

[2] Amartya Sen, *The Argumentative Indian* (New York: Farrar, Straus and Giroux, 2005), 86.

straightforward; it depends on what one means by "development" and the time period under study.

To take an example: the Indian Institutes of Technology (IITs) are one of India's most visible symbols of modernity and most successful institutions. In the waning days of World War II, one of the first acts of the then government was to send 500 Indian students abroad, in 1945, to institutes in the United Kingdom, Canada, and the United States, to meet the "urgent needs of post-war development." Soon after, the Indian government set up a committee to consider technical higher education, which laid out the framework for the Indian Institutes of Technology.[3] The Committee included two young Indians with doctorates from MIT who had "deep knowledge of what an MIT education was and what it might mean for India. The creation of the Indian Institutes of Technology was an act of the imagination, but it was not solely an act of the imagination."[4] It institutionalized what the returning young Indians had learned about engineering education, emphasizing the circulation aspect of international migration and its contribution to new ideas in India, with far-reaching effects.

A few years later, when IIT-Kanpur was being set up, it received about a thousand applications, a fifth of them from the United States and Western Europe. Two-thirds of the Indians chosen as faculty had earned their degrees in U.S. universities. And their contribution to building one of India's finest institutions has stood the test of time. In this small example, a judgment on the contribution of international migration to India's development in the late 1960s would come to a categorical positive assessment.

However, over the next three decades, the initial cashing in on India's "brain bank" abroad, instead of stemming the brain drain, amplified it. A decade after its establishment, a quarter of IIT-Kanpur's undergraduates and a fifth of its master's students had gone abroad, mainly to the United States.[5] It was said that "when a student enrolls at an IIT, his spirit is said to ascend to America. After graduation, his body follows."[6] As you saw in chapter 3, a large number of talented students from IITs (and other similar institutions) continued to leave India over several decades; few returned, and their links with India were personal and familial rather than

[3] The committee, known as the Sarkar Committee, had twenty-two members: nine Britons and thirteen Indians, including some of India's leading scientists, such as J. C. Ghosh and S. S. Bhatnagar, and representatives of India's leading industrial enterprises, such as A. D. Shroff and two young Indians with doctorates from MIT, Anant Pandya and M. D. Parekh, with Pandya sitting on the working subcommittee. Ross Bassett, "MIT-Trained Swadeshis: MIT and Indian Nationalism, 1884–1947," *Osiris* 24, no. 1 (2009): 212–30.

[4] Ibid.

[5] Stuart W. Leslie and Robert Kargo, "Exporting MIT: Science, Technology, and Nation-Building in India and Iran," *Osiris* 21, no. 1 (2006): 110–30.

[6] Ibid.

professional and financial. The IITs became the producers of what wags remarked was the only high-tech product in which India was internationally competitive. Indeed the very absence of some of India's best and brightest contributed to that sad reality. "Dedicated to the Service of the Nation," read the motto of the first IIT (IIT-Kharagpur); by the late 1980s, one could legitimately ask "which nation?"

But as India began liberalizing its economy, slowly in the 1980s and more rapidly in later years, as you saw in chapter 4, the skills, wealth, and reputation of this segment of the Indian diaspora now became an asset. Return rates increased, enhancing India's capacity in knowledge creation.[7]

The effects on India of international migration from the IITs seemed more positive in the 2000s than in the 1980s. And if the nation is constituted as a people rather than territorially circumscribed, then the migration of IIT graduates and their success overseas more than likely benefited the Indian nation in the aggregate. Hence, if development is about people rather than a territory, then surely the development outcomes, by this measure, are positive. But this must be measured against some counterfactual—what if these graduates had never left or if their patterns of migration and return been different?

Instead of providing a simple bottom line, this book contributes to our understanding about the effects of international migration on the political economy of sending countries in three ways. One, it builds on an analytical framework consisting of four channels—prospect, absence, diaspora, and return—and identifies the mechanisms within each channel through which international migration affects the country of origin. Two, the book makes an empirical contribution by designing and creating several original data sets. And three, the book leverages the theoretical framework and mechanisms to the empirical data to examine specific effects.

In this concluding chapter, I summarize the principal economic and political effects of international migration for India. These consequences suggest a somewhat paradoxical finding—the primacy of the domestic in mediating the effects of globalization. One cannot a priori posit whether international migration is "good" or "bad" for a country. The outcomes depend heavily on the policies of the country of origin—which of course can (and do) change over time. This conclusion challenges the breathless invocations of international migration and diasporas as portending a future of deterritorialized nations and transnationalism as an alternative modernity. However, the movement of peoples across borders does raise

---

[7] To take an example, in 2009, a fifth of the over 3800 scientists and engineers at General Electric's technology center in Bangalore were recruited abroad. Bhupesh Bhandari, "Frugal Innovation," *Business Standard*, June 13, 2009, available at http://www.business -standard.com/india/news/frugal-innovation/360886/ (retrieved on June 15, 2009).

a key normative question: how should we think about citizenship and the political community in deterritorialized nations?

How Has International Migration from India Impacted Its Political Economy?

The analysis in this book provides several insights into the complex ways in which international migration can affect the country of origin. The book's empirical material focused on the Indian diaspora in the United States, for reasons discussed in chapter 2. As I argued, the effects of international migration are strongly mediated by the selection characteristics of the migrants and the characteristics of the destination and source country. Furthermore, the status of émigrés and their mode of incorporation in host societies will clearly affect the nature of their links to the origin state. Consequently, given the sheer heterogeneity of international migration from India, it would be foolhardy to attempt to come up with a simple bottom line regarding the net impact of emigration on India. One can, however, look at the effects within specific domains, which I summarize in the following.

Economic Effects

The economic consequences of international migration have been mixed for India. The migration of less-skilled labor (especially to the Middle East) has had positive effects both because this is the more abundant factor in India and because of the large inflow of remittances. In the regions of high emigration, labor markets tightened, raising wages for those left behind and drawing in poorer migrants from other parts of India. In addition to the obvious positive impact for recipient households, financial remittances have had considerable systemic effects on India's balance of payments, allowing much greater trade deficits than would otherwise have been possible, stabilizing the rupee exchange rate, and thereby giving India's central bank greater monetary policy autonomy.

However, the migration of the highly skilled has had more ambiguous consequences. On the positive side, since the skilled migrants were mainly drawn from the upper castes, their exit bolstered political stability, which is usually healthy for any economy. Their success overseas has had positive reputational externalities for India. In addition, this segment of the diaspora has woven a web of cross-national networks, thereby facilitating the flow of tacit information, commercial and business ideas, and technologies into India. It has also facilitated "in-sourcing," as exemplified by the rapid growth of India's diamond cutting and polishing industry.

The implications of the diaspora's role in amplifying ongoing growth trends in India are less clear. India's economically successful diaspora has developed a comparative advantage in white-collar skilled services such as information technology (IT) and tertiary medical services. Consequently, the investments they have influenced into India have also been in these sectors, rather than blue-collar labor-intensive manufacturing sectors (the diamond industry is an exception).

The Indian example illustrates a broader point about how the sectoral expertise acquired by emigrants overseas diffuses back to the country of origin. Parallels can be draw with the Chinese example, where the economically successful Chinese diaspora (especially in Hong Kong, Southeast Asia, and Taiwan) made its wealth (and acquired relevant capabilities) in labor-intensive manufacturing, and therefore its investments into China were in related sectors as well. However, wherever diasporas are engaged primarily in low-skilled jobs (Indians in the Gulf, Mexicans and Central Americans in the United States), the skills acquired are too limited to have any significant sectoral impact on the country of origin.

The loss of significant numbers of the highly skilled has undoubtedly also had negative effects as well, perhaps most manifest in reducing the supply of professionals with the managerial and technical capabilities to run institutions and organizations, be they colleges or hospitals, statistical systems, or research laboratories. There is widespread perception that professional standards in Indian have eroded (for instance, the ethics of India's medical profession), and it is likely that the departure of so many of the better-trained professional might have contributed to this. However, this linkage is speculative, and this book does not offer any evidence to support this view. A prime example of these adverse effects can be seen in India's higher-education system.[8] The 1950s and 1960s were halcyon days for Indian higher education, as universities expanded and a host of new institutions of higher education, including its famed IITs and Indian Institutes of Management (IIMs), as well as new science and technology research institutes, were set up, all at state expense. Many of the key personnel in these institutions were trained abroad and returned to India, inspired by the heady days of "nation building." But by the late 1960s, more and more of India's best and brightest began to go abroad, never to return. The small number who did were sufficient to maintain the high standards of a small number of institutions, but not their expansion, and the number of graduates from these elite institutions remained virtually unchanged for four decades. Meanwhile, the replenishment of talent in

---

[8] This discussion draws from Devesh Kapur, "Indian Higher Education," in *American Universities in a Global Market*, ed. Charles Clotfelter (Chicago: NBER, University of Chicago Press, forthcoming).

universities and research institutes began to decline as fewer returned. Last, when return migration picked up at the turn of the century, few saw public institutions as a viable career alternative. This has been an important reason why Indian universities (virtually all public) have deteriorated. As mediocrity has become entrenched, it has become even more impervious to change. The Indian prime minister has grimly noted that the country's university system "is, in many parts, in a state of disrepair . . . almost two-thirds of our universities and 90 percent of our colleges are rated as below average on quality parameters."[9] Various indicators employed to study the quality of higher education in India, such as research output, infrastructure and placement of graduates, point to low quality.[10]

An important component of any university system, necessary in order for it to expand and become a net producer of knowledge, is the health of its doctoral programs. Despite India's emergence as one of most rapidly growing economies since the 1980s, its rank in publications in major international journals dropped. Between 1985 and 2002, the ratio of the number of PhDs to bachelor's degrees in science and engineering in India dropped from 2.2 percent to just 0.66 percent. (During the same period in the United States, this ratio doubled, from 4.1 percent to 8.4 percent.) In the social sciences, the number of PhDs produced by India's premier economics faculty (Delhi School of Economics) dropped from about 4.5 a year in the 1970s and 1990s to barely 1.5 a year in next decade. As a result, Indian social sciences are faced with a "severe, and increasing, shortage, of qualified researchers,"[11] and overall faculty vacancies in universities were reaching nearly 45 percent.[12] Meanwhile, universities around the world (and especially in Anglo-Saxon countries) are flush with high-skilled talent from India.

While there are many complex reasons for the travails of Indian higher education, these have been amplified by the manner in which the system has been a net exporter of talent. Any system that hemorrhages talent over the long run will struggle to survive, let alone prosper. There have been considerable cognitive effects as well: one example is the migration

[9] Prime Minister Manmohan Singh's address at the 150th Anniversary Function of University of Mumbai, June 22, 2007, available at http://pmindia.nic.in/lspeech.asp?id=555.

[10] In the Times Higher Education World University Rankings 2008, of the top 200 universities, two were Indian; the Academic Rankings of World Universities by Shanghai Jiao Tong University also ranked only two Indian universities in the top 500.

[11] The Indian Council of Social Science Research, "Restructuring the Indian Council of Social Science Research," Report of the Fourth Review Committee, March 2007, 22. New Delhi: ICSSR, 2007.

[12] University Grants Commission, "Report of the Committee to Review the Pay Scales and Service Conditions of University and College Teachers." New Delhi: UGC, 2008.

of liberal economists, which left few behind and weakened the counter-argument to the dominant leftist discourse in Indian academia. A stark example is the state of West Bengal, where three decades of communist rule have so politicized its institutions of higher education that the large number of excellent researchers from this state can be found all over the world, but far fewer in the state itself.[13]

Political Effects

This book has argued that international migration has had a significant positive impact on Indian politics: first, by influencing the commitment to liberal democratic politics among Indian elites, and second, by promoting India's democratic durability and stability through elite "exit." The analysis points to the less salubrious effects on India, arising from support for extremist nationalist and separatist groups by members of the Indian diaspora. However, the evidence suggests that the systemic effects of this support is relatively modest compared to domestic variables and much less important than critics suggest.

In chapter 5, I demonstrated that the *international exposure and return migration* of Indian elites contributed to several key ideas that have shaped India: its commitment to a democratic form of government at the time of independence and, more recently, to economic liberalization. This is not to say that these two critical characteristics of contemporary India have been shaped only or even primarily by international migration, but it has played an important role in shaping the sensibility of Indian political and policy elites.

Additionally, international migration has had a key political impact on the endurance of India's democracy. As I argued in chapter 6, elite "exit" through emigration eased the political ascendancy of India's numerically dominant lower castes. The exit possibilities provided by international migration have reduced the insecurity of India's upper-caste elites—thereby making them less implacably opposed to the political ascendancy of hitherto marginalized social groups. In turn, this has made Indian politics less contentious, providing greater stability than might otherwise have been in the absence of the possibility of exit for India's upper-caste elites.

In the context of religious conflict within India, scholars have suggested that globalization "has had its greatest impact on how religion has come to be deployed as a group identity in Indian politics" due to "the role of India's diaspora in the Hindu nationalist imagination."[14] The evidence

---

[13] There are exceptions, of course, but they simply prove the rule.

[14] Vibha Pingle and Ashutosh Varshney, "India's Identity Politics: Then and Now," in

presented in my analysis suggests that this is only partly true. In chapter 8, evidence on long-distance nationalism in the Indian diaspora suggests that while elements of the diaspora have been strong supporters of Hindu nationalism, this support may be less stringent than previous arguments suggest. The evidence that the diaspora has been an important, let alone primary, cause of anti-Muslim violence in India is rather thin, notwithstanding the overheated rhetoric on this issue.

Because international migration has contributed to a political trend that did not happen (or happened much less than the counterfactual)—namely, intraelite political conflict between extant upper-caste elites and rising elites representing members of hitherto socially marginalized groups, leading to democratic breakdown—this effect has been less visible than in the context of religious conflict, where the diaspora's limited role in long-distance nationalism has been more visible and hence appears more significant. Nonetheless, the analysis presented in this book indicates that the converse may in fact be true: migration's less visible impact on India's democratic traditions may far have outweighed its more visible impact on religious tensions in India.

Last, the political effects of international migration on India also extend to India's foreign policy. As I argued in chapter 7, the diaspora presents opportunities but also serious challenges to India's foreign policy. An overarching point is that the diaspora's foreign policy impact will depend on a combination of the nature of the destination country, the relationship between the Indian government and the diaspora, and the nature of Indian domestic politics. In established industrialized democracies, where the Indian diaspora enjoys full citizenship rights and is also in a privileged economic position, the diaspora is likely to facilitate Indian foreign policy goals to emerge as a "bridging power" that "provides the essential connective tissue, the connectivity that a fragmenting world requires."[15] In contrast, the diaspora's impact on India's foreign policy will be more circumscribed in countries where it enjoys limited citizenship rights and forms a mix of an economic underclass as well as middle-class professionals and businesspeople (as is the case in the Middle East and Gulf states). In these cases, the diaspora is likely to continue to weave a limited web of ties between India and the Middle East and play a stabilizing role in the region. The third group of countries, where the Indian diaspora is of older vintage and where citizenship rights are contested with other ethnic groups, will pose the greatest problems. These include countries in India's neighbor-hood and in others such as Fiji and Malaysia. While in the first two categories of countries there is relatively little uncertainty about the sta-tus of the diaspora, in the third instance there exists the potential for unpleasant surprises and serious challenges to Indian foreign policy.

Reaping the Benefits of Globalization: The Primacy of the Domestic?

> The fault, dear Brutus, is not in our stars,
> But in ourselves, that we are underlings.
>
> —*William Shakespeare*[16]

Given the degree to which globalization has become a favorite whipping boy for so many of humanity's current travails, if Shakespeare were to rewrite his classic line today he would probably be reassuring Brutus that the fault is all in our stars. Why worry about one's own actions if one's fate is so overdetermined? But as this book has tried to show, by examin-ing the effects of international migration from India, globalization offers both opportunities and risks. That the statement is both a truism and a cliché does not render it invalid. But the evidence in this book suggests that the balance depends principally on the policies and politics of the country of origin rather than something intrinsic to this specific mecha-nism of globalization. This is even more true of a giant country like India. Whether diasporas attenuate or amplify national power, whether they lobby for the country of origin in foreign capitals or instead help raise funds for separatist movements, whether a "brain drain" becomes a "brain gain," and whether they invest in factories in the country of origin or one-way tickets for their compatriots to leave the country of origin by and large depends on factors endogenous to the country of origin. It must be remembered that citizens leave their country for a reason. And when they leave, the factors that led them to leave do not disappear. Under-standing these factors is critical to understanding the varying behaviors and effects of diasporas on the country of origin.

In the early 1970s, a time when India's economy was anemic, a well-known Indian parliamentarian, Piloo Mody, asked the then Indian Prime Minister Indira Gandhi, "Can the prime minister explain why Indians seem to thrive economically under every government in the world except hers?"[17] As long as India's economic policies were anti-business, this state of affairs would continue. In those years, when the Indian community was thrown out of East Africa, socialist India pressed the United Kingdom to

---

[16] William Shakespeare, *Julius Caesar* (I, ii, 140–41).

[17] Zakaria, Fareed, *The Future of Freedom—Illiberal Democracy at Home and Abroad* (New York: Norton, 2003), 53.

admit them, seeing little benefit in attracting the community's commercial skills and capital back to India. And when the British government finally gave in to pressure from India, it was seen as a major foreign policy achievement.[18]

Both China and India have large successful overseas diasporas. Looking back, it is hard to imagine that in the nineteenth and early twentieth century, upper-caste Hindus traveling overseas faced social ostracism. And from the late fourteenth century to the end of the nineteenth century, imperial law in China criminally punished Chinese who went overseas without an approved reason.[19] It was only late into the twentieth century, after they opened up their economies, that the diasporas of the two countries became important for their economic development.

India's IT and diamond sectors have done well because facilitative government policies allowed the diaspora to leverage its own strengths with India's comparative advantage. However, in the absence of favorable policies, the disapora's role is more limited. The well-known infrastructural and policy weaknesses in manufacturing have steered the diaspora's role in IT more toward the software side, rather than developing the hardware sector. The decades of migration from Kerala have made it a remittance-dependent economy, but one that has been unable to capitalize on this any further because of political and policy constraints in the state. For instance, in the aftermath of the global economic slowdown in 2008, returnees to Kerala from the Gulf found themselves unable to build on the skills they had acquired. As one migrant said, "After 21 years in Bahrain, I came back here and am not doing anything now because of problems here. One can't do anything in Kerala."[20]

The dominant presence of the Indian-origin diamantaires in Antwerp notwithstanding, India's two-decade-long project to set up the Bharat Diamond Bourse in Mumbai is not likely to replace Antwerp's World Diamond Centre as the global locus of diamond trading. This is not only because of the very different quality of physical infrastructure in the two cities, or the periodic law and order issues in Mumbai, but also, ironically, because India itself is not as open to foreigners coming and working in the country as Antwerp has been. In the hubbub of India trying to engage its diaspora, it has overlooked migrants and diasporas within India itself. India had long hosted numerous diasporas from Africa and the Middle East prior to the onset of colonial rule.[21] After the arrival of the British,

[18] Sunanda K, Datta-Ray, "Showcasing Gujarat," *Business Standard,* April 25, 2009.

[19] Wang Gungwu, *The Overseas Chinese* (Cambridge: Harvard University Press, 2000).

[20] http://www.ndtv.com/news/diaspora/kerala_facing_reverse_migration.php.

[21] On African diasporas in India, see Richard Pankhurst, "The Ethiopian Diaspora in India: The Role of Habshis and Sidis from Medieval Times to the End of the Eighteenth Century," in *The African Diaspora in the Indian Ocean,* eds. Shihan de Silva Jayasuriya and

just as Indians began going abroad under the umbrella of the British Empire, many immigrant trading communities—Armenians, Parsees, Chinese, Baghdadi Jews—settled in India and expanded trade between India and the outside world.[22] However, post-independence, these communities dwindled, in part because of decades of economic policies that reduced their economic opportunities (in the case of Armenians), better outside options (especially for the Jewish community, which migrated to Israel), discrimination (Chinese, especially after the 1962 Indo-China war) or simply Westernization (Parsees).

Post-independence, migration into India was largely from its neighbors, whether looking for work (Bangladesh, Nepal) or refugees fleeing civil strife and oppressive governments (Afghanistan, Myanmar, Tibet, and Sri Lanka). Despite these large inflows (India is the seventh largest destination for immigrants in the world), it has not passed laws for resettling refugees, choosing to opt for a case-by-case approach. This allowed India to calibrate its response to the refugees/migrants to its relationship with the country of origin. While sound *realpolitik*, the consequences on the migrants have been less than salubrious as they often struggle to earn a living at the margins of law and with handouts from agencies and relatives. India loves to celebrate its migrants who make it big abroad, but it is wary of allowing the same opportunities to those who come into the country.

The political impact of diasporas depends on the cleavages and conflicts in the country of origin. In India's case, the cleavages in its domestic politics have clearly hurt its efforts to engage the diaspora. While the BJP-led National Democratic Alliance (NDA) government began a more concerted effort to strengthen links between India and its overseas migrants, it appointed as ambassador-at-large for NRIs and people of Indian origin (PIOs) in its Washington embassy a partisan associated with the Overseas Friends of BJP, the international wing of the ruling party.[23] This move exacerbated divisions within the Indian American community and created a rivalry between Indian foreign ministry officials and an individual whom the U.S. government declined to even accord diplomatic status. The Congress-led UPA government went one better, appointing as minister for overseas Indian affairs a person dogged by controversy over his role in the 1984

Richard Pankhurst (Trenton, NJ: Africa World Press, 2001), 189–221; Fitzroy A. Baptiste, "African Presence in India," *Africa Quarterly* 38, no. 1 (1998): 75–90.

[22] Sushil Chaudhury, "Trading Networks in a Traditional Diaspora: Armenians in India c. 1600–1800," in *Diaspora Entrepreneurial Networks: Four Centuries of History*, eds. Ina Baghdiantz Mccabe, Gelina Harlaftis, and Ioanna Pepelasis Minoglou (New York: Berg, 2005), 51–72.

[23] Bhishma Kumar Agnihotri was then chancellor, Southern University Law Center, Baton Rouge, LA.

264 • Chapter 9

anti-Sikh riots in New Delhi. Protests from overseas Sikhs curtailed his travels sharply, limiting his effectiveness. Meanwhile, the state with the most affluent overseas community, Gujarat, was also unable to suitably leverage this community; the state's chief minister was beset by his own travel problems, which arose from his role in the anti-Muslim riots in Gujarat.

International migration has meant that political conflicts will reverberate abroad and ricochet back. If anything, the intensity of this "blowback" will only increase if countries do not handle internal conflicts with greater sagacity. In India's case, this phenomenon has been even greater because of the propensity of some of its neighbors to fish in troubled waters. If federal authority in India weakens, it will provide opportunities for regional parties to manipulate diasporas from their states to further parochial political agendas and undermine efforts to engage the diaspora for the formulation of a coherent foreign policy that advances the collective national interest.

To be sure, the Indian government has mounted many initiatives to both improve welfare and leverage its diaspora. Efforts to safeguard the interests of Indian emigrants go back to 1843, when the Governor General in Council was authorized to appoint a Protector of Emigrants at Calcutta. In 1871, when the UK Foreign Office was contemplating a proposal from the Spanish Government for supplying labor from India, the Government of India protested "very strongly . . . on the ground that no sufficient guarantee could be afforded for the proper protection of the emigrant." The dispatch expressing views of the Government concluded: "[C]onsidering how deeply Cuba is imbued with slave-holding and even slave-dealing traditions, and having regard to the political situation, both of the island itself and its mother country, it would be the last colony to which we should wish to see emigration extended."[24]

For more than a century and half, the Indian government has required emigration clearance for low-skilled workers and young women going to certain countries, to try and ensure that this vulnerable group is not exploited by unscrupulous labor contractors. Aside from that, however, the government did little else until the 1970s, when it took steps to attract financial remittances from the burgeoning labor migration to the Middle East. Its efforts to reach out to the diaspora become more pronounced in the new millennium. In 2001, the Indian government set up a Commission on the Indian Diaspora. Two years later, it organized the first *Pravasi Bharatiya Divas* (an annual celebration and gathering of overseas Indians) in New Delhi and created a dedicated ministry (Ministry of Overseas

---

[24] J. Geoghegan, *Note on Emigration from India* (Calcutta: Office of Superintendent of Government Printing, 1873), 60.

Indian Affairs). At one level, the event signaled that India was becoming more proactive in trying to leverage its diaspora. Since then, governments in India—both at the national and state levels—have been making greater efforts to cultivate relationships with overseas Indians. In 2002, the Indian Government created the Person of Indian Origin (PIO) card, which granted modest privileges to foreign citizens of Indian origin. Subsequently, the Citizenship Act was amended to allow for the registration of persons of Indian origin holding foreign citizenship as Overseas Citizens of India (OCIs).[25] The nomenclature, however, is a misnomer since it excludes any political rights or even the right to own agricultural land.

Concurrently, the Indian government also mounted initiatives to ensure that Indian workers overseas (for instance in the Gulf) have minimal statutory protections such as minimum monthly salary, stipulated hours of work, medical care, overtime payment, access to consular services during a crisis, insurance schemes for workers going overseas, and efforts to address the predicament of deserted Indian women.[26] In 2009, the government constituted a Prime Minister's Global Advisory Council to facilitate a dynamic two-way engagement between stakeholders in India and the overseas Indian community.

While these schemes have certainly benefited Indian workers overseas, the overall impact of these initiatives for India have been modest, principally because they are stand-alone enclave-type initiatives and are rarely embedded in the wider national and international policies of the Indian government. Take the case of education. Although India has hemorrhaged talent overseas since the mid-1960s, there is broad recognition that the human and financial capital of overseas Indians can be a tremendous asset for the country. The Indian Government has attempted to access this talent pool in three ways: (1) promote a "PIO/NRI" university; (2) launch a program called Collaborative Projects with Scientists and Technologists of Indian Origin Abroad; and (3) create an India Development Fund (IDF) to channel contributions from NRIs toward philanthropic activities in India in a wide range of activities. Their good intentions notwithstanding,

[25] As of June 1 2008, a total of 256,097 OCIs had been issued. The largest were from the United States (96,648), followed by the United Kingdom (25,133), Australia (24,480), Canada (21,792), and Sri Lanka (10,362). If the 17,229 issued to PIOs in India are excluded, the four Anglo-Saxon countries accounted for two-thirds of all OCIs. Source: Ministry of Overseas Indian Affairs. By November 2009, the number had nearly doubled (crossing half-a-million), perhaps as a hedging strategy against the economic crisis in the West.

[26] For instance, it signed a bilateral agreement with Qatar in 1985 and another one in 2007 to extend these benefits to informal workers. It also has agreements with Kuwait, and Bahrain and similar agreements with other Gulf countries and Malaysia are at an advanced stage as well as discussions with countries like Canada and Poland for better treatment of Indian migrant workers.

these initiatives will at best have modest results unless accompanied by fundamental changes that address the severe governance problems and the lack of autonomy of educational institutions within India. Entrenched domestic political interests make the latter difficult. Similarly, the OCI scheme did little to leverage a key asset of the Indian diaspora—its intellectual capital—because of barriers to recognizing overseas professional qualifications, even from countries with far better educational systems.[27] In 2009, the Indian prime minister announced that OCIs with professional qualifications would be able to practice their professions in India, but the legal changes were not yet in place at the time of this writing. Most importantly, perhaps, although India's public sector—ranging from defense-related research to health to higher education—is desperately short of talent, India has proscribed OCIs from getting jobs in the public sector.

The Indian Government's schemes to tap the financial capital of its diaspora have focused on remittances—and on this front, it has been quite successful. As you saw in chapter 4, overseas Indians send greater financial flows than overseas Chinese in the form of remittances but far less as foreign direct investment (FDI), in part because of the attractive financial terms of bank deposit schemes (a risk-free, high-yield asset) and the high transactions costs at the local government level of starting an enterprise. The schemes to invest remittances in risk-free, high-yield assets in India's banking system, together with the income from convertible foreign exchange accounts totally exempt from income tax, reduced incentives for diaspora FDI. But the schemes have created a powerful interest group—especially in the Indian state of Kerala, a state with a delicate political balance—and consequently, despite their declining national benefits, they will continue.

Domestic politics also explains (at least in part) why, despite the very large number of high-skilled Indians working in industrialized countries, India has had only modest success in reaching "totalization" agreements. (These agreements exempt citizens in one country working temporarily

[27] For instance, a dentist trained in Canada and wanting to practice in India needs to provide documents and credentials as well as details of the degree program from which she/he graduated (including admission, academic, clinical, and evaluation requirements) to the professional council (in this case the Dental Council of India, DCI), which can then make a recommendation to the Ministry of Health and Family Welfare (MH&FW). However, the latter has been refusing to grant approval, arguing that registration as a dentist may only be granted to an Indian citizen as per the Dentist Act 1948, and OCIs do not qualify. Given the number of dentists trained in India who work abroad, this may seem to be a bit self-defeating. A simple issue requiring the recognition of dental degrees in a country with higher standards needs approvals by three ministries—MH&FW, Ministry of Overseas Indian Affairs (MOIA), and Ministry of Home Affairs (MHA)—which neither deny registration nor grant it!

in another, usually for 5 to 10 years, from paying social security taxes to both countries.[28]) The failure was particularly glaring in the case of the United States—by 2009, the United States had signed totalization agreements with 24 countries, but not with India, even though Indians constitute one of the largest groups of overseas workers in that country. India's inability to seal totalization agreements has been costing the country hundreds of millions of dollars in social security taxes, which its workers pay but do not collect, since they return home before working for the minimum number of years.[29] Although the Indian Government had put together a draft agreement by 2004, it did not come to pass, largely because these agreements primarily exist among countries that have a nationwide social security system, which India lacks. This could have been redressed by pushing through policy changes allowing individual IRA accounts and a pensions regulator. However, a bill to create a pensions regulator languished in Parliament because of opposition from India's communists, who feared that it would lead to the privatization of the sector. Better that India lose an estimated half a billion dollars in forfeited social security taxes annually than sacrifice ideological principles.

These examples underline a banal reality. Initiatives to strategically engage a country's diaspora need to be embedded in the government's wider national and international policies in order to be successful. In the Indian case, addressing these problems requires the engagement of key ministries that are significantly more powerful as compared to the very modest resources of a stand-alone ministry.[30]

As is the case with India, other developing countries are also making efforts to tap their diasporas, especially for economic development purposes. But specific narrow benefits directed toward a country's diaspora raises several questions. One, if members of the diaspora are treated more favorably than citizens at home, might it not create incentives to leave or arbitrage possibilities?[31] Two, why should a country's diaspora be treated more favorably than other external-based actors in cases such as financial flows—does the source of money matter rather than its terms and uses?

[28] By early 2009, India had reached reciprocal social security totalization agreements with Belgium, France, Germany, and Netherlands and was negotiating with several others.

[29] High-skill workers enter the United States under the H1-B visa, which is valid for three years and renewable once. An individual must contribute social security taxes for at least 40 quarters (10 years) before she is eligible for social security payments. Hence, unless the individual manages to convert the H1-B visa and becomes a permanent resident, her visa will lapse before the minimum contribution period for social security eligibility.

[30] The annual budget of the Ministry of Overseas Indian Affairs in 2007–2008 was barely about $10 million.

[31] There are good reasons to believe that special benefits accorded to financial remittances to India and diaspora FDI in the case of China have led to considerable round-tripping in both cases.

And three, if reaching out to emigrants and one's diaspora residing in other countries is such a laudable idea, other countries might do the same. The presumption is the migrants are in rich countries. But given the large migration flows among developing countries, how open will developing countries be to overtures made by another developing country toward its diaspora residing inside their borders?

Citizenship and the Political Community in Spatially Unbounded Nations

International migration is resulting in subtle but important changes to an idea that is at the heart of nationhood—citizenship and the basis of a political community. Around the world, international migration has deepened anxieties, as countries are forced to grapple with settled comfortable assumptions about "national identity." In the closing years of the twentieth century, dual citizenship, once an anathema for nation-states, has become increasingly accepted as countries react to international migration and seek to maintain ties with their migrants, presumably to reap economic and political benefits.[32] Alternatively, this may be perhaps because the "imagery of common citizenship within the territory is inadequate because nationalism most often seeks its ultimate value and justification beyond its territorial figuration."[33]

In India's case, international migration has subtly reshaped notions of citizenship, from one rooted in *jus soli* (territorial based) to a more *jus sanguine* (based on ethnicity or by blood) conception of citizenship. In the early part of the twentieth century, the Congress Party campaigned for better treatment of Indians in the colonies and sent emissaries to help them; they were operating on a concept of "empire" in which Indians were seen as entitled to the same rights as white subjects, wherever in the empire they found themselves. The defense of the interests of Indians abroad was driven more in terms of securing rights of Indians settled overseas than some notion of racial or blood connection. In 1946, Nehru had even suggested a common nationality between India, Ceylon, Burma, Malaya, and Indonesia as a way to address the problems of Indians living in those countries. India proposed the idea of a reciprocal common citizenship during the negotiations of the terms of India's membership in the Commonwealth—one reason being that it would allow the interests of

---

[32] Tanja Brøndsted Sejersen, "I Vow to Thee My Countries"—The Expansion of Dual Citizenship in the 21st Century," *International Migration Review* 42, no. 3 (September 2008): 723–38.

[33] Prasenjit Duara, "Transnationalism and the Predicament of Sovereignty: China, 1900–1945," in *The Chinese Overseas*, Routledge Library of Modern China, vol. 1, ed. Hong Liu (New York: Routledge, 2006), 375.

overseas Indians to be upheld.[34] However, the idea was not acceptable to other members (especially the "Old Dominions"—Australia, Canada, and South Africa—because of its implication for their racial immigration policies) and was dropped from the final agreement of April 1949.

Even as independent India was coming into being, the intertwining of migration and citizenship was evident, most starkly in the huge (and bloody) migrations surrounding the partition of British India. Controlling the spatial mobility of people across borders emerged as the critical means of defining nationhood and citizenship. Soon after partition, debates during the framing of the Indian constitution about defining the rights of common Indian citizenship brought to the fore tensions arising from internal migration and preferential policies for "sons-of-the-soil" (members of local ethnic groups) in jobs and admission to educational institutions. Unlike the case of affirmative action for India's socially marginalized groups, the justification for preferences was based neither upon minority status nor upon past discrimination. Indeed, the demand for preferences for sons-of-the-soil was made on behalf of the majority in relation to a minority on the grounds that the group's unequal status (be it education, employment, or income) in relation to other "outside" groups migrating into the state. At the time, Dr. Ambedkar, the key architect of the Indian constitution, argued that residential requirements "subtract[ed] from the value of a common citizenship." Nonetheless, he felt compelled to concede that "it must be realised that you cannot allow people who are flying from one province to another, from one State to another as mere birds of passage without any roots . . . just to come, apply for posts and so to say take the plums and walk away."[35]

The Indian Constitution eventually tried to strike a balance between the principle of a common citizenship and the need to respond to local concerns.[36] However, it also left a loophole, giving Parliament the exclusive right to set residential requirements in state services as and when the need arose.[37] The need to "balance" between these principles was periodically emphasized, as epitomized by the Indian Prime Minister Indira Gandhi's statement in Parliament: "While we stand for the principle that any

---

[34] R. J. Moore, *Making the New Commonwealth* (Oxford, UK: Clarendon Press, 1987).

[35] *Constituent Assembly Debates* VII (November 30, 1948): 700.

[36] Articles 14, 15, 16(1), and (2) of the constitution guarantee equality of all citizens before the law and bar discrimination on grounds of religion, race, caste, sex, and place of birth. Article 19 guarantees all citizens the right to move freely throughout the territory of India and to reside and settle in any part of the country.

[37] Article 16(3), which states that: "Nothing in this article shall prevent Parliament from making any law prescribing in regard to a class or classes of employment or appointment to an office under the government of or any local or other authority within a state or union territory any requirement as to residence within that state or union territory prior to such employment or appointment."

Indian should be able to work in any part of India, at the same time, it is
true that if a large number of people come from outside to seek employment . . . that is bound to create tension in that area. Therefore, while I do
not like the idea of having any such rule, one has to have some balance
and see that the local people are not deprived of employment."[38] Numerous Indian states put in residential and language requirements in matters
of employment and admission to educational institutions, which leads to
large number of cases on these issues before India's courts. But the courts'
pronouncements have lacked coherence, especially in guarding the principle of a common citizenship against rank political opportunism.[39]

Ironically, even as internal migration challenged the idea of a common citizenship within India, with special rights granted on the basis of
ethnicity, international migration has created incentives to shift (albeit
to a limited extent) the definition of Indian citizenship from birth in
India or naturalization as the sole legal criterion to encompass ethnicity
as well. Initially, when the Indian government was contemplating the
creation of an Overseas Citizen of India (OCI) category, it announced
that the privilege would be granted only to the diaspora from selective
(mainly industrialized) countries, seemingly privileging money politik.
Responding to strong criticism, it settled on a more uniform principle
wherein anyone who left India after the Indian republic came into being
(January 26, 1950), but excluding Bangladesh and Pakistan, could become an OCI.[40] Although OCIs were extended most privileges available
to nonresident Indians (NRIs)—i.e., Indian citizens living abroad with
an Indian passport—they were not granted any political rights or the
right to own agricultural land.

These developments marked a subtle shift in the basis of Indian nationalism from a pure civic and territorial one to ethnic nationalism. If the Indian citizenship act was originally rooted in a *jus solis* principle, in the last
two decades—and especially this decade—the wheel has again turned.
Critics have argued that "the construction of diaspora membership focuses

[38] *Lok Sabha Debates* XXII (December 13, 1972): 13, quoted in Myron Weiner, M. F.
Katzenstein, and K. V. Narayana Rao, *India's Preferential Policies: Migrants, the Middle
Classes, and Ethnic Equality* (Chicago: University of Chicago Press, 1981), 25.

[39] For a good analysis of the India courts rulings on this issue, see T. M. Joseph and S. N.
Sangita, "Preferential Policies and 'Sons-of-the-Soil' Demands: The Indian Experience,"
Ethnic Studies Report XVI, no. 1 (1998): 73–102.

[40] A foreign national who was eligible to become a citizen of India on January 26, 1950
(when India became a Republic), or was a citizen of India on or at anytime after January
26, 1950, or belonged to a territory that became part of India after August 15, 1947, and
his/her children and grandchildren, provided his/her country of citizenship allows dual
citizenship in some form or other under the local laws, is eligible for registration as an
OCI. Applicants who have ever held citizenship of Pakistan or Bangladesh are not eligible
for OCI.

on professional success, ecumenical Hinduism, and multicultural incorporation ... [and] betrays a continuing anxiety over the terms of Indianness."[41]

It is certainly the case that the Indian government's cultivation of its diaspora has followed a realist logic, favoring those in industrialized democracies rather than those such as the stateless people of Indian origin in Myanmar, where India is competing with China for influence. However, this differential approach is also a recognition that strengthening links with the diaspora will be perforce smoother in countries where the nation-building project has been long settled. As the Malaysian example in chapter 7 illustrated, in countries where the nation-building project is still a "work in progress" (which includes virtually all countries that were under colonial rule, including India), anxieties about diasporic minorities (especially from bigger countries) will be much more pronounced, and therefore any active cultivation of minority diasporas could easily further jeopardize their well being.

However, and contrary to the contention that the construction of the diaspora favors ecumenical Hinduism, an active cultivation of the diaspora may actually serve as an anchor for securing minority rights in India. India's claims to speak on behalf of the human rights of Indian-origin minorities in other countries would run aground pretty quickly if it was seen as consciously and consistently violating the rights of minorities within its own borders. It could be argued that the BJP government tried to do both—promoting the diaspora abroad while being hostile to minority rights at home—but such contradictions can only go so far.

Meanwhile, what lower-skilled Indian workers are doing in the Gulf and higher-skilled workers are doing in the United States, Indians from poorer regions of the country are trying to do within the country by moving to the more prosperous regions. Ironically, the backlash they are facing is sometimes worse than if they had gone abroad. Natives—whether in cities like Mumbai or India's Northeast or Kashmir—believe that they are being swamped by outsiders and worry that their distinct regional identity is under threat from "uncivilized" migrants. Migrants are blamed for a range of ailments, from a spurt in the crime rate to adding to the welfare burden on the state exchequer. As India celebrates its overseas migrant community, regional politicians revel in chauvinism, passing legislation for employment and education quotas for natives and even instigating violent campaigns against migrants.

These are familiar refrains worldwide. If anything, these complexities underscore how the mobility of people presents both transcendental

---

[41] Jen Dickinson and Adrian J. Bailey, "(Re)membering Diaspora: Uneven Geographies of Indian Dual Citizenship," *Political Geography* 26, no. 7 (2007): 757–74.

possibilities and singular challenges. Although trade and financial flows have been key drivers of globalization in the last half-century, international migration is in many ways the more powerful force, bringing in its wake dual citizenship and political rights in multiple jurisdictions and fundamentally altering what constitutes a political community. Territorially unbounded nations could conceivably be the pathway for a global cosmopolitanism—but with what implications for democratic processes and practices? At a minimum, that pathway will be lined with growing anxieties among those who are not mobile, and there will undoubtedly be numerous political entrepreneurs willing to fan the flames of these anxieties.

Globalism is likely to result in people sharing identities with more than one group, not just their nation-state or homeland. The mobility of people across borders may mean that citizenship will come to symbolize multiple political alliances rather than a singular political identity. This raises the question of what happens when these different alliances and identities come into conflict. Is it conceivable that as spatial boundaries of people expand, becoming more "cosmopolitan," they transfer their membership allegiance vertically, away from the national to the international, or downward to the subnational? As countries dip into nostalgia in seeking to tap their diasporas, it is not the past but rather the future that is driving them. But that future may be rather different from what they may have bargained for.

Survey of Emigration from India (SEI)

SURVEY METHODOLOGY

THIS SURVEY WAS inserted as an additional module to the Indian Readership Survey (IRS), 2003, one of the largest and the most comprehensive media and market research surveys in India. Established in 1995, the IRS is widely used by the media and marketing professionals. The IRS 2003 was jointly conducted by Media Research Users Council (MRUC), a nonprofit body, along with Hansa Research Group (HRG), which undertook the entire responsibility of the survey, from conception to implementation and delivery.[1]

The prime objective of the IRS is to collect detailed information about individual and household consumption of all types of media products, fast-moving consumer goods (FMCG) products usage, and ownership of consumer durables from a cross section of individuals. The information is primarily used by advertising agencies for media planning, brand profiling, market sizing, and reaching their desired target audience.

COVERAGE

The IRS is a household survey, with a sample size exceeding 200,000 covering about 1100 towns and 2800 villages. The survey covers 22 of India's 28 states. The excluded states—Arunachal Pradesh, Manipur, Mizoram, Nagaland, Sikkim, and Tripura (the small states of the Northeast)—account for less than one percent of India's population of 1.028 billion as per the 2001 census. The IRS even reaches villages without electricity, attesting to its wide coverage. Given its purpose, the IRS sample has an urban bias. The sample is approximately two-thirds urban and one-third rural, the inverse of India's population distribution. However, this is suitable for the purposes of this study since (in contrast to internal migration) international migration from India is largely an urban phenomenon.

[1] The MRUC comprises members drawn from major advertisers, advertising agencies, publishers, broadcasters, and other media members. It was incorporated with the sole purpose of organizing accurate, timely, efficient and economical media research in the country, across all forms of media. It has currently over 170 members.

The IRS questionnaire is primarily divided into two sections—the household section and the individual section. The household section is administered to the housewife of the household and includes questions on ownership of various household durables (TV, refrigerator, etc.). The second part—the individual section—is administered to a 12+ individual randomly selected from among the household members. This random selection is done using the Kish Grid. The IRS 2003 fieldwork period was spread across eight months, from July 2003 to February 2004.

SAMPLING

The universe on the estimated number of households and the estimated 12+ population is determined based on the 2001 census. The urban sampling is based on classifying all towns in urban India into six groups:

Class I	4 million+
Class II	1 million—4 million
Class III	500,000 to 1 million
Class IV	100,000 to 500,000
Class V	50,000 to 100,000
Class VI	Below 50,000

While all towns above 100,000 population are sampled, only some of the below 100,000 towns are randomly selected. Sample allocation for each town is done in such a way that every class in every state is proportionately represented in the sample. Each state has been broken up into several clusters of districts (called ISDs) depending on their geographical contiguity and other sociocultural and linguistic aspects. Each ISD is represented in the sample in proportion to its population size.

For rural sampling, all villages have been classified into three groups, with each village class represented in every ISD in proportion to its population size:

Class I	Population greater than 5000
Class II	Population between 1000 and 5000
Class III	Population below 1000

HOUSEHOLD AND INDIVIDUAL SELECTION

The IRS adopts a systematic random sampling method using electoral rolls as the sampling frame. An individual is first selected randomly from the electoral rolls, and then the other individuals are selected at regular intervals. The households to which these individuals belong are chosen as cluster head households. Interviews are done in these households and a predetermined number of households around this cluster head household. In the largest cities (Class I and Class II), boosters are done after purposively choosing SEC A households in SEC A heavy clusters. Once a successful household interview is conducted with the housewife, an individual over 12 years of age is selected from the same household (HH) using a Kish Grid.[2]

SAMPLE SIZE AND DISTRIBUTION

The sample size was 210,000, with the following distribution:

Town/Village Class	Class Definition	Universe of Towns/Villages	Sampled Towns
		Urban	
Class I	Above 4 million	7	7
Class II	1–4 million	28	28
Class III	0.5–1 million	36	36
Class IV	0.1–0.5 million	317	317
Class V	0.05–0.1 million	395	275
Class VI	Below 50,000	3,398	500
		Rural	
Class I	Above 5000	18,008	558
Class II	1000–5000	205,092	1,532
Class III	Below 1000	391,080	600

The sample was weighted to correct for certain demographic variables (available from the 2001 census), adding to the statistical validity of the survey. The IRS weighting takes into account two census variables for weighting—namely, age and gender. These two variables are available in

[2] The Kish grid is used to randomize the selection of respondents such that each 12+ member gets an equal opportunity to get selected. There are two axes on the Kish grid. The abscissa is the interview number in the cluster, and the ordinate is the number of active members in the household. The respondent is selected by first arranging the names of the family members in the households in decreasing order based on their ages. Thus, the oldest member is the first name, and the youngest is the last. From the Kish grid, the number of the selected person is obtained and the interview conducted with the same person. If the respondent is not available, the interviewer tries to contact the respondent six times, after which if the interview still does not occur, the interview is treated as a casualty.

the census for the smallest weighting unit in IRS. In calculating weights, the universe for the cell is then divided by the raw counts in that cell to arrive at the weight for that particular cell. This weight is then multiplied to all the records in that cell at the time of projection to get universe estimates.

SURVEY QUESTIONNAIRE

1(a). Do you personally know anyone living abroad among _____ (READ OUT)?

ASK 1(b) ONLY IN CASE CODED '2' FOR ANY OF THESE, OR ELSE MOVE TO Q6.

1(b). How many of the _____(READ OUT FOR THOSE CODED '2') that you personally know live abroad?

	No	Yes	1(b) Numbers Staying Abroad
Members of immediate family	1	2	
Members of extended family	1	2	
Friends	1	2	

ASK '2' ONLY IF MEMBERS OF IMMEDIATE FAMILY STAYING ABROAD.

2. You mentioned that _____(MENTION THE NUMBER OF IMME-DIATE FAMILY MEMBER/S LIVING ABROAD) member/s of your immediate family live abroad. Can you please tell me about their

(a) Age
(b) Gender
(c) Education
(d) Occupation
(e) Yrs since staying abroad

Please start with the member who has been abroad for the longest duration.

START WITH THE MEMBER WHO HAS STAYED ABROAD FOR THE LONGEST DURATION.

RECORD ACTUAL AGE, CIRCLE GENDER, TRANSFER APPROPRIATE EDUCATION AND OCCUPATION CODES FROM THE GRID, RECORD YRS. SINCE STAYING ABROAD FOR MAX 3 MEMBERS OF FAMILY STAYING ABROAD.

	Age	Gender M	F	Education	Occupation	Years Since Staying Abroad
Member 1						
Member 2						
Member 3						

3. Can you please tell me, for each member, which country/region is he/she (ARE THEY, IN CASE OF MORE THAN 1 MEMBER STAYING ABROAD) living in?

	Member 1	Member 2	Member 3		Member 1	Member 2	Member 3
U.S./America			1	Asia (other)	6	6	6
Middle East			2	Africa	7	7	7
UK			3	Australia/			
Europe (other				New Zealand	8	8	8
than UK)			4	South America	9	9	9
Southeast Asia			5	Other			
				(specify———)	10	10	10

4. Does your household receive remittances from members of the family staying aboard? SINGLE CODE

1		2		3
Yes		No		DK/CS

CONTINUE IF CODED '1' OR ELSE MOVE TO

5. Can you please tell me how much remittance did your household receive in the past one year from the family member/s staying abroad? SINGLE CODE

278 • Appendix I

None	1	Rs. 30,001−Rs. 50,000	6
Less than or equal to Rs. 5000	2	Rs. 50,001−Rs.1 lakh	7
Rs. 5001−Rs. 10,000	3	Rs. 100,001−Rs.2 lakh	8
Rs. 10,001−Rs. 20,000	4	> Rs. 2 lakh	9
Rs. 20,001−Rs. 30,000	5	DK/CS	10

6. Do you have children? SINGLE CODE

| Yes | 1 | No | 2 |

CONTINUE ONLY IF CODED '1', OR ELSE MOVE TO

7. Do you believe that your children's future will be better if they live abroad? SINGLE CODE

| Yes | 1 | No | 2 | DK | 9 |

CONTINUE ONLY IF CODED '1', OR ELSE MOVE TO

8. If yes, in what way do you think living abroad will be better? MAX 3 CODE POSSIBLE

Better professional opportunities abroad	01	Better standard of living abroad	07
India has less/no professional opportunities	02	India has poor standard of living	08
Can earn more money abroad	03	Less corruption abroad	09
Difficult to earn more money in India	04	More corruption in India	10
		Other (specify————)	11
Less discrimination abroad	05	DK/CS	12
More discrimination in India	06		

9. Do you believe that your children are likely to live abroad? SINGLE CODE

| 1 | 2 | 3 | 4 |
| Very Likely | Likely | Not Likely | Don't Know |

CONTINUE ONLY IF CODED '1' OR '2' OR ELSE MOVE TO___

10. What would be your first three choices of countries where your children should live, if they live abroad?

	First Choice	Second Choice	Third Choice		First Choice	Second Choice	Third Choice
U.S./America	1	1	1	Asia (other)	6	6	6
Middle East	2	2	2	Africa	7	7	7
UK	3	3	3	Australia/			
Europe (other				New Zealand	8	8	8
than UK)	4	4	4	South America	9	9	9
Southeast Asia	5	5	5	Other			
				(specify———)	10	10	10

SOCIOECONOMIC CLASSIFICATIONS (SEC) I. URBAN

Education		Illiterate	School Up to 4th/ Literate but no Formal Schooling	School 5th to 9th	SSC/ HSC	Some College But Not Graduate	Graduate/ Postgraduate (General)	Graduate/ Postgraduate (Professional)
Occupation		−1	(2/3)	−4	−5	−6	(7, 9)	(8, 10)
1. Unskilled workers		E2	E2	E1	D	D	D	D
2. Skilled workers		E2	E1	D	C	C	B2	B2
3. Petty traders		E2	D	D	C	C	B2	B2
4. Shop owners		D	D	C	B2	B1	A2	A2
5. Businesspeople/	None							
industrialists	1−9	D	C	B2	B1	A2	A2	A1
with number	10 +	C	B2	B2	B1	A2	A1	A1
of employees		B1	B1	A2	A2	A1	A1	A1
6. Self-employed professionals		D	D	D	B2	B1	A2	A1
7. Clerical/ salespeople		D	D	D	C	B2	B1	B1
8. Supervisory level		D	D	C	C	B2	B1	A2
9. Officers/ executives (junior)		C	C	C	B2	B1	A2	A2
10. Officers/ executives (middle/senior)		B1	B1	B1	B1	A2	A1	A1

SOCIOECONOMIC CLASSIFICATIONS (SEC) II. RURAL

Education	Type of House		
	Pucca (Permanent)	Semi-pucca	Kuccha (Temporary)
Illiterate	R4	R4	R4
Literate but no formal school	R3	R3	R4
Up to 4th standard	R3	R3	R4
5th to 9th standard	R3	R3	R4
High school	R2	R3	R3
Some college but not graduate	R1	R2	R3
Graduate/postgraduate (general)	R1	R2	R3
Graduate/postgraduate (professional)	R1	R2	R3

Survey of Asian Indians in the United States (SAIUS): Methodology

A FUNDAMENTAL PROBLEM in conducting a survey of an immigrant group is how to construct a random sample without incurring prohibitive costs.[1] In rare cases where the immigrant group is present in large numbers and is spatially concentrated, this is possible (for instance, immigrants from Mexico in the United States). But in most cases, the numbers are small relative to the population. Thus, although immigrants from Indian were the top five groups coming to the United States during the 1990s, by the end of the decade they still accounted for just 0.6 percent of the population. Simply conducting a random sampling of the population would require an extremely large sampling frame. One can improve upon this by sampling only those areas where Asian Indians are spatially concentrated. According to the 2000 U.S. Census, half of Asian Indians live in five urban areas, three-fourths in twenty, and four-fifths in thirty (table AII.1). However, the share of the Asian Indian population in these urban areas is still meager— 1.91%, 1.39%, and 1.25% respectively. The highest density is the San Francisco/Oakland/San Jose urban area (4.81%). However, sampling in just this urban area—which encompasses Silicon Valley—would not be representative of the Asian Indian population, since an unusually high fraction of the Asian Indian population in this area is engaged in high-tech occupations.

Another route is to tap immigrant organizations for member lists. This has three obvious problems. Constructing the universe of such organizations and persuading them to share information about their membership lists is nontrivial and creates sample bias as regards members of those organizations who are unwilling to share this information. Most critically, however, since members are self-selected, sample bias is a major problem, and it is unclear how one would know the extent of the bias, and how to correct for it.

---

[1] "Asian Indian" is the term used for people of Indian origin in U.S. Census surveys.

TABLE AII.1
Spatial Distribution of Asian Indian Population, 2000

	Percent of Total Asian Indian Population	Population of Urban Areas as Percent of Total U.S. Population	Asian Indian Population as Percent of Total Population
Top 5 urban areas[a]	50.86	15.95	1.91
Top 20 urban areas	75.54	32.52	1.39
Top 30 urban areas	79.59	38.04	1.25
Total	1.68 million	281 million	0.597

Source: 2000 U.S. Census.

[a] Ranked by numbers of Asian Indians. In descending order: New York/New Jersey/Connecticut; San Francisco/Oakland/San Jose; Chicago; Los Angeles; and Washington, DC/Virginia/Maryland.

INDIAN LAST NAMES

Indian last names are an excellent instrument to analyze international migration. Indian last names are for the most part unique, which makes it relatively easy to track people of Indian origin. This is particularly the case for the migration to North America, Europe (except the United Kingdom), and Australia, which has taken place after the mid-1960s. This group of migrants is drawn from the upper end of India's human-capital endowment. The households from which this migration pool is drawn are part of communities and classes that occupy a relative privileged position in India—essentially, they are part of India's urban middle and upper classes. Evidence for this comes from the Survey of Emigration from India (SEI), explained in appendix I. This is important, since this pool is most likely to have a telephone.

In order to obtain a comprehensive list of Indian last names, I merged the phone directories of four of the six largest Indian cities located in different parts of India: Bangalore, Delhi, Mumbai (Bombay), and Hyderabad. The number of telephone entries was 4,060,203, which represented 8.3 percent of India's fixed-line telephone subscribers as of the end of October 2002.[2] The frequency distribution of last names is given in table AII.2.

All last names with a frequency of five or more were then matched to a

[2] The total number of telephone subscribers as of October 31, 2002, was 48,960,414. Source: Ministry of Communication and Information Technology, Lok Sabha, Unstarred

Table AII.2
Frequency Distribution of Indian Last Names from Indian Telephone Directories

Total last names	213,622
Total last names with a count of 1	128,966
Total last names with a count of 5 or more	38,386
Total last names with a count of 10 or more	22,517
Total last names with a count of 50 or more	6628

commercial database available from InfoUSA of 110 million households. However, the procedure encountered an unexpected problem. The total count was 22,638,845 (out of 110 million records), and 16,961 surnames did not match to the InfoUSA consumer file. The latter was not a problem (since many groups do not migrate, or at least not to the United States). However, the former posed a major problem in that the total number of Asian Indians in the 2000 census was just 1.7 million. However, when examining the list of last names and matching frequency in the United States, the reason became obvious. There are foreigners living and working in India (particularly in the four cities under question), and their names were also listed in Indian telephone directories. Although those last names have a low frequency in India, they occur very frequently in the United States. Thus, a name like "Smith" had a frequency of about 300 in India and nearly one million in the United States.

To address this problem, I adopted a two-track approach. In the first step, only those last names with a frequency greater than 10 in the combined phone lists from India were included in the search. After excluding those last names that did not find any match in the InfoUSA database, the list of names was pruned to 13,418. In the second step, I assigned a code to each last name. All persons with last name *extremely likely* to be Indian were coded 1; all persons with last name *extremely unlikely* to be Indian were coded 2; and all last names whose ethnicity was not immediately apparent were coded 3. Subsequently, all records corresponding to last names coded 1 were included, while all records with last names coded 2 were dropped. In the case of all last names coded 3, I used a second filter: this filter was a list of about 9000 Indian first names constructed from various Indian baby-name websites and books. This list includes only those last names coded 3, but which also had a *first* name that matched any of the names from the database of Indian first names.

question no.4481, December 18, 2002. The breakdown by city was as follows: Bombay— 1,864,944; Delhi—1,717,484; Hyderabad—226,225; Bangalore—251,550.

TABLE AII.3
Survey of Asian Indians in the United States: Phone Survey Responses

Total calls made	**8370**
Completed	**2132**
Answering machine	4550
Busy	154
Disconnected	412
Not of Indian origin	64
Not interested	1017
Refused	20
Other (phone number wrong, not valid, not in service, do not call)	21

This methodology resulted in the creation of a database of Asian Indians with just over 400,000 records. The vast majority (380,000) corresponded to those coded 1, where I was absolutely sure that the last name is Indian. The other 20,000 odd names were those under status 3, with an Indian first name. Given the census count (of 1.68 million in 2000), this represents about three-fourths of all Asian Indian households in the United States.

There are two types of errors that could result from such a methodology. First, errors of inclusion may arise from miscoding names that are not of Indian ethnicity, or at least are not solely of Indian ethnicity, as Indian. There is only way one to test this, and that is the phone survey itself. In conducting the phone survey, a random sample of names was chosen from this database, and the survey was conducted using a call center in India. The first question each respondent was asked was "Are you of Indian origin?" If the person answered "yes," then the surveyor continued to ask the next question; if the person said "no," the respondent was thanked and the interview was terminated. A total of 8370 calls were made; in 4704 cases no contact could be made either because of an answering machine (4550) or because the number was busy (154).[3] In the remaining 3666 cases, just 68, or less than 2 percent, said they were not of Indian origin (table AII.3).

Errors arising from omission of Indian last names pose more difficult methodological problems.

First, can phone directories of four cities representing about four percent of the country's population be an exhaustive source of Indian last names? Phone penetration in India is less than five percent of households, and it is

---

[3] Each number was called three times at different hours of the day before further contact was terminated.

concentrated in the large metropolitan cities. More importantly, with the exception of migration from Kerala to the Gulf and from rural Punjab to the United Kingdom and Canada, the vast majority of Indian overseas migration is an urban phenomenon. For example, the likelihood of an urban household in India having a family member in the United States is more than an order of magnitude greater than a rural household.

Second, last names drawn from Indian phone directories will also include foreigners living in India, such as embassy employees, members of the media and the press, or employees of multinational corporations. Including these names in a directory which is then used for global searches would mistakenly include non-Indian names and give an upward bias to the results. However, the frequency of occurrence of a foreign last name in India (e.g., Rosenzweig) is likely to be very small. Consequently, I eliminated all names that occur with a frequency *less than ten* to address this problem. That eliminated 93.7 percent of all last names, and obviously all these cannot be foreigners. However, it is very unlikely that households with names that occur with such low frequency in India will have members who have migrated out of India, given the low overall probability of the latter to begin with. To confirm this, I did a random sampling of last names of frequency less than ten in India on U.S.-wide phone directories.

Third, the last names of Indian Muslims and Christians may not be unique to the country. This is particularly the case with the former group, who share common last names with other South Asian Muslims, especially in Bangladesh and Pakistan. In the case of Indian Christians, however, many of their last names are also unique to India, especially the large number of Keralite Christians.[4] However, Indian Christians from Goa, a former Portuguese colony, share some last names with those from other Portuguese colonies (especially Brazil). In both cases, these last names were coded 2, which created a bias in the sample. For reasons mentioned earlier, this bias is likely to be greater in the case of Indian Muslims. However, my Survey of Emigration from India (the SEI survey) allows me to get data on emigration of Indian Muslims by country and check how much bias might arise.

A fourth potential problem arises from the possibility that people of Indian origin have changed their last name after migration. This is much more likely to be the case with Indian women, where the probability of changing the last name after marriage is greater (than Indian men). Their exclusion could bias the results on linkages between the diaspora and the country of origin. However, data from the U.S. Census indicates that the propensity of Asian Indian women to marry outside the ethnic group is small (and, as a result, the bias will be small). Of the major Asian American

[4] About one-third of India's Christian population is from Kerala.

Table AII.4
Survey Response Rate by Income Level

	Answering Machine, Busy, or Disconnected	Refused, Not Interested	Completed
Low income	29.76%	28.79%	23.85%
Middle income	37.01%	36.43%	36.37%
High income	33.23%	34.78%	39.77%

ethnicities (Chinese, Filipino, Indian, Japanese, Korean, and Vietnamese), Asian Indian women are *most likely* to marry within the ethnic group (92 percent). In part, this may be because a substantial majority of the adult Asian Indian population is first generation.[5] For those raised in the United States (defined as those who were either born in or immigrated to the United States at age thirteen or younger), the figure drops to 62.5 percent, which, however, is still the highest among any of the aforementioned Asian American ethnicities.

A fifth potential problem is a selection bias resulting from respondents who refused to answer or whose numbers were busy. This is true of any survey, but in this case I checked on some characteristics of respondents who completed the survey and those who did not. If we look at respondents by income level, there does not appear to be a sampling bias (table AII.4).

Last, there could be potential problems in that a particular minority may totally exit (for instance, because of bias or persecution), and hence the names of such groups are likely to occur with very low frequency in India. In such a scenario, there could be many more from this community outside the country than in India. While India is an extremely heterogenous country with high levels of conflict in certain parts of the country, I do not know of any instance where an entire community has migrated. In other words, while conflict has indeed led to greater levels of migration among certain communities (e.g., Sikhs in the 1980s), it is definitely not of such extreme magnitude as to virtually eliminate last names of specific Sikh clans and subcaste groups in India. One exception is the Indian Jewish community that migrated to Israel over the 1950s for economic reasons, leaving a tiny minority in India.

[5] This is confirmed by the fact that Vietnamese Americans, another relatively recently arrived community, has the highest overall rate of endogamy among Asian Americans (slightly more than Asian Indians). However, the rate for women is less than for Asian Indians.

APPENDIX III

Survey of Asian Indians in the United States (SAIUS): Questionnaire

1(a). Do you have children?

SINGLE CODE

Yes	1	No	2

CONTINUE ONLY IF CODED '1', OR ELSE MOVE TO 4a

1(b). Do you believe that your children's future will be better if they live abroad?

SINGLE CODE

Yes	1	No	2	DK/CS	9

CONTINUE ONLY IF CODED '1', OR ELSE MOVE TO Q3

2. In what way do you think living abroad will be better? MAX 3 CODE POSSIBLE

Better professional opportunities abroad	01	Better standard of living abroad	07
India has less/no professional opportunities	02	India has poor standard of living	08
Can earn more money abroad	03	Less corruption abroad	09
Difficult to earn more money in India	04	More corruption in India	10
Less discrimination abroad	05	Other (specify_____)	11
More discrimination in India	06	DK/CS	12

3(a). Do you believe that your children are likely to live abroad?

SINGLE CODE

Very Likely	1	Likely	2	Not likely	3	Don't know	4

CONTINUE, ONLY IF CODED '1' OR '2' OR ELSE MOVE TO 4a

3(b). What would be your first three choices of countries where your children should live, if they live abroad?

	First Choice	Second Choice	Third Choice		First Choice	Second Choice	Third Choice
U.S./America	1	1	1	Asia (other)	6	6	6
Middle East	2	2	2	Africa	7	7	7
UK	3	3	3	Australia/			
Europe (other				New Zealand	8	8	8
than UK)	4	4	4	South America	9	9	9
Southeast Asia	5	5	5	Other			
				(specify_____)	10	10	10

4(a). Do you have any family members or friends who live abroad?

SINGLE CODE

Yes	1	No	2

CONTINUE ONLY IF CODED '1', OR ELSE MOVE TO NEXT SECTION

4(b). Does your HH receive remittances from abroad?

SINGLE CODE

Yes	1	No	2	DK/CS	9

CONTINUE ONLY IF CODED '1' OR ELSE MOVE TO 5a

4(c). Can you please tell me how often does your household receive remittances from abroad?

Once a month	1	Once a year	5
Once in 2−3 months	2	Less often	6
Once in 4−6 months	3	As and when required	7
Once in 7−11 months	4	DK/CS	9

4(d). Can you please tell me how much remittance did your household receive in the past one year from abroad?

SINGLE CODE

None	1	Rs. 30,001–Rs. 50,000	6
Less than or equal to Rs. 5000	2	Rs. 50,001–Rs. 1 lakh	7
Rs. 5001–Rs. 10,000	3	Rs. 100,001–Rs. 2 lakh	8
Rs. 10,001–Rs. 20,000	4	> Rs. 2 lakh	9
Rs. 20,001–Rs. 30,000	5	DK/CS	10

ASK 5b ONLY IN CASE CODED '2' FOR ANY OF THESE, OR ELSE MOVE TO NEXT SECTION

5(a). How many of the _____ (READ OUT FOR THOSE CODED '2') that you personally know live abroad?

5(a)	No	Yes	5(b) Numbers staying abroad
Members of immediate family	1	2	
Members of extended family	1	2	
Friends	1	2	

ASK '5(c)' ONLY IF MEMBERS OF IMMEDIATE FAMILY STAYING ABROAD

5(c). You mentioned that _____ (MENTION THE NUMBER OF IMMEDIATE FAMILY MEMBER/S LIVING ABROAD) member/s of your immediate family lives abroad. Can you please tell me how many years each of them have been staying abroad? Can you tell me the age and gender of each member? What is the occupation of each of these members? Also tell me the highest completed education for each of these members?

START WITH THE MEMBER WHO HAS STAYED ABROAD FOR THE LONGEST DURATION. RECORD ACTUAL AGE, CIRCLE GENDER, TRANSFER APPROPRIATE EDUCATION, OCCUPATION CODES, COUNTRY OF STAY FROM THE GRID, RECORD YRS. SINCE STAYING ABROAD, AMOUNT OF RE-MITTANCES AND LIKELIHOOD OF RETURN FROM GRID FOR MAX 4 MEMBERS OF FAMILY STAYING ABROAD.

| | Relationship to You (See Grid) | Age | Gender | | Education | Occupation | Number of Years Staying Abroad | Country of Stay (See Grid) | Amount of Remittances in the Last One Year | Likelihood of Return (See Grid) |
			M	F						
Member 1			1	2						
Member 2			1	2						
Member 3			1	2						
Member 4			1	2						

RELATIONSHIP GRID

	Code		Code
Son	01	Father	05
Daughter	02	Mother	06
Brother	03	Other	07
Sister	04	DK/CS	0

COUNTRY GRID

	Code		Code
U.S./America	01	Africa	08
Middle East	012	Middle East	09
UK	03	South America	10
Europe (other than UK)	04	Other (specify)	
Southeast Asia	05	Other (specify)	
Australia/New Zealand	06	Other (specify)	
Asia (other)	07	DK/CS	99

LIKELIHOOD OF RETURN GRID

Likelihood of Return	
Very likely	01
Likely	02
Unlikely	03
Very unlikely	04
DK/CS	09

6(a). What services did you use to receive money from abroad?

Demand draft	1	Family member himself/herself brings	6
NRI account	2	Through friends relatives	7
Internet-based money transfer service	3	Any other way	8
		DK/CS	9
Other money transfer services	4		

6(b). Can you tell me the purpose for which you spend money received from abroad?

Household expenses	1	Real estate	6
Festivals	2	Special occasions (marriage,	
Bank deposits, investments in		travel, etc.)	7
stocks, mutual funds	3	Other (specify)	8
Business	4	DK/CS	9
Medical emergencies	5		

7(a). Does your household *send* money abroad?

SINGLE CODE

Yes	1	No	2

CONTINUE ONLY IF CODED '1', OR ELSE MOVE TO NEXT SECTION

7(b). Can you please tell me how much money you send abroad?

SINGLE CODE

Less than or equal to Rs. 5000	1	Rs. 50,001–Rs.1 lakh	6
Rs. 5001–Rs. 10,000	2	Rs. 100,001–Rs.2 lakh	7
Rs. 10,001–Rs. 20,000	3	Rs. 2 lakh–Rs. 5 lakh	8
Rs. 20,001–Rs. 30,000	4	More than Rs. 5 lakh	9
Rs. 30,001–Rs. 50,000	5	DK/CS	10

THESE TWO QUESTIONS COULD EITHER BE INSERTED UP FRONT IN THIS SECTION OF THE SURVEY OR IN THE BEGINNING OF THE SURVEY ITSELF

1. Has anyone in this household started a business in the last 12 months?

SINGLE CODE

Yes	1	No	2	DK/CS	9

2. Can you tell me what types of business-related investments were made in the last 12 months?

Buildings	1	Land	5
Machinery	2	Animals	6
Office equipment	3	Other (specify)	7
Transport equipment (vehicles, etc.)	4	DK/CS	9

Database on India's Elites (1950–2000)

The objective of this database was to determine the overseas exposure of India's elites. The database was designed to address three issues:

- Who qualifies as an elite?
- What does an overseas exposure mean?
- How does one get a consistent source for the first two issues over time?

The database covers elites in the following fields:

- Politicians
- Scientists
- Bureaucrats
- Industrialists

The first step involved searching for the various sources that could provide a consistent data set about the Indian elite from 1950 to 2000. Elites do not change annually. I therefore chose three periods of time that encompass independent India's first half-century: 1950, 1980, and 2000.

I have used the following sources (in rough order of importance) in full or in part in constructing the database. (The figures in brackets are the time periods for which the particular source was relevant.)

- *India News and Feature Alliance (INFA): Who's Who* [1980, 2000]. New Delhi: INFA Publications, Durga Das Pvt. Ltd.
- Chattopadhaya, Anjana. *Biographical Dictionary of Indian Scientists: From Ancient to Contemporary. Indian Scientists* [1900–2000]. New Delhi: Rupa & Co., 2002.
- *Lok Sabha Yearbooks* [1950–2000]. New Delhi: Reference Division, Indian Parliament Library.
- *Rajya Sabha Yearbooks* [1953–2000]. New Delhi: Reference Division, Indian Parliament Library.
- *Indian Council of States* [1950]. New Delhi: Reference Division, Indian Parliament Library.
- *Handbook of Cabinet Ministers* [1950–2000]. New Delhi: Reference Division, Indian Parliament Library.
- *Who Was Who* [1900–1980]. New Delhi: Durga Das Pvt. Ltd.
- *Eminent Indians* [1950–1980]. New Delhi: Durga Das Pvt. Ltd.

- *Times of India Yearbooks* [1980–2000]. Mumbai: Times of India Press.
- *Saur Indian Biographical Archives* [1950–1995]. Munich: K.G. Saur Verlag.
- *Committees and Commissions in India* [1975–1985]. Concept Publishing Co., 1993.
- *Nalanda Yearbook* [1950]. *Nalanda Yearbook and Who's Who in India and Pakistan, 1950–51. An Indian and International Annual of Current Statistics, Events and Personalities*. Edited by Tarapada Das Gupta. Calcutta.

The following sources were used to obtain archival material.

- The Indian Institute Library, Oxford University, United Kingdom
- The Marshall Library, University of Cambridge, United Kingdom
- The Teen Murti Library, University of Delhi, India
- The National Library, Calcutta, India

Politicians

Consistent data on politicians was relatively easy to obtain. The following criterion was adopted for including an individual: all members of the Lok Sabha, Rajya Sabha, and all cabinet ministers were included. This would encompass both houses of the Parliament, and therefore include any individual with some influence on national policy. This criterion, however, does not hold for 1950. The Rajya Sabha came into existence only after 1952. This data for 1950 covers members of the Indian Council of States, supplemented with members of the newly formed Rajya Sabha. The logic for including the latter is that any individual who was part of the first Rajya Sabha was probably in a position to be included in an elite list for 1950.

Data sources used for India's political elite were the Lok Sabha and Rajya Sabha yearbooks, the *Handbook of Cabinet Ministers*, and the *Handbook on the Indian Council of States*.

Scientists

Here the problem was how to define "elite scientists." The database covers each discipline within the sciences, including earth sciences, physics, chemistry, and mathematics, and leading practitioners within each discipline. The two major sources for this data were:

- *INFA database* [1980–2000]. New Delhi: INFA Publications, Durga Das Pvt. Ltd.

- Chattopadhaya, Anjana. *Biographical Dictionary of Indian Scientists: From Ancient to Contemporary*. New Delhi: Rupa & Co., 2002.

The criteria for inclusion in these databases included heads of major scientific institutions in India, citations, and published papers. The INFA yearbook database provides data for the years 1980 and 2000, with a breakdown by discipline. The individual-level data are not very comprehensive, but it suffices for the questions that the database seeks to ask. The selection methodology is somewhat subjective. The recently published *Biography of Indian Scientists*, which included scientists from 1900–1980, provides more comprehensive biographies of the major contributors to different scientific fields. The selection method here is also subjective, depending on the editors' knowledge of scientific institutions in India. However, it is a more comprehensive source than the INFA database.

Data for 1950 draws solely from the *Biography of Indian Scientists*. The method of selection was as follows. All scientists born before 1910 and still alive in 1950 were included. The logic was that scientists attain renown only after a certain period. I have used a minimum age of 40 years, balancing the minimum age needed to attain broad recognition with some confidence that the individual had enough productive years in front of her/him to make a difference.

For 2000, all entries in the 2000 INFA yearbook are included. Recognizing that using two different databases for the end-years (1950, 2000) might result in noncomparable entries, for 1980 I compared entries from both sources. Fortunately, there was a large overlap between the two sources for this year. Entries from INFA completely span the individuals mentioned in the *Biography* and exceed it by 17 individuals. In percentage terms, this was a minor difference. I therefore chose to use INFA for 2000 without making any changes.

BUREAUCRATS

The list of bureaucrats was compiled from the INFA *Who's Who*, and there were no problems with consistency. However, data on the bureaucratic elite in 1950 have proven to be more difficult. There seem to be no records held in any of the sources I consulted.

A second database was compiled from the list of all current (as of mid-2004) serving officers of the Indian Administrative Service (IAS), based on the record of the Ministry of Personnel, Government of India. This helps track different cohorts of the India's bureaucratic elite over the past thirty-five years. Given the source of the database, the accuracy and consistency of this data are very high.

Business and Industry

The simplest way to rank individuals in this category is to use a money metric scale. The INFA yearbook claims to follow this approach, for both 1950 and 1980 selecting the top 300 richest individuals in India. However, there is a disparity with their data, as there were 54 more entries in 1980 compared to 2000. However, the data appear to be rigorous to a variety of cross-checks (discussed in the following) to which the data were subjected.

A more important problem is the lack of data for 1950. For this, I draw from a recent history of Indian business (Dwijendra Tripathi, *The Oxford History of Indian Business*, Oxford, UK: Oxford University Press, 2004), supplementing it with data from reports prepared to implement the Monopolies and Restrictive Trade Practices Act, which detail the largest industrial groups at the time.

General Comments

I have tried as far as possible to test the data for consistency from other sources that are not by themselves comprehensive, but nonetheless act as a useful cross-check. Most of these sources do not have a specific methodology behind their selection of the individuals. What I have done is to compare my database with all these databases to see whether there are significant differences.

One important source that spans 1900–1995 is the Indian Biographical Archives (IBA), published by Saur Verlag. While this database is highly inconsistent and comprises an ad hoc collection of a variety of sources, which differ from year to year, it does allow us to see whether the database we have constructed compares favorably: I found that for all categories, the overlap between my database and the IBA database was *at least* 90 percent. I also cross-checked my database with the standard yearbooks, including the Times of India yearbooks, the Nalanda Yearbook (1950 only), and a publication titled *Eminent Indians, 1900–1980*.

Bibliography

Abernethy, David. *The Dynamics of Global Dominance: European Overseas Empires, 1415–1980*. New Haven, CT: Yale University Press, 2000.

Acemoglu, Daron, and James A. Robinson. "Why Did the West Extend the Franchise? Democracy, Inequality, and Growth in Historical Perspective." *The Quarterly Journal of Economics* 115, no. 4 (November 2000): 1167–99.

Acemoglu, Daron, S. Johnson, and J. A. Robinson. "Reversal of Fortune: Geography and Institutions in the Making of the Modern World Income Distribution." *Quarterly Journal of Economics* 117, no. 4 (2002): 1231–94.

Acharya, Shankar. *India's Economy: Some Issues and Answers*. New Delhi: Academic Foundation, 1976.

Adams, James. *The Financing of Terror*. New York: Simon & Schuster, 1986.

Agarwal, Reena, and Andrew W. Horowitz. "Are International Remittances Altruism or Insurance? Evidence from Guyana Using Multiple-Migrant Households." *World Development* 30, no. 11 (2002): 2033–44.

Agrawal, Ajay, Devesh Kapur, and John McHale. "How Do Spatial and Social Proximity Influence Knowledge Flows? Evidence from Patent Data." *Journal of Urban Economics*, 64 (2008): 258–69.

Ahluwalia, Montek Singh. Interview by Manik Suri, August 23, 2004, New Delhi.

Albright, Madeleine. Interview by Manik Suri, October 12, 2004, Washington, DC.

Allport, Gordon W. *The Nature of Prejudice*. Cambridge, MA: Addison-Wesley, 1954.

Almond, Gabriel, and Sidney Verba. *The Civic Culture: Political Attitudes and Democracy in Five Nations Culture*. Boston: Little, Brown, 1963.

Altemeye, Bob. *The Authoritarian Specter*. Cambridge, MA: Harvard University Press, 1997.

Ambirajan, S. "Ambedkar's Contributions to Indian Economics." *Economic and Political Weekly* 34, no. 45 (1999): 6–12.

Anderson, Benedict. *Imagined Communities: Reflections on the Origin and Spread of Nationalism*, revised ed. New York: Verso, 1997.

Appel, Hilary. *A New Capitalist Order: Privatization and Ideology in Russia and Eastern Europe*. Pittsburgh, PA: University of Pittsburgh Press, 2004.

Appiah, Kwame Anthony. "What Was Africa to Them?" *New York Review of Books* 54, no. 14 (September 27, 2007). Available at http://www.nybooks.com/articles/20600.

"Are We Entitled to the Moral Leadership of the World?" *Black Dispatch* 4 (August 15, 1919): 123. Quoted in Alfred L. Brophy, *Reconstructing the Dreamland: The Tulsa Riot of 1921: Race, Reparations, and Reconciliation*. New York: Oxford University Press, 2002.

"Arvind v Arvind." A review of *India's Turn: Understanding the Economic Transformation* by Arvind Subramanian. *The Economist*, June 26, 2008.

Awaaz South Asia Watch Limited. "In Bad Faith? British Charity and Hindu Extremism" (February 26, 2004). Available at http://www.awaazsaw.org/ibf/ibflores.pdf.

Babb, Sarah. *Managing Mexico: Economists from Nationalism to Neoliberalism.* Princeton, NJ: Princeton University Press, 2001.

Bajpai, Kanti, and Siddharth Mallavarapu, eds. *International Relations in India: Bringing Theory Back Home.* New Delhi: Orient Longman, 2005.

Balachandran, G. "Circulation through Seafaring: Indian Seamen, 1890–1945." In *Society and Circulation: Mobile People and Itinerant Cultures in South Asia 1750–1950*, edited by Claude Markovits, Jacques Pouchepadass, and Sanjay Subrahmanyamy. New Delhi: Permanent Black, 2003.

Ballard, Roger. "Emigration in a Wider Context: Jullundur and Mirpur Compared." *New Community* 11, no. 1 (1983): 117–36.

Banerjee, Abhijit, Pranab Bardhan, Kaushik Basu, Mrinal Datta-Chaudhuri, Ashok Guha, Mukul Majumdar, Dilip Mookherjee, and Debraj Ray. "Strategy for Economic Reform in West Bengal," *Economic and Political Weekly* 37, no. 41 (October 12, 2002): 4203–18.

Baptiste, Fitzroy A. "African Presence in India." *Africa Quarterly* 38, no. 1 (1998): 75–90; no. 2: 91–126.

Barber, William J. "Chile con Chicago: A Review Essay." A review of *Pinochet's Economists: The Chicago School in Chile*, by Juan Gabriel Valdés. *Journal of Economic Literature* 33, no. 4 (December 1995): 1941–49.

Bardhan, Pranab. *The Political Economy of Development in India.* New Delhi: Oxford University Press, 1999.

Barro, Robert, and Jong-Wha Lee. "International Data on Educational Attainment: Updates and Implications." Center for International Development Working Paper No. 42. Cambridge, MA: Harvard University, 2000.

Bassett, Ross. "MIT-Trained Swadeshis: MIT and Indian Nationalism, 1880–1947." *Osiris* 24, no. 1 (2009): 212–30.

Bellin, Eva. "The Robustness of Authoritarianism in the Middle East: Exceptionalism in Comparative Perspective." *Comparative Politics* 36, no. 2 (January 2004): 139–57.

Bermeo, Nancy. *Ordinary People in Extraordinary Times: The Citizenry and the Breakdown of Democracy.* Princeton, NJ: Princeton University Press, 2003.

Bhagwati, Jagdish. *In Defense of Globalization.* New York: Oxford University Press, 2004.

———. *India in Transition.* Oxford, UK: Clarendon Press, 1995.

———. *International Factor Mobility.* Cambridge, MA: MIT Press, 1983.

Bhagwati, Jaimini. "Return on FCA," *Business Standard*, December 14, 2006. Available at http://www.business-standard.com/india/news/returnfca/267918/.

Bhandari, Bhupesh. "Frugal Innovation." *Business Standard*, June 13, 2009. Retrieved on June 15, 2009; available at http://www.business-standard.com/india/news/frugal-innovation/360886/.

Bhardwaj, Surinder M. *Hindu Places of Pilgrimage in India.* Berkeley: University of California Press, 1973.

Bhattacharjee, Debashis, Karthik Krishna, and Amol Karve. "Signalling, Work Experience, and MBA Starting Salaries." *Economic and Political Weekly, Review of Management and Industry* 36 (November 24, 2001): 46–47.

Bilefsky, Dan. "Indians Unseat Antwerp's Jews as the Biggest Diamond Traders." *Wall Street Journal*, May 27, 2003.

Blauer, Ettagale. "The Diamond Industry." *New York Diamonds* 77 (July 2003): 62–63.

Blumer, Herbert. "Race Prejudice as a Sense of Group Position." *Pacific Sociological Review* 1 (1958): 3–6.

Boix, Carlos. *Democracy and Redistribution.* Cambridge, UK: Cambridge University Press, 2003.

Borjas, George J., Richard B. Freeman, and Lawrence F. Katz. "Searching for the Effect of Immigration on the Labor Market," *American Economic Review* 86 (1996): 247–51.

Bornstein, Charlie. "Antwerp Perspectives." Interview by Martin Rapaport, December 9, 2003. Available at http://www.diamonds.net/News/NewsItem .aspx?ArticleID=8922.

Brewer, Marilynn B. "The Psychology of Prejudice: Ingroups Love or Outgroups Hate?" *Journal of Sociological Issues* 55 (1999): 429–44.

Brophy, Alfred L. *Reconstructing the Dreamland: The Tulsa Riot of 1921: Race, Reparations, and Reconciliation.* New York: Oxford University Press, 2002.

Brown, John Seely, and Paul Duguid. *The Social Life of Information*, 4th ed. Cambridge, MA: Harvard Business Press, 2002.

Bunce, Valerie. "Comparative Democratization: Big and Bounded Generalizations." *Comparative Political Studies* 33 (2000): 6.

Burt, Ronald S. *Structural Holes: The Social Structure of Competition.* Cambridge, MA: Harvard University Press, 1992.

Byman, Daniel L., and Kenneth M. Pollack "Let Us Now Praise Great Men (and Women): Restoring the First Image." *International Security* 25, no. 4 (spring 2001), 107–47.

Chanda, Nayan. *Bound Together: How Traders, Preachers, Adventurers, and Warriors Shaped Globalization.* New Haven, CT: Yale University Press, 2007.

Chaudhry, Kiren Aziz. "The Price of Wealth: Business and State in Labor Remittances and Oil Economies," *International Organization* 43, no. 1 (1989): 101–45.

———. *The Price of Wealth: Economics and Institutions in the Middle East.* Ithaca, NY: Cornell University Press, 1997.

Chaudhry, Lakshmi. "The Great Indian Dream." *Wired Magazine*, April 4, 2000. Available at http://www.wired.com/culture/lifestyle/news/2000/04/35308.

Chaudhury, Sushil. "Trading Networks in a Traditional Diaspora: Armenians in India c. 1600–1800." In *Diaspora Entrepreneurial Networks: Four Centuries of History*, edited by Ina Baghdiantz Mccabe, Gelina Harlaftis, and Ioanna Pepelasis, 51–72. New York: Berg, 2005.

Chehabi, Houchang E., and Juan Jose Linz, eds. *Sultanistic Regimes* Baltimore, London: Johns Hopkins University Press, 1998.

Cherian, Joy. *Our Relay Race.* New York: University Press of America, 1997.

Chibber, Pradeep. *Democracy without Associations*. Ann Arbor: University of Michigan Press, 1999.

Chiswick, Barry R. "Are Immigrants Favorably Selected?" In *Migration Theory: Talking Across Disciplines*, edited by C. B. Brettell and J. F. Hollifield, 61–76. New York: Routledge, 2000.

Coleman, Simon. *Pilgrimage: Past and Present in the World Religions*. Cambridge, MA: Harvard University Press, 1995.

Collier, Paul, Anke Hoeffler, and Catherine Pattillo. "Flight Capital as Portfolio Choice," World Bank Working Paper No. 2066 (2000): 55–80.

Commander, Simon, Mari Kangasniemi, and Alan L. Winters. "The Brain Drain: Curse or Boon? A Survey of the Literature." In *Challenges to Globalization: Analyzing the Economics*, edited by Robert E. Baldwin and L. Alan Winters, 235–78. Chicago: University of Chicago Press, 2004.

Commission on International Migration Data for Development Research and Policy. *Migrants Count: Five Steps toward Better Migration Data*. Washington, DC: Center for Global Development, 2009.

Courbage, Youseff. "Fertility Transition in the Mashriq and the Maghreb." In *Family, Gender, and Population in the Middle East*, edited by Carol Obermeyer, 80–104. Cairo: American University in Cairo Press, 1995.

Dahl, Robert. *On Democracy*. New Haven, CT: Yale University Press, 1998.

Darwin, John Gareth. "Civility and Empire." In *Civil Histories: Essays Presented to Sir Keith Thomas*, edited by Peter Burke, Brian Howard Harrison, and Paul Slack, 321–36. Oxford, UK: Oxford University Press, 2000.

Datta, Romita, and Aveek Datta. "Mainstream Politics Not for Us, Says Koteshwar Rao." *Mint*, May 28, 2009.

Datta-Ray, Sunanda K. "Showcasing Gujarat." *Business Standard*, April 25, 2009.

Davis, Kingsley. *The Population of India and Pakistan*. Princeton, NJ: Princeton University Press, 1951.

"Delhi Dreams—Face Value." *The Economist*, December 23, 2006.

De Ridder-Symoens, Hilde. "Training and Professionalization. In *Power Elites and State Building*, edited by Wolfgang Reinhard, 149–70. New York: Clarendon Press, 1996.

Desai, Mihir, Devesh Kapur, and John McHale. "Sharing the Spoils: Taxing International Human Capital Flows." *International Tax and Public Finance* 11, no. 5 (2001): 663–93.

Desai, Mihir, Devesh Kapur, John McHale, and Keith Rogers. "The Fiscal Impact of High-Skilled Emigration: Flows of Indians to the U.S." *Journal of Development Economics* 88 (2009): 32–44.

Diamond, Jared M. *Guns, Germs, and Steel: The Fates of Human Societies*. New York: W. Norton & Company, 1997.

Dickinson, Jen, and Adrian J. Bailey. 2007. "(Re)membering Diaspora: Uneven Geographies of Indian Dual Citizenship," *Political Geography* 26, no. 7 (2007): 757–74.

Diwanji, Amberish. "The India Caucus Still Has a Long Distance to Go," *Rediff*, September 18, 2000.

Docquier, Frederic, and Abdeslam Marfouk. *Measuring the International Mobility of Skilled Workers*. Policy Research Working Paper No. 3381. World Bank, 2004.

Dominguez, Jorge. *Democratic Politics in Latin America and the Caribbean.* Baltimore, MD: Johns Hopkins University Press, 1998.

———. *Technopols: Freeing Politics and Markets in Latin America in the 1990s.* University Park, PA: Penn State Press, 1997.

Dowding, Keith, Peter John, Thanos Mergoupis, and Mark van Vugt. "Exit, Voice and Loyalty: Analytic and Empirical Developments." *European Journal of Political Research* 37 (2000): 469–95.

Dreazen, Yochi. "Iraq Sees Christian Exodus." *Wall Street Journal*, September 27, 2004, A17.

Dreze, Jean, and Amartya Sen. *India: Economic Development and Social Opportunity.* New Delhi: Oxford University Press, 2002.

Duara, Prasenjit. "Transnationalism and the Predicament of Sovereignty: China, 1900–1945." In *The Chinese Overseas*, Routledge Library of Modern China, edited by Hong Liu, vol. 1, 375. New York: Routledge, 2006.

Dugger, Celia. "U.S. Plan to Lure Nurses May Hurt Poor Nations." *New York Times*, May 24, 2006.

Dumm, Christopher. Interview by the author, August 13, 2004, Washington, DC.

Dumont, Jean-Christophe, and Georges Lemaître. "Counting Immigrants and Expatriates in OECD Countries: A New Perspective." Social, Employment and Migration Working Papers No. 25. Paris: OECD Directorate for Employment, Labour, and Social Affairs, 2005.

Dutta, Rumi. "The Next Outsourcing Wave—Lab Tests." *Business Standard*, April 19, 2004.

Eckstein, Harry. *Division and Cohesion in Democracy.* Princeton, NJ: Princeton University Press, 1966.

Embassy of the United States of America. *Report on the Official Visit of Prime Minister Atal Bihari Vajpayee to the United States*, September 13–17, 2000.

"Employment Statistics in India." *Economic and Political Weekly*, May 3, 2003.

"Expatriation Rates for Doctors and Nurses, circa 2000." In *International Migration Outlook*, edited by John P. Martin. Paris: Organisation for Economic Co-operation and Development (OECD), 2007.

Fair, C. Christine. "Diaspora Involvement in Insurgencies: Insights from the Khalistan and Tamil Eelam Movements." *Nationalism and Ethnic Politics* 11. no. 1 (2005): 125–56.

Faiz, Faiz Ahmed. "Sochne do." In *Nushkhaha-e vafa.* Lahore, Pakistan: Maktaba-e Karvan, 1967.

Feldhaus, Anne. *Connected Places: Region, Pilgrimage, and Geographical Imagination in India.* New York: Palgrave Macmillan, 2003.

Feliciano, Cynthia. "Educational Selectivity in U.S. Immigration: How Do Immigrants Compare to Those Left Behind?" *Demography* 42, no. 1 (2005): 131–52.

Fernandes, Edna. "Indian Manufacturers' Designs on the World." *Financial Times*, October 6, 2002.

Finnemore, Martha, and Kathryn Sikkink. "International Norm Dynamics and Political Change." *International Organization* 52, no. 4 (1998): 887–917.

Fischer-Tiné, Harald. "'Indian Nationalism and the World Forces': Transnational and Diasporic Dimensions of the Indian Freedom Movement on the Eve of the First World War." *Journal of Global History*, 2 (2007): 325–44.

Fish, M. Steven. "Islam and Authoritarianism," *World Politics* 55, no. 1 (October 2002), 35.

Fitzgerald, David. *A Nation of Emigrants: How Mexico Manages Its Migration.* Berkeley: University of California Press, 2009.

Foner, Nancy. "What's So New about Transnationalism? New York Immigrants Today and at the Turn of the Century." *Diaspora* 6, no. 3 (1997): 354–75.

"The Foreign Exchange of Hate: IDRF and the American Funding of Hindutva." Mumbai, India: Sabrang Publishing, Ltd., 2002. Available at http://stopfundinghate.org/sacw/.

Foster, Andrew D., and Mark R. Rosenzweig. "Imperfect Commitment, Altruism, and the Family: Evidence from Transfer Behavior in Low-Income Rural Areas." *Review of Economics and Statistics* 83, no. 3 (August 2001): 389–407.

Fox, Jonathan "Exit Followed by Voice: Mapping Mexico's Emerging Migrant Civil Society." In *Alternative Visions of Development: Rural Social Movements in Latin America*, edited by Carmen Diana Deere and Fred Royce. Gainesville: University Press of Florida, 2009.

Frankel, Francine. *India's Political Economy, 1947–1977: The Gradual Revolution.* Princeton, NJ: Princeton University Press, 1978.

Frey, Frederick. *The Turkish Political Elite.* Cambridge, MA: MIT Press, 1965.

Frieden, Jeffry. "Actors and Preferences in International Relations." In *Strategic Choice and International Relations*, edited by David A. Lake and Robert Powell, 39–76. Princeton, NJ: Princeton University Press, 1999.

Fukuyama, Francis. *State-Building: Governance and World Order in the 21st Century.* Ithaca, NY: Cornell University Press, 2004.

Gabaccia, Donna R. *Italy's Many Diasporas.* Seattle: University of Washington Press, 2000.

Ganachari, Aravind. "Purchasing Indian Loyalties I: Imperial Policy of Recruitment and 'Rewards.'" *Economic and Political Weekly* 40, no. 8 (February 19, 2005): 779–88.

Gellner, Ernest. *Nations and Nationalism.* Ithaca, NY: Cornell University Press, 1983.

Geoghegan, John. "Note on Emigration from India." Calcutta: Office of Superintendent of Government Printing, 1873.

Gibson, Campbell, and Kay Jung. "Historical Census Statistics on the Foreign-Born Population of the United States: 1850 to 2000," Working Paper No. 81. Washington, DC: U.S. Census Bureau, 2006.

Gibson, Campbell, and Emily Lennon. "Historical Census Statistics on the Foreign-born Population of the United States: 1850–1990." Technical Paper No. 29. Washington, DC: U.S. Bureau of the Census, 1999.

Goldberg, Pinelopi, and Nina Pavcnik. "Trade, Inequality, and Poverty: What Do We Know? Evidence from Recent Trade Liberalization Episodes in Developing Countries." In *Brookings Trade Forum 2004*, edited by S. M. Collins and C. Graham, 223–69. Washington, DC: Brookings Institution Press, 2004.

Goldstein, Judith, and Robert O. Keohane. "Ideas and Foreign Policy: An Analytical Framework." In *Ideas and Foreign Policy*, edited by Judith Goldstein and Robert Keohane, 3–30. Ithaca, NY: Cornell University Press, 1993.

Goodman, Gary L., and Jonathan T. Hiskey. "Exit without Leaving: Political Disengagement in High Migration Municipalities in Mexico." *Comparative Politics* 40, no. 2 (January 2008): 169–88.

Gordon, Jim, and Poonam Gupta. "Understanding India's Services Revolution." Paper presented at the IMF-NCAER Conference, *A Tale of Two Giants: India's and China's Experience with Reform*, November 14–16, 2003, New Delhi.

Gorringe, Hugo. *Untouchable Citizens—Dalit Movements and Democratisation in Tamil Nadu*. New Delhi: Sage Publications, 2005.

Goswami, Manu. *Producing India: From Colonial Economy to National Space*. Chicago: University of Chicago Press, 1973.

Gourevitch, Peter. "The Second Image Reversed: The International Sources of Domestic Politics." *International Organization* 32 (1978): 881–912.

Government of India. *Report of the High Level Committee on the Indian Diaspora*. New Delhi: Ministry of External Affairs, 2001.

Granville, Austin. *The Indian Constitution: Cornerstone of a Nation*. New Delhi: Oxford University Press, 1966.

Green, Donald P., and Rachel L. Seher. "What Role Does Prejudice Play in Ethnic Conflict?" *Annual Review of Political Science* 6 (2003): 509–31.

Grewal, David. *Network Power: The Social Dynamics of Globalization*. New Haven, CT: Yale University Press, 2008.

Grix, Jonathan. *The Role of the Masses in the Collapse of the GDR*. Basingstoke/New York: Macmillan/Palgrave, 2000.

Groth, Alexander, and Donald Rothschild. "Pathological Dimensions of Domestic and International Ethnicity." *Political Science Quarterly* 110, no. 1, 69–82 (1995).

Guarnizo, Luis Eduardo, Alejandro Portes, and William Haller. "Assimilation and Transnationalism: Determinants of Transnational Political Action among Contemporary Migrants." *American Journal of Sociology* 108, no. 6 (2003): 1211–48.

Guha, Ramchandra. "The Ones Who Stayed Behind." *Economic and Political Weekly* 38, nos. 12 and 13 (March 22, 2003): 1121–24.

Guha, Ram. *The Hindu*, November 23, 2003.

Gumpert, David. "An Unseen Peril of Outsourcing," *BusinessWeek*, March 3, 2004.

Gupta, Shekhar. "Masters in Illiberal Arts." *India Express*, August 23, 2009. Available at: http://www.indianexpress.com/news/masters-in-illiberal-arts/505446/0.

Haas, Peter M. "Epistemic Communities and International Policy Coordination." *International Organization* 46, no. 1 (winter 1992): 1–35.

Hagopian, Frances. "What Makes Democracies Collapse?" *Journal of Democracy:* 15, no. 3 (2004): 166–69.

Hall, Peter A. *The Political Power of Economic Ideas*. Ithaca, NY: Cornell University Press, 1989.

Haniffa, Aziz. "US Senate India Caucus," March 31, 2004. Available at US-India Friendship.net

Hart, Matthew. *Diamond: A Journey to the Heart of an Obsession*. New York: Walker Publishing Company, 2001.

Hatton, Timothy J., and Jeffrey G. Williamson. *Global Migration and the World Economy: Two Centuries of Policy and Performance*. Cambridge, MA: MIT Press, 2005.

Heller, Patrick. "Degrees of Democracy: Some Comparative Lessons from India." *World Politics* 52. no. 4 (July 2000): 484–519.

Hermann, Margaret, and Charles Hermann, "Who Makes Foreign Policy Decisions and How: An Empirical Inquiry." *International Studies Quarterly* 33, no. 4 (December 1989): 361–87.

Hirschman, Albert G. *Exit, Voice and Loyalty: Responses to Decline in Firms, Organizations, and States*, 76. Cambridge, MA: Harvard University Press, 1970.

Honig, Bonnie. *Democracy and the Foreigner*. Princeton, NJ: Princeton University Press, 2001.

Horgan, John, and Max Taylor. "Playing the Green Card: Financing the Provisional IRA Part 1." *Terrorism and Political Violence* 11, no. 1 (1999): 1–38.

———. "Playing the 'Green Card'—Financing the Provisional IRA: Part 2." *Terrorism and Political Violence* 15, no. 2 (2003): 1–60.

Huang, Yasheng. *Selling China: Foreign Direct Investment during the Reform Era*. Cambridge, UK: Cambridge University Press, 2003.

Huntington, Samuel. "The Erosion of American National Interests." *Foreign Affairs* 76, no. 5 (1997): 28–49.

———. *Who Are We? The Challenges to America's National Identity*. New York: Simon and Schuster, 2004.

Hussain, Akmal "Pakistan: Land Reforms Considered." In Sociology of Developing Societies of South Asia, edited by H. Alavi and J. Harris. New York: Monthly Review Press, 1989.

Iliffe, John. *Africans: The History of a Continent*. London: Cambridge University Press, 1995.

Inderfuth, Karl. Interview by Manik Suri, November 12, 2004, Washington, DC.

Indian Council of Social Science Research. "Restructuring the Indian Council of Social Science Research." Report of the Fourth Review Committee, New Delhi: Indian Council of Social Science Research, 2007.

Integrated Risk Control Applications (IRCA). "The Indian Gems and Jewellery Sector." Industry Comment, July 2006. Available at www.forcesofindia.com/headhunting/resources/presentations/Gems&Jewellery-200607.pdf (cited June 12, 2009).

International Initiative for Gujarat (IIJ). "Threatened Existence: A Feminist Analysis of the Genocide in Gujarat." December 19, 2002. Available at http://www.onlinevolunteers.org/gujarat/reports/iijg/.

Irvine, Steve. "Ajeya Singh: Head of India, Lehman Brothers." In *Euromoney*, 39. London: 1998.

———. "Seen from India's Ivory Tower." In *Euromoney*, 38. London: 1998.

Jaffrelot, Christopher. "Gujarat: The Meaning of Modi's Victory," *Economic and Political Weekly*, April 12, 2008, 12–17.

———. *India's Silent Revolution: The Rise of the Lower Castes in North India*. New York: Columbia University Press, 2003.

Jalal, Ayesha. The State of Martial Rule. Cambridge, UK: Cambridge University Press, 1990.

Johnston, Alastair Iain. "Treating International Institutions as Social Environments." *International Studies Quarterly* 45, no. 4 (2001): 487–515.

Jones-Correa, Michael. *Between Two Nations: The Political Predicament of Latinos in New York City.* Ithaca, NY: Cornell University Press, 1998.

Joseph, T. M., and S. N. Sangita. "Preferential Policies and 'Sons-of-the-Soil' Demands: The Indian Experience." *Ethnic Studies Report* XVI, no. 1 (1998): 73–102.

Juster, Kenneth. Interview by Manik Suri, December 14, 2004, Washington, DC.

Kanigel, Robert. *The Man Who Knew Infinity: A Life of the Genius Ramanujan.* New York: Pocket Books, 1991.

Kannan, K., and K. S. Hari. "Kerala's Gulf Connection—Emigration, Remittances and Their Macroeconomic Impact 1972–2000." CDS Working Paper No. 328. Thiruvananthapuram, Kerala, India: Center for Development Studies, 2002.

Kapur, Devesh. "The Indian Diaspora as a Strategic Asset." *Economic and Political Weekly* XXXVIII, no. 5 (February 1–7, 2003): 445–48.

———. "Indian Higher Education." In *American Universities in a Global Market*, edited by Charles Clotfelter. Chicago: University of Chicago Press, forthcoming.

———. "The Janus Face of Diasporas." In *Diasporas and Development*, edited by Barbara J. Merz, Lincoln Chen, and Peter Geithner, 89–118. Cambridge, MA: Harvard University Press, 2007.

———. "Remittances: The New Development Mantra?" In *Remittances: Development Impact and Future Prospects*, edited by S. M. Maimbo and Dilip Ratha, 331–60. Washington, DC: World Bank, 2005.

Kapur, Devesh, and John McHale. "Cosmopolitanism and the 'Brain Drain.'" *Ethics and International Affairs*, 20, no. 3 (fall 2006): 305–20.

———. *The Global War for Talent: Implications and Policy Responses for Developing Countries.* Washington, DC: Center for Global Development, 2005.

———. "Sojourns and Software: Internationally Mobile Human Capital and High-Tech Industry Development in India, Ireland and Israel." In *From Underdogs to Tigers: The Rise and Growth of the Software Industry in Some Emerging Economies*, edited by Ashish Arora and Alfonso Gambardella, 236–74. New York: Oxford University Press, 2005.

Kapur, Devesh, and Pratap Bhanu Mehta. "Mortgaging the Future? Indian Higher Education." In *Brookings-NCAER India Policy Forum 2007–08*, edited by Suman Bery, Barry Bosworth, and Arvind Panagariya, vol. 4, 101–15. New Delhi: Sage Publications, 2008.

Kapur, Devesh, and Moises Naim. "The IMF and Democracy." *Journal of Democracy*, 16, no. 1 (January 2005): 89–102.

Kapur, Devesh, and Urjit Patel. "Large Foreign Currency Reserves: Insurance for Domestic Weakness and External Uncertainties?" *Economic and Political Weekly* XXXVIII, no. 11 (March 15, 2003): 1047–53.

Kapur, Devesh, and Arjun Raychaudhuri. "NRI Deposits for Core Sector." *Business Standard*, January 7, 2007.

Kenny, John. "Mobilizing Diasporas in Nationalist Conflicts." PhD thesis, University of Chicago, 2000.

Kerala Public Expenditure Review Committee. "First Report." May 2006. Thiruvananthapuram, Kerala, India: Finance Department, Government of Kerala, 2006.

Kessinger, Tom. *Vilayatpur 1848—1968: Social and Economic Change in a North Indian Village*. Berkeley: University of California Press, 1974.

Khadria, Binod. "Of Dreams, Drain, and Dams: Metaphors in the Indian Emigration of Talent." *India International Center Quarterly* 26, no. 3 (1999): 79–90.

———. *The Migration of Knowledge Workers: Second-Generation Effects of India's Brain Drain*. New Delhi: Sage Publications, 1999.

Khalidi, Omar. *Khakhi and Ethnic Violence in India*. New Delhi: Three Essays, 2003.

Khatkhate, Deena. "Brain Drain as a Social Safety Valve." *Finance and Development* 18, no. 1 (1971): 34–39.

———. "Looking Back in Anger." *Economic and Political Weekly* 38 (December 27, 2003): 51–52.

Khilnani, Sunil. *The Idea of India*. New York: Farrar, Straus and Giroux, 1999.

———. "India as a Bridging Power." In *India as a New Global Leader*, edited by Prasenjit K. Basu, Brahma Chellaney, Parag Khanna, and Sunil Khilnani, 1–15. London: Foreign Policy Centre, 2005.

King, Charles, and Neil J. Melvin. "Diaspora Politics: Ethnic Linkages, Foreign Policy, and Security in Eurasia." *International Security* 24, no. 3 (1999): 108–38.

Kotkin, Joel. *Tribes: How Race, Religion, and Identity Determine Success in the New Global Economy*. New York: Random House, 1993.

Kudaisya, Gyanesh. "Indian Leadership and the Diaspora" In *The Encyclopedia of the Indian Diaspora*, edited by Brij V. Lal, 82–89. Singapore: Editions Didier Millet, 2006.

Kuklinski, James H., Michael D. Cobb, and Martin Gilens. "Racial attitudes and the 'New South.'" *Journal of Politics* 59 (1997): 323–49.

Kull, Steven, and Doug Miller. "Global Public Opinion on the US Presidential Election and US Foreign Policy." Questionnaire (2004). University of Maryland/Washington, DC: Program on International Policy Attitudes/Globescan, September 8, 2004.

Kuntamukkala, Ajay. Interview by Manik Suri, December 14, 2004, Washington, DC.

Kurzman, Charles, and Erin Leahey. "Intellectuals and Democratization, 1905–1912 and 1989–1996." *American Journal of Sociology* 109, no. 4 (January 2004): 937–86.

Lall, M. C. *India's Missed Opportunity. India's Relationship with the Non Resident Indians*. London: Ashgate, 2001.

Lasswell, Harold. *Politics: Who Gets What, When, How*, 13. Cleveland, OH: Meridian Books, 1936.

Leonard, Karen. "South Asians in the Indian Ocean World: Language, Policing, and Gender Practices in Kuwait and the UAE." *Comparative Studies of South Asia, Africa and the Middle East* 25, no. 3 (November 2005): 677–86.

Leslie, Stuart W., and Robert Kargo. "Exporting MIT: Science, Technology, and Nation-Building in India and Iran." *Osiris* (2006): 110–30.

Lever-Tracy, Constance, David Fu-Keung Ip, and Noel Tracy. *The Chinese Diaspora and Mainland China: An Emerging Economic Synergy.* New York: Macmillan Publishing Company, 1996.

Levi, Scott. *The Indian Diaspora in Central Asia and Its Trade, 1550–1900.* Leiden, The Netherlands: Brill Academic Publishers, 2002.

Levitt, Peggy. "Social Remittances: Migration Driven Local-Level Forms of Cultural Diffusion." *International Migration Review* 32, no. 4 (winter 1998): 926–48.

———. *The Transnational Villagers.* Berkeley and Los Angeles: University of California Press, 2001.

Lewis, Arthur. *The Evolution of the International Economic Order.* Princeton, NJ: Princeton University Press, 1984.

Lijphart, Arend. "The Puzzle of Indian Democracy: A Consociational Interpretation" *American Political Science Review* 90 (June 1996): 258–68.

Linden, Leigh. "Are Incumbents Really Advantaged: The Preference for Non-Incumbents in Indian National Elections." Draft 2004; available at http://econ-www.mit.edu/graduate/candidates/download_res.php?id=89 (accessed December 12, 2005).

Linz, Juan, and Alfred Stepan, eds. *The Breakdown of Democratic Regimes: Crisis, Breakdown and Reequilibrium.* Washington DC: Johns Hopkins, 1978.

Linz, Juan, Alfred Stepan, and Yogendra Yadav. "Nation State or State Nation: Conceptual Reflections and Some Spanish, Belgian and Indian Data." Background paper prepared for the Human Development Report. New York: United Nations Development Program, 2004.

Lipset, Seymour Martin. "The Social Requisites of Democracy Revisited," American Sociological Review 59, no. 1 (February 1994): 1–22.

Lipset, Seymour Martin, and Aldo Solari, eds. *Elites in Latin America.* New York: Oxford University Press, 1967.

Lloyd-Roberts, Sue. "Zimbabwe's precarious survival." *BBC News,* September 8, 2007. Available at http://news.bbc.co.uk/2/hi/programmes/from_our_own_correspondent/6982183.stm.

Mainwaring, Scott, Guillermo O'Donnell, and J. Samuel Valenzuela, eds. *Issues in Democratic Consolidation: The New South American Democracies in Comparative Perspective.* Chicago: University of Notre Dame Press, 1992.

Markovits, Claude. *The Global World of Indian Merchants: Traders of Sind from Bukara to Panama.* New York: Cambridge University Press, 2000.

———. "Structure and Agency in the World of Asian Commerce During the Era of European Colonial Domination (c. 1750–1950)." *Journal of the Economic and Social History of the Orient* 50, nos. 2–3 (2007): 106–23.

Mathew, J. T., S. Irudaya Rajan, and K. C. Zachariah. "Impact of Migration on Kerala's Economy and Society." *International Migration* 39, no. 1 (2001): 63–85.

McDermott, Jim. Phone interview by Manik Suri, November 18, 2004.

McKinley, James. "Mexican Leader to Visit U.S., Outside the Beltway," *New York Times,* February 9, 2008, A3.

McNamara, Kathleen R. *The Currency of Ideas.* Ithaca, NY: Cornell University Press, 1998.

Menon, Tanya, and Jeffrey Pfeffer. "Valuing Internal versus External Knowledge: Explaining the Preference for Outsiders," *Management Science*, 49, no. 4 (2003): 497–513.

Merchant, Khozem. "I Make Films for Every Indian Everywhere," *Financial Times*, February 10, 2004, 12.

Mill, John Stuart. *Considerations on Representative Government*. New York: Liberal Arts Press, 1958.

Miller, Henry. *Big Sur and the Oranges of Hieronymus Bosch*. New York: New Directions Publishing, 1957.

Ministry of Labor, Government of India. Annual Report, 2004.

Mohan, C. Raja. "Indian Diaspora and 'Soft Power.'" *The Hindu*, 6 January, 2003.

Moore, Robin J. *Making the New Commonwealth*. Oxford, UK: Clarendon Press, 1987.

Mosca, Gaetano. *The Ruling Class*. New York: McGraw Hill, 1939.

Mullan, Fitzhugh. "Doctors for the World: Indian Physician Emigration." *Health Affairs* 25, no. 2 (2006): 380–93.

Nanda, Meera. *Prophets Facing Backward: Postmodern Critiques of Science and Hindu Nationalism*. Piscataway, NJ: Rutgers University Press, 2003.

Nandy, Ashish. *The Illegitimacy of Nationalism: Rabindranath Tagore and the Politics of Self*. New Delhi: Oxford University Press, 2004.

———. *The Intimate Enemy*. New Delhi: Oxford University Press, 1988.

National Science Board. *Science and Engineering Indicators, 2004*, figure 3-32. Available at http://www.nsf.gov/sbe/srs/seind04/.

———. *Science and Engineering Indicators 2008*. Arlington, VA: National Science Foundation, 2008.

Nayyar, Baldev Raj. *India's Quest for Technological Independence*. New Delhi: Lancer Publishers, 1983.

Nayyar, Deepak. *Migration, Remittances and Capital Flows: The Indian Experience*. New Delhi: Oxford University Press, 1994.

Nayyar, K. P. "Masks of Conquest." December 26, 2007. Available at http://www.telegraphindia.com/1071226/jsp/opinion/story_8707952.jsp.

Nehru, Jawaharlal. *Selected Works of Jawaharlal Nehru*, edited by Sarvepalli Gopal. New Delhi: Jawaharlal Nehru Memorial Fund, 1993.

Neuburger, Mary. *The Orient Within: Muslim Minorities and the Negotiation of Nationhood in Modern Bulgaria*. Ithaca, NY: Cornell University Press, 2004.

North, Douglas. *Institutions, Institutional Change, and Economic Performance*. Cambridge, UK: Cambridge University Press, 1990.

Northrup, David. *Indentured Labor in the Age of Imperialism, 1834–1922*. Cambridge, UK/New York: Cambridge University Press, 1995.

Nussbaum, Martha C. "Genocide in Gujarat: The International Community Looks Away." *Dissent* (summer 2003): 15–23.

Nye, Joseph. *Soft Power: The Means to Success in World Politics*. New York: Public Affairs, 2004.

O'Rourke, Kevin H., and Jeffrey G. Williamson. "The Heckscher Ohlin Model Between 1400 and 2000: When It Explained Factor Price Convergence, When It Did Not, and Why." NBER Working Paper No. 7411. Cambridge, MA: National Bureau of Economic Research, 1999.

Obstfeld, Maurice, and Kenneth Rogoff. "The Six Major Puzzles in International Macroeconomics: Is There a Common Cause?" National Bureau of Economic Research Working Paper No. 7777. Cambridge, MA: National Bureau of Economic Research, 2000.

Omissi, David. *Indian Voices of the Great War: Soldiers' Letters, 1914–18.* New York: St. Martin's Press, 1999.

Ong, Aihwa, and Donald Macon Nonini. *Underground Empires: The Cultural Politics of Modern Chinese Transnationalism.* New York: Routledge, 1997.

Osella, Filippo, and Caroline Osella. "Islamism and Social Reform in Kerala, South India." *Modern Asian Studies* 42, nos. 2/3 (2008): 317–46.

———. "Migration and the Commoditisation of Ritual: Sacrifice, Spectacle and Cntestations in Kerala, India." *Contributions to Indian Sociology* 37 (2003): 109–39.

Pankhurst, Richard. "The Ethiopian Diaspora in India: The Role of Habshis and Sidis from Medieval Times to the End of the Eighteenth Century." In *The African Diaspora in the Indian Ocean*, edited by Shihan de Silva Jayasuriya and Richard Pankhurst, 189–221. Trenton, NJ: Africa World Press, 2001.

Parfitt, Tudor. "Tribal Jews." In *Indo-Judaic Studies in the Twenty-First Century*, edited by Nathan Katz, 181–96. New York: Palgrave MacMillan, 2007.

Parsons, Craig. "Showing Ideas as Causes: The Origins of the European Union." *International Organization* 56, no. 1 (winter 2002): 47–84.

Paul, Swraj. *Beyond Boundaries: A Memoir.* New Delhi: Viking-Penguin India, 1988.

Pedraza, Silvia. *Political Disaffection in Cuba's Revolution and Exodus.* New York: Cambridge University Press, 2007.

Percot, Marie, and S. Irudaya Rajan. "Female Emigration from India: Case Study of Nurses." *Economic and Political Weekly* 42, no. 4 (2007): 318–25.

Pettigrew, Thomas F. "Intergroup Contact Theory." *Annual Review of Psychology* 49 (1998): 65–86.

Phadnis, Urmila. "The Indo-Ceylon Pact and the 'Stateless' Indians in Ceylon." *Asian Survey* 7, no. 4 (April 1967): 226–36.

Pingle, Vibha, and Ashutosh Varshney. "India's Identity Politics: Then and Now." In *Managing Globalization: Lessons from India and China*, edited by David Kelley and Ramkishen Rajan, 353–86. Singapore: World Scientific Book Corporation on behalf of the Lee Kuan Yew Center for Public Policy, 2007.

Piore, Michael. *Birds of Passage: Migrant Labor and Industrial Societies.* London: Cambridge University Press, 1979.

Portes, Alejandro. "Globalization from Below: The Rise of Transnational Communities." In *The Ends of Globalization: Bringing Society Back In*, edited by D. Kalb, M. van der Land, and R. Staring, 253–72. Boulder, CO: Rowman and Littlefield, 1999.

———. "Immigration Theory for a New Century: Some Problems and Opportunities." *International Migration Review* 31 (1997): 799–825.

"Proud Hindu, Not a Proud Indian." *Times of India*, April 10, 2004.

Przeworski, Adam, Michael E. Alvarez, and Jose Antonio Cheibub. *Democracy and Development: Political Institutions and Well-Being in the World, 1950–1990.* Cambridge, UK: Cambridge University Press, 2000.

Puri, Sanjay. Interview by Manik Suri, August 13, 2004, Washington, DC.

Pushpangadan, K. "Remittances, Consumption and Economic Growth in Kerala: 1980–2000." Working Paper No. 383. Trivandrum, Kerala, India: Centre for Development Studies, 2003.

Putnam, Robert, Robert Leonardi, and Raffaella Nanetti. "Attitude Stability among Italian Elites." *American Journal of Political Science* 23, no. 3 (1979): 463–94.

Rajagopal, Arvind. *Politics after Television: Religious Nationalism and the Reshaping of the Indian Public.* Cambridge, UK: Cambridge University Press, 2001.

Ratha, Dilip, and Zhimei Xu. *Migration and Remittances Factbook 2008.* Washington DC: World Bank, 2008.

Rauch, James E. "Business and Social Networks in International Trade." *Journal of Economic Literature* 39, no. 4 (December 2001): 1177–1203.

Rauch, James E., and Vitor Trindade. "Ethnic Chinese Networks in International Trade." *Review of Economic Studies* 84, no. 1 (February 2002): 116–30.

Ravishankar, Nirmala. "Voting for Change: Turnout and Vote Choice in Indian Elections." PhD Dissertation, Harvard University, 2007.

Reserve Bank of India. *Handbook of Statistics on the Indian Economy*, table 135. New Delhi: Direction of Foreign Trade, 2004.

Richmond, Yale. *Cultural Exchange and the Cold War: Raising the Iron Curtain.* University Park, PA: Penn State University Press, 2003.

Rodrik, Dani, Arvind Subramanian, and Francesco Trebbi. "Institutions Rule: The Primacy of Institutions over Integration and Geography in Development," NBER Working Paper No. 9305. Cambridge, MA: National Bureau of Economic Research, 2002.

Romer, Paul. "Idea Gaps and Object Gaps in Economic Development." *Journal of Monetary Economics* 32, no. 3 (1993): 543–73.

Rosenthal, David. "Deurbanization, Elite Displacement and Political Change in India." *Comparative Politics* 2, no. 2 (1970): 169–201.

Rostow, Dankwart. "The Study of Elites" *World Politics* 18, no. 4 (1966): 690–717.

Rule, Brendan Gail, Gay L. Bisanz, and Melinda Kohn. "Anatomy of the Persuasion Schema: Targets, Goals, and Strategies." *Journal of Personality and Social Psychology* 48, no. 5 (1985): 1127–40.

Sachs, Jeffrey D., and Andrew M. Warner. "Fundamental Sources of Long-Run Growth." *American Economic Review* 87 (1997): 184–88.

Sarkar, Sumit. "Meanings of Nationalism in India." New Delhi: Nehru Memorial Lecture, 2005.

Sassen, Saskia. *The Global City: New York, London, Tokyo,* 1st ed. Princeton, NJ: Princeton University Press, 1991.

Saxenian, Annalee. *Local and Global Networks of Immigrant Professionals in Silicon Valley.* San Francisco: Public Policy Institute of California, 2002.

———. *Silicon Valley's New Immigrant Entrepreneurs.* San Francisco: Public Policy Institute of California, 1999.

Sedanius, James H., and F. Pratto. *Social Dominance: An Intergroup Theory of Social Hierarchy and Oppression.* Cambridge, UK: Cambridge University Press, 1999.

Sejersen, Tanja Brøndsted. "'I Vow to Thee My Countries'—The Expansion of Dual Citizenship in the 21st Century." *International Migration Review* 42, no. 3 (September 2008): 723–38.

Sen, Amartya. *The Argumentative Indian*. New York: Farrar, Straus and Giroux, 2005.

———. "Open and Closed Impartiality." *The Journal of Philosophy* XCIX, no. 9 (2002): 445–69.

Sennott, Charles M. *The Body and the Blood: The Middle East's Vanishing Christians and the Possibility for Peace*. New York: Public Affairs, 2002.

Shain, Yossi. "Ethnic Diasporas and U.S. Foreign Policy." *Political Science Quarterly* 109, no. 5 (winter 1994–1995): 811–41.

———. *Kinship and Diaspora in International Affairs*. Ann Arbor: University of Michigan Press, 2007.

———. *Marketing the American Creed Abroad: Diasporas in the U.S. and Their Homelands*. Cambridge, UK/New York: Cambridge University Press, 1999.

Shain, Yossi, and Aharon Barth. "Diasporas and International Relations Theory." *International Organization* 57 (2003): 449–79.

Shain, Yossi, and Martin Sherman. "Dynamics of Disintegration: Diaspora, Secession and the Paradox of Nation-States." *Nations and Nationalism* 4, no. 3 (1998): 321–46.

Shankardass, Amit. "Ask the Expert." *CIO Magazine*, September 24, 2003, 25.

Sheth, D. L. "Caste, Ethnicity and Exclusion in South Asia: The Role of Affirmative Action Policies in Buislind Inclusive Societies," Background paper for *Human Development Report*, 13 (2004). New York: United Nations Development Program, 2004.

Simpson, Edward. "Migration and Islamic Reform in a Port Town of Western India." *Contributions to Indian Sociology* 37 (2003): 83–108.

Siriyavan, Anand. "Caste on the Couch." *Himal*, April 2003.

Skowronek, Stephen. *Building a New American State: The Expansion of National Administrative Capacities, 1877–1920*. New York: Cambridge University Press, 1982.

Slaughter, Anne-Marie. *A New World Order*. Princeton, NJ: Princeton University Press, 2004.

Smith, Tony. *Foreign Attachments: The Power of Ethnic Groups in the Making of American Foreign Policy*. Cambridge, MA: Harvard University Press, 2000.

Special correspondent. "Manmohan Voices Concern over Unrest in Malaysia." *The Hindu*, December 1, 2007. Available at http://www.hinduonnet.com/2007/12/01/stories/2007120155721400.htm.

Srinivas, M. N. *Social Change in Modern India*. Delhi: Orient Longman, 1995.

State Department Press Release. *United States–India Joint Statement on Next Steps in Strategic Partnership*, September 17, 2004. Available at http://www.state.gov/r/pa/prs/ps/2004/36290.htm (accessed February 4, 2005).

Sukhatame, S. P., and Indira Mahadevan. "Brain Drain and the IIT Graduate." *Economic and Political Weekly* 23, no. 25 (June 18, 1988): 1285–93.

Swami, Praveen. "Jihad in the Cyber City." *The Hindu*, March 8, 2008. Available at http://www.hindu.com/2008/03/08/stories/2008030854911200.htm.

———. "Lethal remittance." *Frontline* 21, no. 1 (January 3–16, 2004). Available online at http://hinduonnet.com/fline/f2101/stories/2004011600320600.htm.

Teichman, Judith A. *The Politics of Freeing Markets in Latin America: Chile, Argentina, and Mexico.* Chapel Hill and London: University of North Carolina Press, 2001.

Teltumbde, Anand. *Ambedkar in and for the Post-Ambedkar Dalit Movement*, 55. Pune, India: Sugawa Prakashan, 1997.

Thapar, Romila. "Syndicated Moksha." *Seminar* 313 (September 1985): 14–22.

Tharoor, Shashi. "Growing Up Extreme: On the Peculiarly Vicious Fanatacism of [Indian] Expatriates." *Washington Post,* July 15, 1993, C5.

Tripathi, Dwijendra. Interview with the author, Ahmedabad, India. June 2004.

———. *The Oxford History of Indian Business.* New Delhi: Oxford University Press, 2004.

Tseng, Wanda, and Harm Zebregs. "Foreign Direct Investment in China: Some Lessons for Other Countries." In *China, Competing in the Global Economy,* edited by Wanda Tseng and Markus Rodlauer, 68–88. Washington, DC: International Monetary Fund, 2003.

Turner, Frederick Jackson. *The Frontier in American History.* New York: Dover Publications, 1996.

Tushman, Michael L., and Thomas J. Scanlan. "Boundary Spanning Individuals: Their Role in Information Transfer and Their Antecedents. *The Academy of Management Journal* 24 (1981): 289–305.

Uberoi, Pia. *Exile and Belonging: Refugees and State Policy in South Asia.* New Delhi: Oxford University Press, 2006.

University Grants Commission. "Report of the Committee to Review the Pay Scales and Service Conditions of University and College Teachers." New Delhi: University Grants Commission, 2008.

US-India Friendship.net. "Congressional Caucus on India and Indian Americans." Available at http://www.usindiafriendship.net/congress1/housecaucus/caucuson india.htm.

"Vaiko's Visit Pre-empted Solution to Sri Lankan Tamil Issue." *The Hindu,* August 20, 2006. Available at http://www.hindu.com/2006/08/20/stories/20060820 13360100.htm.

Varshney, Ashutosh. *Ethnic Conflict and Civic Life: Hindus and Muslims in India.* New Haven, CT: Yale University Press, 2002.

Venkitaramanan, S. "The Prodigals Return." *The Telegraph,* February 3, 2003.

Vigdor, Jacob L. "Measuring Immigrant Assimilation in the United States." Manhattan Institute, Civic Report No. 53. New York: Manhattan Institute for Policy Research, 2008.

Wadhwa, Vivek, Annalee Saxenian, Ben Rissing, and Gary Gereffi, "America's New Immigrant Entrepreneurs," Duke Science, Technology & Innovation Paper No. 23 (January 2007). Available at SSRN: http//ssrn.com/abstract=990152.

Wallia, Kaajal. "Indian Diaspora Renews Love Affair with Bollywood." *Times of India,* July 18, 2002.

Walt, Stephen M., and John Mearsheimer. *The Israel Lobby and U.S. Foreign Policy.* New York: Farrar, Straus and Giroux, 2007.

Wang, Gungwu. *The Overseas Chinese*. Cambridge. MA: Harvard University Press, 2000.

Weber, Max. *Essays in Sociology*, edited, translated, and introduced by H. H. Gerth and C. Wright Mills. Oxford, UK: Oxford University Press, 1946.

Weidenbaum, Murray, and Samuel Hughes. *The Bamboo Network*. New York: Free Press, 1996.

Weiner, Myron. *The Child and the State in India*. Princeton, NJ: Princeton University Press, 1990.

———. *The Indian Paradox: Essays in Indian Politics*. New Delhi: Sage Publications, 1989.

———. *Sons of the Soil: Migration and Ethnic Conflict in India*. Princeton, NJ: Princeton University Press, 1978.

Weiner, Myron, Mary F. Katzenstein, and K. V. Narayana Rao. *India's Preferential Policies: Migrants, the Middle Classes, and Ethnic Equality*. Chicago: University of Chicago Press, 1981.

Westwood, Sallie. "A Real Romance: Gender, Ethnicity, Trust and Risk in the Indian Diamond Trade." *Ethnic and Racial Studies* 23, no. 5 (2000): 857–70.

Wilentz, Sean. *The Rise of American Democracy: Jefferson to Lincoln*. New York: W. W. Norton, 2005.

Wilkinson, Steven. "Consociational Theory and Ethnic Violence" *Asian Survey* XL (October 2000): 767–91.

———. *Votes and Violence: Electoral Competition and Ethnic Riots in India*. New York: Cambridge University Press, 2004.

Wood, Elisabeth Jean. *Forging Democracy from Below: Insurgent Transitions in South Africa and El Salvador*. Cambridge, UK: Cambridge University Press, 2000.

Woodruff, Christopher, and Rene Zenteno. "Remittances and Microenterprises in Mexico." UCSD, Graduate School of International Relations and Pacific Studies Working Paper (August 14, 2001). San Diego: University of California, 2001.

World Bank. *Priorities and Strategies for Education: A World Bank Review*. Washington DC: Education Section, Human Development Department, World Bank, 1995.

Yadav, Yogendra. "Electoral Politics in the Time of Change: India's Third Electoral System, 1989–99." *Economic and Political Weekly* 34, nos. 34–35 (1999): 21–28.

Yochi, Dreazen. "Iraq Sees Christian Exodus." *Wall Street Journal,* September 27, 2004, A17.

Zachariah, K. C., and S. Irudaya Rajan. "Economic and Social Dynamics of Migration in Kerala, 1999, 2004: Analysis of Panel Data." Working Paper No. 384. Trivandrum, Kerala, India: Centre for Development Studies, 2007. Available at http://cds.edu/download_files/wp384. pdf.

Zachariah, K. C., E. T. Matthew, and S. Irudaya Rajan. "Impact of Migration on Kerala's Economy and Society." *International Migration* 39, no. 1 (2001): 63–87.

Zakaria, Fareed. *The Future of Freedom—Illiberal Democracy at Home and Abroad*. New York: Norton, 2003.

Zaller, John. *The Nature and Origins of Mass Opinion*. Cambridge, UK: Cambridge University Press, 1992.

Zamindar, Vazira Fazila-Yacoobali. *The Long Partition and the Making of Modern South Asia: Refugees, Boundaries, Histories*. New York: Columbia University Press, 2007.

Zelliot, Eleanor. *From Untouchable to Dalit*. Delhi: Manohar, 1988.

Index

Note: Page numbers for entries occurring in figures are followed by an *f*; those for entries occurring in notes are followed by an *n*; those for entries occurring in tables are followed by a *t*.

Patel, I. G., 145, 150
patent filings, 75–77, 121
patriarchy theory, democracy, 164
Paul, Swaraj, 107
Pavcnik, Nina, 7
Person of Indian Origin (PIO) card,
212n4, 265
philanthropy, diaspora-based, 213, 246–47
Philippines, 24, 79, 120
physicians. *See* health care sector
pilgrimages, as idea transmission
mechanism, 11–12
PIO (Person of Indian Origin) card,
212n4, 265
Pitroda, Sam, 154
Planning Commission, 147, 149
Poland, 79, 265n26
Polish Americans, post-World War II
influence, 191
political beliefs, diaspora evidence, 218–21
political community, migration effects
summarized, 268–72
political effects: as absence channel example, 27–28; analysis opportunities, 7–9,
13–14; as diaspora channel example,
28–32; overview, 210–12, 256, 259–61,
263–64; as prospect channel example,
24–25. *See also* democracy's endurance;
long-distance nationalism
political elites, 137–38, 145–48, 153–54,
156–58, 173–74, 294
political partisanship, as emigrant selection
characteristic, 78–79
political remittances, in analytical
framework, 31–32
politics of belonging, 185
Pol Pot, 40–41
Portes, Alejandro, 37, 214
poverty study, data problem, 7
Pravasi Bharatiya Divas, 15, 54, 124, 264
prejudice, defined, 222. *See also*
anti-Muslim prejudice, survey approach
prospect channel, in analytical framework,
16, 23–25, 41–45
Protector of Emigrants, 55, 264
Przeworksi, Adam, 164–65, 168
public goods, 21, 25, 119
public sector, travel effects, 12. *See also*
bureaucratic elites
Punjab: and anti-Muslim survey, 225–26;
civil conflicts, 35, 37, 39, 202, 209, 226;

emigrant patterns, 52, 79, 90, 179; film
industry, 96; land settlement program,
146; remittances impact, 114–15
Punjabi speakers. *See* anti-Muslim
prejudice, survey approach
Putnam, Robert, 136

Qatar, 265n26
Qian Xuesen, 125
quantity variable, 42–43

racial prejudice, 132–33. *See also* anti-
Muslim prejudice, survey approach
Rai, Lala Lajpath, 148
railways, as idea transmission
mechanism, 12
Raj, K. N., 143
Ramadoss, Anbumani, 157
Ramanna, Raja, 143
Ramanujan, Srinivasa, 139
Ramesh, Jairam, 147
Rangarajan, S., 150
Rao, Koteshwar, 220
Reagan, Ronald, 193
region, as selection characteristic: British
Empire expansion, 89–90; indentured
laborers, 52; linguistic group comparisons, 79, 80t; and long-distance nationalism, 218
region, in anti-Muslim survey,
225, 235
religion: in anti-Muslim survey, 229–34,
238, 239t, 251t; in civic nationalism
survey, 240, 241, 242–44, 246; ideation
effects, 144–45; and philanthropy
support, 246–47; as selection characteristic, 67–68, 77–78
remittances: in analytical framework,
29–31; as diaspora channel example,
29–31; distribution by states, 116t; as
economic impact mechanism, 18, 262;
growth of, 111–13; human-capital
effects, 119–21; indentured laborers, 52;
in Mexico, 10; and microenterprise
liquidity, 113–15; philanthropic types,
246; political economy consequences,
115, 117–19, 256; in poverty study, 7;
as selection characteristic consequence,
50–51. *See also* financial flow
mechanisms
representation patterns, 173–76

Republican identification, as emigrant selection characteristic, 78–79

reputational assets, disapora networks, 84, 86–89, 91–92, 95, 122–23

research methodology: data sets, 45–48, 273–96; overview, 48–49. *See also* analytical framework

Reserve Bank of India (RBI), 130, 154

return channel, in analytical framework, 17, 38–45

Roma people, 253

Rosen, Steven, 70

Rosy Blue, 101–2

rural *vs.* urban households, selection characteristics, 56–60, 61, 62–63, 64

Rushdie, Salman, 214

Russia, 90–91, 98, 125, 204, 205

SAIUS (Survey of Asian Indians in the United States), 17, 46–47, 281–92

Sangh Parivar, 203, 216–17, 220

Sarin, Arun, 107

Sarkar Committee, 254*n*3

Saudi Arabia, 30, 78, 127, 144–45, 203

savings rate, indentured laborers, 52

Saxenian, Annalee, 92–93, 94–95

Sayyid Qutb, 40–41

scholarship about migration, overview, 4–6

scientific elites, 93, 120–21, 126, 138–39, 140*t*, 294–95

seafarers, ideation effects, 144

SEI (Survey of Emigration from India), 17, 46, 273–80

selection characteristics, emigrants: age, 62, 71, 73; in analytical framework, 42–43; caste, 80–82; data sources, 51, 54–55, 70, 71, 73, 75–77; in democracy argument, 20; destination, 64–67; education, 62–64, 72–77; ethnicity, 79, 80*t*; gender, 61–62; historical patterns, 51–54, 82–83; overview of potential consequences, 50–51; and political beliefs, 218–19; political partisanship, 78–79; religion, 67–68, 77–78; socioeconomic status, 55–60, 61, 68–70, 71*t*, 72–73, 74*t*, 80–82, 177–78; timing of departure, 60–61

Sen, Amartya, 132–33, 253

Senegal, soccer example, 24

separatist movements, diaspora support, 201–3, 209

Sewa International, 246

Shain, Yossi, 191

Sharma, Kapil, 195*n*30

Shourie, Arun, 150

Shroff, A. D., 254*n*3

Sikh diaspora: in anti-Muslim survey, 230, 238, 248; conflict/separatism support, 35, 202, 209, 264

SIMI (Students Islamic Movement of India), 203, 221

Simpson, Edward, 144

Sindh, emigrant patterns, 90

Singapore, 53, 154, 176, 204

Singh, Ajeya, 155

Singh, Manmohan, 150, 153, 154

Singh, V. P., 153–54, 155, 181

Sinha, Jayant, 155

Sinha, Sachidanad, 145*n*47

Sinha, Yashwant, 188

Sirimavo-Shastri Pact, 206

skilled labor migration, overview, 3, 26–27

Skowronek, Stephen, 131*n*22

slave trade, 2, 8–9

soccer, as prospect channel example, 24

social mobility, as absence channel example, 27–28

social remittances. *See* idea transmission

social science research, 160–61, 258

social security systems, 5, 267

social unrest, migration effects, 7–8. *See also* ethnic violence, as long-distance nationalism

socioeconomic characteristics: in democracy predictions, 164–65; and democracy support, 173; and ethnic violence support, 220; as selection factor, 56–60, 61, 68–70, 71*t*, 72–73, 74*t*, 80–82, 177–78

soft power, 126, 186–88, 191–201

South Africa, 8, 90, 103, 268–69

Soviet Union, 125, 126

Spain, 127, 264

Sri Lanka, 35, 37, 205–7, 265*n*25

Srinivasan, T. N., 149–50

start-up statistics, business, 92–95

status argument, ethnic violence support, 214–15

structural hole, defined, 200*n*47

Students Islamic Movement of India (SIMI), 203, 221

support indicator, India's democracy, 173